The Hardball Times Baseball Annual 2015

Featuring contributions by FanGraphs & THT staff writers:
Dave Allen • Tony Blengino • Dave Cameron
Matthew Carruth • Carson Cistulli • Karl de Vries
August Fagerstrom • Frank Jackson • Brad Johnson
David Kagan • Jason Linden • Jack Moore
Matthew Murphy • Dustin Nosler • John Paschal
Mike Petriello • Alex Remington • Eno Sarris
Greg Simons • Alex Skillin • Dave Studenmund
Jeff Sullivan • Matt Swartz • David G. Temple
Shane Tourtellotte • Steve Treder • Neil Weinberg
David Wiers • Jesse Wolfersberger • Bradley Woodrum
Miles Wray • Matthew Yaspan • Jeff Zimmerman

With additional contributions by guest writers:
Warren Corbett • Bill James
Alan M. Nathan • Chris St. John
Kevin Tenenbaum • Craig Wright

Produced by Dave Studenmund & Paul Swydan
Edited by Joe Distelheim, Jason Linden & Greg Simons

The Hardball Times Baseball Annual 2015

A FanGraphs production

New content daily at hardballtimes.com and fangraphs.com

Edited by Joe Distelheim, Jason Linden and Greg Simons
Cover design by Travis Howell
Typesetting by Paul Swydan

Published by FanGraphs and The Hardball Times

ISBN-13: 978-1503263901
ISBN-10: 1503263908
Printed by CreateSpace

What's Inside

The 2014 Season

Commentary

History

Analysis

Et Cetera

Welcome to Our Book

This is the 11th *Hardball Times Annual*—we've been around for a while—and many of you are returning friends. Welcome back. You'll find much that is familiar here. If you're new to these pages, allow me to introduce you.

The Hardball Times Annual is divided into four sections. First, there are reviews of the 2014 season. These are organized into the six American League and National League divisions and include 10 things of interest in each division. That's 60 fascinating things about last year. Continuing the quantitative trend, we offer our unique ChampAdded review of the postseason. We like to think that these seven articles, with their division standings graphs, offer a useful permanent record of the past year.

We call the next section Commentary, and it includes a whole lot of different things. A *Hardball Times Annual* tradition is the "GM in a Box," in which we analyze the traits of a different general manager each year. This year, Ned Colletti, who did that job for the Dodgers for eight years, gets boxed by Mike Petriello. John Paschal continues an *Annual* tradition started long ago by Will Leitch and continued by Craig Calcaterra for many years, offering a humorous take on the major events of the season. Baseball shouldn't be taken seriously all the time, after all.

Our other commentary articles tend to be a bit more on the serious side. Sabermetric legend Craig Wright researches the epidemic of UCL injuries and what can be done about them, while the soon-to-be-legendary Jeff Sullivan wonders if all the new-fangled technologies have helped defenses more than offenses. Jason Linden investigates the lasting impact of *Moneyball* vs. *The Book*. Which do you think has had the bigger impact on the game?

There are a lot of other thoughtful pieces in the Commentary section, but I want to highlight our other sections, too. Our History section, which comes next, features the writings of Bill James, former Mariners assistant GM Tony Blengino and THT stalwart Steve Treder. Steve and Tony's articles make fine back-to-back reading, as they both deal with the historical context of one of the most significant trends in the game today: the rise of the strikeout.

Out final section is called Analysis. Here you'll find rich articles of a more analytic bent, for those of you who find fascination in the numbers of the game, on and off the field. Matt Swartz has a nice piece investigating the rise of "salary insurance." This article is a nice companion piece to Dave Cameron's Commentary article on wins and payroll, not to mention Matthew Murphy's insights into the impact of salary arbitration.

Other Analytic articles pick apart such subjects as defensive shifts (a hot topic these days) and how quickly catchers wear down. We even have two baseball physicists on board…Alan Nathan gets into the physical properties of non-wood bats, and David Kagan has some real detail on how wind affects pitchers.

Several case studies are on hand in the *Annual*. These are relatively short pieces that deal with specific players, such as Jay Bruce, Phil Hughes and the entire Cubs farm system. Also, Carson Cistulli has contributed his unique and wonderful leaderboards—stats you may not have heard of but are fun anyway.

You may not like everything in the *THT Annual*—that's what comes of trying to please many audiences—but I feel pretty confident you'll find a lot to like. We've been practicing this particular craft for a while now, and I believe this book reflects our experience.

As you can imagine, many eyes, ears and hands were involved in the production of the Annual. In addition to our writers, crack editors Joe Distelheim, Greg Simons and Jason Linden spent many hours poring over each and every verb, noun and gerund. The most amazing feats were performed by THT's Grand Poobah, Paul Swydan, who has taken over total production of the *THT Annual*. From organizing writers to typesetting articles, Paul has turned this concept into a reality.

Paul also manages the Hardball Times website. Be sure to check it out every day for a new article at hardballtimes.com.

I'm pretty proud of this *Annual* thing that we started 11 years ago, but it's now time for me to move on. Paul has successfully taken over production of the *Annual*, and I go now to find my own new, special place in the sun. So many people have supported me and the Hardball Times that I hesitate to name anyone in particular. But I would be remiss without thanking the original THTer, Aaron Gleeman, Bryan Tsao, David Gassko, David Appelman, Tangotiger, Sean Forman and John Dewan.

Oy. That's only the beginning of a long, long list. If I haven't mentioned you yet, may I just say "thank you deeply" and leave it at that? I know who you are and so, I hope, do you.

May first base rise up to meet you. May the wind be always at your back at bat. May the sun shine in the eyes of that outfielder trying to catch your pop fly.

Happy Baseball,
Dave Studenmund

The One about Studes

Since its inception in 2004, Dave Studenmund has been the lead editor and driving force behind The Hardball Times website and its annual publication, *The Hardball Times Baseball Annual*. But nothing lasts forever, even if we wish it could.

It's hard to know where to begin when talking about what Studes has done for the baseball analysis community, so I'll just start off with his scouting ability. And by scouting, I don't mean player scouting, I mean scouting for analytic minds.

Many baseball analysts got their first real opportunity at The Hardball Times (myself included) and as someone who personally has had to staff a baseball site, I've continually been amazed at Studes' ability to pull talent from the noisy landscape of baseball blogging.

Major league front offices and prominent baseball publications are littered with former contributors who were all at one point noticed and recruited by Studes.

And perhaps what makes Studes such a great assessor of talent is the old saying, "it takes one to know one."

Studes has penned countless insightful articles of his own, including his must-read weekly column "Ten Things I Didn't Know Last Week." Not to mention he has both championed and popularized many sabermetric concepts that we now consider part of every day baseball analysis, including batted ball data, win probability, and the general visualization of baseball data (let us not forget Studes' other website, baseballgraphs.com).

"The One About Win Probability" article that Studes wrote back in 2004 has been the go-to win probability primer for the past 10 years, and he basically invented the modern day win probability graph.

Yet on top of all his baseball accomplishments, what makes Studes really special is that he's a wonderful person. And while that may sound trite, I can't honestly think of another person who is so unanimously liked in our industry. (Really, ask anyone.)

All of us in the baseball community owe Studes a debt of gratitude for his hard work, mentorship, and commitment to excellence that The Hardball Times has exhibited throughout the years. Things will certainly not be the same without him, and I hope he'll pop in from time to time to share with us some things he didn't know last time around.

I think Rob Neyer put it best when he called Dave Studenmund a "national treasure." Seriously.

David Appelman
Founder, FanGraphs

The 2014 Season

The American League East View

by Alex Skillin

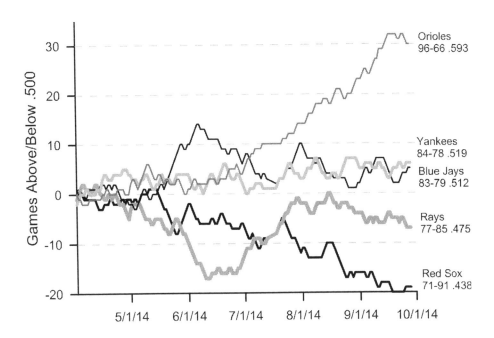

Perennially one of baseball's best divisions, the AL East experienced a down year in 2014. Yearly contenders, the Red Sox and Rays, struggled through disappointing campaigns that culminated in each club selling off important veterans at the trade deadline. The Yankees and Blue Jays both flirted with playoff contention, but injuries and a lack of depth ultimately kept them from making any serious push for the divisional crown. Indeed, the Yanks missed the playoffs for the second straight season, even while saying farewell to Derek Jeter and welcoming Masahiro Tanaka into the fold. That left the Orioles to run away with the AL East title, the organization's first since 1997. Shrewd moves from general manager Dan Duquette and a lineup that led the majors in home runs helped Baltimore earn its second postseason berth in three years.

Derek Jeter's Farewell Tour

For the second year in a row, the Yankees bid farewell to a legend, as Derek Jeter announced in February that 2014 would be his final big league campaign. Much like

Mariano Rivera the year before, Jeter was showered with praise and parting gifts throughout the season, earning tributes in every road park the Yankees traveled to. Unlike the retirements of Rivera and former teammates such as Andy Pettite and Jorge Posada, however, Jeter's final season marked the tangible end of an era in the Bronx. The Yankees captain was the last player remaining from New York's late-'90s and early 2000s championship teams, and his retirement after 20 years served as a reminder of just how far the organization was from those days of dominance.

Although Jeter was celebrated throughout the summer, his on-field performance was anything but stellar. Save for an injury-riddled 2013, it was the worst year of his career at the plate; at 40, he batted .256/.304/.313 with just four home runs. His second half was even worse, as he posted a .274 on-base percentage over 62 games, and continued to play subpar defense at shortstop as the Yankees fell out of playoff contention.

Even still, Jeter's impact on the Yankees and major league baseball is hard to overstate. He finished his career with the most hits, doubles, stolen bases, and games played in franchise history. He ranks second all-time for the Yankees in runs scored, third in total bases, fourth in extra-base hits, and ninth in home runs. Jeter will be remembered as one of the best shortstops ever, and he is a sure bet to be enshrined in Cooperstown and Monument Park at Yankee Stadium.

That Jeter played his entire career in pinstripes in the free agent era only adds to his legend. He became synonymous with New York and the sport itself in ways hardly seen in this day and age. It is fitting, then, that Jeter's No. 2 will be the final single digit number the Yankees retire, up there on the right field façade at Yankee Stadium with numbers worn by the likes of Ruth, Gehrig, Mantle, and DiMaggio.

Jeter's final game at Yankee Stadium, moreover, was the perfect send-off to his career in the Bronx. The Yanks led by three runs before the Orioles tied the game in the top of the ninth inning, setting Jeter up for one more moment of heroics. With a runner on second base in the bottom of the ninth, Jeter lined a one-out single through the hole between first and second base to score the winning run. The moment could not have been scripted any better, and it served as a great reminder of why we watch and analyze sports with such passion and fervor. Even in the twilight of his career, everyone expected—no, knew—Jeter was going to come through with a hit. And he did.

Trade deadline fall-out

In one of the busiest non-waiver trade deadlines in recent memory, AL East teams made a flurry of moves, and even dealt players within the division as the clock wound down on July 31.

Given their unusual status as sellers, the Rays and Red Sox traded away big pieces, but what they received in return indicates both clubs envision competing again in the near future. Although their trade of David Price for Drew Smyly, Nick Franklin, and shortstop prospect Willy Adames left some underwhelmed at the time, Tampa Bay did receive two players who can and did contribute right away. Indeed, Smyly impressed mightily for the Rays down the stretch, posting a 3.07 FIP and allowing no more than three runs in any of his seven starts, two or fewer in six of the seven. Franklin should give the Rays further positional versatility, and his performance in Triple-A indicates his bat will play in the majors better than it has thus far.

The Red Sox also eschewed the chance to land prospect packages, choosing instead to add players with major league experience when dealing starters Jon Lester and John Lackey. Nabbing Yoenis Cespedes gave Boston some sorely needed power, and the additions of Allen Craig and Joe Kelly injected further talent onto the team's major league roster. The Red Sox will hope Craig can get over a foot injury that hampered his 2014 production, and Kelly should give them some dependable innings in a rotation that now lacks veteran pedigree.

For the first time since 1997, meanwhile, the Yankees and Red Sox made a trade just before the deadline. Boston sent Stephen Drew, who struggled at the plate after re-signing with the team in June, to the Bronx in exchange for Kelly Johnson. The Yanks also dealt for Martin Prado after bringing in Chase Headley and Brandon McCarthy earlier in July. Brian Cashman's ability to upgrade the Yankees lineup and rotation in exchange for little of value gave his club a chance at the postseason down the stretch. McCarthy was a huge boost to New York's rotation, and both Prado and Headley provided strong contributions. The trades represented yet another example of Cashman's ingenuity in finding useful pickups, even as the Yankees farm system remains relatively barren.

The Blue Jays didn't make a big trade prior to the deadline, and the Orioles were largely quiet as well, though they did add a dominant bullpen arm in another inter-division trade, landing Andrew Miller from Boston for lefty pitching prospect Eduardo Rodriguez. Miller was lights out during his brief time with the Orioles, giving up only three runs in 23 appearances, and striking out 34 batters against just four walks.

All Toronto could muster was a trade for utility man Danny Valencia, who is a decent platoon option, but didn't provide the Jays with anything they lacked. With the team in the midst of playoff contention, failing to add any pieces of note before the deadline proved a costly mistake for Toronto.

Masahiro Tanaka mania grips baseball

The buzz surrounding right-hander Masahiro Tanaka began long before Opening Day when Tanaka's team in Japan, the Rakuten Golden Eagles, posted the right-hander, affording all 30 major league teams the chance to sign him. Changes to the posting system between MLB and Nippon Professional Baseball in the offseason meant that any club willing to bid $20 million could negotiate with Tanaka. In effect, this created an open market for his services, enabling teams to present lucrative, long-term offers to Tanaka in a process akin to free agency.

Rarely does someone so young—Tanaka was just 25 at the time—enter the free-agent market, which made him a uniquely valuable commodity. When the Yankees prevailed in the negotiation process—they landed Tanaka with a seven-year, $155 million contract—no one was surprised. The Yanks needed depth and youth in their rotation, and Tanaka's signature completed another offseason of rampant spending in the Bronx that saw the club sign Brian McCann, Jacoby Ellsbury and Carlos Beltran to lengthy and expensive deals.

Yet Tanaka proved to be better than anyone—the Yankees included—could have expected. From the start, he was remarkably consistent, as he pitched into the seventh inning in 10 of his first 11 outings and allowed no more than three earned runs in every start through the month of June. Tanaka's first season in the big leagues was better than that of any previous Japanese pitching import, even Yu Darvish, who drew more praise than Tanaka during his time in Japan. What stood out most about Tanaka was his command—he walked just 21 batters and struck out 141 over 136.1 innings.

With the Yankees an otherwise middling team, Tanaka's starts every fifth day soon became a story that overshadowed nearly everything else. Through the season's first three months, he propped up an aging and underachieving Yankees ball club, almost single-handedly keeping them in the playoff race.

But after two bumpy starts to begin July, the Yankees found a partial tear in the ulnar collateral ligament in Tanaka's right elbow. They shut him down immediately, and speculation grew that, like a bevy of other pitchers that season, he would require Tommy John surgery. Instead, Tanaka chose to rest and rehab the injury, and he ultimately returned in late September, though it was too late for him to have much impact on the team's playoff hopes.

In a way, Tanaka's right arm signifies the tenuous position in which the Yankees currently find themselves. Sure, his return in September provided reasons for optimism, yet the team has a lot resting on his partially torn elbow. With the roster aging and Jeter now retired, the Yankees don't have a lot in the way of youthful promise, pitcher Dellin Betances notwithstanding. Tanaka gives them hope and a chance to compete in any game he starts, but the organization's fortunes are firmly tied to his ability to stay healthy.

Rays, Red Sox fall to AL East basement

The struggles of perennial contenders in Boston and Tampa Bay were one of the biggest reasons why the AL East was so weak in 2014. Save for the 2006 campaign, the division had sent two teams to the playoffs and had at least two 90-win clubs in every season dating back to 2002.

No one expected the Red Sox to slump to last in the AL East following a World Series title, but widespread underperformance throughout the roster saw Boston scuffle through a disappointing campaign. After handing full-time roles to young-sters Jackie Bradley Jr., Xander Bogaerts and Will Middlebrooks, the Red Sox saw all three struggle at the plate as their lineup failed to replicate the production of the 2013 championship squad. Offseason acquisitions A.J. Pierzynski and Grady Sizemore didn't contribute either, and both were designated for assignment before the All-Star Break. Add in Dustin Pedroia's injury-plagued campaign, and the Red Sox offense fell from one of baseball's best to one of its worst in 2014.

Boston's starting staff fared better, with Jon Lester producing a career year and John Lackey duplicating his 2013 success, but both were dealt at the trade deadline. Others in the Red Sox rotation struggled. Clay Buchholz got off to a horrid start and never fully recovered, while Jake Peavy's susceptibility to the long ball caught up to him in Fenway Park before he was also traded in late July. After falling out of the playoff chase, the Red Sox handed opportunities to young starters Rubby de la Rosa, Allen Webster, and Anthony Ranaudo, but none gave any indication they deserved a future rotation spot.

Down in St. Petersburg, the Rays offense was even more anemic than Boston's. Tampa Bay finished last in the American League in runs scored, with Evan Longoria enduring a subpar season. Wil Myers regressed from his strong rookie campaign and missed over two months with a wrist injury that sapped his power. That left Ben Zobrist, James Loney, Desmond Jennings and a number of role players to pick up the slack on offense. Joe Maddon did his best to mix and match hitters in the lineup, but Tampa's bats simply lacked the necessary firepower to score enough runs.

Adding to the Rays' problems was a pitching staff beset by injuries to begin the season. Matt Moore underwent Tommy John surgery after making only two starts, and both Alex Cobb and Jeremy Hellickson missed significant time in the first half. This forced Tampa Bay to depend on Erik Bedard, Cesar Ramos and Alex Colome in the opening months, which went about as well as anyone would expect.

Despite these poor campaigns, neither the Rays nor the Red Sox should be down for long. Even after trading David Price, Tampa Bay still boasts a deep, young rota-tion with Cobb, Chris Archer, Jake Odorizzi and Drew Smyly. Health from Myers and a bounce-back season from Longoria will be critical for the club's offense.

Up in Boston, the Red Sox have a bevy of exciting young players. Bogaerts began showing his potential again with the bat in September, and Mookie Betts was a success after earning playing time in the second half. Add in Cuban import Rusney Castillo, and Boston's offense should be much improved in 2015.

Dan Duquette finds more diamonds in the rough

The Orioles won the AL East going away, but their season didn't turn out as planned by any means. Matt Wieters required Tommy John surgery 26 games into the year; Manny Machado started and ended the season on the disabled list (and he didn't produce at his 2013 levels even when he was healthy); and Chris Davis plummeted from MVP contention to below-average hitter before testing positive for amphetamine use.

But as he has in the past, Baltimore GM Dan Duquette pulled all the right strings in adding depth to the club's lineup. In an era when every GM is looking for cheap, under-the-radar bargains, Duquette again showed a knack for finding diamonds in the rough even after a decade-plus absence from the majors. With outfielder/designated hitter Nelson Cruz still a free agent in February, Duquette scooped him up on a one-year, $8 million contract. Although Baltimore had to forfeit a second-round pick as compensation, Duquette shrewdly recognized that Cruz could thrive in a home park like Camden Yards, and at 33, Cruz responded with an major league-leading 40 home runs. Overall, he had his best season at the plate since 2010.

Duquette also hit the jackpot with first baseman Steve Pearce, whom the Orioles designated for assignment in April before re-signing seven days later. Pearce went on to bat .293/.373/.556 with 21 home runs in 383 plate appearances, more than making up for Davis' woeful year. Though Pearce had experienced modest success in limited playing time in the past, his power output came as a big surprise. He finished second on the team in wins above replacement at 4.9.

Delmon Young, too, proved a useful pickup even as Duquette endured some ribbing in the media for signing him to a minor league deal back in January. The 29-year-old outfielder/designated hitter responded by hitting 20 percent better than the league average over his 255 plate appearances. Even smaller-bore acquisitions like David Lough and Alejandro De Aza played well for the Orioles. Lough didn't impress at the plate like De Aza did in his brief time with the club, but both provided plus value on defense, Lough in particular.

The Orioles ran away with the AL East while lacking pitching depth. Ubaldo Jimenez was anything but the staff leader Baltimore was seeking, and the Orioles greatly benefited from the remainder of the starting staff—Wei-Yin Chen, Chris Tillman, Bud Norris and Miguel Gonzalez—all outperforming their peripherals.

Duquette's latest signing from Asia, Suk-min Yoon, was shelled in Triple-A Norfolk after agreeing to a three-year deal in the offseason. More costly, Jake Arrieta, who the Orioles traded to the Cubs in 2013, had a breakout season in Chicago, showcasing the talent that had made him a top prospect with Baltimore a half-decade earlier. So, Duquette was far from perfect. But, in a year in which offense was at a premium, Duquette showed that he is still capable of finding it at every corner of the market.

Orioles grab hold of division in Aug. 7 matchup with Blue Jays

By the time the trade deadline rolled around, the Orioles had assumed the top spot in the AL East, but the Blue Jays sat only 2.5 games back. Less than a week later, on Aug. 5, Baltimore and Toronto began a three-game series at Rogers Centre with divisional supremacy on the line. The clubs split the first two games of the series, setting up the proverbial rubber match for the night of Aug. 7.

J.A. Happ took the mound for the Jays, with right-hander Miguel Gonzalez (another under-the-radar pick-up Dan Duquette made two seasons ago) starting for the Orioles. Both pitchers were sharp, neither allowing a run through the first three innings. Overall, the two teams combined for just nine hits all game.

The O's got on the board first, with the type of production that drove their offense all season long: a home run. Catcher Caleb Joseph belted one to left field off Happ in the fourth, scoring J.J. Hardy ahead of him. Those were all the runs Gonzalez and the Baltimore bullpen needed, though Anthony Gose pulled a run back for Toronto in the fifth inning with a solo home run of his own.

Fittingly, trade-deadline acquisition Andrew Miller came on to pitch a scoreless seventh inning, striking out Gose and Ryan Goins in the process. Darren O'Day and Zach Britton did their parts as well, and overall the Orioles bullpen didn't allow a hit over three innings in relief of Gonzalez to secure the 2-1 win.

The victory extended Baltimore's lead to five games atop the division, and from there, Toronto only fell further back in the race. In many ways, the game highlighted the Jays' shortcomings throughout the season. Third baseman Danny Valencia, the only addition the club made at the deadline, went 0-for-4 on the night (he would go on to bat .240/.273/.364 in a Blue Jays uniform). In contrast, Miller put in a strong performance in his one inning of relief for the Orioles.

Even though Happ gave Toronto one of his best starts of the season, giving up only two runs over eight innings, the Jays still couldn't take advantage. Goins went 0-for-3 out of the eight hole, further adding to his sub-replacement level production at second base after the Blue Jays failed yet again to upgrade the position.

The Orioles proceeded to go 31-17 down the stretch to win the AL East going away, and on the whole, the game showcased two teams moving in opposite directions.

The Blue Jays miss their chance

The 2013 season proved disastrous for the Blue Jays, who came into the year with high expectations after adding Jose Reyes, R.A. Dickey, Josh Johnson, Mark Buehrle and Melky Cabrera. That didn't mean Toronto would scuffle again in 2014, however. In fact, with improved health, better luck and some bounce-back seasons, one could imagine the Blue Jays battling back into contention in the AL East, especially when the season started and there appeared to be no dominant team.

Yet they did need a few upgrades, especially to a pitching staff that finished with the third-highest ERA in the AL during the year prior. Sure, the club was set to welcome back Drew Hutchison from injury, though given his lack of big league experience the team didn't really know what to expect from him. And with Dickey and

Buehrle both underwhelming during their first year in Toronto, the team's pitching depth looked awfully thin again.

This reality made the organization's reluctance to add anyone of note in the offseason (or during the 2014 campaign) a bit curious. Toronto had already gone all in with upgrades in the previous winter; standing pat now, when the club needed just a few more wins to be a credible contender, was a head-scratching decision. Free agents like Scott Kazmir, Bartolo Colon and Phil Hughes all signed with other teams on fair-market deals. Ervin Santana, who the Jays were linked with throughout the winter, didn't sign until March, and even then, his signature required only a one-year, $14.1 million commitment.

Toronto's reluctance or inability to add to its payroll turned out as costly as expected. The Blue Jays were in first place after the month of June, and had the best run differential in the division. Even on Aug. 1, the day after the non-waiver trade deadline—during which they added only Danny Valencia—the Jays were within 2.5 games of the AL East lead and had a firm grasp on the AL's second Wild Card spot. They finished the season's final two months with a 23-28 record, however, as Baltimore pulled away in the division and the Royals, Mariners, Indians and Yankees all passed them in the Wild Card hunt.

The Blue Jays simply didn't have enough quality pitching even after Hutchison and Buehrle gave them solid innings and rookie Marcus Stroman established himself as a legitimate big league starter. Dickey struggled, Brandon Morrow got injured, and Toronto was forced to turn to never-were's like Dustin McGowan, J.A. Happ and Liam Hendricks to fill in the rest of their starts.

The Jays' core will remain intact for another season or two, and the club's offense will continue to hit plenty of home runs. But Toronto missed a golden opportunity in 2014 after failing to upgrade its pitching staff. Rarely are both the Rays and Red Sox so down and out, and it's unlikely the Yankees hover around .500 for a third-straight season. General Manager Alex Anthopoulos went all in with his moves two winters ago, but his inability to follow up and add depth to the Jays roster cost the club a chance to make a serious run at a postseason berth that has now eluded the organization for over two decades.

The Yankees grow more stagnant and boring

For the first time since 2008 and just the second time in two decades, the Yankees missed the playoffs in 2013. Even more discouraging, the franchise's outlook didn't portend much reason for hope as an aging and thin roster was fortunate to reach 85 wins. Mariano Rivera and Andy Pettitte finished their final seasons, CC Sabathia turned in the worst year of his career at the age of 33, and the Yankees scored fewer runs than they had in a single season since 1990.

In response, the Yankees did what they always do in times of trouble: spend. The club signed Brian McCann, Jacoby Ellsbury and Carlos Beltran to expensive long-term contracts in hopes of reviving a flailing offense, though they lost Robinson Cano to the Mariners when they curiously wouldn't meet his asking price. But then in January, the Yankees spent more money when they locked up Masahiro Tanaka. Although Tanaka's talent was undeniable, New York's continued inability to upgrade its roster without outspending everyone else felt increasingly monotonous.

This sentiment only intensified when the Yankees scuffled through a disappointing season again in 2014. Despite the offseason upgrades, the offense was one of the AL's worst. McCann posted an OBP below .300 in the first of a five-year deal, Beltran couldn't stay healthy and another year of aging didn't help Derek Jeter or Mark Teixeira's production. Tanaka was the lone bright spot in a rotation decimated by injuries. Sabathia's future is uncertain after he underwent season-ending knee surgery in July, and Tanaka, Michael Pineda, and Ivan Nova all spent significant time on the DL.

From one perspective, the fact that the Yankees remained in playoff contention despite these setbacks is reason for encouragement. From another, New York's roster isn't getting any younger, and the club was fortunate to win even 84 games considering its -31 run differential. The organization's persistent problems developing youngsters down on the farm have forced them into a pattern of rampant spending. As a result, the front office keeps returning to the free-agent market to replenish the roster, continually investing in expensive players on the wrong side of 30.

The outspending the others strategy has grown stale, especially as the on-field product has deteriorated (not to mention the fact that the Dodgers can compete with them dollar for dollar now). The Yankees are no longer the juggernaut they once were, and despite the last-place finishes of Boston and Tampa Bay, their deeper farm systems have them better positioned for the future.

What the Yankees can do to improve is an open question. They don't have the upper-level prospects to make a major trade, and their core is aging more and more with each passing year, making many of their players untradeable. Injuries certainly hampered the Yankees in 2014, but continually investing big money in free-agent veterans comes with such risk.

Red Sox searching for year-to-year consistency

While the Yankees have stayed consistently boring the past couple of years, the Red Sox have been just the opposite. Only a year after winning the World Series, the Red Sox find themselves faced with a number of questions heading into the offseason once again. 2014 represents the second time in three years that Boston fell to last place in the division, the type of inconsistency the organization will surely look to avoid in the future. Yes, the Red Sox were due for some regression after a surprising World Series campaign in 2013, but the widespread underperformance throughout the roster is something the team must solve moving forward.

Speaking at Saber Seminar in Boston in August, Sox general manager Ben Cherington made clear the club's front office was asking itself some pressing questions. Most important of all, perhaps, was whether so many players underperforming on the roster was simply random variation—a product of bad fortune—or something else entirely?

To that notion, Cherington acknowledged the Red Sox were searching for ways to get "more of [the team's] players to operate at the high end of their projection." Is such success "random," Cherington wondered, "or is there a way to achieve that year after year?"

Cherington didn't divulge any juicy answers, but his thoughts demonstrated how much Boston was grappling with the team's on-field inconsistency. He also admitted the talent gap that used to exist among major league clubs (say, the early 2000s Red Sox and Yankees) had all but disappeared.

"Talent is more easily distributed across the league now," Cherington said, "which makes optimizing player performance only more important."

The challenge facing Boston this offseason will be not only building its starting staff, but also figuring out better ways to integrate young players into the major league fold. Xander Bogaerts battled through an up-and-down season, Jackie Bradley Jr. was one of the league's worst offensive players, and none of the team's numerous young starters grabbed hold of a rotation spot with their shaky performances down the stretch.

That doesn't mean the Red Sox are doomed to another last-place finish in 2015. More talent is set to arrive from the upper minors, including and especially left-handed pitcher Henry Owens, and some offseason spending will add depth to a roster that already has many pieces around which to build.

Yet that doesn't change the reality that Boston, one of baseball's richest clubs, has finished with one of the baseball's worst records twice in three years. Even with a World Series title sandwiched in between, improved stability on an annual basis will be the goal for those on Yawkey Way.

A flurry of youngsters make their debuts

Things weren't all doom and gloom for the AL East in 2014, as the division welcomed a bevy of impressive youngsters who figure to stick around for a long while.

The most hyped was Boston's shortstop Xander Bogaerts. After debuting for the Red Sox the previous year prior, he ranked among the top three prospects in baseball heading into the season, according to every major outlet. However, Bogaerts' rookie campaign was a nice reminder of the growing pains and adjustments even the most talented youngsters must face in the majors. He started the year well, but fell into a nasty slump in the summer months, batting .161/.206/.254 in 268 plate appearances from June to August. A hot September rekindled the optimism about his future, and one must remember he will be just 22 on Opening Day next season.

With Bogaerts slumping, another—more unexpected—Red Sox prospect stole many of the headlines. Mookie Betts began the 2013 season in Low-A Greenville, but a near-unprecedented run through the minors saw him debut in Boston just 14 months later. Betts tore through each stop on the minor league ladder and didn't have much trouble adjusting to major league pitching once he got consistent at-bats. The athleticism and raw ability are clear—a second base prospect, he adjusted to playing a new, difficult position in center field in a matter of weeks. The only question regarding Betts is what position he will play in Boston, with Dustin Pedroia entrenched at second base and the outfield picture crowded.

Despite their thin farm system, the Yankees did find themselves a dominant reliever a year after saying farewell to Mariano Rivera. A failure as a starting pitcher over seven seasons in New York's farm system, big right-hander Dellin Betances was converted to relief pitching in 2013, and he has taken to it amazingly well. In 2014, in his first full season in the majors, he broke the club's single-season record for strikeouts by a reliever, topping Rivera's 1996 mark with 135 punch-outs in 90 innings. He formed a potent combination with closer David Robertson in the back of Joe Girardi's bullpen, which helped pick up the slack from the injuries to the club's starting rotation. Betances led major league relievers in innings pitched and finished with an ERA 64 percent better than league average.

Although the Blue Jays fell prey to pitching woes, they welcomed an impressive young starter to the fold in right-hander Marcus Stroman. After Toronto drafted Stroman out of Duke in 2012, some questioned whether he could hold up as a starter in the majors given his lack of prototypical size. The 5-foot-9 hurler silenced nearly all of his doubters with an impressive run in Toronto's rotation. Beginning in late May, Stroman made 20 starts for Toronto, and posted a 3.29 ERA with 103 strikeouts and 27 walks in 120.1 innings. Stroman's aggressiveness with his mid-90s fastball and willingness to attack the zone stood out, and his slider also showed good potential.

The Rays might have missed out on the playoffs, but Kevin Kiermaier established himself as their center fielder of the future. A 31st-round pick in the 2010 draft and hardly a top prospect, Kiermaier arrived on the scene in mid-May and showed off plus defense and speed in center field, which was expected. Yet his bat played far better against major league pitching than anyone anticipated. He ended the season with 33 extra-base hits and the fifth-best isolated power (.186) among big league rookies. Even if his defense and power don't continue at their 2014 levels, Kiermaier will be a valuable player for the Rays for years to come, and in Desmond Jennings, Wil Myers and Kiermaier, the Rays will have a very solid outfield.

The American League Central View

by August Fagerstrom

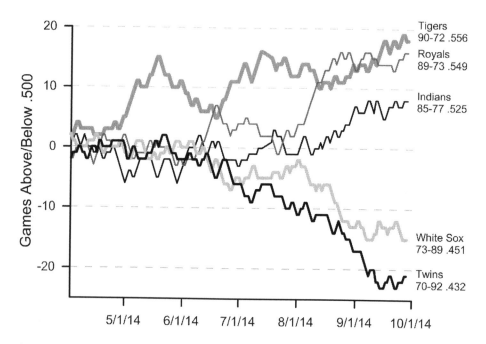

A t the top and the bottom, the American League Central went as expected. The Detroit Tigers at the top. The Minnesota Twins at the bottom. No big surprises there.

But if you want surprises, look no further than the Kansas City Royals, who made the playoffs for the first time since 1985.

The Cleveland Indians followed up their first postseason bid since 2007 with another solid season, hanging around until the end but ultimately falling just short.

The Chicago White Sox found a superstar in Jose Abreu, but lacked a supporting cast to make his breakout rookie season worth anything.

The Minnesota Twins got off to a good start thanks to Brian Dozier, but a second-half dropoff and injuries that limited Joe Mauer and Ricky Nolasco led to a third last-place finish in four seasons.

And the Detroit Tigers slugged their way to a division championship for the fourth consecutive year, but again came away empty-handed because of their defense and bullpen.

And it was those very things which led the Kansas City Royals to being the true champions of the division in the end, despite what the regular season standings might say.

The Royals run away with 2014

If you're looking for the biggest story of the American League Central Division in 2014, look no further than the Royals. By some measures, the Royals weren't too remarkable. They didn't even finish first in their own division. They were last in the major leagues in home runs, isolated slugging percentage and walks. Their starting pitchers had a 3.60 ERA and a 3.84 FIP—which is good, but not great, in this now pitcher-dominated era of baseball.

But what matters is not those numbers. What matters is that the Royals made the playoffs. The Kansas City Royals made the playoffs. That sentence hasn't been true since 1985, but it is now.

Despite their lack of offense, their lack of star power, their lack of experience, the Royals found a way.

They found a way through speed. Their 153 steals led the majors by 15. Not only did they run often, they ran efficiently, evidenced by their 81 percent successful steal percentage, tied for the best in the majors. Jarrod Dyson had 36 steals, including an American League best 10 swipes of third base. Alcides Escobar swiped 31 bags, Lorenzo Cain 28. Nori Aoki and Alex Gordon pitched in, with 17 and 12, respectively.

They found a way through defense. Their outfield's 46 Defensive Runs Saved ranked first in majors. Catcher Salvador Perez and the rest of the infield held their own, but the Royals' outfield is what separated them from the pack. Their 11 errors were fourth-fewest in the major leagues. Gordon and his eight outfield assists led all left fielders in DRS, at 27. Cain split time between center and right field and was among the best at either position, finishing fourth in the majors with 24 DRS. And when Cain was in right, Dyson manned center to the tune of a 14 DRS. To put it in simpler terms: There was no better defensive outfield than Kansas City's in 2014.

They found a way through relief pitching. The Royals' bullpen racked up a major league-best 5.9 Wins Above Replacement. Their 3.30 ERA was 10th-best, their 3.29 FIP was sixth. Closer Greg Holland was steady as ever, racking up 46 saves with a 1.44 ERA and 1.83 FIP, but Wade Davis was the true star. Davis had a breakout season, throwing 72 innings with a 1.00 ERA and 1.19 FIP. The last part of the three-headed monster, Kelvin Herrera, carried a 1.41 ERA and 2.69 FIP over 70 innings. The Royals starting pitching wasn't the greatest, but it doesn't matter as much when you play six-inning games.

We generally think of hitting and starting pitching as the linchpins of a team. The Royals didn't exactly have those in spades, but they made up for it by being awesome at everything else.

For now, "The Trade" is a gem

When the Royals traded top prospect Wil Myers and pitching prospect Jake Odorizzi to Tampa Bay for pitchers James Shields and Wade Davis, the question was, "Will this work out for the Royals?"

When Myers won the American League Rookie of the Year award in 2013, Davis proved he couldn't be a starter and the Royals missed the playoffs, the question became "How bad is this trade going to be for the Royals?"

When Myers played in just 87 games in 2014 due to a stress fracture in his wrist—and performed poorly while he played—and Davis became one of the most dominant relievers in baseball and the Royals made the postseason for the first time in 29 years backed by a second solid season from Shields, the question shifted to "Has this trade worked out for the Royals?"

That's still a tricky question to answer. The answer really depends on your definition of a successful trade from Kansas City's viewpoint.

On one hand, Shields is a free agent this offseason, and is all but guaranteed to be too pricy for Kansas City to retain. Davis, while cheap thus far, has a $7 million team option for 2015, which goes up to $8 million in 2016 and $10 million in 2017. Even with Davis' resurgence as a dominant bullpen weapon, that's a significant amount of money to pay a reliever heading into his 30s. Odorizzi put up solid numbers as a rookie in 2014. Most notably, he struck out 16 percent more batters than he walked, which was 21st-best among qualified starting pitchers, and was fifth-best among rookie starting pitchers. And let's not forget that Myers is still just 24 years old, likely to rebound from the past season's numbers if he stays healthy, and is under cheap team control through the 2019 season.

But…but…the Royals made the playoffs. Which, frankly, is all the fan base needed for the trade to be rendered a success, something that quickly became evident if you watched any of their postseason run. No other fan base in the sport was more starved for a playoff appearance, and Shields helped lead them there, which was the leading reason behind the trade in the first place. The Royals didn't trade away Myers and Odorizzi, for what they knew would be two years of James Shields, for their future. They made the trade for an immediate chance to play postseason baseball, and got their money's worth with their astounding run to the Fall Classic.

We'll never be able to truly evaluate the trade until the players' careers are over, and by that point, will anyone really care? The answer to "Has this trade worked out for the Royals" likely depends on your relationship with the Royals. If you're a fan of the team, you likely don't have a care in the world because you just witnessed the Royals play World Series baseball, possibly for the first time in your life. If you're an outsider, you may still be skeptical about the long-term impact. Which means the easiest way to settle the question is with a cop-out answer: It remains to be seen. But for the present, it appears to be a rare win-win trade for both clubs involved.

The Twins have outfielder Byron Buxton, who is the consensus top all-around prospect in baseball. They hoped he would crush Double-A, and perhaps Triple-A pitching in 2014 with a chance to impact the club at the major league level as early as 2015. The Twins also have third baseman Miguel Sano, a consensus top-15 prospect with some of the best raw power tools in the entire minor leagues. The Twins hoped he would crush Triple-A pitching in 2014 with a chance to impact the club that year or the following year.

What the Twins hoped, unfortunately, isn't what the Twins got.

Buxton suffered a wrist injury in spring training that caused him to open the season on the disabled list. Several setbacks to the wrist kept him largely out of live game action until the middle of August. Shortly after his return, a nasty outfield collision resulted in a concussion, and the Twins decided to shut Buxton down. He played in just 31 games, and struggled in those games.

But that's more than Sano can say. In the year of the Tommy John surgery, not even third basemen were safe. Sano was diagnosed with a torn ulnar collateral ligament in his throwing elbow and missed the entire 2014 season following the surgery.

With the major league club offering little in the way of hope, all the Twins have is their future. And with lost seasons from Buxton and Sano, that future essentially was pushed back a year.

How the future of the Twins organization will pan out certainly falls strongly on the careers of Buxton and Sano, but it's not all them. First baseman Kennys Vargas and shortstop/center fielder Danny Santana both made major league impacts in their rookie seasons. The organization is still holding out hope for guys like outfielder Aaron Hicks and catcher Josmil Pinto, and infielder Eduardo Escobar flashed the potential to be a useful major league player.

In addition, the resurgence of free agent signee Phil Hughes gave the Twins what appears to be a legitimate front-of-the-rotation pitcher, something the team has been desperately lacking in recent years. And the Twins seem to have moved on from the pitch-to-contact organizational philosophy that has failed the team over the last decade-plus: Their farm system is now littered with high-velocity arms.

And it's not as though the injuries to Buxton and Sano are expected to derail their careers, it's just a road bump in the Twins' rebuilding plan. The future in Minnesota still appears to be bright. The future will have to stay healthy to fully realize it.

The long Gardenhire era ends

Two things have remained consistent in the American League Central Division since the early 2000s: The Kansas City Royals never making the playoffs, and Ron Gardenhire being at the helm of the Minnesota Twins. In three quick days, those statements were both rendered false as the Royals clinched a Wild Card spot on Sept. 26 and the Twins fired Gardenhire on Sept. 29.

Gardenhire's 13-year tenure in Minnesota was the second-longest of any active manager in the major leagues behind Mike Scioscia's 15 years with the Los Angeles Angels of Anaheim. Although the Twins never appeared in a World Series under him, they were a perennial contender during Gardenhire's first nine seasons with the club, appearing in six postseasons and posting a .550 winning percentage. Gardenhire won the American League Manager of the Year award in 2010, capping off this stretch.

But from there, it was all downhill. The Twins haven't returned to the playoffs since 2010 and posted a meager .409 winning percentage in that time frame.

It's tough to determine how much of the blame for the Twins' shortcomings in the past four seasons can be placed on Gardenhire. With a tight budget and a pitch-to-contact organizational philosophy that hasn't produced an elite pitcher since Francisco Liriano's breakout in 2006, Gardenhire never had much to work with in his rotation. Chronic injury problems that have plagued the careers of homegrown heroes Joe Mauer and Justin Morneau in recent years limited the Twins offensive potential, and it's hard to see many managers having much success with the recent talent at Gardenhire's disposal.

Regardless, not many managers survive four consecutive 90-plus loss seasons, and Gardenhire was no exception. New manager Paul Molitor has big shoes to fill, but also will be armed with a plethora of exciting young talent.

In Chicago, a great retires quietly

A city wished one of its all-time greats a farewell this season. He had worn his club's white and black uniforms for nearly two decades. Despite his status as a hero in his franchise's history, he largely remained private. He always played hard, and he always respected the game.

No, I'm not talking about Derek Jeter. I'm talking about Paul Konerko.

Konerko didn't get the same gaudy farewell tour that Jeter received. Then again, Konerko isn't Jeter. Unless, of course, you ask a White Sox fan.

Konerko retires as the White Sox all-time leader in total bases, with 4,010. Only Frank Thomas hit more home runs and drove in more runners in a White Sox uniform than Paul Konerko. He sits fourth in runs scored and walks.

Konerko was never the best player in the league; he wasn't even always the best player on his own team. But for 16 years, he was solid.

His final home game didn't conclude with a historic walk-off single like Jeter's did, but that's a special kind of moment that seems almost reserved for a player like Jeter, who had a flair for the theatric.

Instead, the agenda of Konerko's final home game was a bit more dull, but still great—an embodiment of his career. His No. 14 jersey was retired, and Konerko was surprised with a statue of himself, placed next to Thomas'. Konerko was also surprised with the game ball from perhaps the biggest moment of his career—the grand slam in Game Two of the 2005 World Series, which the White Sox went on to win, giving the franchise its first championship since 1917.

Jeter's absence in the Big Apple leaves a gaping hole at shortstop that hasn't needed to be filled for 20 years. Surely, the Yankees will be active in the free agent market, but they are looking to replace a man who cannot be replaced. The White Sox seem to have already found their replacement, and a decent one at that. Cuban defector Jose Abreu smacked 36 homers in his first season in the major leagues, and he missed two weeks with an ankle injury.

Still, no matter what numbers Abreu posts in his time with the White Sox, he will never be Paul Konerko to White Sox fans. For while he may not have been The Captain, for eight seasons, he was the White Sox captain, and for 16, he was the heart and soul of their team.

There's only one Kershaw, but...

The best position player in baseball is Mike Trout. The best starting pitcher in baseball is Clayton Kershaw. These are opinions, and opinions are not facts, but these opinions are about as close to facts as baseball opinions come.

The Chicago White Sox don't have Clayton Kershaw. He pitches for the Los Angeles Dodgers. What the White Sox do have, though, might be the closest thing we have to Clayton Kershaw today.

Kershaw is a lefty with an unusual, deceptive motion, which makes the ball hard to pick up. He relies heavily on a slider as his secondary pitch, and he led his league in both swing-and-miss percentage and strikeout rate in 2014. He has a history of allowing weak contact, which leads to low ERAs.

Chris Sale is a lefty with an unusual, deceptive motion, which makes the ball hard to pick up. He relies heavily on a slider as his secondary pitch, and he led his league in both whiff percentage and strikeout rate in 2014. He has a history of allowing weak contact, which lead to low ERAs.

There's more to it than just that, obviously, and Kershaw is a little better than Sale across the board, but the comparison is obvious.

Despite all the similarities, there are bound to be some differences. We are dealing with individual human beings, after all. The big one is the groundball rate. Kershaw had a top-15 groundball rate for starting pitchers in 2014; Sale was in the bottom 20. This makes Kershaw's home run prevention, thus low ERA, seem far more sustainable than Sale's. Then again, Sale used to get more grounders than he does now, and Kershaw used to get fewer, so maybe this evens out in the future.

Another difference is that Kershaw won his league's Cy Young Award, and Sale didn't. Early in the year, it wasn't certain that Kershaw would be able to win it, due to the handful of starts he missed to begin the season. Sale missed some starts early on as well, but he (a) wasn't quite as dominant as Kershaw, and (b) had stronger competition in his league, from Felix Hernandez and Corey Kluber.

Clayton Kershaw is in a league of his own, but if I had to bet on one guy having a Kershaw-like season in 2015, it would be Chris Sale.

With different guys, Tigers don't change their spot

The sums of the parts were similar for the Detroit Tigers in 2014. They won the American League Central for a fourth consecutive season, led by a booming offense and a rotation of workhorse starting pitchers.

But the parts themselves changed a bit. During the Tigers' recent four-year domination of the Central Division, two names have consistently led the way: Miguel Cabrera and Justin Verlander. This past year was a little different. The Miggy we've gotten used to over the past few seasons was a Triple Crown winner and perennial MVP candidate, capable of 40 bombs and an on-base percentage over .400. The 2014 Miggy was still a great hitter, hitting 25 home runs with a .371 on-base percentage, but he wasn't *Miggy*.

But no worries, Miggy had some friends who more than picked up the slack.

The most obvious is Victor Martinez, who put up the best numbers of his career in his age-35 season, posting career bests in average (.335), on-base percentage (.409), home runs (32) and strikeout rate (6.6 percent). Even more surprising than Victor's resurgence was the breakout of another Martinez—J.D.

J.D. Martinez was waived by the Houston Astros—yes, the Astros—in the offseason, before being claimed by the Tigers in March. After making some changes to his swing plane, he realized the raw power everyone knew he had. Martinez clubbed 23 homers in just 480 plate appearances, with a .358 on-base percentage.

But perhaps the most underrated part of the Tigers lineup was Ian Kinsler, who was acquired in a trade for slugger Prince Fielder in the offseason. Kinsler maintained a similar level of offensive performance as he had his previous two seasons in Texas, but more importantly, he brought two things to the Tigers lineup that had been sorely lacking in previous years. He brought speed, grading out as the American League's most valuable baserunner, taking the extra base 63 percent of the time and racking up 15 steals. And he brought defense, with Gold Glove-caliber play at second base with a major league-leading 20 Defensive Runs Saved.

For Verlander, a slight step back in 2013 turned into a full-on tumble in 2014. Verlander was the Tigers' worst starting pitcher, posting a 4.54 ERA and the lowest strikeout rate since his rookie season. Rick Porcello, however, continued the opposite trend of Verlander, cracking 200 innings for the first time in his career and posting a career-best 3.43 ERA.

If you had known that Verlander would become the Tigers' worst starting pitcher and Cabrera would suffer a near-200-point dropoff in OPS, you might have thought the Tigers would finish second, or perhaps third, in the AL Central and miss the postseason altogether. But thanks to steady performances from the rest of their roster, plus big additions in Kinsler and J.D. Martinez, with breakouts from Victor Martinez and Porcello the Tigers were able to continue doing what they've done for four consecutive years. They just did it a little differently.

The returns on Price aren't in yet

Come late July, despite their division-leading record, the Tigers felt they needed some extra firepower. Oakland general manager Billy Beane had just added Jon Lester and Jonny Gomes to earlier trade catches Jeff Samardzija and Jason Hammel, and the Athletics appeared to represent the biggest roadblock between the Tigers and a potential American League pennant.

So Tigers GM Dave Dombrowski did something he's no stranger to, as proven by his moves in recent offseasons: make a big splash. The Tigers, in a three-team deal with Seattle and Tampa Bay, shipped out center fielder Austin Jackson and starting pitcher Drew Smyly for Rays ace David Price. Dombrowski hoped Price would bolster an already great rotation and help the Tigers make a deep postseason run, looking for their first World Series championship since 1984.

Instead, the Baltimore Orioles, in a demoralizing 3-0 sweep, eliminated the Tigers in the first round of the playoffs.

One could look to Price's 3.59 ERA with the Tigers and deem his performance a disappointment, but Price was far from the Tigers' biggest problem. First, his underlying peripherals were even better in Detroit than in Tampa Bay, thanks to an increased ground ball rate and a home run rate that was cut in half. That was easy to overlook, given a Tigers defense that was bottom-five in major leagues and a bullpen that absolutely imploded in the playoffs. Neither of these are issues new to the Tigers, who have to make some changes if they want to see better results.

So the Price trade isn't what hurt them. In fact, it could still pay dividends through next season, so long as the Tigers improve their defense and pitching, because the Tigers may need Price's contributions more than ever.

Max Scherzer is a free agent who will be commanding big money on the free agent market, and it remains to be seen whether the Tigers are able to commit that sort of money. Further, Justin Verlander continues to decline and Anibal Sanchez continues to be plagued by shoulder problems.

While ERA might make it look like the Tigers didn't get the version of David Price they were hoping for, the underlying numbers show he was even better than expected. The Tigers traded for Price in an attempt to make a World Series run in 2014, but his presence in an ever-thinning rotation for 2015 may end up being the bigger factor.

The American League West View

by David Wiers

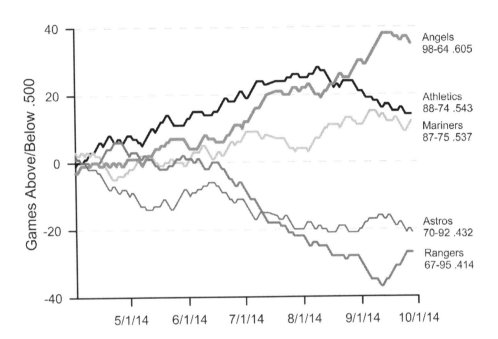

The American League West race started out with one team smashing the opposition and ended with one team smashing the opposition. It happened that they were two different teams.

As in the speech from *Men in Black* where Agent K gives the "for 500 years everybody knew the earth was flat" speech, the AL West had a specific period of time where we thought we know who the best team was. For the first three months of season the Oakland Athletics blew the competition away and chalked up the best run differential in the league.

The second half, though, told a different story, as the Los Angeles Angels caught fire, gained ground and ultimately passed the A's, leaving Oakland to fend off the hard-charging Seattle Mariners. At least the Texas Rangers put their fans out of their misery quickly and efficiently, wasting no time joining their state mate, the Houston Astros, in the cellar.

The sweep

By the time the calendar reached Aug. 28, the Angels had surpassed the A's for a narrow two-game lead in the division. The A's came stumbling into the series with a 2-8 record in their past 10 games; the Angels rolled in with seven wins in their past 10. The first game began with the A's spotting the host Angels three runs in the bottom of the second. Starter Sonny Gray would settle down and ultimately last seven innings. And when the A's offense cobbled together three runs—two in the fifth and the tying run in the sixth—the responsibility for the outcome was entrusted to the bullpens.

Each relief corps did its job well. They kept further damage off the scoreboard until the 10th inning, when the Angels put the game away with a walk-off sac fly to win 4-3. They now had a three-game lead.

One of the beautiful things about baseball is that there is almost always a tomorrow. For the A's, the 29th had both good and bad omens. The good was that the A's were throwing their ace, Jon Lester. The bad? Anaheim was trotting out Jered Weaver, who despite no longer being in peak form, outdueled Lester. Again the Angels bullpen didn't allow a run and won a coldly efficient game 4-0. Make that a four-game lead.

After dropping the first two games, the A's were hoping to win the last two and break even. The A's turned to recent acquisition Jeff Samardzija to help salvage the series, and he was electric on the night. He tossed a four-hit complete game, and allowed just a pair of runs while striking out nine Angels hitters. Unfortunately for him, Anaheim used eight pitchers to hold the A's to three hits and zero runs, and won 2-0. The five-game lead for Anaheim after the Aug. 30 win was a complete reversal of the five-game lead the A's had held just eight weeks ago.

The last game of the series was over almost before it got started. The A's had set their top starters—Gray, Lester, Samardzija and Scott Kazmir—against their divisional foes, but the Angels were up to the challenge. They blasted Kazmir for six runs early, and chased him after just one and a third innings. Anaheim's bullpen allowed its first run of the series in the eighth inning, but the game ended in an anticlimactic 8-1 romp.

It took barely two months of play for the Angels to roar past the Athletics, and it all came to a head in this series. By the time season ended, Anaheim had tacked on another five games and won the division by 10 games, the third-largest margin of victory for any division winner in baseball. The teams were headed in different directions by the time of the Aug. 28 series, and by the end of the sweep, both teams could just about see the writing on the wall.

Building a bullpen in Anaheim

Speaking of that Angels bullpen, it was in full effect for much more than that one series in Oakland. The Angels led baseball with 167 shutdowns in 2014. (A shutdown is defined as increasing a team's Win Probability Added—WPA—by six percent or more. The opposite, a meltdown, is when a relief pitcher decreases his team's chance of winning by six percent or more.)

Anaheim's bullpen wasn't your older brother's bullpen, stacked with homegrown guys like Francisco Rodriguez or Troy Percival, but rather a collection signed via free agency or acquired via trade. Of the nine relievers who faced at least 100 batters for Anahem, only three—Kevin Jepsen, Michael Kohn and Michael Morin—were drafted by the Angels.

In April, Ernesto Frieri was tabbed as the club's closer, but he was sent to the Pittsburgh Pirates for Jason Grilli before June concluded. Grilli had been roughed up in the Senior Circuit, mostly due to his home run rate, which was nearly double his career mark. His numbers snapped back to normal once in Anaheim, and while he was fortunate to not allow a single dinger in his time with the Angels, his statistics for the season weren't far off his average.

Despite his strong numbers, Grilli managed just one save—but 12 shutdowns—as Joe Smith, signed over the offseason, was already recording saves as early as April. It wasn't a cheap deal; a three-year, $15.8 million contract for just about any reliever is a significant investment. But Smith made year one look good, continuing his ground-ball-inducing ways. His strikeouts ticked up to a career-best level as well.

Other trade acquisitions—Fernando Salas, Vinnie Pestano and Cory Rasmus—all brought what a good reliever should: the ability to miss bats. Among the three right-handed relievers, Rasmus' 9.16 K/9 was the lowest of the group. It's hard to get on base, let alone score runs, when opposing batters are swinging and missing so frequently. The group posted a collective 31 shutdowns, impressive for relievers who generally weren't seeing action in the late and highest-leverage innings before they got to Anaheim.

Perhaps the team's best in-season bullpen acquisition was closer Huston Street. He finished the season with a sparkling 1.71 ERA with the Angels, and while he didn't join the club until July 18, led the team with 17 saves.

These relievers helped power the Angels to the best record in the game, but they did come at a cost. The club surrendered most of what its limited farm system could give up, particularly Taylor Lindsey and R.J. Alvarez. Selling the future for current wins is nothing new, but at least with the Angels the immediate dividends were clearly paid.

Trouble in the Texas rotation

Where the Angels found success with their pitchers, the Rangers had almost nothing but trouble with their staff. Pick any ERA estimator you'd like, be it FIP, xFIP or SIERA, and the results match up. Or better yet, don't—the Rangers were so bad you don't need estimators to show it. The club allowed 771 runs, third-most in baseball, and 160 home runs, more than any American League team but the Yankees.

Home runs and fly balls tend to go hand-in-hand, and given what we know about Globe Life Park, one could reasonably expect a pitching staff to be built around ground ballers in an attempt to keep baseballs out of the outfield bleachers there. Unfortunately for the Rangers pitchers, their 38.6 percent fly ball rate was the second-lowest in baseball.

Inarguably their best starter, Yu Darvish, is a fly ball pitcher, and that is something they have to live with, as Darvish is a star. However, he was limited to just 22 starts this past season. The Rangers' next-best pitcher is Derek Holland. He didn't make a start until September, and he doesn't pump out the grounders, either. Among those who did last in the starting rotation, the worst offender was Colby Lewis. His 170.1 innings featured flyballs 44.2 percent of the time and 25 home runs allowed—both team highs.

Both Nick Tepesch and Nick Martinez threw more than 125 innings with less-than-ideal batted ball rates. Tepesch burned worms at a decent 41.6 percent clip, but Martinez kept just one third of his balls in play on the ground. His 32.9 percent groundball rate was the sixth-lowest in baseball among starters with at least 120 innings pitched.

The bullpen didn't fare much better. Rangers relievers allowed fly balls at the fourth-highest clip in the game. Of the 10 Rangers relievers who faced at least 100 batters, only Jason Frasor accrued grounders at the league-average rate. As a unit, the Rangers bullpen netted grounders less than 40 percent of the time.

Dexter Fowler beats the doubters

Many doubted what Dexter Fowler's offense would be once he joined the Houston Astros via trade from Colorado. The criticisms that he was the latest Coors Field mirage were grounded in fact: His home vs. road splits had been quite different. In six seasons with the Rockies, Fowler posted an away weighted runs created plus (wRC+) north of 100—which is league average, with 101 representing one percent better than league average—only once.

At home, the numbers got flipped; in only one season did his numbers at Coors Field show a wRC+ less than 100. Even though he wasn't a power hitter, Fowler's home field had had a clear effect on his offensive output. His move from the best hitting environment in the majors to Houston—a neutral field—raised questions about how useful Fowler would be.

Like Matt Holliday before him, Fowler responded with the best offensive season of his career. His 138 wRC+ at home and a 112 wRC+ on the road is a decent gap, but that's not the point. Once he left Coors Field, he adapted just fine to his new ballpark. A .276/.375/.399 line from a center fielder is nothing to scoff at.

Overall, the season wasn't a banner success for Fowler—he had nagging injuries, and his defense—perhaps related to those injuries—took a turn for the worse. But he answered the question of whether he would hit in a different uniform in resounding fashion. Fowler may not be a flawless player, but he was not a Coors Field illusion either.

The other Angel in the outfield

Coming into the 2014 season, two-thirds of Anaheim's outfield was set. Josh Hamilton was expected to handle one of the corners and some guy named Mike Trout would patrol center field. And in the other corner? Enter Kole Calhoun, a player who had socked eight home runs in 222 plate appearances in his first real big-league action in 2013.

Calhoun, an eighth-round pick in 2010, rocketed through the Angels system and got his first taste of big league action in 2012. Despite the rapid ascent, he didn't break camp with the club in '13 and wasn't recalled again until late July. (Thanks Super Two deadline!) However, once Calhoun did make it back to The Show, he worked his way into regular playing time.

Looking back at his minor league rates, Calhoun had pop, speed and a good batting eye. His power manifested itself in the form of seven home runs in rookie ball and again in 2011 in High-A, where he smacked 22 long balls and his speed shone through with 20 steals. Of course, the California League is a notorious hitter's environment so it was an easy performance to overlook. The Angels didn't overlook it, and skipped him straight to Triple-A to begin 2012, only two seasons after drafting him.

He rewarded their aggressive promotion in the equally hitter-friendly Salt Lake City—first in 2012, and then again in 2013. Overall, he launched 26 home runs and nabbed 22 steals across 687 plate appearances in Triple-A, before giving the Pacific Coast League pitchers a break by being promoted.

Calhoun has not run as often in the majors, as he hit in front of Mike Trout, and you don't want Trout to be distracted (an early-season ankle injury likely didn't help matters either) but he still performed very well. He hit 17 home runs in 537 PAs and his 125 wRC+ was the third-best mark on the team, edging out that Albert Pujols fellow.

It's hard to not believe in Calhoun's power at this point. The Angels hit him leadoff for most of the season and he continues to reward their faith in him. From eighth-round pick to All-Star caliber, Calhoun has arrived.

Is Choo running out of steam?

Following Sin-Soo Choo's strong 2013 in Cincinnati, where he posted the third 20-20 season of his career, many were excited for him to move to Texas and help anchor that lineup with Adrian Beltre. Instead, he was shut down before the end of August with an elbow injury and when he did play, he was a shell of himself.

The season opened with Choo as a staple atop the Rangers lineup. He hit leadoff where his mix of power, speed and, most importantly, on-base prowess would best fit. Things started off well for him when he hit well above league average in April and May, but that didn't last into the summer.

Choo's batting average on balls in play plummeted from .338 to .235 once the calendar flipped to June, and while arbitrary endpoints shouldn't be too heavily considered, batted ball fluctuations were not the only issue with him. His strikeouts were also on the rise.

He began the season with a 20.6 percent K rate in April, just under his 21.4 percent career strikeout rate. In May, it climbed to 21 percent, and then to 24.1 percent in June. The strikeouts just begat more strikeouts. July saw his K rate climb up to 27.3 percent, and it hit a crescendo in August, at an eye-popping 32.2 percent.

Choo had no drastic shift in his batted ball profile—his ground ball to fly ball rate in 2014 was identical to 2013, he swung and missed at a rate under his career average, he made contact with the same frequency he always had.

That leaves where the ball was going and how well he was striking it. Choo hits very well to the opposite field and to center, but his pull numbers have begun to decline. It started in 2013, when he hit 24 percent worse than league average to right field. This year, he declined even further, as he hit 46 percent worse than league average when he pulled the ball. It's possible that extreme shifts are robbing Choo of a great deal of his production.

It's also possible that he played in pain a great deal of the season. Choo is now coming off of surgery to his elbow as well as his ankle as we hurtle towards the 2015 season. If he can't regain some of his lost ability to pull the ball effectively—and with subpar pull numbers in three of his past four seasons that seems unlikely—then perhaps we've seen the best of him.

A powerful infielder in Seattle

Robinson Cano's arrival in Seattle was much heralded, but the Mariners did have another power-hitting infielder in the person of Kyle Seager. For the third straight season, Seager's home run total went up, as did his power numbers and his offensive output overall. His walk rate isn't particularly special, but if a league-average walk rate is the biggest complaint about a hitter in SafeCo Field, that's a pretty good hitter.

The 2014 season was Seager's third full season in the majors and having played his age 26 season, he's tapped into his power potential. That comes as a bit of a surprise, as his high-water mark in the minors was a 14-homer 2010 season in High-A. He tacked on 40 doubles that year, and that is when people began to notice him, though not enough for him to crack any major Top 100 prospect list.

Seager continued to progress through the M's minor league system, but tallied a mere seven home runs in the 2011 season between both Double and Triple-A. He still hit plenty of doubles—33 between both leagues—and joined the Mariners. Although he only appeared in 53 games in the big leagues, Seager managed to sock 13 doubles—but only three home runs.

In 2012 and 2013, some of his doubles began clearing the walls rather than bouncing into them. In both seasons, Seager tallied at least 30 doubles and 20 home runs, and in both seasons, he was the Mariners' best hitter. This past season, his 30-doubles streak ended—he still smacked 27—but he made up for it with his first 25-homer season.

Seager's minor league track record didn't lend itself to obvious power projection, but three consecutive seasons of 20-plus home runs speak for themselves. With his power, better than league average strikeout rate and solid batting eye, Seager has answered any questions about his offense.

A special platoon situation in Oakland

Platoons are nothing new. Lefty/righty splits have been an factor for managers and players for decades. Catchers getting worn out behind the plate has been a problem for much longer than platoon issues, so why not address both issues simultaneously? Oakland used Derek Norris and John Jaso in this fashion for most of the season. Jaso eventually went down with a concussion and was replaced by Geovany Soto, but for 148 games the system worked.

With 93 games started, Norris was the bigger half of the behind-the-dish platoon. Norris, a right-handed hitter, obliterated opposite-handed pitchers—in 179 plate appearances agsinst southpaws, he hit .311/.393/.470, which was 48 percent better than league average. Against righties, which he faced 269 times, he hit a more pedestrian .244/.340/.359—still six percent better than league average.

Norris was forced to see so many PAs against righties because lefty Jaso was limited to 47 starts at catcher. When healthy, Jaso hit right-handed pitchers 28 percent better than league average. Jaso's brutal numbers against southpaws made the platoon necessary, and the A's adhered to it pretty strictly. Where Norris recorded more PAs against his weaker side, Jaso stepped in just 27 times against lefty pitchers versus 317 against right-handers.

Soto, the late-season addition, saw limited action; he made 14 starts for the A's in the final six weeks of the season. When he did play, he didn't always have the luck of hitting against his strong platoon side, as both he and Norris are right-handed hitters. Still, Soto performed well enough behind the dish to get the starting nod over Norris in the Wild Card game.

The three A's catchers, Norris, Jaso and Soto, combined to hit .267/.351/.411, which was 21 percent better than league average, good for the fourth-best mark in the game, and overall they were the fifth-most valuable catching corps. Of the four teams that finished ahead of the A's in WAR, each had premium catchers—Jonathan Lucroy, Buster Posey, Russell Martin and Yan Gomes. The A's didn't have that star power, but with this formidable platoon they kept their catchers fresh and played to each individual's strength.

Offspeed is on point for Collin McHugh

After two poor stints in the majors with the New York Mets and the Colorado Rockies, right-hander Collin McHugh owned a FIP on the wrong side of 4.50 and an ERA north of 8.00 in 46.1 innings pitched. All that changed in 2014 with a breakout season in his first year with Houston.

McHugh found the right balance of pitches in the American League: He began throwing more sliders. His 31.5 percent slider usage rated sixth highest among starters with at least 150 innings pitched. McHugh wasn't shy about attacking hitters with his curveball, either. He threw the deuce at a 23.5 percent clip, the 11th-highest frequency. It should come as no surprise, then, to see McHugh's 40 percent fastball rate as the fifth lowest in baseball, fourth lowest if you don't count knuckleballer R.A. Dickey (which you shouldn't).

The off-speed pitches kept hitters off balance, and McHugh posted the highest strikeout rate of his career. The strikeouts went hand in hand with batters whiffing at his offspeed pitches: His 10.8 percent swinging strike rate was also a career high. Factor in the lowered contact percentage and the improved batted ball rates and he essentially had everything working.

The effective mixing of pitches even helped McHugh's batted ball rates. He posted a nearly league average ground ball rate, but his home run to fly ball rate was cut virtually in half—from 18.4 percent in past seasons to 9.5 percent in 2014. That's no small feat, considering that Minute Maid Park is on par for home runs with Coors Field, and much friendlier for home run hitters than is Citi Field (Coors and Citi Field being his two previous home addresses).

McHugh also benefited from a strong .259 batting average on balls in play versus a .340+ mark in small sample sizes in 2012-13. Again, impressive considering the Astros' defense was either one of the 10 worst or one of the two worst by the two main advanced defensive metrics housed at FanGraphs.

It's hard to put faith in something as fickle as BABIP going forward, but the gains in the swinging strike and subsequent strikeout rate are real. Even if—or when—McHugh's BABIP regresses to something more closely resembling a league average, expect the strikeouts to remain.

Had McHugh pitched for a better team, or had he accumulated enough innings to qualify for the pitching triple crown, he probably would have garnered a lot more attention. Now, he just needs to make sure his arm doesn't fall off from all the breaking pitches.

Game 162s matter

Since 161 games wasn't enough to determine the final AL Wild Card participant, the final day of the regular season decided if a Game 163 would be needed. The A's clung to a one-game lead over the Mariners. If they lost and Seattle won, then Game 163 would have been on. Both teams had sputtered to the finish—the A's had lost six of their last 10, and Seattle had recently lost five in a row.

Both teams put their best foot forward on the final day. The M's had Felix Hernandez on the mound to face the Anaheim Angels, while Oakland had Sonny Gray pitching versus the Texas Rangers. First pitch for the Oakland/Texas showdown was set for 3:05 p.m. and the Mariners/Angels match would start soon after at 4:10 pm. Both teams would doing some scoreboard-watching during their games.

The A's were the first team to strike, as they scratched off two runs in the top of the second. Brandon Moss doubled and later scored off a Josh Reddick triple. Stephen Vogt would then bring Reddick home on a single for the 2-0 lead.

By the time the Mariners game started, if they were looking, they saw their season beginning to end. They didn't relent, and scored a run of their own in the bottom of the second to give King Felix an early lead. Logan Morrison dropped a single in center field and was driven in by the next batter, Michael Saunders, on his wall-ball double to center.

At this point Gray was probably too busy mowing down the Rangers batters to see the Mariners score. He didn't allow a baserunner in the second or third innings, and only an infield single sullied his fourth inning. Gray was at 53 pitches through four innings, had allowed just a pair of hits and had set down five Rangers on strikes.

Hernandez was cruising as well. The Mariners ace had coughed up just one hit in the first four innings and fanned seven Angels batters, including all three in the third. He got more run support as the M's offense tacked on an additional three runs to make it 4-0 entering the fifth. And he just kept slamming the door on the Angels' offense.

Unfortunately for the Mariners faithful, Gray maintained his stranglehold on the Rangers. After a double and an infield single to open the fifth inning, he struck out Luis Sardinas and then induced an inning-ending double play from former teammate Adam Rosales. Gray kept his clean sheet intact and concluded the sixth inning at a tidy 70 pitches.

The Mariners didn't add to their lead, and they didn't have to, not with Hernandez on the hill. With his pitch count at 63 in the fifth, he induced a C.J. Cron ground-out after five pitches to end his day. Without allowing a run in 5.1 innings, Felix Hernandez left the game—and the season—in the hands of his teammates...and the Rangers.

The Mariners relief corps would do their job, but as the M's bullpen held the Angels scoreless, Gray continued to do the same to the Rangers. His seventh inning consisted of just eight pitches. With the A's hitters silent in their portion of the seventh, Gray took the hill for the eighth inning with a pitch count of 78. He required just 10 pitches to dispatch the four batters he faced. In the top of the ninth, the A's offense came around again to tack on another pair of runs to open a 4-0 gap—the same lead ther Mariners held 2,093 miles away at Safeco Field.

Anaheim finally pushed a run across the board in the top of the ninth inning against Seattle's Danny Farquhar, but he held the lead to win 4-1. It was too little, too late, as the A's had already clinched. Gray threw a six-hit complete game shutout to send Oakland to the Wild Card game. The entire season came down to the last day, and while both teams won their last game of the regular schedule, only the A's earned the right to move on to postseason play.

The National League East View

by Alex Remington

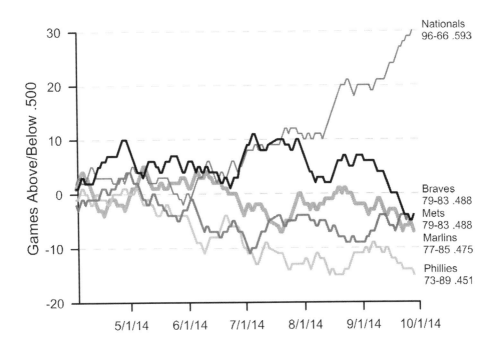

The National League East was arguably the weakest division in baseball—it was the only one with four teams below .500. While the Washington Nationals lived up to their high expectations, the Atlanta Braves fell off a cliff in the second half, and the Marlins, Mets and Phillies more or less did exactly what was expected of them.

The Nationals disappointed their fans, too, losing in the NL Division Series in four games; the franchise has not won a playoff series since the 1981 strike season. The other franchises have even more soul-searching to do, as the offseason began early for all of the other teams. The odds are good that the 2015 season will go better for several of them than the 2014 season did, but that may not be enough to prevent the NL East from remaining the place where teams from other divisions go to collect a few empty wins.

NL East shows the range of Tommy John outcomes

The Tommy John epidemic hit no division in baseball harder than the NL East, where it seriously damaged the hopes of three teams: the Mets and Marlins, whose longshot playoff hopes were utterly dashed when Matt Harvey and Jose Fernandez went under the knife, and the Atlanta Braves, whose payroll flexibility was wrecked when they spent $18 million dollars on free agents Gavin Floyd and Ervin Santana to replace injured starters Kris Medlen and Brandon Beachy. In the end, their pitching was fine, but the lack of payroll flexibility meant that they were unable to upgrade their horrendous offense and bench.

So, a serious medical problem plaguing baseball had massive strategic ramifications in the division, essentially clearing the way for the dominance of the Nationals. In 2013, Fernandez and Harvey looked like two of the best pitchers in baseball. In 2014, they spent nearly the entire year on the DL. Harvey got hurt in August 2013, Fernandez in May 2014. The Marlins and Mets' prayers of contention in 2015 will largely depend on the range of possibilities for their recoveries, and that range is well illustrated by other pitchers in the division.

Washington's Jordan Zimmermann is probably the best-case scenario: Following his 2009 surgery, he took his place at the top of the Nationals rotation and quickly proved himself one of the top starters in the league in 2014, twirling a no-hitter in game 162. His teammate Stephen Strasburg is the next-best-case scenario: He lost a few miles on his fastball, and went from a phenom to merely one of the 15 best pitchers in the game.

The worst-case scenario struck Atlanta's Beachy and Medlen, who in early 2014 both experienced setbacks in their recovery from the surgery, each requiring a second operation. It is unlikely that either will ever again be able to consistently shoulder a full-time starting pitcher's workload.

If the Mets and Marlins are to end their respective nine- and 12-year playoff droughts, they'll need their stars back at full strength. Sports medicine has never been better. But nothing is certain. (For more on Tommy John surgery, please see Craig Wright's article later in this book.)

Hot corner not so hot

The hot corner has become a problem for several of the division teams. The Braves and the Nationals both owe a fair bit of money to third basemen they likely can no longer play at third base, in Chris Johnson and Ryan Zimmerman, and the Mets' David Wright is looking like he may have lost his power for good.

The stone-gloved Johnson was signed to a $23.5 million extension from 2015 to 2017, which looked like a decent deal after his three-win 2013 season. But it started looking like a B.J. Upton-level disaster after Johnson lost 50 points of batting average on balls in play and turned into a replacement-level player in 2014. The worst part is that he still managed a .345 average on balls in play, which is really high, and he still had limited value offensively.

Zimmerman's bat is still potent enough that he can play a corner position lower on the defensive spectrum, like left field or first base, both of which he played for the first time in 2014. But the Nationals owe him another $86 million through 2020, and they didn't expect that he would have to move off his position this soon after signing the deal. Zimmerman signed the extension in 2012, but 2014 was the first year of his new contract. The Zimmerman extension is in a long line of unfortunate deals that were insufficiently future-proofed, with the Phillies' disastrous Ryan Howard contract being the most notable.

Wright signed his extension in 2012, too, and the Mets owe him another $107 million through 2020. But while he's still a league-average player thanks to his positional value, his bat has gone missing. He hasn't hit 30 homers since 2008; he hasn't hit more than 21 homers since 2010. His .105 isolated power—which is simply slugging percentage minus batting average—in 2014 was 35 points below his previous career low, from 2009, the Mets' first year in Citi Field. As long as Wright has hit for a relatively high average, he has been a very good player. But in 2014, Wright's walks went significantly down and his power disappeared, and a late-season MRI revealed ligament damage in his shoulder. That helps explain the poor performance, but it provides cold comfort. Recovering from a shoulder injury is neither easy nor certain.

Fortunately for the Nationals, there is a terrific third baseman in the organization: Anthony Rendon, who played there for much of 2014 (Zimmerman was on the field for only 58 games). The Braves do not have anyone waiting in the wings, which is likely what prompted then-GM Frank Wren to extend Johnson in the first place. The Braves will likely enter the 2015 season with Johnson as their projected third baseman, but they will need to find a decent backup. Thanks to his glove, Wright will stay at third base for the Mets for the foreseeable future, but they have to hope that he has more good years in him. The Wilpons can scarcely afford to write off another $100 million.

The Phillies' third baseman of the future, Maikel Franco, had an indifferent big league audition in 2014. His failure to stay above the Mendoza line as a 22-year old is not much of a concern—and their current replacement-level third baseman, Cody Asche, will not provide much of an impediment to Franco's advancement. But the Phillies' recent track record with homegrown talent provides more reason for worry. Domonic Brown's flawed handling is a big reason that the Phillies have continued to have to rely on their aging core of Howard, Chase Utley, Jimmy Rollins, and Carlos Ruiz. If Franco cannot live up to his potential, the Phillies will continue to flounder at third.

The return of Grady Sizemore

For some players, the "Comeback Player of the Year" award simply doesn't capture how enormous the accomplishment is. If baseball ever decides to create a new award for unlikeliest comeback of the year, it could be called the Bartolo Colon Award. After Colon managed only 257 major league innings from 2006 to 2010, he reemerged to pitch at least 150 innings in each of the subsequent four seasons.

Grady Sizemore would be the 2014 nominee. Injuries knocked him completely out of the majors in 2012 and 2013, and he had not managed 300 plate appearances in a season since 2009. He signed a low-dollar contract with the Red Sox in the offseason, and scuffled to a .216/.288/.324 mark through his first 205 plate appearances.

It wasn't very good, but it was still noteworthy: he hadn't played a game in three years and spent six separate stints on the disabled list during the previous three seasons. In 2014, Sizemore did not miss a single game due to injury, a victory in itself.

But he actually had a second chance. Or, a third chance, depending on your perspective. The Red Sox released him in June and the troubled Phillies picked him up a few days later, eventually installing him as a sort of permanent fourth outfielder, frequently spelling Domonic Brown in left and Marlon Byrd in right. And for his first two months in Philly, he caught fire. He started 27 games and appeared in 14 others, and hit .306/.354/.463 in 130 plate appearances on a league-minimum salary for a team whose best hitter was Byrd. To put it mildly, they needed him.

He cooled in September, going 4-for-41 with five walks, which pulled his season numbers down to a pedestrian triple slash of .233/.299/.354. Still, his numbers with the Phillies were better than they got from elsewhere: Sizemore hit .253/.313/.389 with the Phillies, while Ryan Howard hit just .223/.310/.380, and batting title contender Ben Revere hit just .306/.325/.361. Part of Sizemore's problem in 2014 was poor usage. For his career, Sizemore's weighted on-base average (wOBA) is 74 points higher against right-handed pitchers than against left-handed pitchers, and in 2014 the gap was 93 points. In 2014, his managers allowed him to collect 103 of his 381 plate appearances against southpaws. That was too many.

It wasn't hard to imagine why he might have worn down as the year went on, since it was the most he'd played in six years. But the season was a success by any definition. He battled back to the majors and reestablished himself as a durable performer. It was beautiful to watch.

The devastating Marlins outfield

Giancarlo Stanton is a household name. But few fans realize just how good his outfield mates were in 2014. Quietly, the Marlins have built one of the most productive outfields in baseball: fourth in the majors in on-base percentage behind only the Pirates, Dodgers and Nationals, and fifth in slugging percentage behind the Rockies, Orioles, Dodgers and Pirates.

Scariest is how young they are. All three—Christian Yelich, Marcell Ozuna and Stanton himself—played the entire 2014 season before turning 25. (Next spring training, Stanton will be 25, Ozuna 24 and Yelich 23.) The emergence of an outfield full of young stars is what made it easier for the Marlins to trade 23-year old Jake Marisnick in the Jarred Cosart deal; Marisnick has plenty of tools, but is far from a finished product, and he was going to have a tough time breaking into an outfield this talented.

Of course, you already know about Stanton, who has been one of the most feared power hitters in baseball since his 2010 debut; he was a leading MVP candidate before he sustained a season-ending injury in early September. But he was the only one of the three to have played a full season before 2014. Yelich and Ozuna both lost their rookie status in half-years in 2013, and both produced roughly similar numbers, good for approximately one and a half wins above replacement in just under 300 plate appearances. In 2014, they each crossed the 600-PA threshold and produced closer to four wins above replacement. If they were better known, and on a better team, they would have been All-Star candidates. If they get hot out of the gate next year, they may well be.

Yelich was well known to prospect hounds even before the Marlins selected him in the first round in 2010; his baby face belies his bat, which tore through the minor leagues; he hit .311/.386/.497 in 1,308 minor league plate appearances, and pushed his way into the majors after only 49 games in Double-A. His eventual major league success was not a surprise.

If there was a surprise, it was was Ozuna. A cousin of former major leaguer Pablo Ozuna, he signed with the Marlins as a 17-year old in the Dominican Republic in 2008. He was known for his power, but he was known to be raw and thought to be a long way from the majors. He didn't reach High-A until his fifth season in the Marlins system, in 2012, and didn't reach Double-A until the following season. But then, after all of 10 games in Double-A, he was called up to the majors to fill in for an injured Stanton.

He's been there ever since, as his glove made him a useful player even when his power didn't immediately translate in 2013. But in 2014, it blossomed, and his 23 homers tied for the fifth-highest total among major league center fielders—tied with Carlos Gomez and behind only Matt Kemp, Andrew McCutchen, Adam Jones and Mike Trout. That's pretty good company.

Evan Gattis: Still a pleasant surprise for the miserable Braves offense

The 2014 Braves had one of baseball's worst offenses. They scored fewer runs than any team other than the Padres, but at least the Padres have the excuse of playing in PETCO Park, perhaps the pitcher-friendliest ballpark in baseball.

You can't lay all of the blame on the starting lineup. Braves pitchers had the fourth-worst OPS in the National League, and Braves pinch-hitters had the second-worst OPS in the NL. But you can lay almost all of the blame on the starting lineup. Nearly every Braves hitter who accumulated 100 plate appearances in both 2013 and 2014 hit worse in 2014 than in 2013, with the following exceptions:

- B.J. Upton improved his weighted on-base average (wOBA) 25 points, from .252 to .277, from horrifying to very bad. It was a real improvement, but not enough to prevent his manager from taking him out of the starting lineup and putting him into a platoon with Emilio Bonifacio, who started in center field for 17 of the final

49 games of the season. It also wasn't enough to prevent the general manager who signed him, Frank Wren, from being fired.

- B.J.'s brother Justin turned in another good year and improved his wOBA six points, from .357 to .363.
- And Evan Gattis improved his wOBA by 23 points, from .329 to .352.

Every other starting player declined.

Gattis' numbers were actually very similar from year to year, except for his batting average on balls in play, which improved tremendously.

Evan Gattis Statistics, 2013-2014										
Year	G	PA	HR	R	RBI	BB%	K%	ISO	BABIP	wOBA
2013	105	382	21	44	65	5.5%	21.2%	.237	.255	.329
2014	108	401	22	41	52	5.5%	24.2%	.230	.298	.352

If anything, the improvement in BABIP helped to demonstrate the kind of hitter Gattis is: a relatively low-walk, low-contact, high-power hitter. From 2013 to 2014, he had the sixth-highest isolated power—which subtracts batting average from slugging percentage to get at how many extra-base hits a player is contributing—in the National League. Other than the lack of walks, his biggest problem is staying on the field: he has now gone to the disabled list twice in two years, and this year he missed an additional two weeks due to a combination of strep throat and kidney stones. (Ouch.)

Gattis is already 28, so he doesn't have a great deal more physical projection; barring any major reinventions in plate approach, he's probably as good a hitter as he'll ever be. And if his BABIP stabilizes closer to .260 than to .300, then 2014 may have been a career year. But that's still enough to make him one of the best hitters on the Braves. If the Braves get dead-cat bounces from the rest of their offense in 2015 (or actually improve the roster), that might be enough to allow them to contend for the playoffs once more.

Mets player development of pitchers: From Dillon Gee to Jacob deGrom

The New York Mets' Jacob DeGrom was the best rookie starter in the National League and one of the Senior Circuit's more effective pitchers, period. deGrom was a ninth-round pick in 2010 out of Stetson University in DeLand, Fla., which is also the alma mater of Corey Kluber (2007, fourth round) and Chris Johnson (2006, fourth round).

The Mets deserve major credit for finding a pitcher of deGrom's quality in the ninth round, but the team actually has a pretty good track record in the last few years. In addition to deGrom, the Mets drafted and developed Jon Niese (2005, seventh round), Dillon Gee (2007, 21st round), and even Collin McHugh (2008, 18th round)—whom they traded to the Rockies in 2013 for Eric Young Jr., and who, after he landed with the Astros, ended up being in a group of six pitchers (along with deGrom) who could claim they were the best rookie pitcher in 2014.

The Astros should be lauded for helping McHugh reach his full potential and succeed for the first time at the major league level, but the Mets' scouts deserve a great deal of credit for identifying and signing him in the first place.

The St. Louis Cardinals are often lionized for finding quality major leaguers in the mid- and late rounds of the draft, like Matt Adams (23rd round), Matt Carpenter (13th round), and Allen Craig (eighth round). But the Mets have been a lot better at this than many people realize.

When the Nats pulled away

The Washington Nationals won the division by 17 games, but that belied how close the division race was for most of the year. The Braves were in first place for much of the first four months of the season, before the Nationals took sole possession of first place on July 21, never to relinquish it.

The Nats scuffled for much of the first half of the season, struggling to stay more than a few games above .500. Through 81 games, the team was tied for first place with the Braves, with just a 43-38 record. But the next 81 games were much different, as the Braves went 36-45 and the Nationals went 53-28.

Washington pulled away as the Braves underwent one of the worst offensive collapses in recent memory, but the Nats also caught fire themselves, and their 4-3 victory on July 30 was emblematic. Entering the game with a half-game lead in the division, the Nationals were tied 1-1 with the Marlins after seven innings, before they scored three runs in the eighth on a Jayson Werth sacrifice fly and a two-run Ian Desmond double. They then hung on for the win, despite the fact that Drew Storen allowed a home run to Giancarlo Stanton and an RBI double to Adeiny Hechevarria before picking up his first save of the season. (Unfortunately for the Nationals, Storen's shaky performance prefigured their postseason run.) The Braves lost 3-2 to the Dodgers in 10 innings, and fell a game and a half behind Washington. Atlanta would never get any closer to the division lead.

A day after this win, the Nationals made one of the best moves at the trade deadline, trading Zach Walters for Asdrubal Cabrera, who had worn out his welcome in Cleveland but who in Washington was perfectly capable of filling the black hole at second base caused by the inexplicable disappearance of Danny Espinosa's bat. They then effectively put away the division for good with a 10-game winning streak from Aug. 12-21, after which neither the Braves nor anyone else could threaten their lead.

When the Braves collapsed

Though the Braves and Nationals shared the same record through 81 games, the Nationals probably had a more talented 25-man roster, particularly after the Braves lost Kris Medlen, Brandon Beachy and Gavin Floyd to season-ending injuries. But the Braves' pitching was not their problem. The problem was the offense. Through July 31, the Braves as a team hit .246/.310/.373, and scored 3.8 runs a game—not particularly good, but barely worse than the Nationals, who hit .249/.317/.381 and averaged 4.2 runs a game. However, after that point, the two teams sharply diverged, as the Braves slumped to .230/.294/.334, and scored just three runs a game, while the Nats improved to .261/.328/.416, and scored 4.4 runs a game.

The Braves effectively sealed their own fate when they lost eight games in a row from July 29 to Aug. 6, including a three-game sweep by the banjo-hitting Padres. But few days were more perfectly representative of their season than Aug. 20. Through seven innings, Alex Wood held the Pirates scoreless. He permitted just three hits and no walks, and Atlanta clung to a slender 2-0 lead that was provided by a two-run single in the first inning.

Then, with his pitch count at 90, Wood came out for the eighth inning and promptly allowed a walk and a ground-rule double. Jordan Walden came in and allowed both inherited runners to score, wiping out the lead. In the ninth, with David Carpenter on the mound, the Pirates got a single, a two-base error, and a walk-off sacrifice fly. The Braves managed to lose despite taking a two-run lead into the eighth inning, and Craig Kimbrel, the best closer in baseball, never got a chance to enter the game.

The loss snapped a five-game win streak. But because the Nationals were in the midst of their own 10-game win streak, each Braves win left them exactly six games back in the division, and this loss dropped them seven back. A win on Aug. 31 got them once more to within six games, but with a 7-18 September record, they would get no closer.

The Phillies and Cliff Lee

The Phillies had an execrable season. But perhaps no moment better encapsulated their year than July 31, the day of the trade deadline. Cliff Lee was known as one of the most desirable starting pitchers on the trade market, if the Phillies were willing to trade him.

In the fourth year of a five-year deal, with $37.5 million guaranteed remaining on his contract after 2014, Lee pitched well for the first two months of the season, but then went onto the disabled list for two months with an elbow strain. He returned in mid-July, time enough for the Phillies to showcase him on the trade market. In early July, with Lee on minor league rehab and getting ready to return to the majors, ESPN reported that "other clubs ... expect the Phillies to aggressively attempt to move Lee," and that "teams that have spoken with the Phillies say the club has indicated it is willing to eat a significant portion of Lee's salary."

It stood to reason that the Phillies would do so. The team's slim playoff chances were sunk by a poor offense and by the two-month injury to Lee, and years of win-now trading had left the minor league cupboard nearly bare. But the team's general manager, Ruben Amaro Jr., confounded expectations by failing to sell.

Three hours after the trade deadline had passed on that fateful July 31, Lee took the mound for his scheduled start. He departed after just 30 pitches after suffering the same elbow injury as before. They were his last pitches of the season, and the Phillies had lost their best chance to improve their team for 2015 and beyond.

Jason Heyward, the Alex Gordon of the National League

In 2014, Alex Gordon of the Royals had a dark horse Most Valuable Player campaign. He was a left fielder who hit .266, but drew a bunch of walks, hit for decent power, and was perhaps the best defensive player in the American League. Like the Hall of Fame candidacy of Bert Blyleven, his excellent season provided a teaching moment for sabermetricians to explain the scale of each of the quantities that go into wins above replacement (WAR), to explain how a .266 hitter could plausibly be considered one of the best players in his league.

There was a player in the National League who had a very similar season, but garnered only a fraction of the attention: Jason Heyward. He hit .271 with just 11 homers and a .735 OPS, but thanks to his glove, he was worth five or six wins.

Heyward suffers from the age-old problem of prospect fatigue: After enjoying one of the best 20-year old rookie seasons ever, he endured a classic sophomore slump. Since then, he has never been able to please fans who wanted him to be a five-tool perennial All-Star. (Andruw Jones had the same problem: Many Atlanta fans never forgave him for not being Willie Mays.) But Heyward, who in 2014 was in his age-24 season, has turned in three five-win seasons in his five years in the big leagues, and since his 2010 debut, he has been a top-20 player in the big leagues, according to wins above replacement—just ahead of Ryan Braun and just behind Yadier Molina and Gordon himself. (While Braun's suspension cost him much of the 2013 season, they've spent almost the exact same amount of time on the field thanks to Heyward's frequent injuries: since 2010, Braun actually has five more plate appearances than Heyward.)

Heyward suffers from a problem of perception. He hits for low average and relatively low power, but makes up for it with fine baserunning and an otherworldly glove: He is probably the best defensive player in the National League other than his teammate Andrelton Simmons. His power outage is concerning: 24-year olds aren't supposed to see their slugging percentage decline from .479 to .427 to .384 over a three-year period. But his glove and baserunning have actually improved since he came up, and it's a fair bet that he'll remain a valuable player when healthy for the foreseeable future.

The National League Central View

by Greg Simons

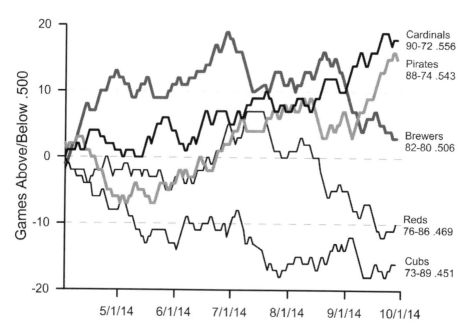

T he 2014 standings for the National League Central division look quite similar to those of 2013. However, the story of how the 2014 season developed—the rises and falls, the heroes and goats, the able-bodied and the infirm—gave a unique texture to how it played out.

Cardinals surge late, reach postseason yet again

Any early-season rumors of the Cardinals' demise proved greatly exaggerated, as the Redbirds once again found themselves playing October baseball, the 11th time in 15 seasons that St. Louis has reached the playoffs. It may be annoying to fans of the rest of the league, but the Cards have continued to tweak their formula from season to season, eschewing one particular way to find success, instead working with the talents of the particular personnel on hand to push into the postseason.

In 2013, St. Louis posted an insanely high .330 batting average with runners in scoring position, allowing the Cardinals to out-produce their expected results at the plate by a wide margin. Their 783 runs scored and +187 run differential comfortably outpaced the rest of the NL. In 2014, it was a totally different story. The Cardinals

---

scored only 619 runs, with a +16 run differential, with neither number leading the division, let alone the league.

St. Louis did excel in one-run games, with a 32-23 record in such contests, second only to San Diego's 33-21. But the Cardinals bullpen wasn't anything special, finishing mid-pack in fWAR and ERA. Ditto the starting pitching, which had a middling fWAR standing despite a top-five ERA finish. That discrepancy can be partially attributed to Busch Stadium's tendency toward favoring pitchers. And the hitting wasn't particularly strong, either, also contributing middle-of-the-road performance in terms of both fWAR and wOBA.

So how did the Cardinals win their division? It's often frustrating to credit impressive or discouraging performances to random chance, but for a team that had a Pythagorean record of 83-79 to finish 90-72, good luck certainly shone.

Obviously, St. Louis has been good more often than it's been lucky, as the previous decade and a half have demonstrated. For the other teams in the division, knowing they couldn't take down the Redbirds when they were vulnerable had to have been frustrating. For the Cardinals and their fans, it was just another chapter in their long-term tome of success.

Oscar Taveras passes away

Baseball lost one its most promising young players in late October when Oscar Taveras and his girlfriend died in a car crash in their native Dominican Republic. The 22-year-old Cardinals outfielder had reached the majors just months before. While Taveras struggled overall in his brief time in the majors, he produced some highlight moments that had fans in his homeland, in St. Louis, and throughout the baseball community anticipating great things from this up-and-coming talent. Now, we have only the memories of his ascension to baseball's grandest stage to dwell upon.

Taveras was signed as a 16-year-old to a $145,000 deal, and he quickly showed that this relatively small investment was quite likely to pay big dividends for the Cardinals. After posting a .257 batting average in his first taste of pro ball in 2009, he never again would have an average under .300 in the minors, peaking at .386 for Class-A Quad Cities in 2011. And that excellent contact swing, combined with acceptable patience and solid power, led many prognosticators to declare Taveras a future perennial batting title candidate who would make multiple All-Star Games.

A Texas League Player of the Year award in 2012 was followed by a difficult 2013 season in which Taveras injured his ankle and played only 47 games. He came out hitting again in 2014 at Triple-A Memphis, performing well enough to earn a promotion to the majors. In his first big-league game—with the falling rain adding to the dramatic atmosphere—Taveras clubbed a home run in his second major league at-bat, helping St. Louis to a 2-0 victory against the San Francisco Giants.

He scuffled for much of the rest of the season, and was even sent back down for a brief stretch in mid-June. He finished the year hitting only .239/.278/.312. However,

Taveras had another impactful performance against those same Giants, this time in the postseason. His pinch-hit, game-tying home run in Game Two of the National League Championship Series helped the Redbirds come back to secure a 5-4 victory.

A stellar minor league career and two key home runs in the majors are much more than most aspiring ballplayers could ever hope for. However, for a fantastic talent like Oscar Taveras, those performances seemed like just an inkling of what was to come. Sadly, for all of us, they are a sobering reminder that the future is not yet written, and that nothing is guaranteed.

The next Ben Zobrist?

Sabermetricians have argued for years that Ben Zobrist is significantly underrated. Sure, he's received MVP votes in three seasons, including an eighth-place finish in 2009, and he's been to two All-Star Games. But a player who posts fWAR in the 5-6 range year after year should be receiving much more recognition, so the thought process goes.

And how does Zobrist continue to rack up big value with so little acclaim? As is often the case, he doesn't excel in any particular area, instead providing a broad base of skills. In 2014, we may have been witness to Zobrist's parallel in the National League in the person of Pittsburgh's Josh Harrison.

An obvious connection between these two players is their defensive flexibility. Zobrist played second base, shortstop and all over the outfield for the Rays in 2014, and he's also manned first and third base on rare occasion in previous years. Harrison covered third base, the corner outfield spots, second base and shortstop this past season, as he had done the previous two campaigns.

The ability of a player to fill multiple defensive spots allows a manager to optimize matchups elsewhere on the diamond as the opposing pitcher and other factors dictate. It gives other players a day off while minimizing performance dropoff, and it provides protection against injuries. What this ability doesn't do much is get the proper attention or credit. Receiving the tag of "utility man" is far from a ringing an endorsement of one's skills.

Zobrist and Harrison also matched up pretty well at the dish. Zobrist batted .272/.354/.395 with 34 doubles, three triples and 10 home runs. Harrison hit .315/.347/.490, with 38 doubles, seven triples and 13 homers. While Zobrist has seen his slugging percentage dry up the last couple of seasons, the bigger difference between these two hitters is their willingness to take a free pass. Zobrist has walked at a 12.1 percent rate over his career and was at 11.5 percent in 2014. Harrison, by contract, has a 3.3 percent career walk rate, with a 4.0 percent mark last season.

The funny thing is, while Zobrist has been underrated because his on-base percentage has been propped up by that strong walk rate, Harrison may be overrated because his on-base percentage is so batting average dependent. Finishing second in the race for the batting title is a fairly high-profile accomplishment, even today, and if Harrison can keep batting .300 every year—which he did frequently in the minors—he'll get some extra hype because of that feat, regardless of whether he ever learns to take a walk.

That's not to say Harrison's BA skills aren't valuable. While batting average has been devalued over time as we've learned that on-base percentage is a more important skill, it's clear that a .315/.350 BA/OBP line is more valuable than a .275/.350 mark, because a walk can advance the runners only a single base, whereas a hit can lead to multiple-base advancements for runners, result in errors, etc.

The 2014 season was Harrison's breakout campaign, his opportunity to show fans throughout the game what he is capable of. Whether he is overrated or underrated, Pittsburgh certainly is pleased that he was a key cog in the Pirates' first repeat playoff appearances since 1990-92.

Reds flop in second half

At the All-Star break, the NL Central was a four-team race. Milwaukee was coasting on the fumes of its blazing-hot 18-6 start, pacing the division at 53-43. (Yes, this means the Brewers still were in first place despite a sub-.500 record from late April to mid July.) The eventual champion Cardinals were a game back, the Reds were 1.5 behind, and the Pirates sat 3.5 games shy of the Brew Crew, though of course Pittsburgh climbed into the first Wild Card spot by season's end.

Milwaukee's steady slide to mediocrity—they finished 82-80—seemed almost inevitable. Cincinnati, however, was expected to contend all season. But the Reds put any postseason aspirations to rest quickly after the season's second half began.

Yes, Joey Votto had been lost to a quad strain for the second time, the first DL stay lasting 23 games and the second the remainder of the year, but one player cannot change a team's fortunes alone. And besides, Johnny Cueto helped counter Votto's absence with his year-long presence, during which he pitched spectacularly.

Additionally, Devin Mesoraco had the breakout Cincinnati had been waiting for, ripping 25 home runs, batting .273/.359/.534 and posting a 149 OPS+. And Todd Frazier made the All-Star Game on his way to a .273/.336/.459 line that included 29 long balls.

The problems, then, rested with the remainder of the roster. In the rotation, Alfredo Simon was a first-half sensation, going 12-3 with a 2.70 ERA. He won only three games the rest of the way, and his ERA climbed to 3.44. Mike Leake and Homer Bailey had identical 97 ERA+ marks, demonstrating thorough mediocrity, though Leake chewed up 50 percent more innings that Bailey. Mat Latos pitched just over 100 frames, and Tony Cingrani learned that big league hitters can catch up to anyone's fastball over time.

On the other side of the ball, Brandon Phillips started to show his age, Zack Cozart's bat regressed, and the trio of Ryan Ludwick, Billy Hamilton and Jay Bruce pretty much defined "second-division outfield."

This isn't an old team, but it's not a particularly young one, either. With its best player missing significant time to injury, its second-highest paid one playing a position—second base—that has historically not aged well, and its ace eligible for free agency after next season, the Reds are coming up to a crossroads. Do they count on returns to prominence from Votto and Phillips, hope Cozart and Bruce get their mojo back, and bank on repeats of Cueto's and Mesoraco's excellent years? Or does Cincinnati decide to rebuild, dealing Phillips and the starting pitchers who are getting ever closer to free agency?

In reality, this winter would be too soon to pack things in. The Reds have made the playoffs in three of the last five seasons, though they failed to reach the NLCS during any of those October ventures. There's lots of talent on the roster, and health and continued development could lead them back to contention. But with the Cardinals a constant threat, the Pirates finally resurgent, the Brewers in a similar spot as the Reds, and the Cubs poised to explode with their young hitters, 2014 might have been Cincinnati's last shot at an NL Central crown for a while.

Hamilton's game-changing speed really didn't change many games

The fastest man in baseball patrols center field for the Cincinnati Reds. As a minor league middle infielder in 2011, Billy Hamilton made everyone take notice by swiping 103 bases in 135 Single-A games. The next year, he set the single-season professional record for steals with 155 between High-A and Double-A. Perhaps bored, or tired of showing off, he pilfered "only" 75 bases in 2013 at Triple-A.

Quite clearly, Hamilton is blazingly fast. What he is not—at least not yet—is particularly wise about when he should steal. While minor league pitchers and catchers gave him few problems—he swiped 395 bags in the minors at an 82.5 percent success rate and probably had the green light all the time—big league batteries have presented a greater challenge.

After breaking into the majors late in 2013 and successfully stealing 13 bases before being caught by the immortal Juan Centeno (file that name away for future trivia games), 2014 was not as easy for Hamilton. He did finish second to Dee Gordon with 56 stolen bases, but he was caught a league-leading 23 times. (Gordon swiped 64 bags and was caught 19 times, a 77 percent success rate.) Hamilton made it only 71 percent of the time, slightly below the major league average of 72 percent.

This means that, for all Hamilton's speed, for all the chaos that supposedly ensues when he reaches first base, he actually hurt the Reds slightly with his base-stealing attempts. This doesn't mean that Hamilton's speed does not provide value overall. FanGraphs credits him with 6.4 base-running runs for 2014, indicating Hamilton's consistent ability to take third on a single, score from first on a double, and generally zoom around the bases more quickly than anyone else does can contribute to his team's success.

If he learns to refine his approach at the game's highest level, Hamilton could wreak havoc with his base-running exploits in a way not seen since Vince Coleman. (Any attempts at a Rickey Henderson comparison would seem absurd.) If he does not adjust his game plan—and if he can't get his on-base percentage above .300—matching Coleman's career will be nothing but a pipe dream for the current fastest man on the base paths.

Ryan Braun struggles

While no one player has too great an impact on any team's fate—perhaps with the exception of guys such as Babe Ruth and Barry Bonds—it's clear the Brewers were counting on much better performance from Ryan Braun than they received. Even though he earned a relatively paltry salary of $10 million for the 2014 campaign while top-tier players are now inking deals valued at more than $30 per annum, the $117 million Braun is owed through 2020 is indicative of the type of performance Milwaukee expects him to produce.

What the Brewers did get in 2014 was a .266/.324/.453 line with 19 homers and 11 steals over 135 games. Factor in Braun's poor defense, and he totaled 1.2 fWAR. That's none too impressive, especially considering Braun totaled 1.6 fWAR in 2013 in only 61 games and had topped 7.0 fWAR in both 2011 and 2012.

The reasons behind this performance drop are many. Braun is now on the wrong side of 30. He dealt with a thumb injury all season long, which almost certainly affected his swing. And, of course, there was the PED suspension at the end of the 2013 campaign. Determining the benefits of that chemical mixture is impossible, but it must be considered.

With Gold Glove winner Gerardo Parra now in the fold, along with Carlos Gomez and Khris Davis, Milwaukee has discussed shifting Braun to first base. If this move occurs, it would place even greater emphasis on his hitting abilities. The Brewers have had enough middling first baseman the last few seasons; they don't need another.

If his thumb heals, and he shrugs off Father Time and any lingering PED questions, Braun could give the Brewers the thumper they need to remain relevant in the division. If not, 2014 may have been the beginning of the end of Ryan Braun as an impact player.

The Cubs really are paying attention to their pitching, too

The Cubs had a parade of young hitters reach the majors in 2014, and 2015 will bring another stud or two to the position player portion of the ledger. Figuring out where to play all these potential stars could be the worst of the team's issues from an offensive standpoint. What Chicago needs to focus on next is the pitching talent necessary to complement its hitters. Fortunately, that work already has begun, though no one should think of Edwin Jackson as a good example of those efforts.

While the North Siders have indicated a willingness to spend big on starting pitching—they put in a waiver claim on Cole Hamels last August, and the Theo Epstein/Jed Hoyer connection has led many to speculate that they'll be in on Jon Lester over the winter—their approach thus far has consisted mostly of low-cost, low-profile acquisitions, the Jackson mistake contract notwithstanding.

Two such examples that worked out quite well in 2014 were Jake Arrieta and Kyle Hendricks. Arrieta was acquired from the Baltimore in July of 2013 as part of the trade that sent Scott Feldman to the O's (the Feldman signing being another example of their methodology). Despite coming up as a promising prospect, Arrieta never had a major league ERA lower than 4.66 in three-plus seasons with the Orioles, and that was back in 2010, yielding an ERA+ of 89 in 100.1 innings. His ERAs climbed to 5.05, 6.20, and finally 7.23 before he was dealt to Chicago.

Something seemed to click, as Arrieta sported a 3.66 ERA in 51.2 frames over nine starts for the Cubbies. Then came 2014. Though he only had 10 wins to show for his efforts in 25 starts, Arrieta posted a 151 ERA+ over 156.2 innings, punching out 167 batters, allowing fewer than one base runner per inning, and sporting a 4.1 strikeout-to-walk ratio. It seems likely that the Cubs front office and player development staffs have found and developed an above-average starter who will be cheap for the next few seasons.

Though he had a shorter run of success, Hendricks' path to the North Side echoes Arrieta's. With the Cubs going nowhere at the 2012 trade deadline, they picked up Hendricks in a deal that sent Ryan Dempster to the Texas Rangers. Hendricks can't match the strikeout wizardry of Arrieta, but he has pinpoint control, never walking more than two batters per nine innings in the minors and issuing only 1.7 free passes per nine in 2014. His lack of Ks may limit his upside, and his 2.46 ERA may be fluky, but Chicago would be quite happy with a cheap No. 4 starter for the next few years.

It's taken a while for Epstein and Hoyer to put their plan in place, but things finally started to come together for Chicago at the end of the year. The glimmer of hope the Bleacher Bums have been waiting such a long time for shone faintly in the second half of the season. Those who were looking for it may have seen the beginnings of something much brighter.

The story of two seasons in the tale of one game

Is it possible to capture the feel of an entire 162-game season in a single game? It may be a stretch, but if any game can do it, the July 11 contest between the St. Louis Cardinals and Milwaukee Brewers is the one.

On this mid-summer day in the more northerly of the beer-making cities these two teams represent, the Redbirds were scuffling. Joe Kelly had lasted all of three innings for the Cardinals, surrendering six runs on seven hits and two walks. The faint silver lining was that he struck three batters. At the plate, they managed only two hits (one by Kelly) in the first three innings, though one of their base runners was erased by a double play.

The Cardinals came out of the gate trailing the lofty expectations placed upon them. Presumed to be the cream of the NL Central crop, St. Louis couldn't sustain a run of any significant length. While they were never awful, a 17-5 drubbing in the middle of May at the hand of the Cubs dropped the Cardinals to 19-20, 5.5 games back, though still in second place.

On the flip side, the home team broke loose with a terrific start. The first three batters in the bottom half of the first inning reached base, and when the inning was over, all three runners had scored. The second frame featured more of the same, as two singles and a pair of triples plated three more runs.

The Brewers' season started like gangbusters also, as they jumped out to a 10-2 start and pushed their record to 18-6 by late April. Two months later, they had nudged their mark to 51-32 and held a 6.5-game division lead.

The Redbirds came to life in the middle innings, breaking onto the scoreboard with a fourth-inning two-run home run from Matt Adams. In the sixth frame, Kolten Wong and Jhonny Peralta ripped homers of their own, and a run-scoring groundout knotted the score at 6-6.

On the year, St. Louis rarely scored with such assertiveness, finishing last in the NL in long balls. However, the Cardinals did have strong bursts of victories. After that blowout at the hands of the Cubs, the Redbirds would immediately climb above .500, winning seven of eight games, and nine of 11. A brief dry spell—similar to the lack of scoring in the fifth inning—quickly was followed by a stretch of eight wins in nine games. By July 12—the day after this specific game—the Cardinals had caught the Brewers for the division lead.

Milwaukee was not shut down completely, getting doubles in both the third and fourth and a single in the fifth, but the Brewers clearly were not the same team that had pounced on the opposition early. Yovani Gallardo stumbled his way through 5.1 innings, allowing five runs via seven hits and a walk. The immortal Rob Wooten then entered in relief and promptly gave up two hits and a walk without recording an out, and Zach Duke was charged with a blown save as he allowed the tying run to score.

Immediately following their surge to that high-water mark of 51-32, the Brewers endured a 1-11 stretch that caused their division lead to evaporate completely. While they did retake sole possession of first place, and maintained their lead to the end of August, it was at this juncture the good vibes from their strong start had evaporated, and it was clear they were holding knives in a gunfight.

The Cardinals couldn't make a move as the game swept through the seventh and eighth innings, garnering just one single in those two frames. However, Matt Holliday struck yet another long ball—the Redbirds' third of the day—with two outs in the ninth, putting St. Louis in the driver's seat heading into the last of the ninth. But things didn't go smoothly—they rarely did—for young closer Trevor Rosenthal, who gave up a leadoff single, giving the opposition a chance.

After stumbling along through the second half of July and all of August—almost perfectly paralleling catcher Yadier Molina's time on the disabled list with a thumb injury—on Sept. 1, the Cards moved into sole possession of first place. While their lead quickly swelled to 4.5 games, they made the end exciting by allowing their opposition to get within a single game before putting away the NL Central crown on the second-to-last day of the season.

The Brewers gave it a good effort, putting at least one runner on base in each of the final three innings, but their heady start served only to mask their weak finish. Four of their final nine outs were via strikeout, and they couldn't plate a run. Two whiffs and a groundout to finish off the ninth sent Milwaukee to the showers on the wrong end of a 7-6 final score.

The Brew Crew struggled through a 1-13 slide in late August and early September that saw the division title slip away for good. The season's final month was particularly unkind, as Milwaukee went 9-17, stumbling and tumbling to third place, a full eight games behind St. Louis.

Reds wave the white flag

In 2013, Cincinnati reached the postseason as the second Wild Card. In 2014, the Reds were expected to contend for an October invitation again. The actual results failed to live up to expectations: The Queen City nine finished the year 10 games under .500 and out of the playoff chase several weeks before the season ended.

Cincinnati's July 28 home game against Arizona was an excellent example of the suffering the Reds and their fans endured as the summer went along. There was promise early on, a long stretch of "eh," and a painful ending. How about some specifics?

After a horrible start to the year that saw him post a 6.15 ERA in April, Homer Bailey took the mound to start the game after having improved significantly from that beginning, reducing that ERA mark to a still-middling 4.22. He was terrific in this game, going eight innings and surrendering only a single run. All he needed for the victory was a decent showing by the Reds' bats. That's all. But he wouldn't get it.

Things looked promising early on at Great American Ballpark, as Devin Mesoraco led off the bottom of the second with a deep solo homer to left. (He would add another hit later in the game and finish 2-for-5, the Reds' offensive star of the game.) A double and single followed, nearly scoring a second run, but Brayan Pena was thrown out at the plate.

The Diamondbacks responded in the top of the fourth, with their double-single combo plating the tying run. And then...nothing happened for a very...long...time.

The Reds certainly missed Joey Votto, in this game and many others. His consistent .400-plus on-base percentage and overall excellence may not have been enough to turn the team's season around, but he might have kept them on the good side of .500. In this contest, Pena played first base, an obviously precipitous drop-off in performance, though he did have two hits in the game. The legendary Kristopher Negron, playing second base in place of Brandon Phillips, also had two hits. And that was the sum total of the Reds' offense.

Keep in mind that this was against the D-backs, not exactly a juggernaut of the league this past season. Chase Anderson started the game for Arizona and limited the Reds to one run over seven innings before turning the game over to the bullpen. And the 'pen kept Cincinnati off the scoreboard for quite a stretch.

Hurting the Reds' cause were these performances:

- Billy Hamilton, 0-for-6, three strikeouts
- Jay Bruce, 0-for-4, three Ks
- Todd Frazier, 0-for-6, four whiffs
- Chris Heisey, 0-for-6, two strikeouts

Hamilton, as we discussed above, wasn't much with the stick. And as you will read later in this book, Jay Bruce was a disaster all season, and Heisey has never been much better than that. So when you throw in one of the better performing players in Frazier posting an 0-for-6, you have a recipe for trouble.

So how did this contest end? In the top of the 15th inning, a one-out walk, a groundout, and a single put the Diamondbacks ahead, and their closer, Addison Reed, recorded punchouts for two of the three outs to finish off the game.

This may not have been Cincinnati's worst game of the season, but it's certainly very near the bottom. And it demonstrated the futility of the Reds' attempts to remain relevant in the playoff race. With the loss, they dropped below .500. Though they bubbled up above break-even a little while longer, the Reds slumped badly over the last several weeks, wrapping up the 2014 campaign in fourth place, 14 games out.

Catching on in Pittsburgh

Remember when Russell Martin was such a weak-hitting catcher, batting only .249/.350/.330 with a dozen total homers over his last two seasons with the Dodgers? All he could land was a one-year, $4 million contract with the Yankees, which was followed by another one-year deal, though this one was for $7.5 million after his power came back, as Martin had hit 18 home runs.

He hit 21 more long balls in his second year in pinstripes, but his batting average was an intolerable .211. Though the Yankees had no clear successor behind the dish, they had some fuzzy, self-imposed financial limitations that "prevented" them from signing Martin to a long-term deal. Of course, this is when the big-money Pirates swooped in and out-bid the Bronx Bombers with their two-year, $17 million outlay, the largest contract Pittsburgh ever had given to a free agent.

From there, everything played out as expected. New York failed to make the playoffs over the next two seasons, while Martin led Pittsburgh to the postseason in both his years with the Pirates. It was inevitable. (The actual inevitable part was when the Yankees spent big on catcher Brian McCann, who then failed to outproduce Martin, despite playing in 29 more games.)

Okay, there may have been a few others factors involved in each team's destiny, but Martin certainly made his mark in Pittsburgh. Pitchers love throwing to him, his defense is highly rated by both the eyes and the numbers, and his gritty attitude endears him to the fans.

Martin's second career renaissance was particularly important to the Pirates. His .402 on-base percentage (buoyed by a career-high 15 hit-by-pitches) was second in the NL to teammate Andrew McCutchen's .410 mark, among players with 450-plus plate appearances. Martin's .290 batting average and 11 homers helped, too, pushing his wRC+ to a career-best 140.

And while evaluating defense continues to be a work in progress, Martin's framing skills are highly rated, the advanced metrics are fond of him, and he threw out 38.5 percent of potential base stealers.

What's not to like? For the Pirates over the past two seasons, the answer has been "almost nothing." Yes, they have a perennial MVP candidate in McCutchen, who is flanked by emerging talents Starling Marte and Gregory Polanco in the outfield. Their starting rotation had a couple of successful reclamation projects in Francisco Liriano and Edinson Volquez to go along with young stud Gerritt Cole. And the bullpen featured multiple standout performances. But Russell Martin was as crucial as anyone to the Pirates' success over the last two seasons.

The National League West View

by Dustin Nosler

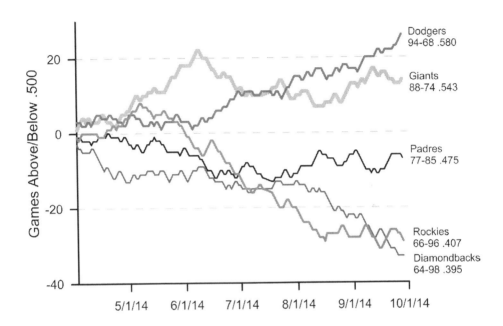

The National League West was always the Los Angeles Dodgers' for the taking in 2014. Over the winter, they were the clear favorite of many baseball pundits and analytic systems. PECOTA projections had the Dodgers pegged for 98 wins. They fell short of that projection at 94, and it wasn't as easy a row to hoe as some thought.

Some other story lines deserve recognition—some positive, some not so positive. Suffice it to say, this division—despite the Dodgers' perceived potential dominance—always will be competitive as long as the San Francisco Giants are around. Arizona, Colorado and San Diego all have some nice pieces, but it's going to take a long time for those pieces to come together. Until then, it looks like a two-horse race.

Front office turmoil for most of the division

When a team fails, the general manager is often the one to fall on the sword. For the Arizona Diamondbacks, Colorado Rockies, Los Angeles Dodgers and San Diego Padres, such was the case during and following the season. While no general managers were fired in 2013, the National League West had four of its five GMs displaced, in some fashion, in 2014.

The Padres were the first: They removed Josh Byrnes in June. The Padres' new ownership group hadn't hired Byrnes, and the Padres hadn't improved much over the past couple of years, so it was just a matter of time. Other San Diego front office members left on their own accord. Vice president/assistant general manager A.J. Hinch quit in August to "explore other opportunities." Hinch was part of Byrnes' regime, so he wasn't likely to be in San Diego long term.

Byrnes' missteps included waiting too long to deal Chase Headley, who regressed after his MVP-caliber 2012 season; he was eventually traded to the Yankees for a less-than-formidable return. A contract extension to Cameron Maybin hasn't gone according to plan due to Maybin's injury history, and the jury is still out on the big contract the team gave Jedd Gyorko. The Padres invested their limited resources in players who are and have the potential to be good-not-great. If those players don't perform, it's difficult for a GM to be successful.

San Diego replaced Byrnes with A.J. Preller, formerly of the Texas Rangers. Preller was one of the brightest and youngest candidates on the market, and Padres ownership made a big splash by bringing him aboard. His impact was felt almost immediately, as he poached longtime Dodgers' vice president of amateur scouting Logan White from Los Angeles. White will oversee the pro scouting department and be a special adviser to Preller. Preller worked for White in 2003 and 2004 with the Dodgers, so when Preller called White and offered him a promotion, it was likely too good for White to pass up.

The Diamondbacks were next, firing general manager Kevin Towers in September. He is famous (infamous?) for trading Justin Upton for essentially Martin Prado because Upton wasn't "gritty" enough for now-ex-manager Kirk Gibson. The Diamondbacks—actually, Tony La Russa, who was brought in to run the show—tapped former pitcher Dave Stewart to succeed Towers. It was an odd choice, seeing as Stewart was previously an agent—most notably for Matt Kemp—though Stewart did spend a brief time as a Blue Jays assistant GM. The Diamondbacks also hired DeJon Watson away from the Dodgers to be their senior vice president. La Russa, Stewart, Watson and Co. will have an opportunity to make their mark right away, since the D-backs hold the No. 1 pick in the 2015 MLB Draft.

Dan O'Dowd had been the Rockies' general manager for 15 years. The Rockies haven't been formidable since 2009, when even Dexter Fowler leaping over Chase Utley couldn't save the team in that year's NL Division Series from Jim Tracy's extreme bullpen mismanagement and Huston Street's inability to retire left-handed hitters. And yet, the Rockies felt compelled to offer him a contract extension before he willingly resigned in October.

He leaves new GM Jeff Bridich, who has been with the Rockies for a decade, in charge of a team coming off a 66-96 season, second worst in the majors. While there appears to be help coming from the farm in the form of Jon Gray and Eddie Butler, and while Nolan Arenado and Corey Dickerson (more on him later) join Carlos

Gonzalez and Troy Tulowitzki as premier players, the Rockies have struggled to play well consistently. There is a lot of work to be done to right the ship in Colorado.

Finally, in perhaps the move that might impact the division the most, the Dodgers removed nine-year general manager Ned Colletti from that post during the NL Championship Series. Many will focus on the Dodgers' five playoff appearances in nine years (they had just one from 1988 to 2005, before Colletti was hired), but with sky-high expectations dashed by an early exit from the NL Division Series, a change was going to come.

Finally, in the move that might impact the division the most, the Dodgers removed nine-year general manager Ned Colletti from his post. Many will focus on the Dodgers' five playoff appearances in nine years (they had one playoff appearance from 1989 to 2005, before Colletti was hired), but with sky-high expectations and an unscheduled early exit from the National League Division Series, a change was going to come. Enter Stan Kasten, who lured former Tampa Bay Rays' general manager Andrew Friedman to be the president of baseball operations in Los Angeles. After losing Logan White to the Padres, Friedman was able to pry Oakland assistant general manager Farhan Zaidi away from Billy Beane. While Zaidi is an extension of what Friedman wants to implement in LA, Zaidi is widely regarded as one of the game's brightest minds and was one of the best candidates available. Beane was more afraid of losing Zaidi to a company like Apple or Google, as opposed to another baseball team. Now, the Dodgers now have a forward-thinking front office in place—something that has been lacking since former GM Paul DePodesta was let go following the 2005 season. They also added Josh Byrnes, who will likely focus on scouting or player development. While the moves have drawn praise in many quarters, Friedman, Zaidi and Co. will have astronomical expectations. They'll also have a big budget with which to play, so it will be interesting to see what they come up with in LA.

Dodgers' bullpen leaks

One of the most volatile components of a baseball team is the bullpen. One minute it could be great, the next a disaster. This encapsulated the Los Angeles Dodgers' relief corps in 2014.

Before the season, that bullpen looked like it could be one of the best in recent memory. Kenley Jansen had become a Proven Veteran Closer, Brian Wilson was back after Tommy John surgery, re-signed to a one-year deal with a player option, J.P. Howell was retained to be LA's primary left-hander, Chris Perez was signed to a deal based purely on his stuff, and Chris Withrow was looking to build on his surprising 2013 season. But then, attrition happened.

Jansen was predictably great. It was the other guys who were a problem. Wilson got hurt in the team's fifth game. Howell performed well for five months, but like his teammate Paco Rodriguez—who toiled in Triple-A and the disabled list most of the season—he had a disastrous finish. Perez was simply never good, and Withrow suffered a torn ulnar collateral ligament in May. Jamey Wright was decent, but right-hander Brandon League could not get a left-handed hitter out (though he was surprisingly good against right-handers). With the injuries and subpar performances, the Dodgers had to turn to youngsters like converted third baseman Pedro Baez, Carlos Frias and others.

At the trade deadline, general manager Ned Colletti was unsuccessful in landing any reliever, let alone an impact one. The two relievers traded at the deadline ended up being Joakim Soria and Andrew Miller. The Dodgers had a lot of interest in Joaquin Benoit but couldn't land him. It turned out ownership effectively handcuffed Colletti and didn't allow him to make what could have been deemed as a foolish or panic move.

For the first time in years, the Dodgers had a really good farm system—a system that could have played a part in trading for a reliever. The organization clearly had three prospects it had zero interest in moving, especially for a reliever—outfielder Joc Pederson, infielder Corey Seager and pitcher Julio Urias. But there were other players they could have traded to improve a bullpen that finished in the bottom third of baseball in most important metrics, including ERA (3.80).

The team's lack of quality bullpen options outside of Jansen was never more apparent than it was in October. The Dodgers bullpen was a factor in every game of the NL Division Series. In Games One and Four, Los Angeles stuck with Clayton Kershaw longer than it should have because manager Don Mattingly didn't trust anyone to be the bridge between him and Jansen. In Game Two, Howell gave up a game-tying home run to Matt Carpenter (in a game the Dodgers would eventually win) and in Game Three, Scott Elbert allowed a game-winning, two-run home run to Kolten Wong.

It's entirely possible to conclude the Dodgers missed a chance at the World Series in 2014 because of one of the team's worst bullpens in a decade.

Why the Giants almost missed the playoffs

Every year produces teams that don't seem to have the most talent yet find a way to be in the thick of things come October. In 2014, that team was the San Francisco Giants, after a roller coaster season.

The Giants got out to a fine start, standing at 43-21 after sweeping the New York Mets June 6 through 8, and holding a 10-game lead on the Los Angeles Dodgers. A month later, the Dodgers had a half-game lead on San Francisco. Now, no one expected the Giants to play nearly .650 baseball for the duration of the season, but a 7-20 stretch in midseason was certainly a notable beating from the regression stick.

It wasn't injuries. Sure, Brandon Belt's broken thumb and Angel Pagan's back problems didn't help matters, but the thing that did them in was their pitching. In June, the pitching staff posted a collective 4.31 ERA—fourth worst in the majors—

while striking out fewer batters per nine innings pitched (6.8, also fourth worst) than in any other month.

This is an organization that always has been built on pitching, and in AT&T Park that makes sense. But the starting rotation suffered from general ineffectiveness that almost sunk the team's season. The bullpen wasn't much better. Three of the most important relievers had horrible Junes—Sergio Romo (9.72 ERA), Jean Machi (6.00) and Javier Lopez (6.35). Romo was removed from his closing role in favor of Santiago Casilla.

The Giants' offense also contributed to the midseason near-collapse, scoring only 93 runs in June and a mere 85 in July. For reference, the Toronto Blue Jays scored 165 runs in the month of May alone (a major league high for any month in 2014). Generally known for his defense, shortstop Brandon Crawford was one of the team's best hitters in June. Center fielder Pagan hurt his back (again), and Michael Morse decided that June would be the month he would stop trying to draw walks. The team would give 181 plate appearances to Joaquin Arias, Tyler Colvin, Brandon Hicks and Hector Sanchez, who collectively hit .183/.239/.256 during that period. Soon after, players like Joe Panik and Andrew Susac would emerge from the farm system as valuable pieces of the puzzle, but in June this collection of cast-offs nearly sank the ship.

No-hitters galore

The 2014 season saw five no-hitters, and three of them were thrown by National League West pitchers. While some no-hitters aren't necessarily the greatest pitching accomplishments, they're still impressive. Each of these three had its own character. One was unexpected, one could have been expected to happen eventually and one was a trip down memory lane…to 2013.

The first was thrown by a most unlikely candidate, Josh Beckett. Sure, Beckett always had the ability and stuff to throw a no-hitter, but he was a shell of his former self in recent years and hadn't performed well after he came to the Dodgers in the famed Adrian Gonzalez trade. Beckett twirled his no-hitter in Philadelphia on May 25. It was a career-high 128-pitch performance that saw him with a pitch count of 90 through six innings. He wasn't the same workhorse pitcher he had been in his past, so there were questions about whether Beckett would finish the game. But he needed just 38 pitches for the final three innings, finishing with a strikeout of Chase Utley.

Beckett would battle through a hip injury the rest of the way before throwing his last game on Aug. 3. The no-hitter was the first—and also last—of Beckett's career: He announced his retirement after the Dodgers were eliminated from the playoffs.

The all-but-expected no-hitter came from Dodgers southpaw Clayton Kershaw. Not all great pitchers throw these gems – Pedro Martinez never did, for instance. Kershaw had not yet, either, before June 18 against the Rockies. This wasn't a standard no-hitter; Kershaw did things in this game no pitcher had ever done, like strike out 15 batters without allowing a hit or a walk. His 102 Game Score was the second best of all time, just behind Kerry Wood's 20-strikeout game back in 1998. It was one of the most dominant pitching performances in the game's history and might have been even more so. Hanley Ramirez' throwing error in the seventh inning was the only blemish on an otherwise perfect night for Kershaw.

The final NL West no-hitter was by a return performer. Tim Lincecum has battled adversity over the last few years: His fall from top-five pitcher to back-of-the-rotation starter to relief pitcher has been swift. But on June 25, Lincecum was the Lincecum of days gone by. Pitching at home, he stymied the same team he had no-hit in San Diego less than a year earlier—the Padres. His 2014 no-hitter wasn't as dominant (six strikeouts, one walk) as the 2013 version (13 strikeouts, four walks), but it also wasn't anywhere near as stressful for Lincecum. He threw just 113 pitches in this no-hitter, compared to 148 the first time. Unfortunately for Lincecum, he struggled after the no-hitter, posting a 5.20 ERA in his final 17 appearances.

The decline of Andre Ethier

Like Tim Lincecum, it wasn't long ago that Andre Ethier was a valuable contributor—he even had the moniker of "Captain Clutch." But his decline, too, has been rapid and severe.

When the Guggenheim Group took over the Dodgers in May of 2012, it had a lot of work to do to repair the damage Frank McCourt and Co., did in Los Angeles. One of the group's first moves was to sign Ethier to a five-year, $85 million contract extension. Ethier was set to become a free agent following the 2012 season, and at a time when Yasiel Puig was an unknown and Matt Kemp was hurt, it looked like a prudent decision to stabilize the Dodgers' future outfield. However, the deal has backfired to the point that Ethier was relegated to pinch-hitting duties late in the 2014 season.

After he signed the extension, Ethier played 87 more games in the 2012 season. He hit a respectable .280/.352/.425 with 10 home runs and essentially matched that production in 2013 (.272/.360/.423). But when 2014 came around, Ethier was on a short leash. Puig had proven himself, and when Carl Crawford and Kemp were healthy, the Dodgers had too many outfielders.

Ethier was the one who saw his playing time cut most drastically. It was clear that his bat speed had slowed, and in the end he was essentially a replacement-level player. He hit just .249/.322/.370 with four home runs in 130 games. He had career lows in every major offensive category.

Moreover, since his batted ball distance has dropped so sharply, this doesn't seem like a fluke.

In 2012, Ethier averaged 284 feet on his fly balls (122nd in baseball). Not great, but certainly you could do a lot worse, especially given how many games the Dodgers play at sea level. But in 2013, that dropped to 276 feet (188th) and then in 2014 it fell again to 271 (209th). Combine this drop in both production and raw talent with

Scott Van Slyke's emergence, Crawford's comeback, Kemp's good health and Puig's awesomeness, and there was virtually no playing time left for fan favorite Ethier. If the Dodgers can manage it, he'll be playing elsewhere in 2015.

The rubber match

The Dodgers and Giants effectively decided the National League West in a series Sept. 12-14 in San Francisco. The first two games were routs: The Giants took the first, 9-0, and the Dodgers the second, 17-0. As such, the two teams entered the rubber match the same way the series began, with Los Angeles up by two games. With just 13 games left, the Giants needed to win the final game of this series. They would send the surprising Yusmeiro Petit to the hill, but Clayton Kershaw was his opposite number.

It was a classic Dodgers-Giants rivalry game, with pitching as the star. Kershaw has enjoyed ample success against the Giants in his career, and this game was no different. Normally, an eight-inning, two-run outing from a starting pitcher, which Kershaw delivered, would be praiseworthy, but he set the bar so incredibly high in 2014 that when he allowed more than one run, it seemed like a disappointment. This effort produced just his 18th-best Game Score of 2014 (68).

And it isn't like the Giants pitched poorly. Petit allowed four runs (three earned) in seven innings, and the staff as a whole struck out 11 and didn't allow one walk. But Matt Kemp, enjoying a resurgent second half, hit a two-run homer in the second inning, and the Dodgers won, 4-2.

The teams would meet eight days later in Los Angeles, but by that point the Dodgers had a four-and-a-half-game lead, and it would prove insurmountable. Three days later, the Dodgers clinched the West – and the season series against San Francisco, 10-9.

The Giants would get the last laugh, winning the NL pennant, but the goal of each regular season is to win the division, and winning the rubber match on Sept. 14 helped the Dodgers do so with as little drama as possible.

Kershaw's 2014 season vs. Gibson's 1968

It has been 46 years since a pitcher won the Most Valuable Player in the National League: Bob Gibson in his magical 1968 season. The NL has always been thought of as the pitchers' league, but seven pitchers have won the American League MVP since 1968—Denny McLain (1968), Vida Blue (1971), Rollie Fingers (1981), Willie Hernandez (1984), Roger Clemens (1986), Dennis Eckersley (1992) and Justin Verlander (2011). That's not to say there haven't been pitching seasons worthy of the MVP in the NL (Orel Hershiser in 1988, Greg Maddux in 1994 and 1995, Randy Johnson in 1999). The voters just have not seen it the same way. With no offensive players making a clear case for the award, Kershaw's dominant 2014 seemed worthy of breaking that long streak.

There are a lot of similarities between Kershaw's 2014 and Gibson's 1968. The number that stands out most is Gibson's 1.12 ERA, the lowest for a qualified starter since that time. Pitchers like Maddux and Pedro Martinez have come the closest, but they weren't really that close. Kershaw led the majors in ERA for the fourth consecutive season in 2014 with a career-best 1.77 ERA.

Gibson's and Kershaw's standout seasons—in different eras—had striking similarities:

- Batting average against: Kershaw .194, Gibson .181
- Fielding independent pitching: 1.81, 1.77
- Home runs per nine innings: 0.41, 0.32
- Walks per nine innings: 1.4, 1.8
- Walks plus hits/innings pitched: 0.857, 0.853

Gibson takes the cake in terms of Wins Above Replacement, in part because Kershaw missed a month due to a back/shoulder injury. While Kershaw's 198.1 innings pitched are nothing to sneeze at, doing what Gibson did over 300 innings is pretty amazing. Where Kershaw sets himself apart is strikeouts. His 10.8 strikeouts per nine innings led the majors and marked a career high for him. Gibson struck out 7.9 batters per nine innings, fifth best that season, but we wouldn't consider it dominant outside of his era. Gibson also benefited from a much lower batting average on balls in play (.230 to .278). As such, Kershaw has a case for the better season, especially considering the era. Either way, both were pretty special seasons.

Corey Dickerson emerges

Every year, players who people don't expect much from produce anyway. They may be veterans coming off a few bad seasons, prospects who are getting their first crack at a full-time job or young players who weren't widely regarded. The Rockies' Corey Dickerson falls into the third category.

Dickerson finished his age-25 season with an impressive .312/.364/.567 triple-slash line, with 24 home runs in 131 games. If Dickerson had qualified for the batting title, he would have finished second in slugging percentage in the majors behind Jose Abreu of the Chicago White Sox. It was a down year for slugging in the bigs, but that's still an impressive feat.

Despite a hot start by Charlie Blackmon (which he couldn't sustain), Dickerson worked his way into the lineup, aided by Carlos Gonzalez's injuries. Dickerson made the most of his opportunity and could be the next great hitter for the Rockies.

Two things are working against him: He's a left-handed hitter who needs to hit lefties better, and he needs to hit better away from the friendly confines of Coors Field. Now, that's not to say Dickerson was totally unplayable against lefties—he hit .253/.306/.418 against them with three home runs—but he did that in just 98 plate appearances. The Rockies had Michael Cuddyer (when he wasn't hurt), Brandon

Barnes and Drew Stubbs to play against left-handed pitchers, so playing time wasn't as available for Dickerson.

Dickerson's home-road splits might give some pause. The Rockies always are going to hit better at home, and Dickerson was no exception. He batted .363/.415/.684 at Coors Field with 15 home runs compared to .252/.305/.431 with nine home runs on the road. He did get 18 of his 39 extra-base hits on the road, however, and players like Matt Holliday and Dexter Fowler have hit well once departing Colorado. So, while Dickerson wasn't as good on the road, he likely isn't a mirage, either.

If the Rockies decide to trade Carlos Gonzalez in the offseason, Dickerson figures to slide in as the team's everyday left fielder. One thing is for sure: Dickerson's 2014 performance shows he deserves a chance to be a true everyday player in 2015.

Tyson Ross proves his doubters wrong

Choosing an emerging pitcher who pitches in Petco Park is like choosing an emerging hitter who hits in Coors Field. (You know, like Corey Dickerson.) But the San Diego Padres have someone who could be a thorn in the sides of other National League West teams going forward in Tyson Ross.

Ross, 27, was acquired from the Oakland A's in November of 2012 in what looked like a minor deal—Ross and A.J. Kirby-Jones (who is a real person, it seems), for Andy Parrino and Andrew Werner. After all, at the time, Ross had a career 5.33 ERA, and hadn't found much success as a starter or a reliever in Oakland.

It turned out to be quite the one-sided affair in favor of the Padres. Ross was the Padres' lone All-Star representative in 2014. While that doesn't mean a whole lot, what does are the numbers he put up as the San Diego ace. He struck out 195 batters in 195.2 innings, posted a 2.81 ERA and kept the ball in the yard, with a 0.6 home-runs-per-nine-innings rate. He does it all with a 93-mph fastball that he can bump up to 96-97, but his big weapon is his slider. It's a pitch that FanGraphs rated as 20.3 runs above average—second best in baseball behind some guy named Kershaw in Los Angeles.

Ross became a much more groundball-focused pitcher, as he raised his ground ball-to-fly ball ratio to 2.58, second best in baseball. He also improved other in areas that lead to success. He got more swings outside the strike zone in 2014 than 2013 (33.4 percent compared to 32.9 percent), more swinging strikes (12.5 percent compared to 11.1 percent) and less contact on pitches inside the strike zone (84 percent compared to 89 percent). All of those improvements are factors in his success.

As most pitchers do, Ross benefited from pitching in Petco Park. He had a sparkling 1.88 ERA in 100.2 innings at home in 2014. He was decent on the road (3.79 ERA in 95 innings), but he was Kershawian at home. And he doesn't get knocked around by left-handed hitters: He posted almost identical platoon splits in 2014: .231/.295/.337 against righties, .230/.319/.317 against lefties.

Ross is a big pitcher at 6-foot-5 and has the frame to turn into not only a work-horse starting pitcher, but a quality starting pitcher with a chance to be great, especially if he remains in San Diego. The new front office will have to balance his expected production and cost, which is about to increase in arbitration, but Ross is good enough to pitch significant innings for a first-division team right now. Padres fans hope he won't have to go anywhere to do so.

A miserable D-backs season brings a No. 1 pick

The Diamondbacks came into the 2014 season as a second-place ball club, albeit a .500 one in 2013. Still, they had NL MVP runner-up Paul Goldschmidt and some decent starting pitchers in Wade Miley, Patrick Corbin, Trevor Cahill, Brandon McCarthy and free-agent signee Bronson Arroyo. But before the season even started in Australia against the Los Angeles Dodgers, they lost Corbin to Tommy John surgery, moving everyone up a spot. And not everyone was qualified to move up a spot.

Cahill was atrocious, so much so that he was optioned to the minors. Miley was decent, but not memorable beyond reaching the 200-inning plateau. McCarthy was traded to the Yankees for a bag of balls, then subsequently finished the season with a flourish. Arroyo, who had never spent a day on the disabled list in his career, tore his UCL and needed Tommy John surgery.

As usual, there are some silver linings, no matter how poorly a team plays. The loss of Corbin and Arroyo allowed the D-backs to pitch Josh Collmenter in a starting role, and Chase Anderson—an unheralded prospect—got significant work and performed admirably. Collmenter was the team's best pitcher (3.46 ERA in 179.1 innings), and Anderson showed some ability as a rookie (4.01 ERA in 114.1 innings). But it wasn't enough to make up for the shortcomings elsewhere.

Goldschmidt suffered a season-ending broken left hand in August. Mark Trumbo, acquired for Tyler Skaggs in the offseason, played only 88 games and didn't come close to the 34 home runs he hit in 2013.

The team was 40-56 at the All-Star break. And with a chance to secure the worst record in the league, and subsequently, the No. 1 overall pick in next summer's draft, the Diamondbacks really stepped down...or up, depending on your perspective. They went 24-42 in the second half, "beating out" the Colorado Rockies and Texas Rangers (a team that had the worst record for a good majority of the season) for the dubious honor.

New general manager Dave Stewart has his hands full in trying to rebuild the organization. The farm system isn't as strong as in years past, and there isn't a ton of major league talent on the roster at present. That isn't a good combination for a team in a division with two of the best organizations in the NL in the Dodgers and Giants. Having the No. 1 pick in the draft should help, but it won't pay immediate dividends.

The Story Stat, Circa 2014

by Dave Studenmund

Jeter's Last Game in the Bronx

Derek Jeter's very last game in Yankee Stadium, the last game in which he took the field as a shortstop, was his finest. Silly statement, no? After all, he went just 2-for-5, scored a run and batted in three. Pretty good, but not great, right? Let's review his at-bats from the perspective of Win Probability Added (WPA) instead, and you may see what I'm hinting at.

After Baltimore had taken a two-run lead in top of the first inning, Jeter hit a double in the bottom half, scoring a runner with no one out. He subsequently advanced to third on a wild pitch and scored on an error. In other words, he was in the middle of three different plays in which the Yankees tied the score. Before he batted, the Yankees had just a 37 percent chance of winning. After he was done, they had a 58 percent chance.

In the second inning, with the score still tied, Jeter hit into a fielder's choice to make the last out of the inning. If this had been the first out of the inning, he might have made a significant negative impact on his team's chance of winning. With two outs, however, the impact wasn't as great, and the Yankees' chances dropped from 52 percent to 50 percent.

Jeter struck out swinging in the fifth, another two-point drop in the Yankees' win probability. Not a big loss. But in the seventh inning, with one out, the bases loaded and the score still tied, Jeter hit a ground ball to shortstop that J.J. Hardy booted for an error. Two runs scored on the play, and the Yankees' win probability jumped from 74 percent to 93 percent. Before the inning was over, the Yankees held a 5-2 lead.

On that play, Jeter didn't really make a positive contribution in the form of a hit, a walk or whatever. He was the recipient of a Baltimore error. Still, the play had the same impact as a single and, after all, isn't Jeter known for somehow taking advantage of his opponents' mistakes? Let's acknowledge that we're telling the Story of Jeter here; we're not trying to measure the exact impact of his batting line. The Story is that the Yankees took the lead on a Jeter batted ball.

The Orioles slugged a couple of home runs in the top of the ninth to tie the game, setting the stage for more of the Jeter Story. In the bottom of the ninth, Jose Pirela singled to lead off and was subsequently sacrificed to second. At this stage, the Yankees had a decent chance of breaking the tie, and their probability of winning was 62 percent. Jeter sealed it by singling to right, as you may recall. The run scored, and the Yankees won Derek Jeter's very last home game.

Jeter's final hit was the one that grabbed the headlines, but the remarkable thing about this string of events is that he was centrally involved in all three of the Yankees' scoring displays. He not only singled and doubled, but Jeter took advantage of a wild pitch and two errors. His two outs had minimal negative impact because of when they occurred.

In fact, when you add up all the win probability increases and decreases, you find that this was the finest game of Jeter's career. All in all, his plays added 62.8 percentage points to the Yankees' win. (Kudos to Ben Lindbergh of *Grantland* for pointing it out at the time.) For perspective, the second-best total of his career came on April 11, 2006, when he added 53.2 points to a Yankees win (primarily due to a three-run homer in the bottom of the eighth that handed Mariano Rivera a 9-7 lead).

We figure that each team starts a game with a 50 percent probability of winning. At the end of the game, one team sits at 100 percent and the other sits at zero percent. There are a lot of swings up and down between the beginning and the end, but one way of looking at Jeter's 0.63 WPA is that he made up the difference between the start of the game and winning (and then some) all by himself (0.63 being more than 0.50). Quibble with my approach, but it was a remarkable capstone to a remarkable career.

A Game for the Ages

Jeter's Last Home Game wasn't the biggest batting game of the year, however. That distinction belongs to the Orioles' Nelson Cruz. On Sunday, Sept. 7, when playing the Rays at Tampa Bay, Cruz...

- Singled in the first with two outs (very small impact on his team's probability of winning)
- Grounded out to lead off the top of the fourth (same)
- Homered with a runner on first in the top of the sixth, to put the Orioles on the scoreboard and pull within 3-2 of the Rays (helped a lot)
- Walked in the bottom of the seventh with the Orioles down 4-2 (helped a little)
- Came to bat with the bases loaded and one out in the top of the ninth and the Orioles down 4-2 and tripled to put the O's on top. However, Tampa tied the score in the bottom of the ninth. (almost won the game)
- Homered in the top of the 11th with a man on to put the Orioles ahead for good, 7-5 (won the game)

When you add up the impact of all of these plays, Cruz added 1.24 WPA to the Orioles' cause. This was the biggest total of the year. In fact, this total was historically great; it was the second-highest single-game WPA batting total in the last 40 years (1974 is the first year for which we have complete play-by-play data).

The only bigger game was turned in by Brian Daubach of the Red Sox on Aug. 21, 2000. I'll let you look up the details of that game on the internet.

The funny thing is that Cruz racked up only 2.88 WPA over the entire season, which means he accrued almost half of his net positive total in one game.

The Biggest Game of the Year

You know how we were talking about Derek Jeter and taking advantage of opponents' mistakes? Well, the biggest game of the year ended on a mistake.

When I say "biggest" game, I mean the one with the most in-game drama. When teams swap leads, or just threaten to take a lead, win probability moves up and down a lot. When one team takes an early lead and cruises to a win, win probability basically moves in just one direction.

So I use swings in win probability to quantify how much drama there was in each game. Specifically, I take all the swings in win probability and divide by the number of innings in the game. (If not for this last step, all extra-inning games would be ranked ahead of nine-inning games.)

So it is that the game with the highest "drama" in 2014 was played on May 21 between the Tigers and Indians in Cleveland. The Indians had taken the first two games of the series and were going for the sweep with a victory in the third. This is how the game unfolded:

- The Tigers jumped out to a 4-0 lead in the top of the first against Indians starter Zach McAllister.
- The Indians scored one in the bottom of the first and five more in the bottom of the second to take a 6-4 lead against Max Scherzer, the Tigers' starter and reigning American League Cy Young Award winner.
- The Tigers scored a run in top of the third, and the Indians scored one of their own in the bottom of the third. The Indians maintained a two-run lead.
- The Tigers tied things up, 7-7, with two runs in the top of the fifth. At this point, McAllister was out of the game, but Scherzer was hanging in there.
- The score stayed tied until the top of the eighth, though both teams threatened to score in nearly every inning. There was only one 1-2-3 frame along the way.
- The Tigers took a 9-7 lead in the top of the eighth on a single, walk, error and single. Batters subsequently went down in order in the bottom of the eighth and top of the ninth.
- In the bottom of the ninth, David Murphy hit a home run with Michael Brantley on base to tie the game.
- A few threats were pulled together in extra innings, but no team actually scored until the top of the 13th, when Alex Avila homered for the Tigers.
- The Indians bounced back and won the game in the bottom of the 13th by scoring two runs on a single, sacrifice bunt, hit batter, single, ground out, intentional walk and balk by the pitcher, Al Albuquerque.

Yes, the biggest game of the year ended on a walk-off balk. This is what that the game looked like graphically:

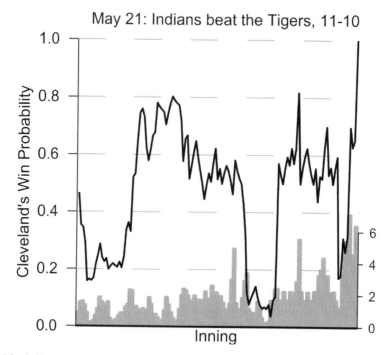

May 21: Indians beat the Tigers, 11-10

The black line shows the Indians' win probability at each point of the game. The gray bars at the bottom are the Leverage Index (scale from 0.0 to 6.0 on the right), which uses WPA to measure the criticality at each stage of the game. For Leverage Index, 1.0 is average. Naturally, as the game progressed, the plays became more critical.

There were lots of other games with big swings in win probability last year. April 10 in San Francisco; April 3 in Chicago (South side); April 23 in Colorado; Sept. 5 in Boston. Look them up, or better yet, watch them on MLB.tv during the offseason. They are sure to be entertaining.

The year's biggest game ended on a mistake, but it wasn't the year's biggest mistake.

Taking Advantage of Mistakes

The biggest mistake of the year occurred in the bottom of the eighth on April 14. The Padres were down by a run and batting against the Rockies with the bases loaded and two outs when Rex Brothers uncorked a wild pitch and catcher Wilin Rosario threw wildly to try to catch the runner. Two runs scored, and the Padres went on to win the game.

I guess that's two mistakes, but it was one play. Okay, the biggest single mistake of the year was a dropped fly ball by Jayson Werth of the Nationals on Sept. 3 against the Dodgers. The Nationals held a one-run lead with two outs in the bottom of the ninth and a runner on first. Jason Turner lofted a fly ball down the right-field line, and Werth seemed to lose it in the sun. The ball glanced off his glove and the runner scored from first, snatching a near-victory from the Nationals. For the moment, anyway—Washington won the game in the 13th.

The batter (or sometimes baserunner) who took the most advantage of mistakes by the opposing team was Asdrubal Cabrera, who garnered 1.31 WPA on opponents' mistakes. He was the runner on third when Albuquerque balked on May 21, and he also reached base on an error against the Pirates in the bottom of the seventh on Aug. 17. The latter play tied the score, and the Nats subsequently won with a run in the ninth.

Altogether, Cabrera was involved in 23 different "mistake" plays by the opposition. Starling Marte was involved in the most mistake plays this past year, 27, but those didn't have quite the same game impact as did Cabrera's. To give you an idea of the types of plays included in my analysis, Marte's total included:

- 12 errors
- 10 wild pitches
- Three errors on fielders' choices
- One passed ball
- One defensive indifference

I know I really shouldn't call defensive indifference a "mistake;" maybe an intentional mistake? Don't worry. The WPA impact of defensive indifference is always extremely small.

By the way, Jeter was involved in 19 mistakes by opponents and ranked 10th in the majors in total "mistake" WPA.

Let's switch sides and ask ourselves "Which pitcher suffered the most from his own team's (and sometimes his own) mistakes?" The answer is Mets reliever Jeurys Familia, who accrued -1.35 WPA (that's a negative) points based on mistakes.

About half of that total was due to nine wild pitches he threw. There were also two errors committed by his fielders, two more errors on sacrifice bunts, an error on a fielder's choice and a passed ball. None of his wild pitches had the same impact that Brothers' did, but nine is a lot for someone who pitched only 77 innings. Familia pitched a lot of high-leverage innings, which is why his mistakes tended to have a bigger impact than the average pitcher's.

Which team took the most advantage of opponents' mistakes? The White Sox did, as they racked up 6.4 WPA points on 60 errors (alone worth nearly 3.0 WPA) and 57 wild pitches (another 2.0 WPA). The Phillies and Twins were close behind the Sox. The team that took the least advantage of mistakes was Colorado, with only 3.1 mistake WPA points. In other words, the difference between the Sox and Rox in taking advantage of mistakes was worth three games in the standings.

Remember that WPA is based not only on how often an event, like a wild pitch, happens, but *when* it happens. The more critical the situation, the bigger impact an event will have. The White Sox saw 57 wild pitches and the Rockies saw 44, but the average Leverage Index of a Sox wild pitch was 1.76, while the Rockies' was 1.23.

Our next-to-last mistake question is: Which team suffered the most from its own mistakes? That would be the Atlanta Braves, with a -6.25 WPA on their own mistakes (followed closely by the Indians and Pirates). Their 73 wild pitches yielded -2.5 WPA, and their errors accounted for another -2.67 WPA. If you're a Braves fan and you thought, "The Braves really hurt themselves with mistakes at the wrong time!" during the season, you were right.

The team that suffered the least from its own mistakes was Cincinnati, with only -3.37 WPA.

For our final thought, let's put the two results together and ask, "Which team most helped its cause by taking advantage of others' mistakes and not hurting themselves with its own?" In other words, which teams had the higher positive "mistake WPA" when batting and the lowest negative "mistake WPA" when pitching?

The answer is the Minnesota Twins, who scored a net positive 1.95 "mistake WPA," followed closely by the Rays. The team that hurt itself the most in this category was Colorado, with a net -2.11 "mistake WPA."

And that was the story of the mistake in 2014. Just for fun though, here's a table with the top five teams by mistake WPA:

"Mistake WPA" Leaders, 2014			
Team	Bat	Pitch	Total
Minnesota	5.9	-4.0	1.9
Tampa Bay	5.7	-3.9	1.8
Arizona	5.6	-4.0	1.6
Washington	5.5	-4.0	1.6
Cincinnati	4.8	-3.4	1.5

The Royals and the Athletics

In general, a team's wins and losses follow a pattern that is predicted by the number of runs it scores and the number of runs it allows. This is called the Pythagorean Formula, and I'll describe it at the end of this article. Suffice to say that when a team scores more runs than it allows, it wins more games than it loses. When it scores a lot more runs than it allows, it wins a lot more games than it loses. As a general rule, every 10-run difference turns a loss into a win in a team's record, and vice versa.

In 2014, the Oakland A's scored 729 runs and allowed 572. This was the biggest run difference in the majors, and you would have expected a team with this many runs scored and allowed to win about 99 games. The A's won 88. The Kansas City Royals, on the other hand, scored 651 runs and allowed 624, which normally would compute to about 84 wins. They won 89 games instead.

Usually, when I see differences like this, I look at each team's record in close games (games decided by just one or two runs). Winning close games is often a key ingredient in making the most of your runs. KC was 22-25 in close games and the A's were 21-28. That's a difference, but not a huge difference.

Let's use WPA instead. On average, American League teams scored 677 runs and allowed 670 (bless the National League!). This means the A's scored 51 runs more than average and allowed nearly 100 fewer runs than average. Since a win is worth about 10 runs, you would expect their batting WPA to be around 5.0 and their pitching WPA to be around 10.0. Unfortunately, for A's fans, those figures were actually 1.75 and 5.3. Let's create two handy-dandy tables to compare the two teams:

Kansas City-Oakland Batting WPA Comparison					
Team	RS	Avg	Exp WPA	WPA	Diff
Oakland	729	677	5.16	1.75	-3.41
Kansas City	651	677	-2.64	-0.55	2.09

Kansas City-Oakland Pitching WPA Comparison					
Team	RA	Avg	Exp WPA	WPA	Diff
Oakland	572	670	9.81	5.33	-4.49
Kansas City	624	670	4.61	8.89	4.27

These are just estimates, but I hope you get the drift. The A's fell short of their batting expectations by nearly three-and-a-half games, and missed their defensive expectations by nearly 4.5 games. The Royals, on the other hand, exceeded expectations by 2.1 and 4.3 games, respectively. As a result, these two teams with vastly different run differentials met as equals in the Wild Card playoff game.

When you see differences like these, timing of events usually plays a key role. The A's probably didn't score runs (and stop runs from scoring) when it counted as well as the Royals did. Timing is often the difference between winning and losing. Timing happens to be what WPA measures.

So let me throw a few numbers at you for perspective. For this next analysis, I'm going to combine WPA and LI into a single stat called Situational Wins (or WPA/LI). The math is as simple as it looks: you divide the WPA of each play by its LI. This takes the criticality out of the situation and simply measures how well each team "won" or "lost" each play on an isolated basis. I'm not going to go into more detail here, but I'll put a link or two at the end of the article for those of you who are interested.

Anyway, using Leverage Index to group events into levels of criticality, we find that AL teams added batting Situational Wins along these lines:

- When LI was between 0 and 1, batting teams posted an average WPA/LI of 0.7 (per 10,000 plays; all the following figures are per 10,000 plays).

- For an LI between 1 and 2, batting teams posted an average WPA of -0.7 (that's a negative; batters lost some ground when the LI rose).

- For LI between 2 and 3, batting teams posted an average WPA of -7.2 (that's a really big drop).

- For any LI above 3, the batting teams posted an average WPA of 2.6. (that's a positive number; for some reason, batting teams bucked the trend at the upper reaches of LI).

Generally, this pattern makes sense. When situations become more critical, pitching teams bring in their best relievers and more strategies are brought into play to stop runs from scoring. Batting teams tend to create fewer Situational Wins when situations get more critical. The head scratcher is that batting teams were actually more productive when LI rose above 3.0. I don't know why this is, but I just love finding more topics to research.

So how did the 2014 A's and Royals batters line up?

Kansas City-Oakland Batting LI Comparison			
LI	Avg	Oak	KC
0-1	0.73	3.49	-15.22
1-2	-0.68	7.34	-3.61
2-3	-7.19	-4.83	22.05
3+	2.55	3.61	10.69

Oakland's bats were good across the spectrum, except for a dip when LI was between two and three. Kansas City, on the other hand, was pretty bad in unimportant situations and much better than Oakland in critical situations. In fact, KC was the worst batting team in the major leagues in unimportant situations (LI under 1.0) and the third-best batting team when LI was between two and three!

Remember, the higher the Leverage Index, the more impact plays have on the eventual outcome of the game. This is why we call it "Leverage Index." The Royals were much better than the A's at leveraging their runs into wins, despite the fact that they scored many fewer runs.

Next, we'll switch sides and view things from a pitching perspective. These average pitching figures will differ from the average batting figures (besides being the negative equivalent) because of the influence of inter-league games. We're just looking at American League teams here.

How did the Oakland and KC pitchers and fielders perform as situations became more critical?

Kansas City-Oakland Pitching LI Comparison			
LI	Avg	Oak	KC
0-1	-0.88	17.45	5.84
1-2	2.76	-2.63	9.92
2-3	7.53	40.37	20.52
3+	1.21	12.51	22.40

Take a good look at that Royals' column. As the criticality rose, so did their performance. It's really striking. They pitched well enough in unimportant situations, but they pitched better and better as situations became more potent.

The A's, once again, pitched really well when it didn't really matter. In this case, they were second in the majors in non-critical pitching (the Nationals were first). They also did well in critical situations (first in the majors with an LI between two and three), but their upward trend wasn't as clear as Kansas City's.

On FanGraphs' website, you can find a stat called "Clutch." It's a measure of how well players impacted their teams' chances of winning. Players who perform relatively better in high-leverage situations have positive clutch scores; those who don't have negative clutch scores.

Among all qualified major league batters last year, the top two leaders in Clutch were the Royals' Alex Gordon and Sal Perez. On the mound, the Royals' Aaron Crow was second in the majors in Clutch (behind the Mets' Carlos Torres).

As a team, the Royals were first in clutch batting; the A's were 15th. On the mound, the Royals were fifth in clutch pitching; the A's were 27th.

Bullpens

There's no doubt Kansas City's vaunted bullpen played a big role in its success. Managers are able to deploy their relievers according to the criticality of the situation. For instance, the average Leverage Index when Wade Davis (he of the 1.00 ERA) entered the game was 1.45. When Aaron Crow (4.12 ERA) entered the game, it was 0.96. When Louis Coleman (5.56 ERA) entered the game, it was 0.52.

This wasn't just smart bullpen management by manager Ned Yost. It was superb performance by KC's best relievers when they were being counted on. WPA is a great way to judge the performance of bullpens, because WPA takes both the performance and impact of the bullpen into account.

Here is a list of the top five bullpens in 2014:

Top Five Bullpens, 2014			
Team	WPA	WPA/LI	LI
KC	7.64	4.04	0.98
SD	7.13	3.72	0.94
BAL	6.24	2.54	1.15
LAA	6.21	3.89	1.06
STL	5.67	3.49	1.26

The Royals led the majors in bullpen WPA and were third in WPA/LI. That's impressive. And while there's a big drop in WPA from fourth to fifth place, I kept the Cardinals in the mix to show that they led the majors in average Leverage Index. One footnote: the Oakland bullpen was second in the majors in WPA/LI but 16th in WPA—proof once again that the A's just didn't perform when it mattered most.

Matchups

Speaking of bullpens, Twins ace Glen Perkins had a couple of interesting matchups against the White Sox last year. In seven plate appearances against Dayan Viciedo, Perkins gave up a home run, triple, double and single. In the other at-bats, Viciedo grounded out, struck out and flew out. Adding up all the pluses and minuses in WPA (that home run was a biggie, giving the White Sox a 7-6 win in the bottom of the ninth of a Sept. 13 game), this was the most lopsided matchup in favor of a batter.

On the other hand, Perkins faced the Sox's Alexei Ramirez seven times—once when the LI was nearly six and two other times when it was over three—and retired him all seven times. Ramirez flied out three times, lined out, hit into two fielder's choices, and struck out. Adding up all the pluses and minuses in WPA, this was the most lopsided matchup of 2014 in favor of a pitcher.

That crazy Glen Perkins. Go figure.

The Best

So who were the winningest batters last year? Here's a list of the top five:

Top Five Batters by WPA, 2014			
Batter	WPA	WPA/LI	LI
Mike Trout	6.88	5.38	0.97
Giancarlo Stanton	5.18	5.42	1.09
Andrew McCutchen	4.90	5.24	0.99
Buster Posey	4.81	3.20	0.97
Jayson Werth	4.68	4.09	1.00

When you rank batters by WPA, you're not really saying these were the best batters. You are saying that these batters arguably had the biggest impact on their teams' records. WPA measures real-time impact, and that's what you see in these numbers.

Of course, we find the usual suspects on this list, but you might be surprised to see Buster Posey at number four—I know I was. Posey had a fine year, but it didn't appear to be on a par with Trout, Stanton or McCutchen. And WPA doesn't care that Posey is a catcher.

But Posey had a Clutch score of 1.78, tied for fifth-best in the majors. The Giants had their winning ways, too.

References & Resources

- Ben Lindbergh, Grantland, "The Captain Bids Adieu: Derek Jeter's Surprisingly, Belatedly Great Good-bye," *grantland.com/the-triangle/derek-jeter-yankee-stadium-farewell-heroics*
- Dave Studeman, The Hardball Times, "10 Lessons I Have Learned about Win Probability," *hardballtimes.com/10-lessons-i-have-learned-about-win-probability-added*
- Dave Studeman, The Hardball Times, "The One About Win Probability," *hardballtimes.com/the-one-about-win-probability*
- Dave Studeman, The Hardball Times, "Talking Situational Wins," *hardballtimes.com/talking-situational-wins*

Pythagorean Formula

The Pythagorean Formula converts a team's Run Differential into a projected Win/Loss record. The formula is $RS^2/(RS^2+RA^2)$. Teams' actual win/loss records tend to mirror their Pythagorean records, and variances usually can be attributed to luck. Invented by Bill James.

You can improve the accuracy of the Pythagorean formula by using a different exponent (the "2" in the formula). In particular, a sabermetrician named US Patriot discovered the best exponent can be calculated this way: $(RS/G+RA/G)^{.287}$, where RS/G is Runs Scored per game and RA/G is Runs Allowed per game. This is called the PythagoPat formula.

A Bumgarner for All (Post)Seasons

by Brad Johnson

This year, we watched two Wild Card winners fight down to the very last pitch in the World Series. It wasn't what pundits predicted at the start of the season, or even at the start of October, yet it led to some fantastic baseball, with no series result easily predictable.

The postseason was bookended by perhaps its most memorable games—the first defining its winner, with the Kansas City Royals running their way past the Oakland A's, the last establishing Madison Bumgarner's 2014 as one of the all-time great World Series performances.

In between were a half dozen extra-inning games, with one running a full 18 innings, the longest postseason contest ever. There was much talk about bullpens—good and bad. There were forgettable performances by regular-season MVP favorites. And there were strangely short playoffs: Prior to the World Series, the teams that advanced to the next level went a combined 20-3.

The World Series was a bit of a reversal. Some of the dullest games were played on the biggest stage, yet the series itself went the full seven. And it ended in properly historic fashion. We'll get to that. But first, some ground rules.

We at The Hardball Times have a pet statistic called Championships Added (ChampAdded). The stat has two components.

The first is Win Probability Added (WPA). Simply put, every game has two possible outcomes—win or lose. We assume that each team has a 50 percent chance at either. Every play in the game moves that percentage. WPA measures the value of each play, taking into account the score, inning, base situation and number of outs. At game's end, one team is at 100 percent Win Probability, the other at zero.

The second ingredient is the Championship Value of each game. As a team moves deeper into a series, its chance to win (or lose) the series increases. Let's turn to the numbers.

Game Seven of the World Series is worth one full championship since it's a winner-takes-all contest. ChampAdded assigns a value of 1.000 to the game, since the winner will receive the Commissioner's Trophy. All other games are worth a fraction of a championship. For example, had we seen a Game Seven of the LCS round this year, it would have been worth 50 percent of a World Series. Below is a chart that notes the total ChampAdded for each game.

Championship Value of Playoff Games										
	0-0	1-0	1-1	2-0	2-1	2-2	3-0	3-1	3-2	3-3
Wild Card Game	0.125	X	X	X	X	X	X	X	X	X
Division Series	0.094	0.094	0.125	0.063	0.125	0.250	X	X	X	X
Championship Series	0.156	0.156	0.188	0.125	0.188	0.250	0.063	0.125	0.250	0.500
World Series	0.313	0.313	0.375	0.250	0.375	0.500	0.125	0.250	0.500	1.000

Once we have our components—WPA and Championship Value—we multiply them together to get ChampAdded. The stat is expressed as a decimal, similarly to many familiar baseball stats like batting average. For example, a hitter may contribute .050 ChampAdded, which also can be read as "five percent of a championship."

Starting with the Division Series round, every team had a 12.5 percent chance of winning the World Series. Teams that fail to win October glory are docked -.125 ChampAdded. In other words, they cede their 12.5 percent chance to another club. The World Champion San Francisco Giants contributed a total of .875 ChampAdded (1.000 minus .125 equals .875).

It is our tradition to use ChampAdded to identify an MVP, a goat and the biggest play of each postseason series. The MVP is the player with the most valuable series. The goat is the player who hurt his team the most. The play with the highest ChampAdded is considered the biggest of the series.

AL Wild Card: Oakland Athletics vs. Kansas City Royals

The Athletics finished the season with only the fifth-best record in the American League, but for much of the season they were considered contenders for the best record in baseball. After racing out to a 51-30 record through the first 81 games, the club dawdled to a 37-44 finish in the second half. Still, the A's were opposed by a Royals unit that seemed unlikely to make a strong postseason impression.

The game turned out to be arguably the best of the postseason. Brandon Moss, whose power bat was conspicuously absent during the A's late-season collapse, opened the scoring with a two-run homer against James Shields. By the end of the third inning, the Royals had clawed their way back against Oakland ace Jon Lester.

The Royals' 3-2 lead held until the sixth inning, when Moss delivered his second home run of the game, this time a three-run shot. The A's tacked on a couple more runs to take a commanding 7-3 lead into the late innings.

Lester cruised through seven frames, but in the eighth he allowed a run and left two base runners to reliever Luke Gregerson. Both runners scored, including Eric Hosmer on a wild pitch. The A's escaped the inning with a 7-6 advantage.

With Kansas City down one in the bottom of the ninth, Josh Willingham reached base with a leadoff single. The Royals pinch-ran with speedster Jarrod Dyson and bunted him to second. Then he stole third base and scored on a sacrifice fly by Norichika Aoki. And with that, we had our first taste of the extra-innings mania that would infect the early rounds of the postseason.

The 12th inning provided the final dramatics. The A's squeaked through a run in the top half of the inning, but the Royals weren't ready to roll over. In the home half, Hosmer tripled and scored on a Christian Colon single. Colon later swiped second base, which allowed him to score the walk-off run on a two-out single off the bat of Salvador Perez.

One important storyline can get lost in the shuffle. Starting catcher Geovany Soto left in the third inning with a thumb injury. The Royals went to town against Derek Norris with a total of seven stolen bases in the game, and those steals were a critical component of the Royals' run-scoring efforts.

Game MVP: When you consult the table above, you can see the Wild Card game is worth .125 ChampAdded. Hosmer contributed 60 percent of that win by reaching base five times in six plate appearances. His two walks, two singles, triple, two runs and one RBI were worth .075 ChampAdded, or 7.5 percent of a championship. He had just one blemish on a fantastic day: He was the only Royals player caught stealing, though even that was Billy Butler's fault.

Game Goat: The Athletics desperately tried to salvage the final inning but came up an out short. Jason Hammel faced just one batter, but he still earns goat honors by our measure. Colon stole an important base on his watch, and Perez delivered the last blow. Despite barely participating in the game, Hammel was responsible for -.055 ChampAdded.

Big Play: Unsurprisingly, Perez's walk-off single in the bottom of the 12th inning was the biggest play of the game. The hit was credited with .049 ChampAdded.

NL Wild Card: San Francisco Giants vs. Pittsburgh Pirates

Compared to the other Wild Card game, this one was exceedingly one-sided. Yet it also foreshadowed perhaps the most impressive storyline of the postseason. Giants shortstop Brandon Crawford belted a grand slam in the fourth inning en route to a stress-free 8-0 win. With Madison Bumgarner controlling the game, the few Giants fans who turned up in Pittsburgh's PNC Park could have left their antacids at home.

Game MVP: Bumgarner received plenty of run support, but he hardly needed it. The star of the postseason threw a complete-game shutout with 10 strikeouts. He allowed just four hits and a walk. The pitching performance was worth .030 ChampAdded, but Bumgarner's hitting brought his game total down to .025 ChampAdded. Pitchers aren't paid to hit, but their offensive contributions (or lack thereof) still affect the outcome.

Game Goat: Edinson Volquez allowed the grand slam, which makes him the obvious candidate for goat by all measures. His five-inning, five-run performance was worth -.028 ChampAdded.

Big Play: Game-winning grand slams are usually the biggest play of the game, so it should come as no surprise to find Crawford's home run here. The blast was worth 2.4 percent of a championship.

AL Division Series: Kansas City Royals vs. Los Angeles Angels

Having tasted extra-inning heroics in the Wild Card series, the Royals produced more against the Angels. Los Angeles was viewed as the heavy favorite, but the Angels' starting pitching depth was questionable due to a series of injuries during the season.

The first game was closely fought, with Los Angeles' Jered Weaver opposing former Angels starter Jason Vargas. The Royals opened the scoring in the top of third to take a 1-0 lead. The Angels immediately responded with a run of their own. When the Royals scored a run in the fifth, Los Angeles tied the game again in the bottom of the inning. The score remained tied into the 11th inning, when Mike Moustakas homered and the Angels finally failed to respond.

Game Two followed a similar script. The Royals struck first in the second inning. The Angels eventually tied the game in the sixth. Kansas City once again worked some 11th-inning magic. This time, Hosmer popped a decisive two-run homer, and Perez added an insurance run on an infield single.

After the first two contests, Game Three was something of a disappointment. Mike Trout offered the first blow with a solo home run (the only hit in 15 plate appearances in this series for the consensus best player in the league). Alex Gordon answered for the Royals with a three-run double. Hosmer and Moustakas contributed home runs. The game was never close after Gordon's double.

Series MVP: Once again, Hosmer was the MVP. He hit two crucial home runs, drove in four runs and scored three times. His 4-for-10 effort with three walks was good for .048 ChampAdded.

Series Goat: Josh Hamilton forgot to bring his bat to the series. The lefty slugger went 0-for-13 with two strikeouts. He did drive in an unimportant run at the end of Game Three, but it was way too little, hours too late. His -.048 ChampAdded makes him the anti-Hosmer.

Big Play: Hosmer's game-winning home run in Game Two was the top play of the series. The hit was worth .040 ChampAdded, or four percent of a championship. Incidentally, it accounts for more than 80 percent of Hosmer's value in the series.

AL Division Series: Detroit Tigers vs. Baltimore Orioles

On paper, this series looked like one of the best matchups of the postseason. The Orioles shared the top record in baseball with the Washington Nationals. The Tigers had plenty of talent with heaps of postseason experience. But both teams possessed a fatal flaw: The Orioles lacked high-quality starting pitching, while the Tigers bullpen was a shambles.

Game One put the Tigers' pen under the microscope. The Orioles held a 4-3 advantage when it came time for them to bat in the eighth. On a team with a better bullpen, Tigers starter Max Scherzer probably would have finished his night after seven innings.

Instead, he came out for the eighth and was relieved after allowing a one-out double. Joba Chamberlain faced two batters without recording an out, although the first reached on an error. Joakim Soria retired one out of five batters he faced. Phil Coke finished the inning after allowing a couple more runs. When the smoke cleared, Baltimore led 12-3.

Game Two was all Tigers—at least until the bullpen reared its ugly head again. The Tigers mounted a five-run fourth against lefty starter Wei-Yin Chen. Carrying a 6-3 lead into the bottom of the eighth, Tigers manager Brad Ausmus went to Chamberlain. He faced four batters, three of whom reached base. With a 6-4 lead, two on, and one out, Soria came in and promptly loaded the bases for pinch hitter Delmon Young. The habitual postseason hero delivered a clutch, bases-clearing double to put the O's ahead, 7-6. Zach Britton slammed the door for Baltimore.

Game Three was all about the pitchers. Tigers starter David Price cruised for eight innings. The only damage came via a two-run homer by Nelson Cruz. Orioles starter Bud Norris managed 6.1 scoreless innings before Andrew Miller turned in a gutsy five-out performance. With a 2-0 lead in the bottom of the ninth, the Orioles again turned to Britton. The Tigers opened the ninth with doubles from Victor Martinez and J.D. Martinez, but Britton buckled down, struck out a batter, intentionally walked another, then induced a series-ending double play.

Series MVP: It had to happen. Delmon Young had just four plate appearances in the series, three of which were outs, yet he's the improbable postseason hero again. Undoubtedly, other Orioles were more essential to the team's success, but Young led the series with .048 ChampAdded.

Series Goat: If Soria was bad in the first game, his appearance in the second game was devastating. His lone pitch to Young wasn't necessarily a mistake; Young took an off-balance swing and pulled a pitch on the outer half. We know it caught too much of the plate because of the outcome, but perhaps that same pitch would work most of the time. Soria is "credited" with -.061 ChampAdded.

Big Play: If the Orioles had won the World Series, "Delmon's Double" might have achieved folklore status. Instead, it will be remembered as a fun moment, one worth .051 ChampAdded. Young came to the plate against Tigers reliever Soria and swung at a first-pitch slider. The announcers barely had time to begin explaining Young's unusual postseason credentials before he delivered his three-run blow.

NL Division Series: St. Louis Cardinals vs. Los Angeles Dodgers

Count nobody surprised that the Cardinals and Dodgers won their respective divisions. Los Angeles had accumulated a bevy of talented superstars in recent seasons while St. Louis performed whatever magic it needs to remain relevant year after year. We may see a reprise of this series in the near future.

This one actually went four games, even if it didn't follow the network's script. Game One was the battle of aces, Clayton Kershaw versus Adam Wainwright. This surely would be a low-scoring game.

And then reality struck. Wainwright was chased after allowing six runs in 4.1 innings. Kershaw was sharp early until an eight-run rally sent him off in the seventh. The Cardinals had a 10-6 lead heading into the Dodgers' half of the eighth inning. Los Angeles cut the lead to two runs. Then in the ninth, they threatened to tie the game. With two outs, the tying run on third, and Yasiel Puig at the plate, Cardinals closer Trevor Rosenthal notched a strikeout to end the game.

The bats went quiet after the Game One outburst. The Dodgers won the second game, 3-2. Matt Kemp supplied the winner, an eighth-inning home run off Pat Neshek. Game Three went the Cardinals' way when Kolten Wong delivered a big two-run homer in the seventh inning. Game Four also was decided with a home run, this time a three-run shot off the bat of Matt Adams. The Dodgers threatened in the ninth, but Carl Crawford grounded out with two runners on, ending the game.

Series MVP: Matt Carpenter had his power stroke working. The Cardinals' left-handed leadoff man went 6-for-14 with three doubles and three home runs. He scored four times and drove in seven runs. His performance was the most valuable of the division series round, with .084 ChampAdded.

Series Goat: Prior to the series, who guessed Clayton Kershaw would play the role of goat? Despite striking out 19 batters in 12.2 innings, Kershaw was dinged for 11 runs and three home runs. He relinquished a large lead in Game One, and Adams was his final batter faced in Game Four. Kershaw was not only the goat; his -.089 ChampAdded made him the second-biggest goat of any single series.

Big Play: Adams' decisive three-run blast in Game Four was the top play. In a series marked by home runs, Adams was credited with .055 ChampAdded for his timely bomb.

NL Division Series: San Francisco Giants vs. Washington Nationals

Washington was the juggernaut of the National League. Armed with a deep and balanced roster, the Nationals were arguably the best-designed team—at least in the regular season.

There is a theory—and it's really just something people talk about around their drink of choice—that depth loses its value in the postseason. An October winner is more about the superlative performances by individuals. It matters less if you can replace a Ryan Zimmerman in your lineup without losing production.

That's the talk anyway. Whether it's real or imagined is for somebody else to investigate. The Giants probably feel like it's real. Their bench wasn't much of anything aside from a defensive replacement for out-of-position left fielder Travis Ishikawa (Juan Perez) and a right-handed pinch hitter (Michael Morse).

The series score was a draw: Each team plated just nine runs in four games. Sequencing decided the series, with San Francisco winning three one-run contests.

One of the sub-plots of the postseason was that of Hunter Strickland, a reliever who emerged as a potential high-leverage option late in the season. The Giants hoped they had found a relief treasure. Instead, Strickland allowed two solo home runs while protecting a 3-0 lead in Game One. The Giants shut the door after escaping some eighth-inning trouble with Sergio Romo, so Strickland's bad day could be swept under the rug.

The second game was an epic. The Nationals nursed a 1-0 lead into the ninth inning behind a gem from Jordan Zimmermann. He recorded the first two outs in the ninth before walking Joe Panik. Nationals manager Matt Williams then called on closer Drew Storen to record the final out. Buster Posey singled, then Pablo Sandoval doubled. Panik scored to tie the game, but Posey was thrown out at the plate to end the inning.

The score remained tied 1-1 through 11 innings, when Giants manager Bruce Bochy turned to Yusmeiro Petit. He would pitch six scoreless innings before Brandon Belt smashed a solo home run in the top of the 18th. Strickland returned to the scene of the crime and notched a critical save.

Game Three could go by an alternate title—The Mortality of Bumgarner. The score was tied 0-0 in the seventh when Washington got its first two men aboard. Wilson Ramos bunted, which set up a throwing error by Bumgarner when he tried to peg the lead runner at third base. Three runs would score in the inning, two earned. It was one of Bumgarner's few mistakes all postseason as his Giants lost, 4-1.

San Francisco won the final game in unusual fashion. The Giants managed a two-run rally in the second via a single, error, bunt single, bases-loaded walk, and RBI fielder's choice. It wasn't an impressive display of hitting, but it worked. Bryce Harper did his best to bring the game back to Washington's favor with an RBI double in the fifth and a game-tying home run off Strickland in the seventh.

The Giants inched out the game-winning run in the bottom of the seventh. With the bases loaded and Pablo Sandoval at the plate, reliever Aaron Barrett bounced a fastball that allowed Panik to score. Barrett wasn't done with the antics. With Posey on third, Barrett uncorked a wild intentional ball, but it caromed back to Ramos in time to catch Posey at the plate. It didn't matter; the game ended 3-2.

Series MVP: Petit delivered a studly extra-inning performance in Game Two. His six shutout innings with the game on the line were worth .067 ChampAdded. It was his only appearance of the series, but it was huge.

Series Goat: Sometimes, the series goat isn't somebody who makes a blatant mistake like Barrett. Instead, it's the player who just didn't contribute anything. Denard Span went 2-for-19 with a walk and no run production. His ChampAdded clocked in at -.054.

Big Play: Belt's midnight blast in Game Two ended the longest game in postseason history with the most valuable play of the series. Winning that game was worth .033 ChampAdded, or 3.3 percent of a championship.

AL Championship Series: Kansas City Royals vs. Baltimore Orioles

Both the Royals and Orioles swept their way to the ALCS. Somebody would have to lose. This time, it was the Orioles. The series had a lopsided result, but it featured four nail-biter games. It easily could have broken in the Orioles' favor.

Game One was the high-scoring match. The Royals took an early lead, but the Orioles clawed back to tie the game, 5-5. That score held until the 10th inning, when the Royals plated three runs on home runs from Alex Gordon and Mike Moustakas. In the bottom of the inning, the Orioles managed only one run, off the bat of Delmon Young.

Fans in search of a repeat of the first game didn't need to wait long. In Game Two, the teams rode a 4-4 tie into the ninth, when a sloppy inning resulted in two runs for the Royals. The Orioles went down quietly to Greg Holland. Baltimore's big chance came in the seventh inning, when they loaded the bases against Kelvin Herrera but failed to score.

Despite two tight ballgames, it wasn't until Game Three that the Orioles held an actual lead. They jumped out to a 1-0 advantage. The Royals manufactured a couple runs on an RBI groundout and a sacrifice fly. It was enough for a 2-1 Kansas City victory.

The fourth contest was a bitter defeat for the Orioles. The Royals scored twice in the first on an error. With runners on second and third, Hosmer hit an easy chopper to first base. The throw came home, but when catcher Caleb Joseph applied the tag, the ball was kicked free. Both runners scored on the play. The Royals eventually won the game, 2-1. Kansas City was heading to the World Series with a sweep and an eight-game playoff winning streak.

Series MVP: The Royals bullpen pitchers—namely Holland, Wade Davis, and Herrera—were the heroes. The three combined for .195 ChampAdded while protecting tied games or narrow leads. Herrera takes top honors with 5.2 of the biggest innings in his young career, worth .079 ChampAdded. Gordon was also quite valuable at .074 ChampAdded. It was truly a team effort.

Series Goat: Poor Zach Britton landed in the wrong place at the wrong time. His damaging appearance came in Game Two, where an inherited runner and an error behind him led to -.086 ChampAdded being assigned to him. He also needed an assist from Darren O'Day to escape a bases-loaded jam in Game One.

Big Play: Gordon's home run in the 10th inning of Game One takes honors as the biggest play, with .055 ChampAdded. However, the Royals actually needed Moustakas' two-run shot to seal the victory.

Honorable Mention: The Royals had a chance to take the lead in Game One in the ninth, but Billy Butler grounded into an inning-ending double play. Those two outs went for -.053 ChampAdded.

NL Championship Series: San Francisco Giants vs. St. Louis Cardinals

When Bumgarner displayed his mortal side in the NLDS, it was due to a throwing error he committed. He made no such error in Game One of the NLCS. He sailed through 7.2 shutout innings en route to a 3-0 Giants victory.

The second game was a seesaw affair, and it will be remembered in St. Louis for reasons beyond the outcome of the contest. The two teams combined for nine runs, but neither managed to score more than once in any inning.

The Cardinals relied on solo home runs for four of their five runs. Matt Carpenter opened the scoring, but the Giants fought back and took the lead in the seventh. Oscar Taveras tied the game with a blast in the bottom of the seventh. Strickland appeared again for the Giants in time to allow another home run—this time to Matt Adams. Rosenthal later blew the save via a bases-loaded wild pitch and narrowly averted disaster. With the game tied in the bottom of the ninth, Wong smashed a walk-off home run for St. Louis.

After a bases-clearing double from Ishikawa delivered the Giants a 4-0 lead in Game Three, the Cardinals fought all the way back to force extra innings. In a 4-4 tie, Cardinals manager Mike Matheny called on lefty specialist Randy Choate to face the first three batters of the 10th inning. Crawford and pinch hitter Perez reached on a walk and single, respectively. Gregor Blanco sacrificed back to Choate, who threw the ball away. A walk-off run scored on the error.

The Giants overcame a 4-3 deficit in Game Four with a three-run sixth. The inning was fueled by an RBI fielder's choice and an RBI groundout. The Giants' reputation for scrounging runs out of the ether became dogma in the process. San Francisco held on for a 6-4 victory.

The Cardinals were on the verge of winning the fifth game. Wainwright somehow outdueled Bumgarner through seven innings. With St. Louis on top, 3-2, relief ace Pat Neshek allowed a leadoff home run to pinch hitter Morse in the bottom of the eighth. Cardinals starter Michael Wacha, called upon to pitch the ninth, allowed a series-ending, three-run home run to Ishikawa.

Series MVP: Ishikawa delivered two massive hits, one in the first inning of Game Three and one to finalize Game Five. He got six of his seven RBI with those two hits as part of a 5-for-13 showing. Those hits were worth nearly nine percent of a championship (.089 ChampAdded).

Honorable Mention: In a tragic twist of fate, Taveras lost his life in a car accident on Oct. 26 upon returning home to the Dominican Republic. Taveras pitched in with .023 ChampAdded in the NLCS. His pinch-hit home run in Game Two probably will stand as the defining play of his all-too-brief career.

Series Goat: Choate's failure in the 10th inning of Game Three saddles him with goat status. The throwing error was bad enough, but the inning itself led to a -.066 ChampAdded.

Big Play: The Cardinals' lone win offered the biggest play of the series, Wong's walk-off home run. The play went for .059 ChampAdded.

Honorable Mention: Rosenthal's wild pitch in Game Three allowed the tying run and was the third-biggest play of the series at -.054 ChampAdded.

World Series: San Francisco Giants vs. Kansas City Royals

The Royals' eight-game winning streak ran headlong into Bumgarner in Game One of the World Series, and the streak broke. The Royals scuffled against Bumgarner before Perez hit a solo home run in the seventh inning. While the Royals searched for their first run, the Giants scored seven. It was another stress-free win for Bumgarner.

Game Two went to the Royals after a five-run sixth put the game out of reach. Strickland continued his offseason woes in that inning. He faced two batters, allowed a double to Perez, gave up a home run to Omar Infante, and got into a shouting match with Perez while Infante circled the bases.

The third game went to the Royals thanks to their magnificent bullpen. The relief corps disappointed in Game Four, however. Tim Collins and Brandon Finnegan allowed the Giants to bust the game open in the sixth and seventh innings. Giants swingman Petit once again saved the day with three innings of scoreless relief after Ryan Vogelsong failed to escape the third.

Game Five was a 5-0 drubbing by the Giants behind another Bumgarner gem. This time, he allowed four hits in a complete-game shutout. The Royals returned the favor in Game Six with a 10-0 shutout via an effectively wild Yordano Ventura (seven innings, three hits, and five walks).

It all came down to Game Seven, and it was an edge-of-your-seat affair. The contest featured Jeremy Guthrie and Tim Hudson as starting pitchers. Analysts wondered how long either would survive before the bullpens were needed. Hudson lasted 1.2 innings and allowed two runs. Guthrie managed 3.1 innings and three runs. On the Royals' side, the big three of Herrera, Davis and Holland shut the door decisively once Guthrie left the game. Unfortunately for those at Kauffman Stadium, a surprise 2.1-inning performance from Jeremy Affeldt and a historic five-inning save from Bumgarner led to the Giants victory.

Despite the dominance of both bullpens, there was plenty of drama. Nobody knew what to expect when Bumgarner came on in relief. He appeared wild when facing his first batter and allowed a leadoff single. Royals manager Ned Yost called on Alcides Escobar to bunt Infante into scoring position. Then Bumgarner settled in to retire Norichika Aoki and Lorenzo Cain quietly.

In total, Bumgarner retired the next 14 batters he faced after Infante singled. With two outs in the ninth, Gordon hit a single that was badly misplayed, and he reached third. Had he been Terrance Gore, the Royals' fastest player, he might have scored on the error. Instead, the ballgame came down to Bumgarner versus Perez. You may recall that Perez was the only Royals hitter to do any real damage against Bumgarner. Any hit would force extra innings, but the free-swinging Perez fouled out to Pablo Sandoval to end the game.

Series MVP: Bumgarner pitched 21 innings, picking up two wins, a save and a shutout while allowing just one run. That superb performance was worth .820 ChampAdded, or 82 percent of a championship.

Series Goat: Perez made the last out of the World Series with a runner on third base, but he was also a negative contributor throughout the series. Despite a good .333/.350/.500 line in the series, Perez made a handful of critical outs and came through when it mattered least. He's assigned -.224 ChampAdded, or 22.4 percent of a championship lost.

Big Play: The series-ending foul out off the bat of Perez was the biggest single play. The out smashed the Royals' 15.1 percent chance of salvaging the game (-.151 ChampAdded).

Playoff MVP: We all know it's Bumgarner. Just his World Series performance smashes the next-most-valuable player. Overall, he's credited with .869 ChampAdded, or nearly 87 percent of a championship. His pitching was worth .936 ChampAdded, but a few untimely outs at the plate prevented him from earning a full championship all by himself.

To give Bumgarner's ChampAdded a little perspective, David Ortiz was the MVP last season with .352 ChampAdded. In 2012, Marco Scutaro was the hero of the playoffs with just .196 ChampAdded. In a normal year, second-place finisher Gordon could have gone home with top honors at .328 ChampAdded.

As we scroll down the list, we see Affeldt buoyed by his critical (and unlikely) Game Seven outing. The Royals' three relief aces are next in line, followed by San

Francisco's three best hitters. The only player to make the top 10 who didn't participate in the World Series was Adams.

2014 Postseason Heroes	
Player	**ChampAdded**
Madison Bumgarner	0.869
Alex Gordon	0.328
Jeremy Affeldt	0.277
Wade Davis	0.229
Kelvin Herrera	0.215
Greg Holland	0.169
Hunter Pence	0.165
Pablo Sandoval	0.143
Michael Morse	0.117
Matt Adams	0.090

Among the goats, Perez's traditionally good statistics contained no whiff of clutch timing. Interestingly, the non-Bumgarner members of the Giants rotation were three of the top six goats. "Big Game James" Shields ranked sixth. He had an ugly postseason with a 6.12 ERA in his five starts and 25 innings pitched. Rounding out the goats is Strickland, who did his best to make the middle innings an adventure just about every time he appeared.

2014 Postseason Goats	
Player	**ChampAdded**
Salvador Perez	-0.292
Tim Hudson	-0.208
Nori Aoki	-0.173
James Shields	-0.162
Ryan Vogelsong	-0.158
Jake Peavy	-0.137
Jeremy Guthrie	-0.130
Brandon Finnegan	-0.101
Brandon Crawford	-0.101
Hunter Strickland	-0.096

References and Resources

For more on WPA:

- Dave Studeman, The Hardball Times, "The One About Win Probability," *hardballtimes.com/main/article/the-one-about-win-probability*

Commentary

The Year in Frivolity

by John Paschal

The 2014 baseball season, like the 2014 Bloomberg TV season, proved a study in serious business. First, before any on-field action took place, Major League Baseball announced that beginning on Opening Day, instant replay would serve as a sage panopticon, righting all wrongs by surveilling marginal swipe tags, contested home runs, and close calls at first base, thus allowing interested viewers to take a bathroom break without having to hit the pause button.

Finding its officious stride, MLB also instituted a new transfer rule, decreeing that should any fielder drop the ball within six days of catching it, the other team not only wins the contest but also assumes ownership of the opposition's vacation homes and riding lawnmowers.

Also, and with an expression so solemn that even Bill Belichick took notice, the league instituted Rule 7.13, i.e., the collision rule, stating unequivocally that each catcher is henceforth required to stand—or, to be fair, crouch—on the coast of Nova Scotia while applying a tag at home plate.

Baseball wasn't kidding around.

What made the offseason even more portentous, however, was the announcement that Yankees shortstop Derek Jeter would retire at season's end, ushering in a time of Jeterless, leaderless chaos whose only order might derive from the recognition that life goes limping on.

Into all this serious business, then, I bring you the year in humorous review, wherein the indisputable facts are succeeded by exceptionally iffy fictions.

March/April

In late March, the major league season officially opens at the Sydney Cricket Ground in Australia with the Dodgers sweeping a two-game series against the Diamondbacks, 3-1 and 7-5. Afterward, Arizona manager Kirk Gibson is surprisingly upbeat, saying he now gets to test the dubious Coriolis effect as it applies to the D-backs going straight down the toilet.

On March 24, just weeks after losing pitcher Derek Holland to a knee injury, the Rangers announce that infielder Jurickson Profar and catcher Geovany Soto will miss extended time due to shoulder and knee injuries, respectively. The team concludes by saying that it already has reached its projected injury quota, so the Rangers will proceed with plans to film *Jackass 4: DamageProof!*

On Opening Day at PNC Park, former Pirate Barry Bonds is booed when he presents Pittsburgh outfielder Andrew McCutchen with the 2013 National League MVP

Award. Later, in a conversation with reporters, Bonds insists that the fans weren't booing but, rather, chanting, "Boo-onds! Boo-onds!"

In related news, Brewers outfielder Ryan Braun is given a loud ovation in his first Miller Park at-bat after serving a 2013 season-ending suspension for using performance-enhancing drugs. Later, Barry Bonds insists that the fans weren't cheering for Braun but, rather, shouting, "Bravo-onds! Bravo-onds!"… which in turn inspires the Bravo network to create *Breaking Braunds*, a reality show in which the two men "test their chemistry" while living in an old, airless RV until one of them "just naturally breaks down."

In his first at-bat of the season, Angels outfielder Mike Trout slugs a two-run homer on a slider from Mariners ace Felix Hernandez. As if to further convince voters they erred in selecting the Tigers' Miguel Cabrera as the American League Most Valuable Player in each of the past two seasons, Trout goes on to solve the Riemann hypothesis in the third inning and to invent a smoother, more spreadable peanut butter in the eighth.

On April 1, Boston's Jonny Gomes wears an American flag-themed jacket during the Red Sox' visit to the White House in honor of their 2013 World Series title. Historians later recall that when members of the notorious White Sox, or "Black Sox," visited a Chicago courtroom after their 1919 World Series loss to the Cincinnati Reds, they wore Monaco flag-themed jackets.

On April 2, in the first stop of his season-long farewell tour, the Yankees' Derek Jeter receives from the Houston Astros a cowboy hat and a pair of custom boots. In efforts to further confirm all the usual stereotypes, Houston also gives the Yankee a "take home plate" with a side of home-style gravy.

In his first mound session since undergoing knee surgery, Texas lefty Derek Holland throws a 25-pitch bullpen session at Globe Life Park. So strong does Holland feel afterward that *Sports Illustrated* decides to put him on its cover, along with Rockies shortstop Troy Tulowitzki, former aces Mark Prior and Carl Pavano, sitcom actor Ted McGinley, 13 ladders, a broken mirror, a black cat named Ted McGinley Jumped The Madden Curse Shark and a Chicago-born billy goat named What Could Possibly Go Wrong?

In an April 3 game at Pittsburgh's PNC Park, Chicago's Junior Lake comes onto the field in the wrong road jersey. Instead of wearing the updated jersey that features CUBS in block lettering across the front, the second-year outfielder wears the traditional Cubs jersey, which features tread marks across the back.

Facing Padres starter Eric Stults in the bottom of the first inning of an April 4 contest, Miami's Giancarlo Stanton belts an epic, 484-foot home run that clears the Budweiser Balcony at Marlins Park. Afterward, Stanton is understandably upset, acknowledging to reporters that if the ball had cleared an adjacent beer-themed deck, it would have established a Guinness record.

On April 9, MLB announces that the annual award for the top reliever in each league will be renamed in honor of former closers Trevor Hoffman and Mariano Rivera. The league also announces that the award for the league's *bottom* reliever will be rechristened the George Brett Preparation H Award.

In the eighth inning of a Red Sox-Rangers game at Fenway Park, Boston DH David Ortiz hits a high drive around the Pesky Pole and then takes a casual 32.91 seconds to round the bases. Afterward, Red Sox manager John Farrell dresses Big Papi in a fine robe, glittering jewelry and comfortable sandals while slaughtering in his honor a fattened calf, reasoning that the last person to come home after such a long time away was the legendary Prodigal Son.

In the eighth inning of game two of an April 17 Twins-Blue Jays doubleheader, Minnesota scores six runs on one hit, eight walks and three wild pitches. In the locker room afterward, the team is delighted when the legendary Treasure of Lima, valued at $260 million, falls from a ceiling panel and directly onto their laps, even as the Brazilian Bikini Team bus breaks down in the players' parking lot just outside the locker room doors.

In the second inning of a game at Fenway Park, umpire Gerry Davis ejects Yankees starter Michael Pineda for having pine tar on his neck. Afterward, Pineda acknowledges in a written confession that he did use pine tar but "only to protest the clearcutting of America's pine forests."

After a series of controversial rulings, MLB announces on April 25 that the strict interpretation of the new transfer rule—umpires have called a no-catch whenever a fielder has dropped the ball while moving it from glove to throwing hand—will now yield to common sense. MLB also announces that common sense will still give way whenever relief pitchers sprint all the way from the bullpen just to hold onto each other during brief brawls in the infield.

News arrives in late April that film director Brett Ratner has acquired movie rights to the story of Dodgers outfielder Yasiel Puig's escape from Cuba. In making the announcement, Ratner says he isn't sure who will play Puig but that he is absolutely certain Clint Eastwood will play the sportswriter.

In late April, the Mets invite "True New Yorkers" to show their support for the team by signing an open letter at mets.com/TrueNewYorker. Peeved by the "True New Yorker" reference, famous Yankees fans Rudy Giuliani and Michael Bloomberg invite famous Mets fans Jerry Seinfeld and Billy Joel to discuss the matter over lunch, and they proceed to do so, quite amicably, first over chateaubriand in Aspen and then over fresh Kona crab in Maui.

May

During a May 1 off day, A's outfielder Josh Reddick attends the Rays-Red Sox game at Fenway Park and, like other fans, receives a Dustin Pedroia bobblehead. When Reddick later reveals that what he really wanted was a David Ortiz bobblehead, he learns that bobblehead makers have been unable to properly capture the Big Papi-glowering-at-the-official-scorekeeper look.

After Miami sweeps a three-game home series against Atlanta, the Braves accuse the Marlins of stealing signs. A subsequent search of the Marlins' dorm room turns up a pair of yield signs and one No Dumping sign, plus Joe Mauer's Gemini necklace and Fernando Rodney's Sagittarius broach.

In a 14-inning game against the Rays, Yankees shortstop Derek Jeter goes 0-for-7 for the first time in his career. Historians later discover that Jeter did go 0-for-6 once, when, during an off day, he met the Delmonico sextuplets, themselves on a day off from Our Lady of Perpetual Chastity Convent.

On May 5, the Yankees honor former closer Mariano Rivera by renaming a street outside the stadium Rivera Avenue. Meanwhile, in San Diego, Padres closer Huston Street realizes that if he continues pitching well, a wonderful opportunity awaits him—that is, he could be traded to a contending team.

The instant-replay era notches its first walk-off ruling when, in the bottom of the ninth inning of a May 6 game, umpires call Pittsburgh's Starling Marte safe at the plate after initially calling him out, giving the Pirates a 2-1 win over the Giants. Later, one purist bemoans the outcome, saying, "Back in my day, replay was never instant—it was always homemade, from scratch, and often caused heart attacks due to the stress it put on our bodies!"

On May 9, Rangers ace Yu Darvish loses a no-hitter with two outs in the ninth when Boston's David Ortiz singles to right. In need of commiseration, Darvish later meets with a climber who fainted just two feet short of the Mount Everest summit and a dudebro who failed to nab the last slice of 'za.

During the first inning of Miami's May 9 game against the Padres, an ailing Jose Fernandez vomits in a dugout garbage can. Later, the pitcher confirms what officials suspect: he leafed through the 2014 Joba Chamberlain Swimsuit Calendar.

Prior to a Diamondbacks-Nationals game in mid-May, a robot throws out the ceremonial first pitch. Convinced that human error will always be part of the game, officials later reprogram the thing to flip the robot finger at umpires.

To honor Derek Jeter's final Subway Series, the Mets give the Captain a piece of art featuring the number 2—Jeter's number—made of New York City Subway tiles. No word on whether the tiles are covered in number one ... or number two.

Dressed in Zubaz—those bodybuilding pants that were big in the early '90s—the Tigers board a Cleveland-bound plane in Boston but soon learn it has broken down. Forced to hitchhike, the team quickly finds a ride in a party bus full of dudes in acid-washed jackets and Aviator glasses, but only because Ian Kinsler is now sporting a tartan skirt and a Rachel haircut.

On a day when the Rangers announce first baseman Prince Fielder will undergo season-ending neck surgery and infielder Jurickson Profar is being shut down due to injury, fans also learn Dodgers Triple-A catcher Miguel Olivo has bitten off part of teammate Alex Guerrero's ear. Fans later learn that during the attack, Guerrero screamed, "*Why?* I'm not a Ranger!"

Facing the Rockies' Boone Logan in the seventh inning of a late-May game, Phillies outfielder Ben Revere hits the first home run of his five-year big league career. Given that Revere famously said "one if by land," experts later concede they expected his first dinger to be an inside-the-parker.

June

During the Dodgers' June 1 home game against the Pirates, manager Don Mattingly and outfielder Andre Ethier engage in what reporters later call a "heated dugout argument." Afterward, Mattingly reveals that he wanted the thermostat set at 78 while Ethier insisted Mattingly just wear mittens.

On June 3, after seven years in the minor leagues, former outfielder Jason Lane returns to the big leagues as a pitcher for the Padres. Following his first appearance, and having forgotten that things got ugly the last time a Jason reappeared after several years away, several nubile teens emerge from a midnight skinny dip and proceed to stumble backward over an exposed root.

Prior to a June 3 game in Detroit, RoboCop throws out the ceremonial first pitch. Intrigued by the idea, the Dodgers decide to issue a similar invitation to Slo-moCop, but only after Josh Beckett completes his police training.

On June 4 comes the 40th anniversary of Cleveland's infamous 10 Cent Beer Night, when thousands of drunken fans rushed the field and wreaked havoc. All of this is news to surviving participants, who don't remember a thing.

Injured Nats outfielder Bryce Harper reveals in a June 6 interview that he will use his PlayStation in efforts to recover from recent thumb surgery. Meanwhile, 40-year-old outfielder Mets outfielder Bobby Abreu says that in efforts to recover from general stiffness, he will push a hoop with a stick.

In early June, the Nationals reveal that a recent hot streak owes itself to the banana and mayo sandwiches players have been eating. In hopes of a similar outcome, the Rangers respond by eating the same sandwich but with one modification, the result being that a dozen players fall ill after ingesting sun-ripened mayo.

On June 10, O's third baseman Manny Machado is suspended for throwing his bat at A's third baseman Josh Donaldson during a June 8 plate appearance. While serving the suspension, Machado quietly contemplates his actions in the Bert Campaneris/Jose Offerman Meditation Garden.

As part of Derek Jeter's retirement tour, the Mariners present the Yankees shortstop with a seat from the old Kingdome, where, in 1995, he made his big league debut and got his first career hit. Given that the Yankees just flew in from Kansas City after a series against the Royals, and that he drank several cups of coffee en route, Jeter is happy to see that the seat is up.

In mid-June, the Brewers auction the "game-used bowl" of unofficial mascot Hank the Dog, a mixed breed the Brewers rescued after he wandered into their spring training facility in March. A week later, the Orioles stick with the theme by telling Chris Davis, mired in a 4-for-36 slump, to sit.

After a poor outing against the Rangers, A's left-hander Drew Pomeranz fractures his non-pitching hand when he punches a wooden chair in the Oakland clubhouse. Given the notorious plumbing problems at O.co Coliseum, many observers are surprised Pomeranz didn't kick a stool.

To boost support for catcher Jonathan Lucroy's All-Star candidacy, the Brewers release a "political attack ad" against incumbent Yadier Molina. In response, the Cardinals invite voters to "Read our lips: no new catchers."

Fresh off the NHL championship, the L.A. Kings visit the Dodgers locker room prior to a June 17 game and invite outfielder Yasiel Puig to pose for a picture with the Stanley Cup. Later, owing to the fact that his teammate is currently wearing it, he declines an opportunity to pose with the Hanley cup.

In honor of the U.S. Men's Soccer Team's World Cup appearance, Cardinals ace Adam Wainwright arrives in the clubhouse one day with the American flag painted across his face. Asked why, specifically, he adorned his visage in Old Glory, the pitcher replies, "I didn't. I decorated it with the American flag, not with any of Tim McCarver's oft-referenced baseball experiences."

Following a controversial call in Pittsburgh, the league tweaks Rule 7.13, which forbids catchers from blocking the plate, by saying that umpires should no longer apply it to force plays. Meanwhile, MLB also decrees water should continue to be wet and the sun should continue to be hot.

Having famously wished a 0-162 season on the Rangers, former Texas second baseman Ian Kinsler celebrates his Arlington homecoming by homering in his first at-bat. After touching home plate, Kinsler turns to the Rangers dugout and *literally* shoots daggers out of his eyes, injuring dozens.

During a Reds broadcast in late June, play-by-play man Marty Brennaman reveals his greatest fear is to "be buried alive...meeting eternity clawing and scratching at the inside of a pine box, screaming in vain." When pressed on the subject, partner Jeff Brantley reveals that his own greatest fear is to work a game—"or really just an inning"—with White Sox broadcaster and relentless homer, Hawk Harrelson.

The Astros reveal on June 30 that a hacker has breached their internal communication system, called Ground Control. Defying expectations, the result isn't that Major Tom continues floating 'round in his tin can but, rather, the common mulberry weed wreaks havoc in the outfield grass.

July

After the Angels and Pirates execute a trade of struggling relievers, Ernesto Frieri and Jason Grilli just happen to cross paths in an O'Hare Airport restroom while each is en route to his new team. Later, as they prepare to leave the restroom, neither makes mention of the toilet paper stuck to the others guy's shoe, Grilli reasoning that Frieri just might need it for the mess he'll make in Pittsburgh, and Frieri reasoning that Grilli will require *at least* that much when he visits Oakland's notoriously defecatory O.co Coliseum.

During an interview with the Associated Press, former big leaguer Johnny Damon claims he can "hit better than at least half the league." Damon later clarifies the comment by allowing that roughly half of all players are pitchers.

A writer claims that when burglars hit the spring training home of David Price and Evan Longoria in 2011, the criminals stole a "pillowcase-sized bag of marijuana." Left unreported is the rumor that while talking to a claims adjuster from the Cheech & Chong Insurance Agency, the players maintained the bag was indeed the size of a pillowcase, "but, like, from one of those *huuuuge* body pillows, y'know?"

After umpires fail to overturn an apparent blown call during a tight A's-Jays game, Toronto's Jose Bautista calls MLB's instant replay system "a joke." When challenged to actually tell the joke, Bautista says, "A replay system and a collision rule walk into a bar. The bartender asks, 'What can I get ya?' The replay system and the collision rule reply, 'A Bud with a good head.'"

In early July, a New York man sues ESPN after the network shows him sleeping during a nationally televised game. Following suit, the Cardinals' Kolten Wong then sues Fox, alleging that during the 2013 World Series broadcast, the network, like the Red Sox, caught him napping at first base.

America learns in early July that Derek Jeter is part owner of Frigo Revolution-Wear, a company selling customized men's underwear that refrigerates the genitals. During subsequent focus group sessions at a local mall, Jeter learns that though the genitals of handsome men who play shortstop for the Yankees just might need the occasional cooling-off period, the genitals of run-of-the-mill non-Yankees might not require such chilling, which is why he immediately introduces his Microwavable GibletsBriefs.

Following the Blue Jays-Rangers game on July 19, Rangers starter Colby Lewis complains that Jays outfielder Colby Rasmus put down a bunt while Toronto led 2-0 in the bottom of the fifth. Lewis later doubles down on his grievance, complaining that Jose Bautista "ran as fast as he could to first base" and that manager John Gibbons "was thinking the whole time."

In mid-July, PETA gives AT&T Park in San Francisco the top spot in its annual ranking of vegetarian-friendly major league ballparks. In a symbolic gesture, a certain San Francisco outfielder quickly renames himself Gatherer Pence.

In a July *Sports Illustrated* article, writer Tom Verducci suggests the league should rule the increasingly popular shift an "illegal defense." Also up for "illegal defense" status are the words "I would never *knowingly* put a banned substance in my body" and "It must have been in that B-12 shot."

America learns in late July that the Cardinals—a franchise whose teams have appeared in three of the past eight World Series—received the third pick in the recent Competitive Balance Lottery. America also learns the New York Yankees have just inherited $455.8 trillion from a rich uncle.

On July 26, the National Baseball Hall of Fame Announces that from this point forward, retired players will remain on the ballot for 10 years instead of 15. In response, Pete Rose issues an angry denunciation, saying in a nutshell that a 50-year period is what he had bet on.

In a late-July promotion at Coors Field, the Rockies embarrass themselves by misspelling the surname of star shortstop Troy Tulowitzki on T-shirt jerseys handed out to fans. Later, the Rockies embarrass themselves again when they refer to righty Christian Bergman as "leftist Agnostic Bergman."

In his Hall of Fame acceptance speech, Greg Maddux defies the usual decorum by telling the crowd that his brother, former big leaguer Mike, "taught me a little bit about science; it has to do with a little methane and a lighter…" Jealous of the crowd response, fellow inductee Frank Thomas immediately creates a new nickname for himself, but ultimately the Big Fart is less of what some wags call "a hit" and more of what others call "a whiff."

After striking out against the White Sox in a July 27 game, the Twins' Oswaldo Arcia responds by breaking his bat, Bo Jackson-style, over his thigh. In further efforts to emulate the former outfielder and running back, Arcia summons Brian Bosworth and summarily cracks the man's sternum.

Pressed into mound duty in the top of the 16th inning of a game at Wrigley Field, Cubs catcher John Baker proceeds to pitch a scoreless frame. In the bottom of the inning, Baker tags at third base on a Starlin Castro fly ball and begins toward the plate as the winning run, at which point he receives the most immediate nickname in big league history: John "Run Home" Baker.

On July 31, the Cardinals' Allan Craig learns via clubhouse television that he has been traded to the Red Sox. Later that day, the Indians' 43-year-old DH Jason Giambi learns via clubhouse telegraph that he is still with the team.

On the month's final night, MLB's new plate-blocking rule takes another hit when Cincinnati's Zack Cozart is ruled safe at the plate despite the throw having beaten him by several feet. The rule then takes a further hit when, during slow-motion replays, fans see Miami backstop Jeff Mathis catch the ball, eat a ham sandwich, order a pair of crotch-cooling underwear and jab a poison-tipped needle into a Rangers voodoo doll before applying the tag.

August

On Aug. 2, Cleveland signs one-time fan favorite Jim Thome to a one-day contract so he can retire as an Indian. Hopeful one of their own also can retire as an Indian—or maybe as a Mariner or an Angel or an Astro or an Athletic—the Rangers explore the possibility of retroactively signing below-the-Mendoza Line catcher J.P. Arencibia to an identical kind of contract.

During a Tigers-Yankees game at Yankee Stadium, one-time Detroit ace Justin Verlander steps out of the dugout to lob a ball to his girlfriend, the model Kate Upton. Having seen a number of similar tosses from Verlander this season, Upton does the usual thing by hitting it for a ground-rule double.

In a blowout loss to the otherwise hapless Rangers, White Sox DH and former University of Texas quarterback Adam Dunn takes the mound in the ninth inning to mop up. Seizing on the college football theme, the Rangers call for a weakside blitz, whereupon Elvis Andrus suffers a debilitating sack injury even as Dunn retreats to a nearby frat party, where he shotguns two kegs of Natty Light and establishes a partnership which, come Monday morning, will have generated a theme paper on the Peloponnesian War.

On Aug. 7, the Indians announce several renovations, including the removal of excess luxury boxes, are planned for Cleveland's Progressive Field. Also among the changes: the addition of thousands of mannequins—most of them wearing *Hot in Cleveland* T-shirts—to fill the otherwise empty seats.

As part of 1980s Turn Back The Clock Day at Wrigley Field, the Tampa Bay Rays wear "fauxback"—i.e., fake throwback—uniforms in a game against the Cubs. Representative of a decade in which the great franchise did not yet exist (hence "fauxback"), each jersey includes not only the player's name and number but also a colorfully clad teenager breakdancing to a Doug E. Fresh song about perestroika, Hillman College and Shermer, Ill.

In mid-August, Smirnoff introduces a vodka bottle decorated with the logo of the Chicago Cubs—its first team-branded bottle. After a tasting, one expert claims that the vodka tastes "like a century of human tears, some bitter and some merely sad, yet softened and even seasoned by droll forbearance and ballpark nacho cheese."

At Globe Life Park in Arlington, reigning Miss Texas Monique Evans spoils a statuesque finishing pose by rolling—yes, *rolling*—the ceremonial first pitch about 15 feet to the left of the catcher. It was still better than 50 Cent's first pitch.

After setting up a walkoff win by stealing second in the bottom of the ninth, Washington's Denard Span explains that his daring alter ego, Span, should get credit for the courageous attempt. Meanwhile, the Padres reveal that due to their chronically boring performance, the team's collective identity—and this, they add, is entirely coincidental—is known as C-Span.

In late August, Texas outfielder Shin-Soo Choo caps an awful season by undergoing surgery to remove a bone spur from his left elbow. While removing the bone spur, surgeons also discover a bone boot, a bone holster and a pair of bone pistols that somehow manage to wound eight Rangers.

On Aug. 26, America celebrates the 75th anniversary of the first televised game in the history of major league baseball. In related news, America also celebrates the 75th anniversary of the first time a player told a postgame reporter, "To be honest, I was just looking for a pitch I could drive."

In late August, the Padres unveil the Selig Hall of Fame Plaza outside Petco Park. Later, in efforts to honor baseball but "in no way to curry favor with the league," the team unveils the Rob Manfred Is A Genius Pavilion and the Joe Torre Can Do No Wrong Koi Pond.

CBS announces in late August that John Rocker, the controversial former pitcher, will appear on the upcoming season of *Survivor*. It is later revealed that as part of the challenge, contestants will take the 7 Train to Ellis Island, where they will acquire a new name, learn a new language, battle trachoma and then set off, virtually penniless, to make a life for themselves in a strange new land where xenophobic rednecks often enjoy a sizable, if paradoxical, advantage.

During a meet-and-greet with fans, the Orioles' Adam Jones upsets local residents when he reveals that his favorite place in Baltimore is the airport, "so I can fly home." Backtracking, Jones later clarifies himself by saying that "*specifically*, it's Terminal 2E."

On Aug. 30, the Rangers establish a major league record when, by activating pitcher Derek Holland from the 60-day disabled list, they place a 60th player on the roster. Later, while preparing for his first start, Holland warms up too quickly and suffers an acute episode of spontaneous combustion, the shrapnel from which sends 249 current and former Rangers to the emergency room.

At August's end, the Padres win their third consecutive extra-inning game, defeating the Dodgers, 2-1, on an Alexi Amarista 10th-inning walk-off single. Later, despite the new Selig Hall of Fame Plaza at Petco Park, MLB denies the team's request that all games begin in the top of the 10th inning.

September

On Sept. 1, Cubs rookie Jorge Soler becomes the third major league player in the past 100 years to record an extra-base hit in each of his first five games. Archivists later affirm the importance of the hyphen when they discover the early box scores of player/manager/team statistician Johnny "Extra Base Hit" Johannsen, who in each of the first five games of his rookie season went 6 for 5 at the plate to put his batting average at a league-leading 1.200.

Following Joc Pederson's Sept. 1 promotion to the Dodgers, the Triple-A Albuquerque Isotopes give away the outfielder's 1994 Buick Century. In need of good cheer, the beleaguered Rangers enter the contest and ultimately receive the consolation prize—a 1958 Plymouth Fury named "Christine."

In related news, the woeful Twins ask fans to select the car that is "most similar to the Twins brand." While acknowledging that the jokes pretty much write themselves—"e.g., Ford: **F**ix **O**r **R**epair **D**aily"—the Twins later reveal the winning entry: "My dad's '72 Gremlin, on blocks in the yard."

The Yankees announce on Sept. 2 that in honor of the retiring Derek Jeter, team members will wear caps and uniform patches that commemorate the Captain. The Yankees also announce that in the ninth inning, players will switch to caps and patches that commemorate his defensive replacement.

In early September, leaders of newly anointed Puig Nation release via Instagram their red, white and blue logo. They also issue a warning to other player-centric governments, saying, "We can, and will, overthrow anyone."

On Sept. 8 comes the news that a Houston furniture store is on the hook for $4 million in payouts after promising customers a refund on their furniture purchases if the Astros lose fewer than 100 games. Perhaps by coincidence, the owner finds the money beneath the cushions of Brian Cashman's couch.

Chicago slugger Jose Abreu acknowledges in a September interview that, someday, he would like to sing the national anthem before a White Sox game. Abreu goes on to say that it is "truly gracious" that the song begins with the words "Jose, can you see?" … especially when the answer is so clearly yes, given his slash line of .321/.383/.598 and his 34 home runs.

In mid-September, baseball suspends Jonathan Papelbon after the closer directs a "rude gesture"—specifically, a crotch grab—at Phillies fans who booed him after he blew a three-run ninth-inning lead in an eventual 5-4 loss to Miami. Hoping to fill the Papelbon role, the Phillies call up Miley Cyrus.

In the top of the sixth inning of a Sept. 17 game at Tampa Bay, Yankees shortstop Derek Jeter strokes a clean single off Rays starter Alex Cobb to break a 0-for-28 slump. Hoping to keep it "kind of low-key," Jeter later celebrates by going 80-for-80 with the Radio City Music Hall Rockettes.

The *Wall Street Journal* reveals in a Sept. 19 article that the Cubs, Red Sox and Rays are using video games as a form of neurological training to help hitters better recognize pitches. As a result, the Cubs announce that for the rest of the season 12-year-old Jimmy Dugan will be batting cleanup.

Due to a heavy downpour in the eighth inning of a game against the Diamondbacks, Twins starter Phil Hughes falls *one out* short of reaching 210 innings pitched on the season and thus earning the $500,000 bonus that would have come with it. Afterward, old-school pundits remark that Hughes should have been more like former Twins great Jack Morris, who, they say, would have "pitched to the storm."

On Sept. 24, Hillerich & Bradsby Company announces it will retire the Louisville Slugger P72 bat model Derek Jeter uses and replace it with an identical model issued under a different name, DJ2. The manufacturer later announces it will also retire the bat that Albert Pujols uses and, likewise, replace it with an identical model issued under a different name: GIDP25.

Following the Dodgers' division-clinching 9-1 triumph over the rival Giants on Sept. 24, special advisor Tommy Lasorda tweets, "If you don't cheer for the Dodgers, there's a good chance you may not get into Heaven." Meanwhile, across town, the Angels issue a counterpoint, saying, "C'mon, think about it, we're the Angels—what we mean is that if you don't root for us, you'll get stuck, like, *forever* in rush hour traffic on the L.A. Freeway."

After the Orioles score three runs in the top of the ninth on Sept. 25 to tie the Yankees, 5-5, Derek Jeter hits a walk-off single to give New York the win in his final home game. After the game, and straying slightly from the script, Jeter enters a burning munitions factory (instead of a burning fireworks factory) to save four three-legged kittens (instead of three four-legged kittens) and then cures influenza viruses A and B (instead of influenza virus C) just before helping an elderly woman cross a busy street...directly to her twin granddaughters' Victoria's Secret modeling shoot.

America learns on Sept. 26 that in the Yankees' final home game, Derek Jeter wore not one but two uniforms—one to keep and one, reportedly, to sell. Armed with this knowledge, America suspects struggling Tigers closer Joe Nathan has worn two uniforms all season—a Tigers uniform and, underneath it, the uniform of whichever team the Tigers are playing.

Upon defeating the White Sox, 3-1, on Sept. 26, the Royals clinch their first playoff berth since 1985. In recognition, the players give themselves three *Cheers* for what they call their *Family Ties* despite citing Mike Moustakas as a potential *Fall Guy* due to his *Diff'rent Strokes*, which, in making his hit tool go *St. Elsewhere*, have threatened a possible *Dynasty* and thus caused the team to consider a *Star Search* because, hey, these are *The Facts of Life*.

In the Braves' Sept. 27 game against the Phillies, Atlanta's B.J. Upton and Justin Upton become the first pair of brothers in major league history to each homer and record an outfield assist in the same game. A day later, Manny and Yvonne Upton become the first parents in American history to have spawned a pair of brothers who together amassed a season total of 344 strikeouts.

On the final day of the regular season, America is treated to an abundance of sweet, bitter and bittersweet events: Derek Jeter's final hit, an RBI infield single; Paul Konerko's final game, an 0-for-3 performance; Bobby Abreu's final at-bat, producing a single; Jordan Zimmerman's no-hitter against Miami, saved by Steven Souza's spectacular catch; and the clinching of two division titles, a Wild Card berth and home field for the AL Wild Card game. And yet since each occurred on Sunday, Sept. 28, much of the country is tuned to the truck-commercial vehicle known as the NFL.

Major League Baseball's Accidental New Era

by Jeff Sullivan

It feels only appropriate that this story should begin with Mike Trout. In many ways, 2014 was a season much like the previous two for the Angels' young superstar. Blending durability with talent in every possible area, Trout once more led all of baseball in Wins Above Replacement. When the Angels signed Trout long term, he appeared to give them a massive bargain, and then he just continued being himself, carrying on perhaps the most impressive career beginning in the history of the sport. So you could say that, in the big picture, nothing changed. Trout started 2014 as the best player in baseball, and he finished 2014 as the best player in baseball. A little underneath the surface, though, one could spot a significant trend.

With the help of Baseball Savant, which is an invaluable resource, let's look at Trout's 2014 month-by-month rates of high fastballs seen. The "high" threshold is arbitrary, but you have to draw the line *somewhere*. I went with pitches at least 2.5 feet off the ground. As for the last column, that's out of players who faced at least 250 pitches in the month.

Mike Trout and High Fastball Rate		
Month	High FA%	MLB Rank
April	29.6%	118
May	34.7%	11
June	34.9%	10
July	39.2%	3
August	43.3%	1
September	41.1%	2

You don't need me to tell you what you can already see. As the season wore on, Trout saw more and more high heat, to the point where he was seeing more of it than anyone else. And don't you dare think this was some coincidence. This was pitchers pitching to Trout's weakness. Here's a selection of Trout's career slugging percentages:

Upper third of zone: .386 SLG
Middle third: .759
Lower third: .709

Trout's a low-ball hitter. He's probably the best low-ball hitter in the world. Down and over the plate is his sweet spot, and it leaks even a little below the zone. But because of Trout's approach and swing path, he's left with a vulnerability up. Given that information, pitchers and catchers increasingly tried to exploit Trout's weakness. His second half of the season was still good, but it was also much worse than his first half, and by the time the playoffs rolled around the Royals were pitching Trout high and tight. There's a book now on how to retire Mike Trout, and every team is in possession.

That's a scouting report, and scouting reports have always existed. There's a whole history of players who've been said to struggle against fastballs up. But with Trout, it isn't a gut feeling. It isn't something based on a small sample of half-decent data. The numbers are there, available to anyone with an internet connection, and they're impossible to argue with. Trout is baseball's best player, and it takes 30 seconds to come up with an informed strategy to put him away.

Maybe you think that's neat. Maybe you think that's troubling. Maybe both. But so much of the stuff we talk about and write about and research these days is made possible by data we didn't have access to ten or nine or eight years ago. Almost all of it is data that just didn't exist. The big bang of information has been endlessly exciting and illuminating, but there's a huge glaring question there that people have missed. We're able to know more about the game and its players than ever. We can see what guys throw and what guys hit, and where those guys hit it. That's all still so hard to believe, and we are blessed as fans. But as every team now employs a department of motivated analysts, has baseball's data revolution worked to the detriment of run production? That is, is there a benefit advantage in favor of the pitchers and defenders?

I'll tell you right now, it's an impossible point to prove, but it's an easy point to hint at. I don't know if major league wide offense is dying, but it's not doing great. You know that we're in an era of suppressed run-scoring, but so that we have a point of reference, here are the average runs per nine innings per team over the past 15 seasons:

MLB Runs per Nine Innings, per Team			
Season	R/9	Season	R/9
2000	5.20	2008	4.69
2001	4.82	2009	4.66
2002	4.66	2010	4.43
2003	4.77	2011	4.30
2004	4.85	2012	4.36
2005	4.65	2013	4.18
2006	4.91	2014	4.08
2007	4.83		

There's a "5" in there, all the way back in 2000, but that feels like ages ago. Since then, the average team has lost more than a run a game, but something interesting you can observe is that run levels in 2001 were the same as run levels in 2007. Only lately has the decline become pronounced. Relative to 2006, offense is down about 17 percent.

It's not exactly a secret that we keep having Years of the Pitcher. Naturally, theories abound. One is that disciplining PEDs more severely evened the playing field, but then we know that pitchers were taking drugs at about the same rate as hitters. There's also the whole thing where it's unclear what, exactly, steroids do to statistics, and furthermore home run rates on contact haven't changed very much.

Maybe we're just gifted with an unusual number of talented pitchers. That can't really be proven, and I suppose it's possible, but it doesn't feel like enough. Not with the trend continuing. The argument has been presented that this is the fault of the increasingly specialized bullpen, but over the past 15 years, starters have consistently thrown 66 percent of all the innings. And, since 2006, starter ERA is down more than 18 percent, while reliever ERA is down 15 percent.

Velocity keeps going up. Have you heard that? Pitchers keep throwing harder and harder. Since 2002, starter fastballs and reliever fastballs have both gained about two miles per hour, on average. But the trend's been developing, not sudden. Starters had gained a tick by 2008. Same for relievers. They've both gained one more tick since, but the drop in offense has gotten steeper.

And then there's the fact that the strike zone keeps changing. It's getting lower and lower, as was discussed in the *THT Annual* a year ago. For one thing, the strike zone is presumably changing on account of PITCHf/x, and that would be a clear example of the information helping pitchers more than hitters. And for another thing, changes in the strike zone can be responsible for only a fraction of the offensive decline. Last year, Jon Roegele estimated the changing zone was responsible for one-third of the offensive drop between 2008 and 2013. If accurate, that's enormous, but it still leaves a lot of the pie.

Maybe it'll help to look at some different numbers. This table shows K% - BB%, by year, for both starting pitchers and relievers. You know that we're also in an era of increased strikeouts. Check out when the increase here got going in earnest.

MLB K% - BB%, Starters & Relievers					
Season	Starters	Relievers	Season	Starters	Relievers
2000	6.7%	7.3%	2008	8.5%	9.3%
2001	8.4%	9.8%	2009	8.9%	9.4%
2002	7.8%	8.7%	2010	9.7%	10.7%
2003	7.6%	8.6%	2011	10.2%	11.2%
2004	7.8%	9.2%	2012	11.2%	12.9%
2005	8.1%	8.7%	2013	11.4%	12.9%
2006	8.0%	9.2%	2014	12.3%	13.6%
2007	8.2%	9.2%			

Numbers for starters were the same in 2001 and 2008. Numbers for relievers didn't really budge until 2010. Starters have gained a few percentage points in just the last few years. It's the same deal for guys in the bullpen, and while people have a whole lot of theories, it's impossible not to notice that these trends have picked up ever since PITCHf/x was installed everywhere and turned into the foundation of practically all worthwhile analysis. To re-state, more clearly: Since PITCHf/x was released, and since people really started understanding how to use it, strikeouts have gone up, and walks and runs have gone down. If trends continue, next year teams could average fewer than four runs per nine innings for the first time since 1976.

What that *isn't* is an obvious bad thing. Some people like the lower scoring environment. One could only imagine how much longer games would take if teams still were scoring like they did at the height of the steroid era. But what this *is* is a fascinating thing, and one has to figure, a presumably unintentional thing. Major League Baseball has tried hard to get rid of steroids and various other performance-enhancers, but it's absolutely possible that the game has reduced its own scoring levels by accident.

I'm far from the first person to raise the possibility. In fact, here's Joe Maddon, talking with MLB.com in June of 2012:

> *"All the stuff that's going on and all this stuff that's talked about, whether it's data, matrixes, all the different stuff that's out there is all slanted toward the pitching and the pitching and the defense," the Rays manager said. "There's no way to slant it toward the hitters. I really think that all the stuff you see out there can only confuse hitters. There's nothing really there definite that the hitter can latch on to when he goes into the box that's really going to help him against [any given pitcher]. He might find a tendency or two, but you just never know if it's going to pop up or not."*

And in case you think Maddon might have changed his mind, here he is again, in September of 2014:

"The hitter's at a total disadvantage right now," Maddon said. *"And there's no advantages on the horizon. I don't see it. That's why it's going to take a lot of creative thinking.*

"It could be just going back maybe to something that had been done before. I'm not sure. But right now, offense is going south, and it's going to continue going south based on pitching and defense. Everything, data, video, all the information benefits them over offense."

Maddon is a strong believer in the idea that the run-prevention side benefits more from big data than the run-production side, and he's been in about as analytical an organization as there is. Not everybody is quite as sure as he is, but it's a difficult theory to argue against, as there are so many little areas for potential advantages.

Think about everything you can do with PITCHf/x and with related ball-in-play information supplied by the non-public but also very much real HITf/x. I've already mentioned that the strike zone is changing, getting bigger—especially at the bottom —presumably due to umpires receiving feedback. Using PITCHf/x information, Mike Fast revealed the significance of good pitch framing on the part of the catchers. It's easier to know now where to position defenders, because there's a log of all balls in play against all pitches. And pitchers can study hitters and their tendencies, if they like. Weak spots aren't just suspected, but confirmed, and pitchers can attack those weak spots with some confidence. Consider the Trout example at the beginning. Trout's data has revealed a seemingly major weakness. And what does Trout have at his disposal to counter that, aside from just changing his swing?

Probably the most conspicuous example of the effects of so much data are all the defensive shifting. Defensive shifts go back about as far as the game of baseball itself, but in the past few years they've gotten more specialized and a heck of a lot more common. There's also no reason for the shifts ever to go away, unless hitters become incredible at evenly spraying balls around.

According to Baseball Info Solutions, there were more than 2,000 shifts in 2011. The next year, that number almost doubled. The next year, *that* number almost doubled. And in 2014, the total shot up again, with some teams employing more than 1,000 shifts each. While defensive shifts haven't reduced hitters to rubble, they've inarguably taken away hits by the dozens or hundreds, and there's only so much that can be done to counter them. Occasionally, a daring hitter will attempt to drop down a bunt, but such attempts are unusual, and as far as full swings are concerned, it's just tremendously difficult to hit a ground ball the other way on purpose.

Some teams shift more than others. Some pitchers don't like it when their infielders shift behind them. This isn't an area where the run-prevention side completely shuts the run-production side down. But, this is an area where the pitchers and fielders get to benefit. It doesn't help hitters to have it known where they're likely to hit the baseball. Even if a hitter does demonstrate some ability to go to the opposite field, he'll just see an adjusted shift in response, with defenders still out of their traditional alignment.

While shifts have been the subject of countless debates, less apparent but still very much real is that pitching staffs now can have customized plans of attack. Any given hitter's tendencies can be examined, whether that be his hot and cold zones, or his inclination to swing at the first pitch, or his preference for fastballs or offspeed stuff. Again, Trout is one example, to stand in for many. A pitcher and catcher can know, going into an at-bat, what the hitter likes, and what he doesn't. A hitter can study a pitcher's own tendencies, to try to at least even the playing field, but a pitcher might not always pitch to his own habits. A hitter will always have his own swing.

Certain hitters always have been pitched differently than others. That part of the game isn't new. But now, adjusted approaches are more informed. "Previously, it was a scout's claim on the hitter's swing, or a pitcher's feel for the hitter's swing," says Joey Votto, "but now the claim and the feel are backed up by evidence."

Brandon McCarthy agrees. "How many at-bats did Trout have this year where in the past the pitcher would've gone, [screw] it, here's my sinker or here's my fastball down, let's see what you're going to do here. Now all of a sudden, someone goes, 'Well, we know up, let's give up a shot.'" The idea being, pitchers can have more confidence in the reports that are getting generated now.

To some extent, observers already could tell what a hitter's skills might be before there was so much information available. C.J. Wilson, for example, could tell that Trout would be a low-ball hitter instead of a high-ball hitter back when he faced him as a rookie in 2011. And hitters can confirm their own hot zones and cold zones, and work with that knowledge. Brandon Moss told Eno Sarris that he knows he struggles high, because his swing doesn't go there, so he tries his hardest to just lay off those pitches. But if you're a hitter with a cold zone in the strike zone, laying off will only result in called strikes. Hitters aren't without their own information weapons; they just seem to be badly outgunned.

To be fair, not everyone is totally in agreement on this point. Sam Fuld, for one, believes it's hitters who get the advantage from having so much data. He thinks a smart hitter can anticipate a pitcher's game plan against him, and then work within that. Jon Lester thinks both sides are helped evenly, and he likes to see what a hitter's swing and stance look like. Sean Doolittle's initial reaction is that all the information helps pitchers and fielders slightly more. Jed Lowrie thinks defenders stand to gain the most.

But then you have Maddon's opinion. You have Votto saying, "all the information being used against us hitters has made for a bit of a pain in the ass." There's McCarthy saying pitchers and defense benefit more, because "hitting is still reactionary." He adds, "there's just more information, just all those little margins that in the past might slip by." And then you have the statistics. Offense is down, and it keeps getting worse. It's correlated with a dramatic increase in the amount of information available to every team in the league. Correlation isn't always causation, but in this case, it's not hard to believe.

Not everyone is equipped to take advantage of the information that's available. Or maybe a better way to put that is, not every pitcher or hitter makes the most of the reports provided. One thing both McCarthy and Wilson stress is the importance of being flexible. Wilson believes there's a benefit to be found provided a given player isn't too stubbornly static about his process. Says McCarthy, "one of the biggest traits you can have as a pitcher that will make you successful is just being adaptable, being willing to change who you are." Speaking about himself, after getting traded to the New York Yankees, McCarthy had it recommended to him that he start elevating more four-seam fastballs, and the result was "tons of easy outs." It wasn't something he'd done much before, but it was an instant suggestion upon his arrival, coming out of an organization that's huge on analysis and information.

And this touches on a developing conversation: Is it better for a guy to pitch to his strengths, or to pitch to a hitter's weaknesses? The prevailing belief within the game is that a pitcher should stick to his guns, and that a sinkerballer should throw sinkers even to particular low-ball hitters. But as pitchers become more willing to be flexible in time, this should diminish in expression. The game now almost insists upon less stubbornness, and a pitcher who's willing to change who he is will be an even more difficult pitcher to prepare for. Ultimately, all the hitter can know is what a pitcher throws, and how he usually throws. Pitchers get to make the decisions. Hitters can do nothing but react to them.

Don't believe for a second that hitters are helpless. There is still scoring. There is still Mike Trout, and Giancarlo Stanton, and Victor Martinez. Trout, in the second half of 2014, posted a 141 wRC+, meaning his numbers were 41 percent better than average. The Royals were pitching to the Trout scouting report in the ALDS, but then in Game Three's first at-bat, Trout authoritatively hit a high, inside James Shields fastball out of the park. Notes McCarthy, "it's still scary how good major-league hitters are and how fast they adjust to something, even if it's really good." But you can understand why offense is falling on harder and harder times. Teams know more than ever about how different hitters should be attacked. They know more than ever about how different hitters tend to put the ball in play. To make matters worse, the strike zone is bigger, and the pitches are faster, and the catchers are, as a whole, better about receiving. Hitting isn't necessarily endangered, but so much of the talk is about adjustments. Adjustments to the pitches. Adjustments to the zone. Adjustments to the shift. It's kind of like the run-prevention side is the performance-enhancing drug, and the run-production side is the testing. The drugs keep a step ahead of the science.

Somewhat anecdotally, one wonders if it's more possible now for pitchers to have sudden breakthroughs. Before 2014, Collin McHugh had allowed 50 big-league runs in 47.1 big-league innings. According to an article in *Business Week* from August, the

Astros liked the way McHugh's curveball looked in terms of its measured spin, and they also liked the potential of his fastball if he'd use it up in the zone, to counter the league's trend toward low-ball hitting. McHugh became one of the true surprises of 2014. Matt Shoemaker was a terrific rookie with a Triple-A ERA in the 5s. Shane Greene emerged out of nowhere to record a strikeout an inning for the Yankees. Offensive breakthroughs still happen, too—this season, we can poit to the cases of the Tigers' J.D. Martinez and the Reds' Devin Mesoraco—but it's not clear the extent to which data played a role. Mesoraco had been a top prospect. Martinez overhauled his whole swing, sensing that his career was at a crossroads.

That's just a theory, a theory within a theory. The bigger theory is that with so much information available to front offices, coaching staffs, and players, offense is at a disadvantage, in large part because hitters might see pitches specifically intended for them, and defensive alignments specifically intended for them. The smaller theory is that this could lead to a greater number of pitcher breakouts, but that's not the most important question. That's something to be investigated separately, and it might be something of interest.

The bigger theory, if true, could be a hell of a case of unintended and significant consequences. It's possible, I guess, that when baseball decided to allow for so much data generation, it figured that might do something to run-scoring levels. More likely, baseball just wanted to know more about itself, and it wanted other people to be able to know more about it, and it didn't think about the potential implications too deeply. It would be hard to blame MLB for that—you don't think of available information as being able to change the look of the game itself. At least, you don't think that information is going to make things more lopsided.

So what's going to happen to offense, then? We're in the middle of a decline, with no indication that we've yet reached the lowest point. For all I know we might even be at the start. Hitters, increasingly, will work on their abilities to beat the shift. Hitters, increasingly, will be selected for their abilities to spray, and for their abilities to cover the whole zone with their swings. Teams will look for hitters who don't have easily exploitable weaknesses, to try to counter the other side's apparent advantage. Relatedly, we could see an increase in emphasis on quality baserunning. Teams could target contact hitters, and quality bunters. If the run-prevention units are responding to the data, there can always be a response to the response, and every team in baseball is trying to figure out how it actually might be able to hit.

Votto thinks, eventually, things will normalize. "This will pass and teams will evolve and adapt and offense will return." McCarthy isn't so sure, barring official intervention. "I think the only way you actually bring hitting back is by adjusting rules against the pitchers. Otherwise I think it just keeps furthering." If his recent quotes are any indication, Maddon sides with McCarthy, as he's not sure hitters have any edge anywhere. Over time, pitchers will only become *less* stubborn. They'll only become *more* willing to have the defense shifted behind them. Offense has dropped, and is still in the process of dropping. At least, that's what the numbers suggest.

Whether you think it's a problem now or not, it might become a problem down the road, so consideration must be given to how this trend might be brought to a halt. And even if you see absolutely nothing problematic, think about where we are, with a baseball game that's apparently changed because people got to learn more about the baseball game. Ted Williams is believed to have said that the hardest thing to do in sport is to hit a baseball. Relative to the major leagues over the course of Williams' career, last year's OPS was lower by 18 points. Hitting a baseball has never been harder, and now teams know better than ever where you're probably going to hit it.

References & Resources

- Special thanks to Brandon McCarthy and Joey Votto for their time.
- Special thanks to Eno Sarris for interviewing Sean Doolittle, Sam Fuld, Jon Lester and C.J. Wilson.
- MLB.com, "Maddon says advanced metrics hurting hitters," *m.rays.mlb.com/news/article/33081024/*
- Bill Chastain, MLB.com, "Maddon, Rays searching for new offensive edge," *m.rays.mlb.com/news/article/95701848/joe-maddon-rays-searching-for-new-offensive-edge*
- Tom Verducci, Sports Illustrated, "Why MLB teams are shifting on defense more than ever," *si.com/mlb/2014/04/29/mlb-emphasis-defensive-shifts-astros-yankees*
- John Dewan, Bill James Online, "How Do Shifts Affect League-Wide BABIP?," *billjamesonline.com/how_do_shifts_affect_league-wide_babip_*
- Joshua Green, *Business Week*, "Extreme Moneyball: The Houston Astros Go All In on Data Analysis," *businessweek.com/articles/2014-08-28/extreme-moneyball-houston-astros-jeff-luhnow-lets-data-reign*
- Mike Fast, Baseball Prospectus, "Spinning Yarn: Removing the Mask Encore Presentation," *baseballprospectus.com/article.php?articleid=15093*

The Explosion in UCL Injuries

by Craig Wright

Pitching in the third inning of a game on July 17, 1974, Tommy John suffered a complete rupture of the ulnar collateral ligament (UCL) in his elbow. While many pitchers have come back from partial tears of the UCL, a complete tear was essentially considered a career-ending injury.

John became the first pitcher to undergo a new type of surgery that reconstructed the UCL using a relatively unimportant tendon of similar size from another part of the body, usually the palmaris longus tendon in the wrist, as was the case in John's surgery.

John's recovery from his acute injury via this surgical solution was stunning. He actually had a better ERA in the five seasons after his return from the surgery than he had in the five seasons before the surgery.

Tommy John, pre- and post-surgery		
Time Period	ERA	IP
Five years before surgery (1970-1974)	3.14	1,056.1
Five years after return surgery (1976-1980)	3.11	1,182.0

John's amazing success story helped popularize this surgical solution, which has been a boon to other pitchers with serious injuries to their UCLs, and the general results of the surgery have improved over time. The chances of a pitcher coming back to approximate his prior effectiveness have risen from around 75 percent to closer to 90 percent. With this surgery, pitchers have come back to be All-Stars, throw perfect games, and have long careers. David Wells got a record 21 years of big league mileage out of his "new elbow." He had the surgery as a minor leaguer and went on to win 239 games in his long big league career.

The number of Tommy John (TJ) surgeries being done on major league pitchers has rapidly escalated. A dozen years ago, only about five TJ surgeries a year were being done on major league pitchers. The average in recent years is well over 20 and still rising. Jeremy Hefner's second TJ surgery, performed on Oct. 9, put the 2014 tally at 30 major league pitchers.

Some of that rise is just a matter of the surgery being applied more frequently to the less severe UCL injuries, where surgery is more of an option than a clear necessity. A dozen years ago, a pitcher with a partially torn UCL was more likely to opt for the non-surgical solution of "rest and rehab," as was elected by the Yankees'

Masahiro Tanaka this past summer for a manageable 10 percent tear of his UCL. But Tanaka's choice is becoming less common as the significant advantage of the non-surgical option—a faster recovery time—is shrinking due to the advances in rehabilitation for those coming back from the surgery. They now have special braces with adjustable range of motion that protect the recovering elbow while still allowing exercises to keep the overall arm strong, which reduces the amount of time needed to build the arm back up to pitching shape when the elbow is ready. The recovery period has been dramatically shaved, from 18 months to about a year.

Among the major leaguers having TJ surgery in 2014, the coverage of their decision to have the surgery indicates that six had small enough tears that rest and rehab was a reasonable alternative to the surgery. The call was closest for Bobby Parnell of the Mets, whose tear was less severe than the torn UCL of his famous teammate Matt Harvey the year before. It was deemed essentially a coin flip in Parnell's case as to whether the surgery was the better course of treatment over rest and rehab.

Not yet well appreciated as a factor in the rise of TJ surgeries is that the push to shorten the recovery time may be making the pitchers more vulnerable to a *future* tear of their reconstructed UCL. In the days of the more patient 18-month recovery period, the limited data suggested a pitcher with a reconstructed UCL had only about a four to five percent increased risk of a subsequent UCL tear in the next five years when compared to other pitchers. That estimate has been obliterated with the results in recent years. In 2014, six of the major league pitchers having TJ surgery were having it for the second time in five years, or in the case of Johnny Venters of Atlanta, for the *third* time.

But the major force behind the huge number of pitchers having TJ surgery "appears" to be simply an unprecedented increase in the number of significant injuries to the UCL.

Epidemic...or Not?

I wrote "appears" for the moment out of deference to those who argue that we really can't say for sure. In a 2014 *Sports Illustrated* article, a surgeon was quoted saying: "We can't say whether baseball is in the midst of a true Tommy John epidemic or if we are just better at diagnosing an injury that, silently, was just as prevalent in previous generations."

It is a safe bet that before the more definitive tests available today, some significant tears in the UCL were being misdiagnosed as some other type of elbow injury. Even today, the symptoms of the lesser tears in the UCL sometimes are mistaken for something else, especially a strain or tear in the flexor muscle group that runs over the UCL. Often several weeks go by before the lack of recovery leads to further examination and the more involved tests reveal the damage to the UCL.

While a severe tear to the UCL often was considered a career-ending injury before the days of TJ surgery, it actually is possible to pitch without having a UCL at all to stabilize the elbow. Many know the story of R.A. Dickey, who was a fine college pitcher and was the 18th overall pick in the major league draft, only to have a physical examination reveal that he had no UCL in his pitching elbow. He was able to pitch, but the absence of the UCL dangerously stressed the other elements of his elbow joint. As Glenn Fleisig of the American Sports Medicine Institute explained it: "If a pitcher has no UCL, he must compensate with extra compression between his elbow bones [which increases generation of bone chips and possibly bone spurs] and/or extra tension in the other ligaments and tendons."

The solution for Dickey was to convert to being a knuckleballer, where the slower pitch would put less stress on the joint. Again from Fleisig, "Ligaments and tendons are like rubber bands. Stretch them as far as you can and over time they'll develop small tears until they break. If you pitch at submaximal effort, the rubber band doesn't tear at all."

It also seems that the pronounced pain of an extreme but incomplete tear of the UCL is greater and more bothersome than when a pitcher completely ruptures the UCL. Most of the big league pitchers having TJ surgery described their injury as involving pain that made it impossible to pitch—to throw certain pitches and especially to throw hard. Some said it hurt too much to even lightly toss the ball. Pete Moylan said, "I went to the field the next day and tried to play catch and couldn't do it."

Yet Bronson Arroyo, who was one of the few to suffer a complete tear of his UCL in 2014, had six more starts before being shut down and did reasonably well. The OPS of the opposing batters was higher, but not gigantically so, a rise from .722 to .769. He did favor the elbow by reducing the velocity of his fastball to under 85 mph—compared to the 87.2 mph figure he managed the year before.

So, yes, it might be remotely possible that pitchers of other generations were unknowingly tearing up their UCLs at a much higher rate than was diagnosed at the time, and that it was missed because they managed to keep their careers going by gritting their teeth and altering their pitching styles to reduce the strain on their elbows.

But from a baseball common sense perspective, does that really hold water in explaining what is happening today? Even with the advantage of modern drugs helping with the pain and inflammation that Arroyo was suffering, he got to a point where he said, "I couldn't do it anymore…If this was the last year of my career, I could gut through it with anti-inflammatories and different things [but] it would be tough." And he was the rare one to stay on the mound for a month after the significant injury to his UCL.

It is a mistake to think it is the surgery that stops their seasons. It is the severity of the injury itself that stops them, and if this were happening in another era without the surgical option, I'm sure we would be noticing something odd was going on. One would notice 20-plus pitchers in a year suddenly having to be shut down with elbow trouble for lengthy periods—usually the rest of the season—and with some of them never coming back.

That's likely what the scenario would be without the surgical repair. Most pitchers having TJ surgery have experienced a significant tear of the UCL that is not expected to heal well on its own, and even if it did, it would heal so slowly it likely would be a season-ending injury. Look at those who "rested" for a long period of time because the injury was originally assumed to be something else, a muscle strain or tear. A.J. Griffin rested over six weeks without making progress, after which the significant UCL tear was found. He had the surgery 47 days after he had last been able to pitch. Tyler Chatwood was disabled for nearly three months before having the surgery.

I'm fine with not using the hyperbole of the term "epidemic," but I don't doubt that most TJ surgeries among professional pitchers involve a significant enough tear that its impact on the pitcher would be notable in any era. If something similar to what is going on now were happening in 1990 or 1960 or 1930 or 1910, it would have stood out.

Ironically, for something intended to help with UCL injuries, TJ surgery likely has contributed to the number of UCL injuries by weakening our interest in preventing them. The success rate for the surgery has gotten so high that many baseball people view the huge rise in UCL injuries as not that big a problem. And I could add to that perception by pointing out that in the case of young pitchers coming back from the surgery, the year's respite from competitive pitching might actually be beneficial to the long-term health of their throwing shoulders.

But the explosion of UCL injuries does deserve to be treated as a serious problem. If there is an element in the game pushing participants to a high level of injury, then that is a weakness in the sport, one that detracts from its status as a game and its popularity in the future. This is something that needs to be addressed.

In some cases, we might accept an unusually high rate of injury if it were primarily confined to the professional ranks, where participants make an informed and compensated choice. But when this injury problem slips down into the amateur ranks, it is unconscionable not to tackle it as a serious problem. In May of 2014, Dr. James Andrews, perhaps the foremost expert on TJ surgery, said something that should have burned the ears of major league baseball. "It's really depressing to go in and see the number of high school kids coming in with this injury. At this point in my career I'm probably seeing more high school kids with an ulnar collateral ligament injury than I am with college and pros."

Big league baseball drives what happens in amateur baseball by imitation. Something is going on in the major leagues that is making the UCL more vulnerable to serious injury, and it is trickling down into the ranks of amateur pitchers.

The Slider and Elbow Injuries

It is commonly believed that throwing the curve and slider puts more strain on the elbow joint than throwing the fastball. That's why young pitchers are discouraged from throwing curves and sliders until their elbow joints mature and are better able to handle the added strain.

Yet we now have biomechanical studies done by the American Sports Medicine Institute comparing amateur curveballs and fastballs, and the results show that the torque—the force and stress—on the elbow is actually less when throwing a curveball than a fastball. But it is also unclear that these types of studies have a clear handle on the types of forces that are most relevant to arm injuries. One of the stranger findings noted that elbow torque was "significantly higher" for sidearm throwers than overhand throwers. And yet the common perception—and I believe an overwhelmingly correct one—is that sidearmers and submariners have a much lower incidence of arm injury than overhand pitchers.

We do know that throwing the curveball and slider requires changing the backspin on the ball from what is generated by a normal throw, and the motion altering that backspin tends to fight the arm's unstoppable natural pronation motion when making a hard throw. Somewhere in generating all this unnatural motion may be something that is putting additional strain on the elbow.

Before the slider became established in the game, the curveball was routinely blamed for many elbow ailments. The slider has long since surpassed the curve as that villain, and even studies suggesting the curve does not add strain to the elbow do find higher levels of torque on the elbow when throwing the slider than when throwing the curve, primarily because sliders are routinely thrown with significantly higher velocity than curves.

The perception has been that arm trouble is more frequent among professional pitchers known for their sliders, although as with any pitch there are notable exceptions. Randy Johnson had a great slider and threw it a lot but had an unusually long and healthy career. When the rise in UCL injuries began, the slider was considered a key culprit, and anecdotal evidence seems to point in that direction. Jose Rijo routinely was praised for his slider, which often was cited as the best in the majors in the late 1980s and early 1990s. He was the first pitcher to have three TJ surgeries, and he had two other elbow operations. John Smoltz replaced Rijo on the best-slider list in the 1990s and eventually tore his UCL in 2000. Chad Fox relied very heavily on his slider, throwing it about a third of the time; like Rijo, he had multiple TJ surgeries.

A huge 2002 study of amateur pitchers looked at arm injuries in relation to pitch totals and pitch types. The study found pitch totals were a better predictor of arm trouble than pitch types. That study is the basis for most of the pitch limits now employed in youth leagues. But the study also noted that pitch type *did* correlate with whether it was the shoulder or the elbow that was injured. The data showed that "throwing a slider was associated with an *86%* increased chance of *elbow* injury."

A more recent study using data collected from 2006 to 2010 concluded that youth league pitchers who threw sliders had "three times the risk of getting injured" as those who did not throw sliders.

The importance of these findings among the youth pitchers is only partly about the risks of the slider. What those results really are shouting about is how the dangers of pitching are magnified when dealing with young arms with immature elbow joints.

While the risk of abusing an immature joint steadily declines during the advance to maturity, it remains a factor for a significant portion of a *professional* pitcher's career. The joints are the parts of the body that mature the latest, often not completing that maturity until around age 24. Even the bones, the bulk of which complete their maturation by ages 18-20 for most males, still have some "late-bloomers." For example, the growth plate of the clavicle, which has a role in the shoulder joint, does not fully ossify all layers until around ages 23 to 25.

The maturity factor is especially notable in regard to the most famous slider pitcher, Hall of Famer Steve Carlton, who never had a significant tear of his UCL while throwing the fifth-most innings in the Expansion Era (1961-present). What many fans don't realize is that the slider was a late addition to Carlton's repertoire. He did not grow up throwing the slider and did not learn the pitch until right around his 24th birthday, on a postseason trip to Japan. He then used it off and on for a few years before he began relying on it heavily. You might be surprised to know that in 1972, which was easily Carlton's greatest season, he actually was better known for his curveball than his slider. It was when he won his next three Cy Young awards that he relied heavily on his slider, which was judged the best of his era.

While the slider is getting less blame in recent years for the escalation in UCL injuries, a relationship still appears to exist between the pitch and a proclivity for tearing the UCL. Venters, who has blown out his UCL three times, throws (or threw) a slider with above-average velocity and has used it more than 20 percent of the time in all of his big league seasons. Reliever Scott Williamson had a great hard slider in the upper 80s and first tore his UCL at age 25, and then did it again three years later. Francisco Liriano came to the majors with a super slider that some described as "unhittable," and he used it a ton. It was not a big surprise when he blew his UCL when he was only 22.

It would be better if more careers were similar to Carlton's, with the slider adopted in the pitcher's mid-20s, but if pitchers are going to throw sliders in their younger years, it would help to see them use the pitch more sparingly, say, no more than 10-12 percent of the time. Just these past couple of seasons, we have seen two truly great pitchers blow out their UCLs while in their formative years. Both had exceptional hard sliders that they were starting to throw more frequently when they got hurt.

Matt Harvey had a spectacular slider that he threw as hard as any pitcher I have ever seen. He threw it 13 percent of the time in his rookie season and then jumped it up to 18.5 percent in 2013, which is when his UCL gave way in his 26th start of the season. Jose Fernandez threw his slider 12.7 percent of the time in his great rookie season of 2013 at age 20. Then, in 2014, he jumped it up to 21.2 percent and, boom, there went his UCL in his eighth start.

Despite the link between the slider and UCL injuries, there is justifiable reason to look beyond the slider in trying to understand the recent explosion of serious tears of the UCL. You see, the massive escalation of this type of injury is taking place at a time when the use of the slider has remained essentially steady, around 14-15 percent. Clearly, there are other significant factors to be considered.

Are We Throwing Too Hard?

It's no big surprise that every biometric study of the stress being put on the UCL by pitchers shows the force exerted on the elbow, and the UCL specifically, rises when the pitcher is throwing his hardest. Baseball has always—always—put an emphasis on throwing hard, but no era has ever been like the modern one. The near-constant message to young pitchers is that we are looking first and foremost for hard throwers. Those are the guys who are going to get the opportunities, especially to advance as a reliever, which is where the largest increase in big league jobs is taking place.

We no longer care about starters going for a complete game—instead we build larger and more talented bullpens. We are moving away from pitchers used to pacing themselves and finding moments to coast. The default now is to think more in terms of "throw as hard as you can as long as you can."

For most of my career in evaluating major league pitchers, the average fastball was around 88-89 mph. If you could throw 94, you had an elite fastball. By 2008, the average fastball in the majors was 90.9, and just five years after that it was up to 92, perhaps the quickest escalation of fastball velocity in history.

And if the fastballs are faster, then many of the breaking balls tend to be faster, as well, especially the sliders and change-ups. The average speeds of these pitches have increased in almost perfect proportion to the rise of the average fastball. Some of the modern fireballers are now throwing change-ups that are faster than the average fastball was back during my career. Kelvin Herrera, a young reliever for the Royals, steadily averages a 98 mph fastball, and near the end of the season, I was startled to watch a game where I realized he was throwing several change-ups at 90 mph. It wasn't a freak game. I looked it up in the Baseball Info Systems data, and in a sample of over 200 change-ups in 2014, his average velocity was 89.4 mph!

All this velocity is dangerous for the UCL in two ways. Ligaments are not muscles, but that does not mean they don't have a strengthening process; it just isn't as easy or as fast as the strengthening process for muscle. Muscles are far more tied into the circulatory system, giving them better blood flow and access to nutrients. That is why they can build strength so much faster and also recover more rapidly from injury than ligaments and tendons do.

In the past, there was more balance between the development of the strength and elasticity of the UCL and the development of the muscles involved in throwing hard. That's less true today. We've made advances in strength training for pitchers, particularly in building up the back and shoulders, which can advance a pitcher's ability to throw hard. Because this is a muscular development, it can happen in a time frame faster than the development of the UCL can keep up.

Perhaps even more dangerous to the UCL is that the great emphasis on velocity is leading pitchers to develop pitching mechanics that enhance velocity in a manner that puts extra stress on the elbow and UCL. I was taught to be cautious of pitchers with certain types of deliveries: "the drag," when the arm falls behind the rotation of the hips; the "high elbow," above the shoulder line too early in the delivery, and the "inverted W" delivery (don't ask me why it isn't just called the "M" delivery), particularly when that inverted W shape is still well-defined just before the striding foot comes down. These were the pitchers who were deemed vulnerable to future arm trouble, and elbow injuries were deemed a more common result of bad mechanics than were shoulder injuries. If you want to use the word "epidemic," use it to describe the rise in these types of mechanics in this age of speed. They are far, far more common today than they were 20 years ago.

If there is one thing that the biometric studies have brought out, it is that pitching mechanics—totally separate from velocity—can play a huge role in the amount of stress being put on the UCL. It has been shown that with two pitchers throwing their fastball at the exact same speed, one can be exerting *50 percent* more force on his UCL than the other! This an incredibly important point in considering the role of dangerous mechanics in the rise of UCL injuries.

I grew up in Michigan as a Tigers fan, and still follow them even though I've lived most of my life elsewhere. In this era of blown UCLs and dangerous mechanics that juice velocity, the Tigers provide two extreme examples.

Joel Zumaya was one of those guys who could top 100 on the radar gun, and in 2009-2010 was *averaging* 99.3 on his fastballs. But he was doing it by overloading his arm with an exaggerated "high elbow" delivery. He was putting a tremendous strain on his elbow, and on June 28, 2010, he fractured a bone in his elbow while simply throwing a pitch, which is essentially unheard of. Then, in the spring of 2012, he actually did tear his UCL, and his elbow was such a mess that he ended up retiring.

Then along came Bruce Rondon, a massive Venezuelan the Tigers signed in 2007 at age 17. I got to see him pitch briefly in the 2012 World Cup for Venezuela, and you could not help but be both excited and concerned. At age 21, he was firing at 100 mph, but, like Zumaya, he was jacking up his fastball with dangerous mechanics, employing an "inverted W" and getting his elbow too high, too soon. Tigers assistant GM Al Avila said he had seen the kid throw a pitch at 103, and Rondon backed him up by doing exactly that in the 2012 Futures Game. In his rookie season in 2013 it was Rondon—not Aroldis Chapman—who led the majors with the highest average speed on his fastball. He was at 99.3—right up there with Zumaya in his prime, but Rondon was doing it age 22. (When Zumaya was 22, he averaged "only" 97.5.)

Rondon seemed a perfect storm for putting more force on his elbow and UCL than it could handle. When he wasn't throwing blinding fastballs, he was throwing hard sliders on 22 percent of his pitches, and he was doing all this with mechanics associated with extra strain on the elbow. By the end of his rookie season, Rondon was experiencing trouble with his elbow, fortunately only a flexor strain. But five months later, early in the spring exhibition season, he was hit with more elbow pain, and this time, it was a significant tear in his UCL. He was one of the big leaguers to have TJ surgery in 2014.

Are We Interfering with Developing Durability in the UCL?

The notion that the emphasis on speed has helped endanger pitchers' UCLs is a fitting one for a problem that is as prevalent among amateurs as in the professional ranks. Pitchers at every level feel they have to maximize their velocity.

Looking for another factor with a similar broad presence across baseball led me to wonder if the current rage of pitch limits—as predominant, or more, in amateur leagues as in the majors—interferes with developing elasticity and strength in the UCL, which might otherwise provide pitchers a protective durability.

As I wrote in an article for the *2011 Hardball Times Annual*, the use of pitch limits is wrong-headed. To the extent it is claimed to be based on my work in *The Diamond Appraised* involves a leap I did not make or intend and is a severe misreading of my conclusions and recommendations. Rather than aiming pitchers at a set pitch limit and holding them to it, I advocated paying attention to the pitcher's *average* workload and allowing room for significant workload variation as a way of allowing the pitcher to build up his durability. You do that by stretching out his workload when he is at his best and pulling him back when he is not.

I advocated a protective pitch "ceiling" to control that variation for young pitchers and pitchers with health issues. That recommended ceiling was about 25 percent above the average deemed appropriate for that pitcher, making it a ceiling that could be tested only rarely if the average was to be maintained. Consider how different that is from the modern practice of pitch limits that sets a low limit the pitcher is encouraged to push but not exceed every time.

After that article appeared, I did some research that showed a higher standard deviation (variance) within a starting pitcher's seasonal workload in his formative years correlated with fewer injuries and longer, more effective careers.

Much of my work in this area has been focused on the impact of various types of workloads on the shoulder, where there is more long-term damage done with chronic attritional damage, rather than the more sudden acute injuries more common in the elbow. I am not as confident that my research and findings are as applicable to the elbow. There are very distinct differences in addressing the health and aging of the shoulder, which is so much more complex a joint than the elbow.

But that being said, there are a lot of principles in common between the two. I would not be surprised to find that, similar to how pitch limits work against building the durability of the shoulder, they are having the same impact on the UCL, which needs to build elasticity and strength to improve its durability.

Suggestions for Curtailing the Rise in UCL Injuries

As I suggested in 2011, we can abandon the modern practice of pitch limits as the best way to control damaging workloads. We can achieve that goal by focusing on an average pitch count in conjunction with a protective pitch ceiling for the games when the pitcher is being stretched out. Coaches also can be instructed about avoiding other stressors, taking greater care in the buildup of the workload coming out of spring training, and breaking strings of heavy-work appearances with "oasis" outings.

We can do a lot more to improve the elasticity of the UCL with more attention to stretching it out with frequent light throwing on flat ground. I also like long toss warm-ups. They help stretch out the arm, but the action is taking place in a very different plane—an upward plane—from the one in which the arm will be worked so hard during the game.

Obviously, the hardest thing will be getting pitchers to slow the heck down. We can try to discourage some of the more dangerous mechanics, but that won't be easy because it is not something that can be legislated, and it will be fighting against the common desire to throw as hard as possible.

But we can work on changing the modern mindset that has so raised the value placed on throwing hard and has made pitching so much about speed. We can legislate changes in the professional game that would place an emphasis on staff durability over staff velocity. Then, as the major leagues build this image of pitchers relying less on velocity, we can hope kids will imitate that.

We can start by restricting the number of pitchers a team can have on its roster to nine rather than the 12 commonly carried today. That will automatically curtail the growing philosophy of throwing as hard as you can as long as you can. Teams will start thinking about how to get more innings safely out of fewer pitchers. We know it can be done. It was done during the lifetime of most of the people reading this article—and those days involved fewer top-velocity pitches and better, safer mechanics.

In addition, we can legislate against using relievers in a way that has them contribute by simply throwing super hard for a few batters. We can discourage pitching changes within an inning by adding a penalty for doing it. Say, the batter gets first base and every runner on base advances a base. Such a rule would likely eliminate 95 percent of partial-inning relief appearances.

I also would advocate curtailing developing one-inning relievers and particularly ninth-inning closers. It would be as simple as this: If a team wants to start the ninth inning with a new pitcher, the leadoff batter gets an intentional walk. This would get relievers, particularly closers, to develop the skills for two-inning outings, roughly equivalent to requiring them to pitch through the whole lineup. Note that this rule would not automatically penalize a team for using a reliever for a single inning. If your starting pitcher is knocked out early and you need to scramble for pitchers to finish out the game, you can use guys for only one inning. They just have to be used by the eighth. If the guy who pitched the eighth doesn't also pitch the ninth, then the new pitcher is going to start with a penalty runner.

To avoid injuries in the transition from pitchers used to an emphasis on velocity rather than durability, I would suggest the roster reduction be in stages. Rather than immediately limiting the roster to nine pitchers, make the limit 11 the first year, 10 the second, and then settle on nine.

I expect these legislative suggestions also would help with other big concerns about the evolution of the game—the length of the games, the rise in strikeouts that has the unsatisfying result of less involvement of the fielders, and the decline in offense. By eliminating most of the pitching changes within an inning, we will not only speed up games but give them a more enjoyable pace. Shifting emphasis away from velocity to durability will lower the strikeout rates. That in itself likely will help the offense, and so will a reduction of pitcher specialization that exploits hitter weaknesses such as the left-right platoon factors.

These types of legislative changes would be good for the game as a whole, as well as ultimately better for the health of pitchers, and particularly so in regard to elbow injuries.

References & Resources

- *The American Journal of Sports Medicine* (2002). Lyman, Fleisig, Andrews, and Osinski. "Effect of Pitch Type, Pitch Count, and Pitching Mechanics on Risk of Elbow and Shoulder Pain in Youth Baseball Pitchers."
- Mark Derewicz, in *Endeavors Magazine*, which covers research and creative activity at the University of North Carolina. The five-year study was developed and implemented by Fred Mueller, director of the National Center for Catastrophic Sport Injury Research at UNC; professor Stephen Marshall of the UNC Gillings School of Global Public Health, and Barry Goldberg, former director of sports medicine at Yale University. The actual study was conducted by a team led by research associate Johna Register-Mihalik.
- A web article in 2010 by Eric Cressey, referring to a 2009 study in *The American Journal of Sports Medicine* done by "Aguinaldo, Al, and Chambers, H."
- *The American Journal of Sports Medicine* (2008), Dun, Loftice, Fleisig, Kingsley, and Andrews. "A Biomechanical Comparison of Youth Baseball Pitches: Is the Curve-

ball Potentially Harmful?" The results showed greater elbow varus torque and elbow proximal force in throwing fastballs than curveballs.

- *The American Journal of Sports Medicine* (2006), Fleisig, Kingsley, Loftice, Dinnen, Ranganathan, Dun, Escamilla, and Andrews. "Kinetic Comparison Among the Fastball, Curveball, Change-up, and Slider in Collegiate Baseball Pitchers."

- The magnitude of 50 percent being possible comes from *Sports Illustrated* (9/8/2014) Matt McCarthy. "The Cutting Edge." It mentions the analysis of a college pitcher whose max varus torque on his UCL was unusually low at 37.4 Newton-meters. A group with similar velocity is around 55 Newton-meters, or 47 percent higher.

"Moneyball" vs. "The Book"

by Jason Linden

Most any serious baseball talk you hear this offseason will mention sabermetrics. Some will be hoping for a sabermetric approach from their favorite team, others will continue to deride it. The question is, why? What has contributed to sabermetrics' hold on baseball? If you ask this question, plenty of people will trace it back to the Michael Lewis' 2003 book, *Moneyball*. You've probably heard about it. It was kind of a big deal. They made it into a movie starring Brad Pitt.

But, you know, there's been other stuff, too. In fact, in 2006, another book came out. It was called *The Book* and it's less well known. It deals much more in hard statistics. While the general public might be less aware of it, major league front offices aren't. In certain circles, it was every bit as big as *Moneyball*, and maybe even more so. It was so important that we might ask if *The Book* had a bigger influence on the game than *Moneyball*. In fact, let's ask that question, and to start toward our answer, let's see how the books start…

> *I wrote this book because I fell in love with a story.*
> *-Michael Lewis,* Moneyball

> *What you are about to read is an attempt to quanitfy or qualify the ideal strategies in baseball. Each chapter will tackle a particular topic, and ask very specific questions.*
> *-Tango, Lichtman, Dolphin,* The Book

Two books, both alike in dignity, but which one turned the wheels? Which one shoved owners and executives, scouts and even players down the path of the saber? It's a tangled question and a hard one to answer, but I'm going to try. So start with those two quotations taken from the beginnings of each book. They are different. Different enough that through them, we can see that the question is not so much whether *Moneyball* or *The Book* matters more. Rather it is this: What matters more: The story or how it is written?

Undercurrents

We can't pretend that these ideas poofed into existence magically the day Michael Lewis' book (or was it Billy Beane's?) was published. Past is always prologue. Throughout history, astute observers have noted the problems with RBI. Branch Rickey was a proponent of on-base percentage. But these things didn't take hold. They didn't take hold probably because no one forced the issue. People resist change, and they often don't want to ask questions. This goes for the owners and general managers of baseball teams as well as anyone else. To convince someone to change, he or she must be shown not only that there are different questions to ask, but that there is value in seeking the answers to those questions.

Billy Beane was given the Oakland A's and a story he didn't like. No money equals no success. It reminded him of another story he didn't like. That of the sure-thing prospect. The same industry told him both of these stories. He knew one was a lie, so why not question the other? That's the first part. Ask different questions.

But it's not that simple, right? Beane didn't invent sabermetrics. Bill James was there. Rob Neyer had already entered the mainstream. They asked questions. But then, they weren't running major league teams. Beane was. But who showed him there was value in the answers so he could show others in baseball? We can do this for days, but you get the idea. It's complicated.

The Horse's Mouth

So enough tripping down memory lane. It's not 1998 or 2003 or 2006. It's 2014. We have the benefit of at least a little perspective. I put several questions to front office folks around baseball and got answers about the workings of six different teams. The answers I received were as interesting for what they didn't say as what they did say. My first question was very simple: *Moneyball* or *The Book*, which was more important? I got some interesting answers to this question. Most favored *Moneyball*, though, of course, our answer won't be so easy. Among the best I received was this response from Justin Hollander of the Angels:

> *"In the movie* Big, *adult Josh Baskin is at a dinner party, and he ends up teaching algebra to the hosts' son by using the example that if Larry Bird scored 10 points in the first quarter, he will score 40 points in the game. 'That,' according to Josh Baskin, 'is algebra.' Well, not exactly, but he packaged the information in such a way that the kid wants to learn more about algebra, and that is what* Moneyball *did for sabermetrics."*

This is the heart of argument for those who side with the importance of story over process. It puts forward the belief that no one wants to look at process unless you package it with a good story. This rings true for me. In the "real world," I'm an English teacher. And let me tell you something, kids aren't wading into *Pride & Prejudice* unless they think they'll get something they find valuable out of it. As often as not, that value is entertainment. Many of the answers I got to this question were along those lines. *Moneyball* was entertaining, so owners read it, and then they wanted to know more.

But there's always another perspective. Here's what Tony Blengino, who has worked for both the Brewers and the Mariners, said:

> *"The Book, no question. Moneyball told us all how laughable it was to take Prince Fielder in the first round."*

And this is an important perspective, too. Because there is more than a little bit of the fairy tale in *Moneyball*. Lewis did fall in love with a story, and sometimes, when we're in love, it's hard to be completely honest. Fielder obviously has turned into a great major league player. *The Book*, some would argue, is essential because it's all about how you go about finding that value. There were plenty of people around baseball when *Moneyball* came out who didn't need to be converted. They were already questioning the system.

This leads into the second question in my survey, which asked respondents about what moved their organization into sabermetrics. These answers were more specific and tended to suggest that it was something other than *Moneyball* or *The Book*. It is hard not to feel, reading the answers to this question, that there was a movement happening already. That it was, literally, just a matter of time. In a sense, this is what *Moneyball* is about. Things were changing, and it documented part of that change.

This is also where I start to get interesting answers from sources who needed to remain anonymous. There is a lot of talk about ownership and management making a decision to move in a sabermetric direction. *The Book* probably gets more weight here, but it's close, and it doesn't come off as a prime component.

With my third question, things got even more interesting. I asked specifically about how much the ideas from each book were used in the organization. Here, the balance was slanted as heavily as the responses to question one, but in the other direction. The clear choice was *The Book*, with the primary takeaway being that it did, in fact, provide a lot of good tools many organizations haven't managed to improve on enough to see them displaced. It is the kind of book that is just lying around in front offices. One very telling answer came from Josh Stein of the Padres:

> *"The ideas and tools from both books are used and referenced all the time throughout baseball, sometimes still incorrectly!"*

I love the ending of that answer. Of course, if you're paying attention, you know that some teams still are not getting it right, but this confirms that the transformation is far from complete. People still misunderstand; they still get it wrong.

The Other Side of the Ball

Lucky man that I am, I was able to correspond not just with some front office folks, but also with two of the writers of *The Book*, Tom Tango and Mitchel Lichtman.

One thing was made very clear in talking with them. *Moneyball* was a nonfactor as far as the work they were doing was concerned. I expected this answer. Drill down deep enough into anything, and you'll find people working for work's sake. That describes Tango and Lichtman. They weren't doing this for any reason other than that they wanted to. I'll let Mr. Lichtman take it from here:

"It was something we wanted to do, and if it sold 100 copies or 10,000 copies, it didn't really make a difference to us. We knew that lots of people, mostly the hardcore type, would be interested in the work we were doing, and we knew it was good work.

We also thought that there was a void in sabermetric books that we could fill. We felt like our book was an extension of the work done by Palmer and Thorn in The Hidden Game, which was written in 1985, 20 years earlier. We thought that it was time to fill that void and that we could do it. Basically, our book was The Hidden Game II, which is one of the reasons we asked Pete Palmer to write the intro."

It was, simply, something done to fill a knowledge gap. They saw a place to work, and they went there and worked. However, both men do acknowledge that the timing of their work was fortuitous. They were targeting a niche at a time when that niche was rapidly expanding. But that was coincidence.

I also asked both if they were trying to send any kind of message to major league teams. Here's what Tom Tango had to say:

"No, not at all. I was already contacted prior to The Book. *I'm extremely direct, and there's no hidden agenda. I just do what I do, and I figure that are some people that like it, too. I'm just hosting a party, really. And some MLB and NHL teams liked it, too."*

It's Not the Game You Think It Is

The final question I asked in my survey of front offices concerned proprietary stats. Much of *Moneyball* centers on the idea that the A's front office was trying to know more than everyone else. They were trying to figure it out on their own to at least some extent. I figured this approach had spread in baseball, and I was curious to know how much.

Well, let me tell you something, no one wants to talk about it. And in this circumstance, I think it's safe to infer there is a lot going on out there that we don't know about. Indeed, the further down the revenue ladder a team is in its division, the less willing it was to tell me anything.

I can't quote people I was told not to quote, but the little I do know makes me want to question everything I see on the field. This is especially true with regards to defense, where HITf/x, I am told, leaves that which is publicly available in the dust. Of course, all the teams have that, and so, in that sense, they are all on the same playing field. But I got the distinct impression that most of the organizations responding to my survey felt they had something going for them that no one else did. Or, at least, they didn't want to risk letting something new out of the bag. After all, who knows for sure what cards everyone else at the table has until they have to lay them down?

And again, it's hard to say what tipped the scales here. Maybe *Moneyball* showed a lot of teams that they could make their own stats, so to speak, but it was *The Book* that showed them how to do it.

The Party Continues

As part of his response to my question about who the audience for *The Book* was, Mitchel Lichtman had this to say:

> "The audience for sabermetrics has grown exponentially, I think, since around the early 21st century. I would say that although sabermetrics started in the '80s with James and Palmer and a few others (Craig Wright, etc.), it existed in a small niche and somewhat "underground" sometime until the 21st century. Perhaps Moneyball *was one of the major catalysts. I don't really know … At the very least it was a catalyst, if not a major one. These types of evolutions or revolutions (I think the proliferation and popularity of sabermetrics was somewhere in between) rarely hinge on one or two things—it is always a confluence of events and the natural progression of innovation and knowledge. Certainly, the internet was a huge influence in the spread of sabermetrics. In fact, that may be why we saw such a slow progression until the 21st century—the internet."*

This is interesting because it raises a third possibility, that it was neither volume that really affected baseball; it was, rather, the easy spread of information. Indeed, I can provide anecdotal evidence of this, as I came of age with the internet in the late '90s. As a the child of parents who didn't care a bit about baseball, I had no one to guide me. In my pre-computer days, it was all about whatever books I could get from the library and my subscription to *Baseball Digest*. But when going away to college brought with it ready access to the internet, I discovered a new baseball writer named Rob Neyer, and down the sabermetric path I went. I knew *Moneyball* was important, of course, but though it had been on my shelf for ages, I hadn't gotten around to reading it until this year. I doubt I'm alone.

But there is further truth in Lichtman's answer that leads me to my final bit of discussion and an arrival at the closest thing we're going to get to an answer…It's complicated (surprise!). It's never one thing or even two things.

The Book is no doubt essential to the progression of sabermetrics in the game of baseball. *The Book*, I was told, can be found lying around front offices. *Moneyball*, not so much. *The Book* is there in a day-to-day way, even now, that *Moneyball* is not. One respondent to my survey admitted to not having read Lewis' book. In ten or twenty years, there will be more like him.

But in some important ways, *Moneyball* was first, and being first matters. As a writer and a teacher, I've read my share of Shakespeare, and let me tell you, a lot of it is great and some it is not, but damned if it doesn't feel unfair because he got a crack at all those great lines 400 years before I did. *Moneyball* wasn't the first piece of saber-focused writing, but it was the first piece of saber-focused writing that a lot of front office people—and more importantly, a lot of owners—read. Even if they didn't like it. Even if at first they didn't believe what it had to say, it mattered because it showed them there were other ways to think about the game. It doesn't matter if part of it is a fairy tale. It just matters that it made people listen.

Every year, in my intro writing class, I teach a lesson in which I have students combine something from their lives with the kind of great, big world event that students have been writing bad poetry about since the dawn of time. I show them examples, and I talk to them about structure, but the most important part of lesson is a little lecture I give about truth. It goes something like this:

> *There are two kinds of truth. There's the factual truth—what really happened—and then there are the bigger truths we try to express in writing, the things we try to make our readers ask questions about. If you have to pretend something happened to you on a day it did not, it doesn't matter. No one will ever know, and that's not what your poem is about anyway.*

Anyway, I tell them this and they write a poem, and a lot of the time, the poems are pretty good. A few of them, maybe, would figure this out on their own. Most wouldn't. Now you tell me, what matters more, the learning how to write or the writing? The story or the facts that let us write it?

References & Resources

- Special thanks to Tom Tango, Mitchel Lichtman, Josh Stein, Justin Hollander, Tony Blengino, and all others who responded for their time and thoughtful and insightful answers.
- Michael Lewis, *Moneyball*
- Tom Tango, Mitchel Lichtman, Andrew Dolphin, *The Book*

Is The Split-finger Dangerous?

by Eno Sarris

Every pitch has its detractors.

The Baltimore Orioles banned the cutter. Jeff Zimmerman found that heavy slider and curve usage upped a starter's chance of landing on the disabled list. Even an uptick in high-velocity fastballs has shown up as a shared marker in Tommy John surgeries, according to Jon Roegele's research.

The split-finger fastball has enjoyed a recent resurgence in baseball. And there aren't necessarily more of them—1.6 percent in 2002, 1.7 percent last season—but the people throwing them seem to be getting more attention. Koji Uehara dominated the 2013 postseason with his. Hisashi Iwakuma, Roger Clemens, Curt Schilling, Dan Haren, Tim Lincecum, Alex Cobb and Jeff Samardzija are all at the top of the usage lists.

Called a FOSH by some, Lincecum's splitter rolls off his fingers a bit.

And they're receiving that attention for good reason. Some call it the split-finger, others the splitter, and still others the FOSH, but they all refer to the same pitch. (There's also the forkball moniker, though that may be a different pitch—more on that later.) The grip does all the work—there's no need for the pronation associated with most change-ups—and all the pitcher has to do is throw the heck out of the ball like a fastball. With his fingers splayed around the seams, the ball comes out looking like a fastball, smelling like a fastball, and tasting like a fastball…until it drops and hits that area between the catcher and home plate.

Now we have Masahiro Tanaka dazzling with his own version of the pitch. With the highest average whiff rate of any pitch type, heavy use of the splitter helped Tanaka to a top-12 finish in strikeout percentage. If you ask Yankees beat writer Bob Klapisch, it also frayed his elbow ligament. Another pitch, another detractor.

More than just one, actually. The pitch was once the darling of another decade. In the 1980s, Roger Clemens, Jack Morris and Dave Stewart featured the pitch in October. Mike Scott used it to turn himself into a Cy Young Award winner. Bruce Sutter became a Hall of Famer. Roger Craig often was credited with the creation of the split-finger fastball, but the forkball has been around since 1908 and Joe Bush (or James Swift, or Fred Martin), and Sutter feels he taught Craig the pitch himself (and Craig agrees). In any case, Craig told everyone who would listen about the pitch that made him a major leaguer.

But then people began to think it caused injury, particularly when Craig's staff went down. Dave Dravecky. Mike Krukow. Joe Price. Terry Mulholland. Mike LaCoss. Kelly Downs. All of them, injured in one year. But it was impossible to blame them all on the splitter, as Craig himself pointed out to Murray Chass in 1989. "The only problem was Dravecky doesn't throw one and Price doesn't throw it so their problems can't be related to the split-finger. Krukow hurt his shoulder diving for a ball and Mulholland was hit by a line drive."

When reached in his home this fall, Craig minced even fewer words. "It's very easy on your arm," Craig said of the pitch, "I'm not that dumb. If it hurt, I wouldn't teach it to people." He went on to tell the story of one particular curveball, which he felt generally puts more stress on the elbow and the shoulder. This curve was the last pitch he ever threw as a major leaguer—"something snapped in my shoulder."

Despite the lack of a strong correlation between the pitch and injury, baseball itself is still skeptical of the splitter. Mike Scioscia told the Associated Press in 2011 that he thought the pitch was stressful:

> "I think there is a correlation between some stresses put on the arms—some guys have had elbow problems, forearm problems, shoulder problems—and that pitch."

Some teams encourage their pitchers to leave the pitch out of their bag of tricks.

The problem with studying this link—between the splitter and injury—the same way we've studied it with other pitches is that it's still a rare pitch. In the PITCHf/x era, we only have 29 pitchers who have thrown the pitch more than 10 percent of the time. In our slider and curveball research, the threshold for injury was high, over 30 percent in some cases. Only 11 pitchers have thrown the splitter more than 20 percent of the time, and even adding names like Lincecum and Alex Cobb to the list (PITCHf/x labels their splitters as change-ups) doesn't move the needle enough. Here are the 11:

Pitchers w/ Minimum 20% Split-Finger Usage				
Name	FB%	FBv	SF%	SFv
Koji Uehara	55.7%	88.3	35.7%	80.5
Edward Mujica	53.8%	92.0	33.1%	86.5
Hideo Nomo	58.0%	86.3	32.4%	77.4
Hisashi Iwakuma	50.8%	89.5	24.7%	85.2
Joel Peralta	47.9%	90.6	24.3%	81.5
Curt Schilling	57.4%	91.7	22.0%	84.8
Roger Clemens	64.1%	91.9	21.6%	87.2
Jose Valverde	74.4%	93.9	21.3%	85.1
Esteban Yan	61.7%	92.6	20.8%	84.5
Jose Contreras	55.6%	91.8	20.5%	78.1
Steve Trachsel	52.6%	87.2	20.5%	81.8

There are actually only six starting pitchers on that list. Those six played in 87 seasons and went to the disabled list in 32 percent of them. The average starting pitcher hits the DL in 40 percent of his seasons. The sample is still so tiny—too tiny to do anything with these numbers.

When numbers can't be your guide, it makes most sense to ask people who play the sport. Who taught you the pitch? Has is it ever been taken away from you? Have you personally noticed any stress on your arm while throwing the pitch?

Most pitchers actually had a hard time remembering how they learned the pitch. Lincecum was "just messing around with grips" in San Francisco after his rookie year. Angels starter Matt Shoemaker has been throwing it since he was 14. Giants reliever Jean Machi said he idolized Pedro Martinez, and in his effort to figure out a grip that would move like his idol's change-up, he stumbled on the splitter. It just happened for them.

Even if they don't always have a memory of the moment, the pitch has spawned interesting formative memories. Orioles starter Kevin Gausman told Mike Ferrin on SiriusXM's MLB Network Radio that his dad made him sleep with a ball between his fingers to stretch them out. Machi could do him one better—he put a softball between his fingers in order to get enough flexibility for his true, deep forkball version of the splitter.

Craig said that when he taught Scott at the behest of then-Astros president Al Rosen, it took 10-12 days...but Scott wanted to give up after three days.

And then there was the time Craig taught his entire pitching staff the pitch. "I took Mark Davis over to the mound in front of everyone," Craig said, "and I told them you might not need it now, but here's an easy offside pitch that, if you throw it right, won't hurt." And then Davis, who had never thrown a split-finger before that day, demonstrated how the ball sank more the wider he pushed his fingers apart.

The grip that Mike Fetters taught Brandon League.

Brandon League had an interesting connection and perspective on those early days. Fellow Hawaiian Mike Fetters, whose career was over by 2006, taught League his secret. "I came up throwing a circle change, but I couldn't throw that consistently," the Dodgers reliever said. The splitter gave him something he could throw like a fastball. But learning didn't come without pain. "At first, it was really uncomfortable, it felt like your webbing between your fingers was going to split."

Cobb felt that his family was predisposed for splitters—"we all have really stretchy fingers"—and lamented the non-stretchy fingers of a teammate who couldn't learn Cobb's grip from him in the minor leagues. Reds reliever Manny Parra couldn't remember if his fingers were always this loose. Astros reliever Tony Sipp showed me that he could touch his pinky to his index finger without any effort before demonstrating his extreme splitter grip.

Tony Sipp was born with stretchy fingers.

But a little pain between the knuckles isn't what we're talking about here. Stretching in the webbing between your fingers isn't going to make a coach or an organization take the pitch away. And that has happened to many of today's split-finger aficionados.

Samardzija's college coach tried to take the split-finger away from him. "To this day we joke about it," the Athletics pitcher said. "Two years ago, when I first started starting, my numbers on my splitter were really good, and somebody put out an article on how good it was…and I photocopied it and sent it to him."

Those stories are so plentiful that it's hard to ignore them. Parra had his taken away from him a couple times in the minor leagues. Tim Hudson's junior college coach told him he'd hurt his arm. The Rays took the splitter away from Alex Cobb when he first joined the organization. The Royals told current Giants reliever Jeremy Affeldt to stop throwing the forkball when they drafted him.

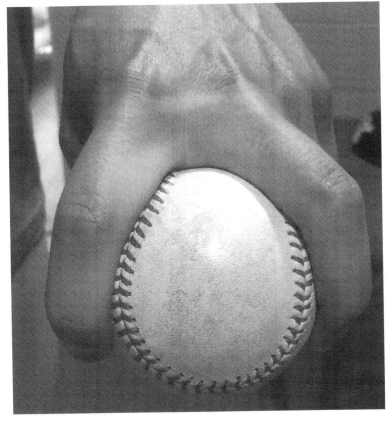

Manny Parra's knuckles didn't hurt long.

The Cardinals took Dan Haren's splitter away at first. He still managed to dominate with the short-season New Jersey Cardinals, but things changed when he was invited to spring training the next year. "They didn't want me throwing it and I was getting hit around," Haren said. "I told them I needed to throw it because it was my second-best pitch."

And that's why the pitch will keep coming back. As Hudson said of the splitter, "It was too much fun seeing those swings and misses." He couldn't quit it.

If you push the pitchers on the subject, you'll start to get some admissions that reach beyond "the team told me not to" and "yeah, my knuckles hurt once."

For example, even Haren, who loves the pitch and had to lobby his own team to use it, doesn't go to the well too often. "I still don't throw it much in bullpens in between starts," Haren told me this year. "I'll throw probably two or three between starts and then I'll throw 15 in a game, so it's not like I'm using it much."

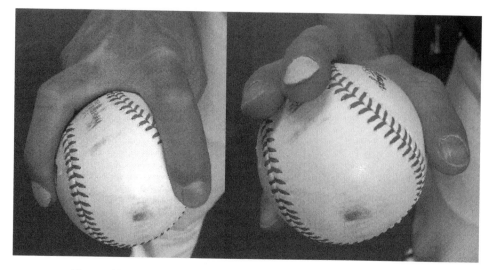

These two Tim Hudson grips are both called splitters by the classification systems. More often than not, though, he's actually throwing the modified change-up grip on the right.

Hudson does something similar, preferring to use his modified change-up grip (on the right in the above picture) over the splitter (on the left) until he has two strikes and really wants a whiff.

And then there are those who have completely eschewed the pitch. Jose Veras was concise: "It blew my elbow out." In his experience, which he said was backed up by conversations with other pitchers, the splitter led to lower velocity and elbow problems. Adam Ottavino has been looking for a change-up forever. "Every time I try the splitter, my elbow barks," the Rockies reliever said.

It's long been assumed that the stretched knuckles lead to some forearm stress. League admitted to as much. Mariners pitcher Hisashi Iwakuma also said that fore-arm strength was important for his split-finger because of the way you splay your fingers.

Affeldt gave a demonstration of how the stretched knuckles related to the forearm and then to the UCL. "You feel the flexor working," he said as he split his fingers wide and mimicked a pitch. "But right down here, that's your ulnar nerve," he said as he pointed to the inside of his elbow. And you can, indeed, feel a difference in the all-important ulnar area of your elbow if you split your fingers wide.

According to Kyle Boddy of Driveline Baseball (and a Hardball Times alum), that isn't necessarily your ulnar nerve you're feeling down there. But that isn't to say that Affeldt is completely wrong. What you feel in your inner elbow are two muscles of the flexor group that are "responsible for stabilizing the elbow joint" as Boddy put it. And the act of moving the middle finger away from the index finger does contract those muscles, and so that "may inhibit their ability to safely protect the UCL during loading." In other words, if your flexor muscles are busy with your grip, it might be possible that they can't help your elbow as much as necessary.

Boddy also admits he has no hard science on the elbow stress of a split-finger—yet—so we return to the words of the players and coaches.

Affeldt doesn't throw splitters when he's working on things and said his elbow hurt in high school back when he threw a forkball. The forkball versus split-finger question could be one of semantics, but look at Robert Coello's forkball below—that's more like the deep-in-the-palm true forkball that was developed by Joe Bush in the early part of the last century. It flutters and works more like a knuckleball. There aren't too many throwing this pitch today.

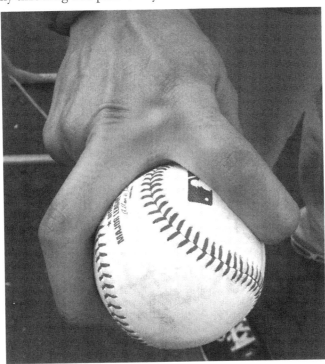

The forkball that flutters like a knuckleball—a throwback to the 1920s.

The modern splitter was popularized by both Roger Craig and Bruce Sutter. It's held more lightly in the fingers than the forkball, and it's thrown like a fastball. If the fastball is supposedly the healthiest pitch, the command of which is the basis of any pitcher's delivery, then another pitch that is thrown like a fastball has to have some health benefits, no?

Alan Ashby, current Astros broadcaster and former Astros catcher, said that the splitter appealed to Mike Scott mostly because it was thrown so much like a fastball. "He said he was happy to be a one-pitch pitcher. He credited the fact that he didn't have to throw a pitch where he turned his wrist…with much of his health and success—everything came out of the same motion, and he said that helped him strengthen his arm and pick up velocity."

And that's why it's often called the split-finger fastball. It's a change-up—the average speed on a splitter last year was 84 miles per hour, about seven mph slower than your average fastball—but it's released like a fastball.

Perhaps the market is telling us that there's something wrong with the pitch. Rob Neyer, co-author of *The Neyer/James Guide to Pitchers: An Historical Compendium of Pitching, Pitchers, and Pitches*, pointed out that the ease of the circle change has led to the demise of other grips designed to take velocity off the ball. Since there's little to no whiff of injury regarding the circle change, young pitchers are faced with what seems like an easy decision.

"I would not discount the significant possibility that the split-finger is a relatively dangerous pitch because of its stature in the marketplace of pitches," Neyer said. Just the fact that the pitch used to be more popular suggests something is at play here. As Mike Scioscia told the AP—"Everyone was throwing that pitch…It was the pitch of the '80s just like the pitch of the '60s was a slider."

And yet…Ashby wasn't sure about that assertion about the popularity of the split-finger. "Not sure it was more prevalent back then—it's used considerably today," Ashby said. And he caught in the '80s, which supposedly was the heyday of the splitter. Craig echoed Ashby, saying that he was "not sure it's thrown any more or less" than it was in the late '80s. Maybe the guys that used it back then were just more visible?

The pitch is as popular as it's ever been in Japan, where health outcomes are generally better. (Tommy John surgeries, at least, are half as prevalent, though the extra day of rest between starts may factor in.) According to Patrick Newman of NPBTracker.com, the splitter represented 6.3 percent of the pitches thrown in 2012 in Japan. That same year in America, 1.7 percent of all pitches were split-fingers, at least by the PITCHf/x algorithm (and 9.8 percent were change-ups).

It certainly seems like most of the pitchers coming over from Japan feature the pitch. Iwakuma shrugged off the possibility that it was due the popularity of Hideo Nomo and instead just said that the splitter was "just a change-up because they don't throw as many other change-ups in Japan." And if the pitchers who come over seem to be having a lot of success with the pitch, he said that he thought the different ball in the United States led to more movement on his splitter.

Perhaps the primary difficulty of studying this question is one of the primary difficulties of studying any pitcher injury question—every pitcher is different.

For example, there are 81 pitchers listed as throwing the splitter more than one percent of the time last season. Alex Cobb, who throws his splitter almost 40 percent of the time, is not on that list. He taught his grip to Jake Odorizzi. Using the same grip, Odorizzi throws a pitch called a splitter by the pitch recognition algorithm.

Cobb throws this splitter, which he calls a "very heavy two-seamer," over one-third of the time.

And so it's hard for us to know who's throwing what exactly, and how. When former Royals pitcher Brian Bannister says that he "loves the pitch," and thinks "it's a shame that it's not encouraged more often," he was probably thinking of the pitch in the same way that Craig thinks of the pitch: "It's just a simple way to get an offspeed pitch." Ashby said Scott felt the same way.

Release it like a fastball. "Throw it as the same pitch," said Ashby. "Trust the grip." What could be so dangerous about that?

References & Resources

- Special thanks to Roger Craig, Rob Neyer, Alan Ashby, Tim Lincecum, Dan Haren, Tim Hudson, Jose Veras, Alex Cobb, Jake Odorizzi, Brandon League, Tony Sipp, Adam Ottavino, Manny Parra, Jeff Samardzija, Mike Ferrin, Jeremy Affeldt, Jean Machi, Robert Coello, Hisashi Iwakuma, Brian Bannister, Patrick Newman and Kyle Boddy for talking to me about the split-finger fastball and injury.
- Jeff Zimmerman, RotoGraphs, "Curveball and Slider Pitchers and the DL," *fangraphs.com/fantasy/curve-ball-and-slider-pitchers-and-the-dl*
- Eno Sarris, RotoGraphs, "Do Cutters Kill Fastball Velocity?," *fangraphs.com/blogs/do-cutters-kill-fastball-velocity*

- Jon Roegele, "Tommy John Surgery and Pitch Frequency, Part II," *beyondtheboxscore. com/2012/11/14/3640648/pre-tommy-john-surgery-pitch-type-frequency-scientific-support*
- Eno Sarris, FanGraphs, "Maybe We Should all Learn the Split-Finger," *fangraphs. com/blogs/maybe-we-should-all-learn-the-split-finger*
- Bob Klapisch, "Surgery could hinder Masahiro Tanaka's lethal splitter," *northjersey.com/sports/klapisch-surgery-could-hinder-masahiro-tanaka-s-lethal-splitter-1.1050290*
- Associated Press, "Split-Finger Fastball, Once Popular, Is Falling Away," *nytimes. com/2011/10/02/sports/baseball/split-finger-fastball-use-of-a-popular-pitch-falls-off-the-table. html?*
- Murray Chass, "Baseball Notebook; Giants' Craig Balks at Criticism of the Split-Fingered Fastball," *nytimes.com/1989/03/12/sports/baseball-notebook-giants-craig-balks-at-criticism-of-the-split-fingered-fastball.html*
- Eno Sarris, Sports on Earth, "The Joy of the Six-Man Rotation," *sportsonearth.com/ article/76156074/major-league-baseball-six-man-starting-pitcher-rotations-tommy-john-elbow-injuries*
- Eno Sarris, FanGraphs, "Jake Odorizzi and Alex Cobb: Two Pitches, One Grip," *fangraphs.com/blogs/jake-odorizzi-and-alex-cobb-two-pitches-one-grip*
- Rob Neyer and Bill James, *The Neyer/James Guide to Pitchers: An Historical Compendium of Pitching, Pitchers, and Pitches*

All pictures by Eno Sarris

GM In A Box: Ned Colletti

by Mike Petriello

On Oct. 14, 2014, a week after the Los Angeles Dodgers bowed out in the National League Division Series, the Dodgers announced that Colletti had been reassigned from general manager to "senior advisor" to CEO Stan Kasten. Though he reportedly received a new contract as part of the switch, and the move was publicly positioned both as a promotion and a decision that Colletti fully agreed with, most viewed it as a way to make room for incoming president of baseball operations Andrew Friedman, formerly of the Tampa Bay Rays. While the specifics of Colletti's new role are unknown, it would seem that his role in baseball operations decisions will be diminshed.

Record and Background

Age: 60

Previous organizations

As an out-of-work hockey writer, Colletti entered baseball on Jan. 3, 1982, in the media relations department of his hometown Chicago Cubs, eventually moving into baseball operations to assist with salary arbitration and player negotiation tasks. The Cubs let him go on Dec. 28, 1993, in the midst of a front office overhaul.

He was out of baseball in 1994, and briefly worked in public relations, then joined the Giants as director of baseball operations following the season. When Giants GM Bob Quinn retired after the 1996 season, Brian Sabean took the top job, and Colletti moved up as his assistant, a position he held until leaving for the Dodgers in the fall of 2005.

Years of service with the Dodgers

Nine. After the Dodgers went 71-91 in Paul DePodesta's second and final season as GM in 2005, owner Frank McCourt hired Colletti on Nov. 16, 2005. Including interim GMs Tommy Lasorda and Dave Wallace, Colletti was the sixth Dodgers GM since longtime company man Fred Claire was fired in the middle of the 1998 season.

At the conclusion of the 2014 season, Colletti's tenure was the ninth-longest in baseball, and the fourth-longest in Dodgers history, behind Buzzie Bavasi, Al Campanis and Claire. (The Dodgers did not officially have a GM before 1950.)

Cumulative record

783-674, including four NL West division titles (2008, 2009, 2013, 2014), one Wild Card appearance (2006), and three trips to the NLCS (2008, 2009, 2013).

Playing career

None, though he played in amateur hockey leagues into his early 40s.

Personnel and Philosophy

Notable changes from the previous regime?

DePodesta was an Ivy League-educated stats aficionado who apprenticed under Billy Beane in Oakland and was among the first of the sabermetrically-inclined GMs. Colletti's blue-collar upbringing included being the son of a Chicago handyman who often struggled to make ends meet for his family. Clearly, the two most recent Dodgers GMs could not be more different, both in personality and approach, although Colletti expanded the team's previous one-person analytics group over the years.

Organizationally, however, Colletti did not make sweeping changes to the front office. He retained assistants Logan White and Kim Ng, each of whom had interviewed for his job, and convinced Terry Collins—who had been viewed as DePodesta's likely choice to replace Jim Tracy as manager—to remain with the organization as director of player development.

Otherwise, changes from the previous regime have been out of necessity as circumstances changed around him. While DePodesta had only one offseason to mold the team (he was hired on Feb. 16, 2004, far too late to have any impact that winter), Colletti survived through three distinct working environments: the end of the McCourt honeymoon (2005-2008), the disastrous financial downfall (2009-11), and the financial excesses of the Guggenheim group (2012-present).

What characterizes his relationship with ownership?

That he managed to keep his job after McCourt was forced to sell the team, when the overwhelming expectation was the Guggenheim group would bring in its own people, says a lot about how he's viewed by ownership. Though it's often seemed as though the team has succeeded in spite of him, rather than because of him, five play-off trips in nine years despite one of the ugliest ownership messes in baseball history are a good track record to fall back upon.

There were more than a few rumors that team President/CEO Stan Kasten is the one really pulling the strings, especially when baseball front office heavyweights Gerry Hunsicker, Pat Corrales and Bob Engle joined the team shortly after it was sold. There's likely some amount of truth to that, but Colletti managed to retain his position through the 2014 season, earning an extension near the end of 2012.

What type of people does he hire?

Several recent hires clearly have come through recent ties with Kasten, like Corrales and national cross checker Roy Clark, who both had been with the Braves and Nationals when Kasten was there. (Clark eventually returned to Atlanta following the departure of GM Frank Wren.)

Colletti clearly prefers former players. Ex-Dodgers Aaron Sele, Josh Bard, Juan Castro and Jose Vizcaino are all currently "special assistants," and Bill Mueller, one of Colletti's first free agent imports, served in that role for approximately six years before becoming a Dodgers scout in 2013 and Cubs hitting coach in 2014. Colletti also values loyalty, as White, VP of player development De Jon Watson, VP of professional scouting Rick Randazzo, and VP of player personnel Vance Lovelace all had served with him at least six years or more. (At the end of the season, Watson left for Arizona and White left for San Diego. Both were promoted.)

Has he ever been outspoken in the media?

Rarely. Aside from an unexpected 2010 radio interview in which he called out Matt Kemp for a slow start, Colletti has learned from his days in public relations, offering the media little.

Even in the face of one of the more uncomfortable press conferences in recent years—following the 2013 NLCS loss, Don Mattingly, clearly unhappy that he had not yet received an extension, visibly chafed while sitting next to Colletti—the GM kept his poker face up. (Mattingly eventually got his contract.) Colletti is seen as very loyal to those he works with, and his emotions rarely come out to the media.

Is he more collaborative or authoritative?

Collaborative. Colletti largely ceded the draft to Logan White, his vice president of amateur scouting/assistant GM, who had been with the team longer than Colletti has and is regularly interviewed for GM openings with other teams. As GM, Colletti has the final word—though with Kasten around, it's an open question as how to how real that is—but he allows the members of his team to operate without a heavy hand, respecting the loyalty that has kept them around for so long.

What kinds of managers does he hire?

Colletti has hired three managers, Grady Little (2006-07), Joe Torre (2008-10) and Don Mattingly (2011-present), all baseball lifers.

Little, best known for managing the 2003 Red Sox to their ALCS collapse against the Yankees, led the Dodgers to a Wild Card appearance in his first year on the job, but the team took a step back in 2007. That year, the Dodgers were wrecked by injuries and reports of clubhouse turmoil as a generation of young stars arrived and butted heads with intransigent veterans like Jeff Kent. Though Little was expected back in 2008, he expressed doubts about returning and eventually was allowed to resign.

After a flirtation with Joe Girardi, Joe Torre was brought in for 2008, bringing in the appropriate managerial star power to a Hollywood team with championship ambitions. Torre led the team to two playoff appearances in three seasons while running into some of the same clubhouse issues Little had, then retired from on-field duty following the 2010 season.

Mattingly, who had followed Torre to Los Angeles after not being offered the Yankees managerial job when Torre left, ascended to the top spot. He had to deal with the worst of the McCourt divorce and bankruptcy mess, particularly during his first season, when legal updates were as interesting as game reports, but his skills at managing a clubhouse generally have outweighed questions about his in-game management.

All three managers follow essentially the same formula: None was particularly loved for his in-game strategy, but all were (or at least were expected to be) able to handle a big-league clubhouse well, an important requirement for a big-market team with big salaries and bigger egos.

How closely does he work with the manager?

Colletti has said on several occasions that he consults his managers on player moves, though how much of that is lip service is unknown. Publicly, Colletti rarely comments on in-game moves or lineup choices, preferring to allow his managers to run the team as they see fit.

Player Development

How does he approach the amateur draft?

By letting White handle it, mostly. Much of the on-field success the Dodgers had during Colletti's tenure came from the draft, including homegrown players like Clayton Kershaw, Matt Kemp, Russell Martin, Chad Billingsley, Jonathan Broxton and Dee Gordon, some of whom were drafted before Colletti arrived. In recent years, the well has dried up somewhat, but some of the blame there lands on McCourt, who destroyed the scouting department when his financial issues were at their worst.

White has interviewed for GM positions elsewhere and is highly regarded throughout the sport, making it a wise choice to leave this mostly to him and his staff. One way in which the Dodgers have flexed their financial muscle to add talent is to spend outside the draft, bringing in international free agents like Yasiel Puig, Hyun-jin Ryu, Alex Guerrero, Erisbel Arruebarrena and Julio Urias, often to great effect, following earlier positive experiences with Hiroki Kuroda and Takashi Saito.

Does he prefer major league-ready players or projects?

Generally, the philosophy has been to find as much talent as possible, whether it's close to the majors or far away. The recent ability to spend wildly on major league and international talent has allowed prospects to develop at their own speed.

Tools or performance?

Tools, because the Dodgers wouldn't have risked so much on a player like Puig, who had barely played in the year before he was signed, without being blown away by tools. That goes for the incredibly young Urias as well, and is probably how Gordon got to the big leagues so quickly. Of course, it's performance that has kept young Dodgers in the bigs, or not, because Kershaw, Kemp, Gordon and others have all made return trips to the minors after pushing to the majors.

High school or college?

High school, mostly, as high-upside picks (including Kemp, Kershaw, and prospects Corey Seager, Zach Lee and Grant Holmes) have been the norm. It's generally "best player available," however, and sometimes that means college players, like 2013 first-round pitcher Chris Anderson.

Pitchers or hitters?

Pitchers, usually. The Dodgers have made 13 first-round picks since Colletti arrived, and nine have been pitchers.

Does he rush players to the majors or is he patient?

Both, depending on the player and situation. Kershaw made his debut at 20 years old in 2008, barely more than two years after being drafted, and there's plenty of talk about how teen sensation Urias could see the big leagues before his 20th birthday. This has sometimes backfired, however, such as when Gordon was rushed to the big leagues in 2011 and struggled on both sides of the ball for a few seasons before putting it together (at a new position) in 2014.

However, Colletti did resist the temptation to promote Pacific Coast League MVP Joc Pederson in 2014 until rosters expanded in September, and Urias never made it above Single-A this year either. Several pitchers have made the jump from Double-A thanks to the high-altitude environments of the team's Triple-A homes in Las Vegas and Albuquerque (the affiliate moves to Oklahoma City in 2015), but for the most part, prospects have had to force their way to the big leagues.

Roster Construction

Is he especially fond of certain types of players?

Good clubhouse guys and former Giants—ideally someone who is both. Colletti is a huge fan of "winners" and "veteran grit," constantly importing players like Skip Schumaker, Nick Punto, Michael Young, Adam Kennedy, Aaron Miles, Mark Sweeney, Garret Anderson, Ryan Theriot and Chone Figgins, even when their on-field utility has clearly vanished.

Though the ex-Giant pipeline has slowed in recent years as Colletti moved further away from his San Francisco tenure, for years players with Giants ties would end up in Dodger blue, including Kent, Mueller, Sweeney, Kevin Correia, the first Roberto Hernandez, Kenny Lofton, Eugenio Velez, Russ Ortiz, Ramon Ortiz, Jason Schmidt, Jack Taschner, Brett Tomko, Brian Wilson and Juan Uribe. Colletti probably wasn't responsible for the two games in 1975 when Giants legend Juan Marichal finished his career with the Dodgers, but let's say that he was.

Does he like proven players or youngsters?

As the above section shows, he's often preferred veterans to young players, particularly in the bullpen. This was notably egregious early in his tenure when Kemp and Andre Ethier were relegated to a platoon or the bench so 39-year-old Luis Gonzalez could man left field. That said, despite his reputation, the team has consistently had young, homegrown players like Martin, James Loney, Kershaw and Kenley Jansen in important roles.

Offensive players or glove men?

Whatever works. Kemp was the regular center fielder for most of five seasons, mostly because of his bat. Hanley Ramirez has lasted longer at shortstop than he had any right to. Before that, Gordon got more than a few chances to prove he could play shortstop, when he never could. But this is a franchise that also has had Uribe and Loney, both excellent defenders at the infield corners, and generally keeps at least one no-offense/plus-defense infield backup—most recently, Miguel Rojas.

Power pitchers or finesse guys?

No preference. For example, at closer, Colletti has had flamethrowers Broxton and Jansen, but he's also had the ground-balling Brandon League and the veteran Saito, who was effective without overwhelming velocity.

Does he allocate resources primarily on impact players or role players?

Since the sale of the team, that's no longer a choice he's needed to make. Who else could lavish $20 million over two years (including a 2015 player option) on setup man Brian Wilson, who had missed most of the two previous seasons with an elbow injury? Or commit $28 million to Guerrero, who came with an impressive bat but little indication that he had a defensive position? Or $25 million to Arruebarrena, who may have the opposite problem? Or $42 million to Puig, who had been all but unknown to most of baseball? Or $22.5 million over three years to League, who long had been an inconsistent setup man before putting together a few great weeks as the Dodgers closer to finish out 2012?

The 2014 Dodgers had eight players making at least $15 million and four more above $10 million. The majority of the payroll goes to the stars, but that hasn't meant the fringes of the roster have had to come on the cheap.

How does he flesh out his bullpen and bench?

With as many veterans as possible. Colletti's Dodgers teams always have had at least one Schumaker or Punto, and while some of those guys have been decent players as well as clubhouse leaders, there's also been more than a few Chris Perez types, overrated or past-their-prime veterans taking up a spot while offering little on the field.

Does he often work the waiver wire, sign minor-league free agents, or make Rule 5 picks?

Rule 5 picks have been very rare, with only one, pitcher Carlos Monasterios in 2010, lasting even more than a few weeks. Like all GMs, Colletti will bring in a dozen or so non-roster types each year, and one or two usually make the team.

When will he release players?

Only when absolutely necessary. A long hallmark of the Colletti era has been the desire to keep as many players under team control as possible, often bouncing those with options back and forth between the majors and Triple-A to avoid needing to designate someone else for assignment. One exception to this was catcher Dioner Navarro, who was sent packing just days before the 2011 roster expansion, an apparent reaction not only to his poor play (.193/.276/.324), but also to reports of a poor work ethic.

On whom has he given up?

One notable departure was catcher Russell Martin, non-tendered following the 2010 season. Martin had been a homegrown star since his 2006 debut, but his fourth and fifth years hadn't held up to his outstanding first three, and a fractured hip that ended his 2010 season early added further uncertainty.

Understandably, the stingy McCourt-era Dodgers were wary of gambling on Martin's hip and let him go. Far less understandably, they instead turned to the inferior Rod Barajas, who gave them a mediocre 2011, while Martin has rebounded to put up several productive seasons for the Yankees and Pirates.

To whom has he given a shot?

Infielder Justin Turner, signed as a minor league free agent after being non-tendered by the Mets following the 2013 season, was outstanding in 2014. He had one of the best bench seasons in Dodgers history. Catcher A.J. Ellis has been in the organization longer than Colletti has, and after years of minor league service, was given a chance at the starting job at age 31 in 2012. He's held that position for three seasons, with varied results. To a lesser extent, he is forever giving chances to scrapheap pitching pickups, like Vicente Padilla, two different Ortizes (Russ and Ramon), David Wells, Tomko, Jamey Wright and Edinson Volquez.

Does he cut bait early or late?

Late, and sometimes not at all. One notable issue during Colletti's tenure is that while he has made several low-cost productive in-season trades—Barajas, League, Juan Rivera, Marlon Anderson and Ted Lilly, to name a few—that have helped the team with an immediate small-sample boost, he's then pressed his luck by paying to bring those players back the next season (or seasons). That has bitten the team several times, when appreciating the production received and moving on would have been the better course.

To his credit, he gave up on Milton Bradley at the right time, sending the talented-but-troubled outfielder to Oakland barely a month after taking over. Simply getting Bradley out of town would have been a win, but Colletti managed to get Andre Ethier in return, a feather in his cap he's lived on for years.

Is he passive or active?

Active. There's always some kind of tinkering around the edges of the roster, and there's been no shortage of high-profile moves over the years.

An optimist or a problem solver?

Problem solver, mostly. I know! I would have thought optimist too, because there' have definitely been times where Colletti has left past-their-prime veterans on the active roster for far too long. That said, he's moved quickly to deal with some of his more high-profile mistakes, replacing Juan Pierre in center with Andruw Jones after just one year, then working out a way to dump Jones immediately after his first year.

Does he want to win now or wait out the success cycle?

There's no question the Guggenheim mandate is to win now, at all costs, and so most of the big-money moves over the last few years have been with that in mind. That said, Kasten and Colletti have been clear that the big initial splash was to fix the McCourt-era lows as quickly as possible, with the long-term plan being to supplement a sizable big league payroll with a stronger farm system.

Trades and Free Agents

Does he favor players acquired via trade, development, or free agency?

No preference. For example, the core of the 2014 team featured drafted players (Kershaw, Kemp, Gordon, Ellis, Jansen, etc.), trade acquisitions (Gonzalez, Crawford, Ramirez, Beckett), international free agents (Puig, Ryu), and domestic free agents (Greinke, Uribe, Wilson, Perez, Howell, Haren, etc.) Talent is talent, no matter where it comes from.

Is he an active trader?

Yes. Colletti has been part of some of the biggest trades of the last several years, from the surprising 2008 deal that brought Manny Ramirez to town to the shocking 2012 Boston trade. As the budget has expanded, trades have been seen as a sibling to free agency, allowing Colletti to bring in players at a lesser prospect cost by agreeing to eat all of the remaining money, a tactic he used twice in dealing with the Marlins to get Hanley Ramirez (in 2012) and Ricky Nolasco (in 2013).

Does he tend to move talent or hoard it?

Though there have been many deserved knocks on Colletti's decisions in his tenure with the Dodgers, the one point that's definitely in his favor is that when he's traded away young talent, it's almost always been the right young talent. That is, very few prospects Colletti has traded away have amounted to anything.

The outlier is Carlos Santana, who has turned into one of the American League's most dangerous hitters, and that deal (which netted the Dodgers Casey Blake) was seen as a mistake by most observers the day it was made in 2008. Otherwise, there aren't many Dodgers fans missing Joel Guzman, or Andy LaRoche, or Ivan De Jesus Jr., or Andrew Lambo, or Jerry Sands, or Allen Webster, or Josh Wall, or Leon Landry, or Lucas May, or Josh Lindblom, or Bryan Morris, or Angel Sanchez, or Logan Bawcom, or Trayvon Robinson, or Blake DeWitt, or Josh Bell or Scott McGough. All are among the prospects the team has traded away.

Other than Santana, the best Dodgers prospect Colletti has traded is probably Nate Eovaldi, who has shown flashes of talent wrapped around a ton of inconsistency in Miami. Even then, he was moved in a deal for Ramirez, who has provided more value than Eovaldi ever would have. Meanwhile, Colletti has resisted the urge to move Seager, Urias and Pederson in recent years, or Kemp, Kershaw and others before that.

With whom does he trade and when?

Anyone, at any time. With the exception of the Detroit Tigers, Colletti has made at least one trade with every team in baseball since he took over. Within the division, the deals tend to be minor and rare—the 2007 trade that brought Sweeney to

Los Angeles is not only the lone time Colletti has matched up with Sabean and the Giants, but is the only trade between the rivals since 1985. Otherwise, he'll deal with everybody.

Will he make deals with other teams during the season?

Absolutely, and the non-waiver trade deadline has not proven to be an impediment, as Colletti has often made August waiver-wire deals to improve his team. Many of the biggest Dodgers trades have come in-season, including the Manny Ramirez deal in 2008 and the massive 2012 Red Sox deal a few weeks after getting Hanley Ramirez from the Marlins, the same team that also sent Nolasco along in July of 2013.

How does he approach the trade deadline?

Usually in a way that terrifies Dodgers fans, though it's been much quieter lately. The 2013 deadline brough only backup catcher Drew Butera, and 2014 saw no movement at all. Prior to that, Colletti was known for making deadline moves, bringing in League, Shane Victorino, Ramirez and Randy Choate in the days leading up to the 2012 deadline, and trading away highly regarded outfield prospect Robinson for what seemed like a collection of spare parts in 2011. (That deal ended up looking far better in retrospect, as Robinson flamed out in Seattle and Baltimore, while Stephen Fife and Tim Federowicz have played small parts for the Dodgers since.)

In 2010, Colletti made three poorly received deals, trading seven prospects for Lilly, Octavio Dotel, Theriot and Scott Podsednik, didn't make a move in 2009, and made a huge splash with Ramirez in 2008.

Are there teams or general managers with whom he trades frequently?

Colletti has particularly worked well with the Cubs (six deals across two regimes) and the Phillies (four).

Has he ever gone to any extremes with his free-agent signings?

How long do you have?

Colletti's early years were defined by several huge free agent disasters. Pierre, a speedy outfielder with a weak arm who didn't get on base enough, received five years and $44 million prior to 2007. He was a starter for one year, then was a reserve for the next two before being dumped on the White Sox with two years left on his deal. Pierre's failure was one reason Colletti gave two years and $36 million to Jones headed into 2008. Jones, who once looked like he would be on a Hall of Fame trajectory with Atlanta, looked uninterested and out of shape in his one year with the Dodgers; he hit a mere .158/.256/.249 in his lone year in Los Angeles. Desperate to unload him, the team agreed to deferred payments that were still going in 2014.

Perhaps most disappointing was the arrival of Jason Schmidt, a former Giants ace Colletti knew well from his days in San Francisco. Despite reports that the medicals on Schmidt's shoulder were troubling, Colletti gave him three years and $47 million heading into 2007. Never healthy, Schmidt made only 10 starts for the Dodgers. League, given a three-year, $22.5 million contract after a few good weeks in 2012, also has proven to have been a mistake, as was reliever Matt Guerrier's three-year deal. Wilson's contract isn't looking so great, either.

Generally, however, Colletti hasn't whiffed on the free agent market nearly as badly in recent years, though it's up for discussion about whether that's because he's learned from his mistakes; because the implosion of the McCourt ownership left him without the money to compete for several years; or because the massive financial resources of the Guggenheim group make it hard for any one contract to stand out. In recent years, most of the big-money Dodgers acquisitions have come via trade or extensions for current players, with one exception being the so far well-received six-year, $147 million contract agreement with Zack Greinke prior to 2013.

Under what circumstances will he sign free agents?

When there are living, breathing baseball players who enjoy copious amounts of money available. Again, Colletti's proclivities have been colored by the fact that he's essentially worked for three different Dodgers organizations. After his initial missteps with Pierre, Jones and Schmidt, he stuck to smaller contracts as the budget shrank, then emerged to sign Greinke after the 2012 season.

Contracts

Does he prefer long-term deals or short?

Since the ownership transition, the Dodgers have had a policy of not signing players past their age-36 season, which necessarily limits some deals. He's signed several long-term deals (Kemp got eight, Kershaw seven, Greinke and Ryu six) and inherited others (Gonzalez had six full years left at the time of the trade, Crawford five).

Does he often backload his contracts?

Less so now that money is no longer a concern, but backloading was the norm during the McCourt debacle when the team had trouble meeting the bi-weekly payroll. (Seriously.) In the winter of 2011-12, Colletti handed out two-year deals to veterans Chris Capuano, Aaron Harang, Mark Ellis, Tony Gwynn Jr., and Jerry Hairston, backloading them all to try to push off financial responsibilities as long as possible since the team's situation was so uncertain. More recent contracts—Kemp, Kershaw, Greinke, etc.—usually have had the first year at the lowest price and then the remaining years spread out relatively evenly.

Does he lock up his players early in their careers or is he more likely to practice brinksmanship?

Colletti's Dodgers rarely have locked up young players to long-term contracts before they absolutely need to, with Kemp, Ethier and Kershaw all coming within a year of free agency before signing. Most pre-free agency deals have been short ones intended to buy out a year or two of arbitration. One exception was Chad Billingsley, who signed a three-year extension covering 2012-14 in the spring of 2011, despite being two full seasons from free agency.

Does he like to avoid arbitration?

Absolutely, Colletti has consistently ensured agreements are reached before the arbitration process is necessary. The Dodgers haven't had a case go to arbitration since relief pitcher Joe Beimel back in 2007.

Anything unique about his negotiating tactics?

Several of his recent deals have included opt-out clauses. Kershaw can opt out of the final two seasons of his deal; Greinke has the ability to opt out of the final three. Puig can't opt out to free agency, but he does have the choice to opt in to the arbitration process once he gets to three years of service time, forgoing the remaining agreed-upon salaries. Ryu also can opt out of the final year of his deal if certain playing time incentives are hit. Reportedly, Guerrero is also able to opt out of his contract at the end of any year in which he's traded.

Is he vocal? Does he prefer to work behind the scenes or through the media?

Behind the scenes. Colletti prefers to keep his negotiations as quiet as possible.

Bonus

What is his strongest point as GM?

After three decades in the game, Colletti seemingly knows everyone.

What would he be doing if he weren't in baseball?

Working in hockey, either for a team or a media outlet.

Short-Term Gains, Long-Term Pains: Recruiting in the Dominican

by Miles Wray

Basketball does not have quite so many problems as baseball when young, international prospects are recruited to the pros.

When a basketball prospect is recruited from outside the United States, his story is unlikely to involve any Sherlock Holmes-ing around for birth certificates, and it is not the norm that extra percentage points will be shaved off his signing bonus from underneath the table. The grind can make for a demanding and lonely life for the basketball prospect, sure—but no more so than the life lived by any sports journeyman.

One revealing sign of the (relative) purity of basketball's international recruiting system is that members of the NBA are gladly willing to be publicly associated with the process.

Take the stirring 2012 documentary *Elevate*, which follows four promising teenage players from the SEED Project (which stands for Sports for Education and Economic Development in Senegal, though sometimes the last 'S' is left out of the acronym) basketball academy in Dakar, Senegal, to private high schools scattered across America, with the players continuing on to play college basketball on scholarship after production on the documentary ceased. Senegal is far from a basketball hotbed, producing nine total NBA players in its history (and only two players who weren't career benchwarmers), and still we see the influence of major NBA figures on the periphery of *Elevate*. On the SEED Project's Board of Advisors we have French-American Joakim Noah, All-Star center for the Chicago Bulls. The director of *Elevate* is Anne Buford, sister of R.C. Buford, who has won five NBA championship rings as general manager of the San Antonio Spurs. The siblings have appeared at screenings together to promote the film.

Compare this to *Pelotero*, the 2012 documentary that chronicles the signings of top Minnesota Twins prospect Miguel Sano and current indie-leaguer Jean Carlos Batista in their home country, the Dominican Republic. In *Pelotero*, a major league scout is taped by Sano's family from a clandestine hole in the wall so that the scout's dishonesty may finally be proved. Before the end credits roll, the chyron announces that MLB "declined our requests to be interviewed for this film." Now, perhaps there is an argument to be made that the SEED documentary garnered more support because it was championed by someone with ownership ties, but there is a stark contrast in transparency between that and a refusal to even be interviewed.

I'm sure that in the extensive annals of international basketball, many a shady deal has been carried out by many a shady character. The point, though, is that there does exist an ethically sound mechanism in basketball where a promising player from Senegal—a country with a basically non-existent basketball history—is the recipient of a college education, earned via his basketball skills.

Given the NCAA's rather thorny stubbornness re: amateurism, this actually may be the more difficult way to go about it. Players from countries as distant and tiny as French Guiana, Cape Verde, and Congo have all, in recent years, joined established, professional European clubs as teenagers. As they worked their way from the club's junior team to senior team, they were appropriately compensated while developing their skills, eventually performing so well that they were drafted by the NBA. This is the case with a player from Cape Verde—an island country of about half a million people off the Western coast of Africa. The system is all the more polished in established basketball superpowers like Spain, France and Lithuania, where professional clubs constantly develop their own youths.

This is a dramatic counterpoint to scouting in the Dominican Republic, which is as close a neighbor to Major League Baseball—not just geographically—as could possibly be. As reported on Opening Day of the 2014 season in an MLB.com press release, 83 of the 853 major league players on major league rosters or disabled lists were from the Dominican, or about one in every 10. The path that must be traveled when bringing a player from French Guiana to the NBA is, for the most part, yet uncharted. The path from the D.R. to majors might as well be a paved sidewalk.

And still that path is laced with scandal and tinged with an unpleasant, lurking sense of feudalism.

Why?

———————————

In the late '80s, sociologist Alan M. Klein spent a significant amount of time immersed in Dominican baseball culture, from teaching English classes for prospects at major league team academies to watching dozens of Dominican League games at revered Estadio Quisqueya. The result is *Sugarball*, a thin, academic book published by Yale University Press.

Although just about everything else about baseball has changed since *Sugarball's* publication in 1991 (even Jamie Moyer has retired), there are depressing similarities between what Klein observed with his eyes and what the creators of *Pelotero* observed with their lens some two decades later. Klein writes that a draft of international players could be around the corner, and with it the hope of increased regulation and oversight. These things are still, as they were, on the horizon. In *Sugarball*, an affiliated scout just might be the biggest antagonist the player and their family will ever meet. Where *Pelotero* observes the scouts, observes the Sano family, and allows the viewers to make up their own mind, Klein pulls no punches in assessing scouts of the '80s: "Their techniques were so reminiscent of those of the West African slave traders of three centuries earlier that I facetiously refer to these unscrupulous scouts as 'blackcatchers.'"

For Klein, the relationship between America and the Dominican Republic over baseball is a contemporary extension of the colonizer-colonized relationship that has dictated so much of the Dominican's history. Klein writes, in a passage that feels like mourning: "How a land so rich in resources and people, so endowed at the outset, could have failed to live up to its potential is the story not only of the Dominican Republic but of the colonial world as a whole." Klein draws a direct line between events like the continuous United States Marines occupation in the Dominican from 1916-24 to the contemporary baseball scene.

One of the more corrosive symptoms that Klein identifies may appear banal, but is only so on the surface: scheduling. Klein writes: "Throughout most of the history of Dominican baseball, organization has been sorely lacking. There was no consistent schedule, teams came and went, and there was little formal structure or governance of play." And it is bizarre that such a baseball-mad country has had so few baseball games actually played within its borders.

Klein assigns credit/blame for the Dominican's lack of domestic games on the sense of ownership that America has historically flexed in acquiring Dominican exports, whether sugarcane or ballplayers. For instance, at the time of Klein's writing, American players who played in the Dominican Winter League were allowed to switch teams within the league, while Dominican players—whether they were in the majors or not—were not allowed free agency within their home country's league. American players also received higher salaries in the Dominican than their Dominican teammates. Klein writes: "For the Dominicans, to be perceived as unworthy of equal wages at home when they have already achieved them in the United States is the final insult."

To imagine the inverse of this being the status quo—if major league players from other countries were granted greater agency and higher salaries than Americans—is ludicrous. And not just because it would be an affront to American machismo: the de jure inequality would be blatantly and obviously backwards to anybody in American society.

Yet inequality has been the state of affairs for so long between baseball in the Dominican Republic and America.

Why, for instance, are American 17-year-olds still allowed time for incubation at the high school level, while a 17-year-old from the Dominican is already too old to sign?

Further complicating the situation is that Dominican ballplayers, as individuals, are compensated adequately for their world-class skills. Baseball provides enough money for academy-level players that they may become the princes of their society. Dominicans who make it to the majors are compensated just as major league players from every nation are, with enough money earned to become a king. Major League Baseball pays its players lucratively, and in a system as close to a pure meritocracy yet devised.

For all his acidity about elements of the Dominican baseball process, Klein does acknowledge that the rules are designed (if not always executed) to treat the individual Dominican player fairly. He writes:

> *It has often been said that the academies exploit their young charges, but this is an ethnocentric argument that is only occasionally true and that overlooks a fundamental reality of Dominican life: the young man who signs with an academy will receive a bonus and a first-year salary that together are roughly seven times his father's annual income (assuming the father is not one of the 30 percent of Dominicans who are unemployed). If the boy plays for only four seasons (two years) he will outdistance all his friends at home. For a time he will eat well, receive medical attention, and perhaps be a hero and a hope to all his less fortunate peers in sandlots and ballfields throughout the Dominican Republic. Disappointing and frustrating his experience may be, but one cannot say that he will be exploited—not if one takes into account the current state of the Dominican Republic. He will have had a reprieve from the streets and from unrewarding labor.*

Even at the darkest moment of Sano's story in *Pelotero*, the greatest danger is that Sano will be paid somewhere below his market value as he enters a major league system—a sum that is still multiple millions of dollars.

So, then, what is the big deal? Why aren't the harrowing chapters of baseball in the Dominican simply examples of crooked, rogue individuals operating away from the revealing light of regulations?

Major League Baseball is a business, and it pays its employees. Must it also be responsible for salvaging large parts of the country's depressed economy? That seems like an awfully unrealistic expectation for a schoolyard game to provide to a nation.

I am reminded of a chapter by Dave Cameron in last year's edition of *The Hardball Times Annual*. In it, Cameron argues that the system used by the 30 major league teams to acquire interns—particularly baseball operations interns—is broken, or at least doomed to break.

Cameron argues that it is broken even though interns voluntarily apply for the positions (with so many more turned away at the door), and he argues that it is broken even though the interns are paid on time.

The interns are, however, not paid very much. They are paid below the poverty line in metropolitan areas where the cost of living is especially burdensome.

The crux of Cameron's argument, with which I fully agree:

Because of the selection process and the requirements that allow an individual to be able to pursue and thrive in these conditions, the primary variable in getting your foot into the baseball operations door may be your family's net worth. As a result, baseball front offices are starting to not only look very similar—they have always been very white and very male, so that isn't a new trend—but are being repopulated with people who often have similar backgrounds and life experiences. And those life experiences often include access to significant amounts of money.

So there isn't really anything morally wrong about the approach that major league teams take in hiring interns. They have more applications from skilled workers than they know what to do with, right?

While this approach may not be wrong, I agree with Cameron in that it also seems like something very far from the best approach. By allowing themselves a quick shortcut in the present tense—paying interns not a cent more than they have to—baseball teams have wounded their future selves with a brutal opportunity cost: they are selecting their most crucial decision-makers from only the smallest sliver of the overall population.

This opportunity cost is not just a moral one—although it may also be that—but it is a competitive cost as well. Out of all the best possible general manager candidates in the world, are more than 90 percent of them white males? Probably not. Here is a market inefficiency that teams have prevented themselves from being able to grab. The short-term shortcut of paying interns next to nil carries a hefty long-term opportunity cost when so many bright candidates can't logistically submit an application, with no familial bankroll to get them through the internship.

If major league teams have been taking shortcuts recently as they construct their analytics departments, recruiting in the Dominican Republic has been a lengthy history of shortcuts. These shortcuts aren't necessarily unscrupulous. But each instance in which MLB has treated Dominican prospects with a different set of standards is a payment that comes due. Not that you can always see it coming.

Here's an example of a shortcut established from the dawn of team academies that is only slowly being rectified in a gradual, decades-long process: games for Dominican prospects to play in.

Perhaps the most bizarre part of *Pelotero*, for me, was watching a full-length baseball documentary that featured no real baseball games. For prospects Sano and Batista, playing baseball is to participate in many tutorials with their trainer—afternoons entirely of double-play pivots, perhaps a stakes-free scrimmage during an official workout—but no games. There are no times when the scoreboard is set at zero and one uniformed team plays against another a full nine innings, with real umpires and real substitution rules, in front of a paying crowd, with the winner advancing one further step in the standings. When they sign their contracts, one could hardly expect Sano and Batista to know how to treat baseball as a team competition: they have been taught only that baseball is a series of endlessly refined individual skills.

Writing in the *2008 Hardball Times Annual,* Jonathan Helfgott quoted the Milwaukee Brewers' Latin American coordinator, Fernando Arango, voicing this as a complaint: "The problem with these kids is that they never play baseball. They only practice." *Baseball America* prospects writer Ben Badler reported the same concerns to me from his observations on assignment in the Dominican: "I remember back in 2008, 2009, one of the most frequent things I heard from teams was, 'We don't get to see these guys in games enough, and by the time we get them and we sign them, these guys are still really raw. We have to teach them a lot of the basic fundamentals of the game sometimes.' They might have tools. They might be a plus-runner and have a plus-arm and a quick bat, or show raw power in batting practice. But, when the game turns on, they were like completely different players because they don't have that game experience, especially in the Dominican Republic."

Badler also describes the quantity and quality of real games for Dominican prospects as improving rapidly and recently: "Over the last several years, you have the introduction of leagues like the Dominican Prospect League and the International Prospect League. There's been a lot more organization of games for these players. If they play consistently they can have the same game experience as a high school baseball season before these guys even sign."

While this bodes well for the future of Dominican prospects gaining early-career game experience, the long past of Dominican prospects not playing in games is unchangeable. Major league teams took the shortcut of not having organized games for their prospects to play in, and it's not hard to imagine the opportunity cost that they have suffered. Certainly there would have been players, their careers dead-ended in the minors, who could have ascended to the big leagues had their careers started with this additional momentum of appearing in games.

This is a small shortcut, and a small opportunity cost. But games are won and lost thanks to those ever-valuable extra percentiles, and it is but one example.

It will be impossible to quantify the opportunity costs that baseball has brought upon itself with its collective shortcuts and ethical failings as it has recruited prospects in the Dominican Republic. But those costs do exist.

What about: How has the overall cheapness of major league teams in the Dominican affected the global popularity of the sport?

In the '70s and '80s, the early days of widespread Dominican recruiting, baseball teams were so interested in this country not just because there were talented players but because there were talented players available to sign for cheap. Klein describes this as an effective ransacking that left domestic Dominican baseball a bare, empty cupboard:

> "In the long run, to mine the baseball riches of the Dominican Republic will impoverish the Dominican game, for the country's supply of baseball talent is not inexhaustible. Not only is amateur baseball being eviscerated by the academies, but the professional winter league teams are increasingly dependent on American major league teams. At the same time successful players returning from play in the United States are increasingly reluctant to play in the winter league—this strikes a devastating blow to the integrity and health of Dominican baseball. The effects of these trends are already being felt, as attendance is falling off at parks around the country."

Since the Dominican Baseball League plays only a truncated winter season thanks to these factors, MLB has removed an important counterpoint from their international environment. The NBA, by contrast, annually schedules preseason games against teams from international leagues, sometimes hosted in America and sometimes abroad. In the October 2013 preseason, for instance, NBA teams traveled to Turkey, Spain, England, the Philippines, Brazil, Taiwan and China for exhibitions.

Sometimes these are exhibitions between two NBA teams, and there are plenty of exhibitions between an NBA team and a professional team from abroad, all squads tuning up for their own country's upcoming regular season. Even America's Major League Soccer, far from a cultural force, hosts Champions League staples like Real Madrid, Manchester United, AS Roma for exhibitions against American teams (or against each other, in front of American audiences).

With both the NBA and the MLS, these are relationships of mutual respect with their global partners: Both leagues acquire international players with the same mechanisms used to acquire American players. Both leagues also see significant amounts of American players take their trade overseas (sometimes to return as members of these exhibition tours).

What a dramatically different scene this is from MLB. Yes, some of that symbiotic relationship exists with Japanese baseball, and also, just starting recently, with Korean and Australian baseball. But these are much smaller inroads than the multidirectional expansion of the NBA and MLS. And, more relevant, neither the NBA nor the MLS have a neighbor whom they are too embarrassed to visit.

What isn't a shortcut is Senegal's SEED Project, which enables prospects to achieve a secondary education, and to do so away from the madly ticking clock of a professional team and its competitive needs. Baseball took shortcuts by plopping down gated academies and grabbing up as many players as possible, uninhibited by the rationing of a draft.

What isn't a shortcut is ensuring that teams sign an international player only through the draft (or after they have been draft-eligible), regardless of who saw them first in their barely pubescent years. It was a shortcut to create an international signing system that, as Badler describes, is so easily and repeatedly circumvented:

> *"Certainly having greater oversight would be the key to having any good system, whether it's a draft or whether it's international free agency with bonus pools or without bonus pools. Whether the signing age is 16 or 17 or 18. I think the key is that, whether it's Major League Baseball or an independent entity, whomever it is needs to have pretty strict oversight over what goes on with players at team academies, with team officials, with MLB officials, and with MLB investigators. Whatever the system is that's in place, I think the most important thing is that the rules are being followed and that the rules are being enforced—especially when it comes to the sort of under-the-table type activity that goes on and is fairly prevalent in Latin American scouting."*

As major league teams and the Commissioner's Office continue to refine operations in the Dominican Republic, and continue to broaden the scope of baseball around the world, I hope that shortcuts are no longer taken, not just for moral reasons but also for the overall health of the game. After all, what kind of world do we want the baseball world to be?

References & Resources

- Special thanks to Ben Badler for his time.
- Alan M. Klein, *Sugarball: The American Game, the Dominican Dream*, 1991, Yale University Press, 179 pages
- *Pelotero*, directed by Ross Finkel, Trevor Martin, and Jonathan Paley, 2012, 77 minutes
- MLB.com, "2014 Opening Day Rosters Feature 224 Players Born Outside the U.S.," *http://m.mlb.com/news/article/70623418/2014-opening-day-rosters-feature-224-players-born-outside-the-us*

The Transition from Czar to CEO

by Jack Moore

The mythology of professional baseball is in many ways more important than its documented history. This mythology comes from the stories we tell to explain how baseball grew from a seed in Abner Doubleday's patriotic mind into the multibillion dollar summerlong pageant it is today. We tell the stories of John McGraw and Christy Mathewson; Babe Ruth and Lou Gehrig; Willie Mays and Mickey Mantle; Satchel Paige and Josh Gibson; Mike Schmidt and Steve Garvey; Mark McGwire and Sammy Sosa. These stories form the backdrop for each new season and give context to new stories crafted from games to come.

The commissioner has his own story, too. It can be found in the history section of Major League Baseball's website, on a page titled "The Commissionership: A Historical Perspective." The page is replete with the standard historical trivia facts, but more critically, the page serves to establish the mythology of the commissioner as the game's moral paragon, the patriarch of baseball. It opens:

> *"Since baseball's beginnings in the mid-19th century, the governance of the game has evolved from an ineffective alliance of players known as the National Association to a central figure with considerable powers called the Commissioner."*

Landis: The Making of a Myth

For 43 years after the National League formed in 1876, the major leagues had no single authority but rather a board of directors composed of team owners and league executives that eventually became the three-man National Commission. Things hardly ran smoothly. Players challenged contractual language such as the reserve clause regularly in the court system from the 1890s through the early 1920s. Other leagues such as the Federal League and Players League popped up to challenge the National Agreement, the laws that ruled the major leagues.

Despite these occasional challenges, this authority lasted until the Black Sox scandal of 1919 threatened disaster. Again, from MLB.com:

> *"The National League proposed to eliminate the National Commission and replace it with one leader, a man 'of unquestionable reputation and standing in fields other than baseball' whose "mere presence would assure that public interests would first be served, and that therefore, as a natural sequence, all exisiting (sic) evils would disappear."*

The names considered are the kinds you'd expect to use in the business of myth-making. They included army generals, Woodrow Wilson's Secretary of the Treasury William Gibbs McAdoo, and even former President William Howard Taft. Baseball's owners were shooting for the moon, but they had good reason to believe men of such import would be interested in such a position. Professional baseball had already pulled in numerous fans in law and political circles, especially around Washington, D.C. A law student at Columbia wrote in 1885, "We have no established church, but base ball is an institution whose welfare our courts will jealously guard." And Taft himself began the tradition of the Opening Day presidential first pitch in 1910.

The man eventually chosen was Judge Kenesaw Mountain Landis, who while not quite at the level of a president or a cabinet member, had made a large name for himself as a trustbusting federal judge in Chicago. In 1907, Landis fined Standard Oil Co. $29,420,000—1,462 separate fines of $20,000 each for accepting a rebate from the Chicago and Alton Railroad for shipping oil on its rails—the largest such fine issued to a corporation in American history at the time. Although the fine was eventually overturned on appeal, it was a symbolic moment for Landis as a man willing to fight against big business.

More important than his status, however, was the fact that baseball's owners already had reason to believe Landis could be the man "of unquestionable reputation" the Lasker plan, named for its originator and Chicago Cubs owner Albert Lasker, called for. In 1915, knowing of Landis's legendary trustbusting, the Federal League sued the National League and American League owners and the three members of the National Commission in Landis' Chicago court. It was the latest and greatest challenge to the reserve clause, the contractual language that allowed major league teams to renew a player's contract in perpetuity until the player was no longer worth the pay.

As recounted in J.G. Taylor Spink's *Judge Landis and Twenty-Five Years of Baseball*:

> The case began Jan. 20, 1915, and many were expecting a quick resolution from the no-nonsense Landis. The Sporting News concurred. "[T]he inference is that he expects to give an early decision in the case," read an article from the Jan. 21 edition. But the article warned, "There is a mass of evidence to be considered and a conclusion may not be reached by the jurist on it for a week or more."

Indeed, Landis would not render his decision that week, nor that month, nor by the time training camps began in the spring, what many assumed was the latest possible deadline for the decision. According to Spink, Landis had "expressed some concern during the trial" that failing to issue a ruling before the season started would leave baseball in a "chaotic mess."

But it should have been obvious to anybody in Landis' courtroom that the Federals never had a real chance. At one point, Landis, a Cubs season ticket holder, declared,

"Both sides must understand that any blows at the thing called baseball would be regarded by this court as a blow to a national institution."

By the 1916 season, the Federal League owners were running out of money and agreed to a rich settlement with the monolith of Organized Baseball. Federal League owners were either allowed to buy into either the National or American Leagues or compensated richly, to the tune of at least $60,000 (over $1.3 million in 2014 dollars, per the Bureau of Labor Statistics). With the Federal League disbanded, the antitrust case against Organized Baseball was dismissed by default. According to Spink, Landis "confided to intimates that he had put off rendering a decision, feeling that sooner or later the rival factions would come together."

That is, Landis knew the law was on the Federal League's side.

Once chosen, Landis was swift to exercise his power over the players, banning the infamous Black Sox for life, but as Irving Sanborn wrote for *Baseball Magazine* in 1927:

> "How much of the public's confidence in the integrity of professional baseball is based on the belief that the crook is certain to be detected and to the knowledge that, when detected, he can be banished from the game for life cannot be estimated. Undoubtedly it is a tremendous factor in protecting the sport from the suspicions of those who judge all others by their own evil standards, and from the poison gas attacks by its enemies in rival fields of commercial pastimeing. That is why the suggestion was made at the start of this freshet of words that some means ought to be found to give the High Commissioner the same czar-like authority over club owners that he has over the players in organized baseball. If that power over the players helps maintain the public's confidence in the game, the same power over the men from whom the players take their orders and salaries certainly would add to the public's confidence.
>
> "In fact it was a veteran member of the fan-public who first impressed on the contents of my skull (in a wholly friendly argument) that the High Commissioner did not have the actual power to rid the game of any club owner who might be found guilty of 'conduct detrimental to baseball,' although he has the power of a permanent expulsion in the case of a player adjudged guilty."

What Sanborn describes was the Landis-era version of the "best interests of the game" clause, the clause used to ban Pete Rose (and, for a time, Willie Mays and Mickey Mantle) for gambling. It was the clause Bowie Kuhn used to suspend players he thought were on drugs. And it was the clause many expected Bud Selig to invoke in the wake of the Biogenesis scandal to ban Alex Rodriguez for life. Such an invocation never came about, likely due to the overturn of a similar ban for Yankees pitcher Steve Howe in 1992 for a cocaine suspension after the Major League Baseball Players Association filed a grievance. It should be noted Landis had no players union or labor arbitration hearings to deal with throughout his tenure.

The clause has been used on owners as well. Former A's owner Charlie Finley was barred from selling his players in response to the dawn of free agency, and most notably, George Steinbrenner was briefly "banned for life" for spying on Dave Winfield. As the *New York Times* reported, however, Steinbrenner actually bargained his suspension "up" from two years to life in order to maintain his status with the United States Olympic Committee. That Steinbrenner was reinstated after two years despite the so-called lifetime ban is an excellent illustration of just how the "best interests" clause works on the owners.

Sanborn's challenge in the pages of *Baseball Magazine*, the most progressive major baseball outlet of the time, was one of few to give the unbalanced power of the commissioner such a treatment. For the majority of the baseball press, Landis remained the czar ruling over baseball with an iron fist. He used that iron fist to stamp out gamblers and other "undesirable characters," such as Benny Kauff, whom he threw out for his alleged involvement in a car-theft ring, even after Kauff was acquitted of the crime. And he used it to maintain the game's color line barring black players from the field of play. His line when pressed by reporters on baseball's unwritten yet obviously standing ban on black players was, unerringly, "No comment."

But come his death in 1944, the same year he was elected to the Hall of Fame, Landis had unquestionably served his purpose in the eyes of the owners. There had been nothing approaching the Black Sox scandal in Landis's tenure, and baseball had clearly risen as America's most popular sport. The moral authority of the commissioner was established.

After Landis: Coming Back to Earth

However well Landis accomplished his primary mission, he did have a mind of his own and was willing to challenge the owners to install his own vision of baseball. Primarily, Landis fought hard against the "chain store" model of the minor leagues that shackled players to parent clubs and allowed teams to keep better players in the minors at low prices—effectively, the model in place today. Landis instituted rules preventing clubs from keeping minor league players on the same team for more than two consecutive years. He also instituted a minor league draft, similar to today's Rule 5 draft, as part of his initiatives to keep the minor leagues competitive.

Reversing this trend was one of the first acts of baseball's second commissioner, Sen. Albert B. "Happy" Chandler. The presentation of Chandler by the media shows the league was consciously trying to distance itself from the judge's cold, stone-faced attitude. *Pittsburgh Press* scribe Harry Grayson wrote in 1945, following Chandler's ascension to the post, "Despite his singing and happy-go-lucky, jovial mien, Chandler is vastly more than an entertainer, back-slapper and handshaker—far from being a clown." A more clear indication of Chandler's softer, cuddlier qualities couldn't be written. To remove all doubt, consider Chandler's response to a comparison to Landis, which borders on parody: "I could never hope to be like him. I'm just Happy

Chandler and will handle problems in my own way." The transition from czar to commissioner had begun in earnest.

The idea of the czar was officially put to rest in 1998, when Bud Selig shed the "acting" tag from his commissioner title. "A commissioner is not a czar sitting above the law," Selig told the Associated Press that July. "Yes, a commissioner has a lot of power, but it must be confined to certain areas." Selig's use of "czar" to describe the position was undoubtedly intentional. Selig earned his undergraduate degree in history at the University of Wisconsin-Madison in the 1950s and has planned to take a position in his alma mater's history department following his retirement. "I don't think people realize," Selig concluded, "how the office of the commissioner has changed since 1921."

Between Chandler and Selig came Ford C. Frick (1951-1965), William Eckert (1965-1968), Bowie Kuhn (1969-1984), Peter Ueberroth (1984-1989), Bart Giamatti (1989) and Fay Vincent (1989-1992). Frick was, as Associated Press writer Charles Chamberlain put it in 1951, a "dyed-in-the wool baseball man," a requirement settled on by the owners after Gen. Douglas MacArthur, who had been removed from his Korean War command earlier the same year, turned down an offer to take the post.

Kuhn, the next man to hold the position for at least a decade, believed wholeheartedly in the owners' myth of the impartial commissioner. As one of Kuhn's bosses, Reds owner Francis Dale, told the Associated Press in 1974, "We must erase the notion that the commissioner is the tool of the owners. The players must feel that he is the impartial administrator—even if the Players Association has to pay half of his salary to make it so."

Ignoring the absurdity of asking the players to pay the commissioner for the privilege of his impartiality, Dale's comment makes the intended role of the commissioner explicit. He is meant to be perceived as an impartial, morally uncompromised arbiter even as his real job is spokesman and mouthpiece for the owners. Kuhn was determined to wedge his way in between the players and MLBPA director Marvin Miller. As the union's consistent victories throughout the 1970s and 1980s, including the elimination of the reserve clause, the adoption of free agency, and the victory in the collusion case of the 1980s show, Kuhn's efforts (and later, Ueberroth's) failed.

AP writer Ronald Blum wrote of Selig in 1998, "He was angered that both Vincent and Peter Ueberroth deemed themselves impartial and immune to owners' wishes." With his knowledge of both baseball and American history, Selig recognized this model of the commissioner was obsolete. The union was never going to be beaten by a man pretending to be on their side, and Kuhn's naivete in this regard was responsible for a number of union victories. Selig's approach was much simpler: make money for Major League Baseball, and position it to make even more in the future.

Even with Selig's failures—the 1994 strike and the consistent steroid issues since the late 1990s—MLB is well positioned for the future. Teams have taken full advantage of the explosion in the cable market. MLB Advanced Media has brilliantly taken advantage of the internet's ability to reach fans old and new. New ballparks continue to pop up, with many—if not most—funded largely by taxpayer dollars. And despite a major economic collapse, the word "contraction" hasn't been uttered for over a decade.

Perhaps these are low standards. Baseball fans, particularly those in Montreal, or those in Minnesota and Miami who endured contraction talk, or those who attended the 2002 All-Star Game, may have bad memories of Bud Selig. But those bad memories have failed to make a long-term impact on Major League Baseball's bottom line, and that is Selig's primary concern.

Conclusion

The commissioner of myth, the perfect moral arbiter, the "man of unquestionable repute" was never a reality and is now unassailably dead. It was a relic of an older sports world, when fans were distanced enough from the men on the field and in the owners box to believe the myths presented in print, over the radio and on the air. It was an appealing idea, the idea that a superman could come in and ensure, as Sanborn wrote nearly nine decades ago, any "crook is certain to be detected and… when detected, he can be banished from the game for life."

As Sanborn also wrote:

> *"Speaking broadly and by the law of averages, humanity and human nature are about the same wherever you find them. There are about so many innately honest men per thousand, and about so many born crooks per thousand, and also about so many persons per thousand who are born neither one nor the other but who are liable to be honest or crooked according to their freedom or exposure to temptation."*

The general law of average applies just as much in 2015 as it did in 1927. Baseball will never be free of scandal or turmoil as long as it is played by—and run by— human beings. Perhaps this is what Bud Selig meant when he told the Associated Press in May 2014 that his successor would have to be someone who understands "the culture" of baseball. "That could be people who do business with baseball or have a lot of knowledge of that," Selig said. "And that's just a judgment call they'll have to make at some point."

The owners settled on Rob Manfred, MLB's chief operating officer, a man who intimately knows how baseball does business. He was deeply involved with the Biogenesis case and the league's Department of Investigations, its multi-million dollar brand police designated to sniff out identity fraud in Latin America and steroid use in the states, among other things.

Manfred, a Harvard Law graduate, marks the full destruction of the mythical commissioner. "I don't think Rob needs or has any notion of being the imperial commissioner," Dodgers president Stan Kasten told the *Boston Globe* in September

2014. Red Sox chairman Tom Werner added, "I think Commissioner Selig was granted, appropriately, extraordinary powers. The next iteration would be more like a CEO reporting to an executive council." The transition from czar to CEO is officially complete.

Maybe there was a time when this would not have been acceptable, when the idea that baseball was like any other business would be too unpalatable to the public. But from the very beginning, from Landis' decision to look the other way when the Federal League's legal case threatened to blow up Organized Baseball, it has been the truth. The commissioner's job was never anything other than protecting the bottom line of the owners who pay his salary. The only difference is they admit it now.

References & Resources

- MLB.com, "The Commissionership," *mlb.mlb.com/mlb/history/mlb_history_people.jsp?story=com*
- Chrisine L. Putnam, "A President Inaugurates a Remarkable Tradition," Baseball Alamanac, *baseball-almanac.com/articles/president_taft_opening_day.shtml*
- J.G. Taylor Spink, *Judge Landis and Twenty-Five Years of Baseball*
- Stuart Banner, *The Baseball Trust: A History of Baseball's Antitrust Exemption*
- Irving Sanborn, *Baseball Magazine*, August 1927
- Murray Chass, *The New York Times*, "Baseball; Faced with Suspension, Steinbrenner Sought an Alternative," *nytimes.com/1990/08/01/sports/baseball-faced-with-suspension-steinbrenner-sought-an-alternative.html*
- Chris Lamb, *Conspiracy of Silence: Sportswriters and the Long Campaign to Desegregate Baseball*

Case Studies: Breaking Out and Breaking Bad

No matter how much we think we know about baseball, there are numerous reminders each season that we really can't know everything, or even most things. Each year brings its surprises. Not all are positive, but such is life.

When Phil Hughes left the Bronx, it was seemingly with his tail between his legs. Next season, he'll almost certainly be the Twins' Opening Day starter, and that's thanks to his revelatory 2014 campaign. Jay Bruce had a similarly revelatory season in Cincinnati, but for all the wrong reasons, and he suddenly finds himself on a team in a car rolling downhill with its brakes cut.

On the way down, the Reds may just pass the Cubs, who in 2014 had one star rebound in a big way (Starlin Castro), one break out (Anthony Rizzo) and three hold their own in their major league debuts (Arismendy Alcantara, Javier Baez and Jorge Soler). Oh, and two of their top prospects sizzled in Triple-A (Kris Bryant and Addison Russell). Not all of them are bona fide stars just yet, and there is a high attrition rate with prospects, but this year several of them played very well at the same time, both at the major league and minor league level, and the team may have that rare, sought-after wave of prospects hit at once.

Phil Hughes
by Neil Weinberg

Phil Hughes knows all about trade-offs. To get something you need, you need to give up something you have. Life is often about working to achieve the right balance, and Phil Hughes found his balance during the 2014 season, his best as a major leaguer and first as a member of the Minnesota Twins.

During his final season of prospect eligibility in 2007, *Baseball America* ranked Hughes as the fourth-best prospect in baseball behind Daisuke Matsuzaka, Alex Gordon and Delmon Young. In the years since, BA has given that honor to Clay Buchholz, Tommy Hanson, Jesus Montero, Dominic Brown, Yu Darvish, Wil Myers and Masahiro Tanaka. It's probably fair to say the fourth slot isn't a guarantee, but it also isn't a graveyard. Hughes was supposed to be a very good starting pitcher.

But that didn't happen. The sum of Hughes' career prior to 2014 wasn't anything to be ashamed of (11 WAR in under 800 innings), but there didn't appear to be much hope for anything more than a league-average peak. Hughes' raw stat line was influenced by the dimensions of Yankee Stadium, but most thoughtful observers were able to recognize that and evaluate Hughes in a reasonably neutral way. He was a league-average starter, at best, and that's exactly what the Twins paid for last November when he signed a three-year, $24 million pact.

But in 2014, Hughes made two important trade-offs that turned him into an above-average starter, if you prefer using runs allowed, or an elite starter if you care more about fielding-independent numbers. Either way, the Twins wound up with a much better pitcher than they could have expected, and Hughes finally had that great season the prospectors foretold.

Hughes' first trade-off was swapping quality defense for a much more reasonable home park. In 2013, the Yankees defense posted 21 Defensive Runs Saved (DRS) and a 12.5 Ultimate Zone Rating (UZR), while the 2014 Twins recorded a horrid -73 DRS and a -34.5 UZR. His old club wasn't a record-setting defensive club, but we're talking about a five- to 10-win difference between the two teams based only on defense. You never know exactly how that impacts each pitcher, but the gap is real.

Hughes was okay with the lesser defenders because he was moving from a park that ate him alive to one that would work for his style of play. Yankee Stadium is only slightly better for offense overall than Target Field (which is how we apply park factors), but the specific type of offense they foster is very different. Yankee Stadium generates home runs, especially for left-handed hitters, while Target Field allows more triples and doubles.

Specifically, Target Field is the third-most difficult park for left-handed home run power while Yankee Stadium trails only Coors Field in supporting bombs from lefties. In other words, a right-handed pitcher with flyball tendencies and an unexceptional change-up couldn't do much better than a move from New York to Minnesota.

In 2013, Hughes was annihilated by lefties at home to the tune of a .405 wOBA against. On the road, he held them to a .331 wOBA. His home/road split against righties was .369 to .301. So while Hughes showed a clear platoon split, it was also a very real home and away split that was propped up by a home run rate that was twice as high at home as it was on the road.

Alternatively, his strikeout and walk rates were much better at home. If he could only escape the Bronx.

He did just that in 2014. Hughes allowed a .287 wOBA at home against lefties compared to a .257 wOBA on the road. Against righties, the split was .325 and .315. He was better for many reasons, but being able to allow a fly ball to a lefty at home without expecting disaster was a huge factor, not just because the damage was limited but also because he didn't have to nibble as much to avoid the long ball.

Hughes was willing to trade defense for a better park, but he also traded pitches out of the zone for strikes. Lots of them.

The story of Hughes' season is unquestionably the way he turned himself into baseball's premier control pitcher. Hughes walked just 1.9 percent of the batters he faced in 2014. Not only did that lead qualified starters, it was the best mark of any pitcher who threw at least 12 innings last year.

This was an entirely new approach for Hughes, who had walked five to six percent of batters at his best and spent much of his career walking eight to nine percent of those he faced. Hughes simply stopped issuing free passes in 2014, and combined with a ballpark that didn't let every fly ball soar over the fence, he became one of the game's best pitchers.

Throwing strikes is certainly important, and pitchers who can't find the zone often don't survive long, but Hughes took strike throwing to an entirely new level. In his career, he had placed 51-54 percent of his pitches in the PITCHf/x zone; during 2014, that number climbed to 61 percent. Batters didn't make much less contact, but more strikes led to more swings and a ball in play is better than a walk if you're a pitcher.

Which is where this gets a little wacky. Normally, we think of a pitcher trading strikeouts for contact, but Hughes' strikeout rate didn't suffer one bit. Instead of falling behind and issuing free passes, Hughes put the ball in the zone and let his questionable defense do the rest. But the balls weren't going to fly out of the park, so even a .324 batting average on balls in play (BABIP)—which was identical to his 2013 mark—didn't hurt nearly that much. Trading strikeouts for balls in play is usually not a great idea with a bad defense, but trading walks for balls in play is usually pretty smart.

The trade-off led Hughes to the best strikeout-to-walk rate since 1901 (11.63 K/BB), easily the best FIP and xFIP of his career and his best ERA as a starter. It's such an interesting story because, of the two things that made Hughes excel, one was entirely unrelated to his performance and one was exclusively within his control.

Hughes' travels to a better home park illuminate that while park factors do well on average, there always will be cases for which they aren't nuanced enough to make proper corrections. Hughes didn't stop allowing fly balls to lefties in 2014. He just moved from a park that killed him for it to a park that protected him, even though the parks support reasonably similar amounts of run scoring.

But the other big change, the decision to throw strikes with reckless abandon, was context independent. Hughes traded his slider for a cutter, used his curveball more and his change-up less, and absolutely attacked the zone against both lefties and righties.

There's no perfect way to pitch. Velocity, movement, location and sequencing can interact in so many different ways that you can't look at any player's year-to-year change and know for certain that he is going to get better or worse, but Hughes arrived in Minnesota ready to make changes and they paid off in a big way.

Instead of trying to avoid the plate and keep batters from sending one into the seats, Hughes was able to attack the zone with his fastball and cutter to great effect. He was somewhere between a four-win and six-win pitcher in 2014, but the earliest projections think he'll be much closer to league average again in 2015.

It's an interesting projection to watch because it anticipates much higher walk and home run rates than Hughes posted in 2014. Can he really continue to throw this many strikes without surrendering more extra-base hits? That's the question he'll have to answer going forward, but that fact that he did it once, in such a big way, is impressive enough to warrant admiration.

People always wondered what Hughes could do if he just got out of Yankee Stadium. They probably expected fewer home runs, but a superhuman walk rate probably didn't factor in. He was able to succeed by averaging one total walk or home run per start. Hughes was a highly touted prospect, but it took him until age 28 to really shine, and that required a complete overhaul in his game.

For all the talk about the Twins drafting and developing strike throwers, their biggest success might turn out to be the one they signed for $8 million per year.

Jay Bruce
by Karl de Vries

Jay Bruce was well into the midst of the most frustrating, humiliating year of his pro career when he stepped into the batter's box in the eighth inning on Aug. 28.

Having already struck out four times, the two-time All-Star needed no reminder of his futility at the plate that day. But just in case, the 21,316 Reds fans at Great American Ball Park felt compelled to voice their disgust at their slugger's year-long slump, greeting him with an angry chorus of boos despite the home team enjoying a 7-0 lead.

Cubs pitcher Kyuji Fujikawa started him off with a high fastball well out of the zone, at which Bruce offered a limp half-swing. Strike one. Next was a fastball at the knees. Strike two. Bruce managed to foul off the next pitch, but when Fujikawa threw a splitter in the dirt off the plate, Bruce waved pathetically, and a moment later he was tossing his bat and helmet toward the Reds' dugout, a look of despondent resignation painted on his face.

Bruce would later call the at-bat "the most embarrassing moment I've ever had on the field," and whether he realized it at the time, the day encapsulated a stunningly terrible 2014 for a player who had been one of baseball's brightest, most consistent stars.

How bad was Bruce? The guy batted .217 for the season. He compiled a disastrous -1.1 Wins Above Replacement (WAR), the fourth-lowest in baseball among qualified hitters. His 18 home runs, while nothing to sneer at, weren't enough to elevate a .288 wOBA, which lagged behind the likes of Adeiny Hechavarria and DJ LeMahieu.

And while it would be unfair to lay the blame for the Reds' disappointing season squarely at Bruce's feet, suffice to say his output didn't do much to help his team avoid a 76-86 record—nor an offense that scored the third-fewest runs in baseball.

This was a player, after all, who had averaged 27 homers and 81 runs batted in since his debut in 2008, and he had improved as he approached his prime, becoming a true 30-HR/100-RBI lineup anchor over the past three years. Entering his age-27 season, there was little reason to doubt Bruce, playing in one of the National League's best hitter's parks, would turn in another standout performance.

What went wrong? How did Bruce go from being one of the game's best players to, statistically speaking, one of its worst in 2014?

To start, it's possible Bruce wasn't completely healthy, as he missed about three weeks in May after undergoing arthroscopic surgery to repair torn meniscus cartilage in his left knee. Only Bruce knows for sure the extent to which the knee affected his season; perhaps not surprisingly, he refused to publicly blame his problems on the injury. But he never missed any significant time the rest of the year and finished with a career-high 12 stolen bases, hardly signs of a hobbled player.

What's certain, however, is that Bruce's batted ball results took a dramatic turn for the worse, according to FanGraphs:

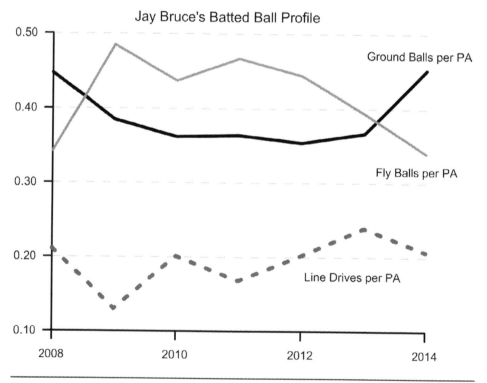

The decrease in fly balls during the 2014 season, of course, continues a less than ideal trend for Bruce, but in the past, he was able to smack enough line drives to maintain a solid batting average. In 2014, however, his groundball rate surged to 45.2 percent. For a home run hitter, that's bad enough, but Bruce also had the misfortune of pulling 57.9 percent of them, his highest rate since his rookie campaign, and he hit into the shift more often than in recent years, according to Inside Edge data.

Meanwhile, Bruce posted the lowest average batted-ball distance of his career, 285 feet, about 10 feet shorter than his usual mark. Not surprisingly, his home run-to fly-ball rate dropped as well, to 15.3 percent, tied for the lowest of his big league tenure, and, combined with the plunge in fly balls, helps explain why Bruce smashed the fewest home runs of his career.

The lackluster batted-ball distribution was accompanied by a more aggressive, and less effective, approach at the plate. This year marked the fifth straight season in which Bruce's strikeout rate climbed, and the third straight in which his walk rate fell. Percentage-wise, he saw the fewest 3-0 counts of his career, and his share of 3-1 and 2-0 counts also was well below his norms, despite seeing roughly the same number of pitches per plate appearance as he had in previous seasons. There's nothing necessarily wrong with attacking more pitches, of course, particularly for a middle-of-the-order power hitter, but Brooks Baseball data show that Bruce swung more frequently at pitches off both corners of the plate in 2014, which likely contributed to the weaker contact.

There was also an unmistakable difference in his plate discipline before and after his knee surgery in May:

Jay Bruce Plate Discipline Percentages										
Period	PA	O-Sw	Z-Sw	Sw	O-Con	Z-Con	Con	Zone	F-Str	SwStr
3/31-5/4	125	25.2	68.1	42.9	48.0	79.1	68.4	41.3	50.4	13.2
5/23-9/28	420	35.8	69.8	48.7	58.0	84.5	72.5	38.0	63.3	13.2
Career	3,951	30.1	73.7	48.5	54.3	83.4	73.0	42.2	58.0	12.7

In late June, roughly a month after returning from the operation, Bruce told C. Trent Rosecrans of *The Cincinnati Enquirer* that he was trying to walk more in 2014, which explains his early decision to lay off balls outside the strike zone and cut down on his swings. That produced a high walk rate in April, and by the time he went under the knife, he was getting on base at a .352 clip.

The problem was, Bruce was hitting only .216 during that span, and when he returned to action, he shelved the passive approach immediately. At first, the change seemed to work: Bruce blasted four home runs over the next five weeks, producing a .454 slugging percentage along the way. But it was a .345 batting average on balls in play (BABIP) that deserved much of the credit, and once the line drives stopped coming, his power largely disappeared.

The loss of key teammates may have contributed, as well. Joey Votto's season was ruined by a quadriceps injury. Brandon Phillips tore a ligament in his left thumb. Shin Soo-Choo, who was an on-base machine for Cincinnati last year, was replaced at the top of the order by Billy Hamilton, who couldn't muster a .300 on-base percentage. Slotted into the cleanup spot more often than he ever had been before at the big league level, Bruce found himself charged with carrying much of the Reds' offense, and one cannot help but wonder if that led him to press too hard at the plate.

Looking ahead to 2015, Steamer, believing Bruce will improve upon the .269 BABIP he posted this year, projects something of a return to form, expecting him to put up around 27 home runs and 83 RBI over the course of a full season. He'll have a full winter to rest his knee and clear his head, and for a guy who won't turn 28 until the first week of April, he still has plenty of prime seasons ahead. And, of course, he'll have the track record of a player who mostly has performed at a high level since he broke into the big leagues back in 2008, one who has earned the benefit of the doubt in his ability to make adjustments.

But in doing so, he'll have to find a way to reverse trends that began well before his miserable 2014, making better contact and fixing his strike zone judgment while building upon the experience of the most difficult season of his big league career.

"It's just one of those things," a dejected Bruce, reflecting on his lost season, told reporters shortly after his five-strikeout nadir. "You have to find a way to take some positive out of it to get better. I think this is going to make me better."

The Cubs Cometh
by Bradley Woodrum

It's been a long night for the Cubs franchise. Since 1945, the end of World War II, the Cubs have had exactly one above-average offense: The 2008 Cubs, who hit .278/.354/.443 for a 104 weighted runs created plus (wRC+). That means—after we control for era and park factors—the Cubs have had an average or below-average offense in 68 of their last 69 seasons. In fact, in only one season (1998) did they hit at exactly league average (100 wRC+), and the group of 69 seasons averages only 89 wRC+.

But dawn is coming.

In 2014, the Cubs lineup was an average of 26.7 years old in a league that averaged 28.2 years of age. The Future appears to be now in Wrigleyville because there is a recent crop of prospects unlike any Chicago has seen since the days of Slammin' Sammy Sosa, and possibly before. And those prospects are starting to reach the majors.

But how did they do? What are the products of this vaunted First Wave? Well, the early returns were mixed. Let's look at the 2014 seasons of these headlining hitters in context.

Anthony Rizzo, 1B: Age 24, .286/.386/.527 in 616 plate appearances

One of the two "grizzled veterans" of the Cubs infield, Rizzo is the organizational favorite whom Theo Epstein and Co. drafted in 2007 for Boston, then acquired again in 2012 from San Diego. From 2011 (his one season with the Padres) through 2013 (his first full season in the majors) Rizzo hit .238/.324/.412 with 39 homers through 1,211 plate appearances. That translated to a 102 wRC+, meaning he hit two percent better the league average. But a down season for a former top prospect did not dissuade the Steamer projection system, which prophesied a .268/.350/.501 slash with 31 homers heading into 2014. A Cubs fan base recovering from the recent, melting disappointments of Bryan LaHair and Micah Hoffpauir might be excused for lowered expectations from first basemen who gashed minor league pitchers.

But Rizzo did not disappoint. In fact, he exceeded his robust Steamer projections. With 32 homers, 28 doubles and a 153 wRC+, he became the core of an otherwise weak Cubs offense. All told, his 5.6 wins above replacement (WAR) put him No. 14 in the majors among position players. In the same way Paul Goldschmidt's success snuck up on East Coast baseball fans, Rizzo's success has no doubt surprised fans of, well, winning teams.

The Cubs have Rizzo under contract through his age-31 season if they so desire. If he can stay healthy—if his back can remain up to the challenge of another grueling, ISOtastic season—the Cubs will have a big piece of their lineup settled for many years to come.

Starlin Castro, SS: Age 24, .292/.339/.438 in 569 PA

The other veteran among the Cubs' young hitters is shortstop Starlin Castro. Like Rizzo, he had bad results in 2013 and a nice turnaround in 2014, and like Rizzo, he is signed long term. Castro is both fun and frustrating: He is the strikeout-resistant, walk-allergic, contact-heavy hitter we might expect from a slap-hitting shortstop, but he hits for decent power.

Compared to his fellow young Cubs hitters, Castro's contact ability stands out:

Comparison of Cubs' Young Hitters, MLB stats					
Player	PA	H%	BB%	K%	HR%
Starlin Castro	3,186	26.6%	5.2%	15.6%	1.6%
Anthony Rizzo	1,827	22.2%	10.8%	19.2%	3.9%
Arismendy Alcantara	300	19.0%	5.7%	31.0%	3.3%
Javier Baez	229	15.7%	6.6%	41.5%	3.9%
Jorge Soler	97	26.8%	6.2%	24.7%	5.2%

Castro has almost twice as many plate appearances as Rizzo despite being almost the same age. Castro is pretty much a known commodity at this point. His career 98 wRC+ (i.e., hitting results two percent worse than league average), is pretty good for a shortstop. It has been punctuated with seasons both great (115 wRC+ this last year) and ugly (72 wRC+ in 2013). To expect Castro to maintain his career-high 5.2 percent walk-rate and near-career-high .146 ISO—isolated power—might be asking for a lot of development from a five-year veteran. But as Adam Jones and Andrew McCutchen have taught, there *is* good reason to be patient with top prospects. Sometimes it takes a few years to get great or, in McCutchen's case, elite.

The dilemma is that Castro's bat plays well at shortstop, but the Cubs have their big fuzzy arms full of high-ceiling shortstops—Javier Baez, minor leaguer Addison Russell and Castro. And it may be that Castro is the worst defender of the bunch. Over his career, he has cost the Cubs an average of about three runs per season. That is not terrible, but for a guy signed through 2020 (albeit cheaply), averaging 3.0 WAR a season may be insufficient in an infield ripe with talent.

Arismendy Alcantara, 2B/OF: Age 22, .205/.254/.367 in 300 PA

Oh, look, another infielder! The Cubs solved their excess-of-infielders problem by shifting Alcantara to the outfield shortly after his arrival on July 9. He split the remainder of the season between second base and center field, with that split favoring time on the grass.

His defensive work in the outfield showed room for improvement. He occasionally took bad routes and misplayed a few easy balls, but he also flexed great range and athleticism. While his defense at second base showed a greater degree of comfort, his outfield game was very much a work in progress.

As was his hitting. In his first 86 plate appearances with the Cubs, Alcantara cracked a .253/.337/.427 line with a 113 wRC+, but when the calendar hit August, he dropped to a .195/.238/.347 slash and a 60 wRC+. The slump worsened to a 42 wRC+ through his final 22 games.

Refer to the table above and we'll notice Alcantara has Castro's low walk rate, but also Carlos Pena's gigantic strikeout rate. That tends to work only if every other batted ball is slapping off ivy or splashing into a bleacher bum's beer. A glance at his PITCHf/x data shows Alcantara took more pitches in the zone and swung at more pitches out of the zone than the league-average hitter. In other words, if he wants to be just average—a low bar for a top prospect—he needs to eat his Plate Discipline Wheaties and improve in both of those components.

Alcantara showed a touch of power in the minors but was more of a high-batting average on balls in play (BABIP), doubles-and-steals type hitter. Steamer forecasts a .247/.296/.394 slash and 15 homers for Alcantara in 2015 and, sadly, that would be a marked improvement for him.

The strikeouts may never go away, but Alcantara has shown enough discipline to walk once every 10 plate appearances in the minors. If he can recapture that, there's a good chance more pieces will fall in place for him.

Javier Baez, SS/2B: .169/.227/.324 in 229 PA

Baez should enter 2015 as the Cubs' starting second baseman. He will be only 22 years old. He will also enter with worse career offensive numbers than Darwin Barney, the likewise former shortstop-turned-second-baseman the Cubs traded away for an A-Ball pitcher. Barney, who was poised for a salary raise, could not hit well enough to figure into the Cubs' long term plans. Baez should.

Baez cranked a solo homer off Boone Logan in his major league debut, helping the Cubs beat the Rockies, 6-5, in extras. But after that, he missed on more than a third of his swings. Imagine that from the pitcher's perspective: If I can just get this hitter to swing, he will miss every third pitch. And he will miss every other breaking ball.

I assume that's an empowering thought, and the fact that Baez struck out in 41.5 percent of his plate appearances suggests pitching against Baez was indeed quite empowering. Among players with at least 200 plate appearances, no player struck out more frequently than Baez. In fact, no hitter with at least 80 PA—just 80 PA—struck out more frequently than Baez.

Needless to emphasize, this is an enormous problem. And despite it, he had a .155 ISO—slugging percent minus batting average. Here is a comprehensive list of players with a K rate above 40 percent and an ISO above .150, minimum 150 PA:

Baez, Javier. That is all.

Oh, yeah, and that's the comprehensive, all-time list—starting in 1871. (Excluding 1897 through 1909 because apparently someone forgot to write down hitter strikeouts for 12 years.)

Now, our list actually gets downright terrifying if we drop it to 100 PA: We see the likes of Brett Jackson (2012), Brooks Conrad (2012), Rick Ankiel (2013), and—yikes—Tom Seaver (1972; a pitcher) and Dave Duncan (1967; a glove-first catcher). These are not the paradigms of hitting potential. And somehow, Javier Baez has the lowest WAR on this list with -0.8. (But, hey, that is more a matter of trivia than anything meaningful; decimal-place WAR and small-sample-size WAR both are trivialities.)

Scared about Javier Baez yet? Well, consider this before you eBay your Baez shirsey: Pitchers are terrified of throwing him a fastball. In a September FanGraphs article, Carson Cistulli observed that Baez, after hitting seven home runs in his first 86 plate appearances, had hit none in the subsequent 66 PA. In that first period of time, pitchers threw him fastballs at a rate slightly higher than the league-average 35 percent. After those seven homers, he saw fastballs at a greatly reduced rate: In September and October combined, he got a 27.6 percent four-seamer rate. His killer ISO in August (.223) cratered in September/October (.079).

Here's the glimmer of hope: The pitch selection ratios for the season are almost identical to pitchers' approach to Baltimore star Adam Jones (lots of off-speed, very little on-speed). And if Jones took a while to figure out breaking balls to an acceptable level, it may take Baez time, too. Or maybe Baez, playing in the longest season of his career (a combined 663 PA), struggled with some fatigue late in the season. This is not an uncommon issue with young prospects who surge through a minor league system quickly.

And if all this fails to encourage the prospect-jaded Cubs fan, remember this: FanGraphs scout Kiley McDaniel chose to look at Baez in a "Scouting Explained: The Mysterious Hit Tool" article and said:

> *I included a video of Javier Baez since he was the first player that came to mind of a guy who, after one swing in BP, is obviously crazy talented. It's a little tough to see with BP swings, but that's what 80 bat speed looks like.*

The scouting number "80," in case you didn't know, translates into a real-world value of OMFG.

Jorge Soler, OF: Age 22, .292/.330/.573 in 97 PA

The only natural outfielder in the bunch, Jorge Soler did not make his major league debut until Aug. 27, but he did so with style. In the top of the second, with Mat Latos pitching, Luis Valbuena and Jorge Soler—in Soler's first big league at-bat—cranked back-to-back cloud-scrapers. Soler, a Cuban ex-pat, finished the season with five homers, eight doubles and a world of renewed expectations.

Fans may be excused for losing their Soler hype leading up to the 2014 season. Soler agreed to terms with the Cubs on June 11, 2012. Ben Badler of *Baseball America* piqued more than a few fans' interest when he wrote: "Power is Soler's best tool, as he shows great bat speed, the ability to hit balls out to all fields and the potential to hit 25 home runs per year." Later, ESPN prospect analyst Keith Law identified Soler as a premium talent: "Had Soler been in this year's draft, he would probably have been a top-five pick on merit, definitely in the top 10."

But in 2013, he started the season in the Rookie-level Arizona League and struggled (.271/.311/.376) despite the league's low talent level. The Cubs promoted him to High-A, and he began to hit well, but had his year severed on June 27 with a stress fracture in his left shin.

Soler then began the 2014 season in Double-A, but a hamstring injury took him out for a month. When he returned in June, he was back in the Rookie level and had been injured twice in the past calendar year. Cubs fans on ObstructedView.net still had Soler ranked No. 3 among their prospects, but the injuries had sullied their high hopes:

The only problem in his development is that he just can't stay healthy. He's dinged both hamstrings, and there's a very real threat that those injuries have sapped both development time and physical projection.
— myles, from "Cubs Top 10 Prospects" on ObstructedView.net

So when Soler arrived with the Cubs and posted a .386 wOBA and 146 wRC+, fear dissipated quicker than an Old Style spilled on Waveland in the middle of July. But what does Soler's future look like? That is a bit tougher. He is still a corner outfielder with a history of leg issues. At the moment, first base is well occupied by Anthony Rizzo. Could injuries or a regression of batted-ball luck (given his .339 BABIP in 2014) stunt his sophomore campaign? It is certainly possible. But until that happens, the Steamer projection of .271/.330/.470 certainly won't quell any Cubs fans' hopes.

Addison Russell, SS: Age 20, .295/.350/.508 in 280 PA (minors)

Acquired in the Jeff Samardzija/Jason Hammel blockbuster deal, young middle infielder Addison Russell could make his major league debut yesterday and probably impress the average fan. His defense may well astound. As Eno Sarris found out in his piece for the *2014 Hardball Times Annual*, Russell has not only the physical defensive tools for shortstop, but the mental. He actively focuses on the pitcher's pitch selection and discretely alerts his fellow infielders when it looks like the pitching battery is going for a ground ball or a fly out.

Therron Brockish of *Baseball America* saw Russell in October 2014, and said the young Cubs infielder "may prove to be a prospect that has a long-lasting impact at the big league level for the Cubs." Heading into the season, FanGraphs' Marc Hulet named Russell the top Athletics prospect and a player who "could eventually develop into a 20-20 threat at the plate while playing above-average defense."

Given a healthy season, Russell might have made his major league debut in 2014, but instead a hammy issue took him out for half the year. He spent the majority of his time with the Tennessee Smokies (the Cubs' Double-A affiliate) where he clocked in at 4.5 solar years younger than his competition. And he still cranked 12 homers in 205 plate appearances (a 5.9 percent HR-rate; wow). Add to that a 17.5 percent K-rate for the 2014 season, and we have a strong defensive shortstop with a dandy combo of contact and home-run ability.

Where does he fit with the Cubs right now? Well, he doesn't. Even if the Cubs moved Castro to third and left Baez at second and Alcantara at center, they would still have one premium player left without a place to play—and he just might be the most important.

Kris Bryant, 3B/OF: Age 22, .325/.438/.661 in 594 PA (minors)

Bryant rounds out the Cubs' Super Infield. Drafted in the first round in 2013, Bryant has done nothing but fuel the nightmares of minor league pitchers. In his

36-game romp through the Rookie, High-A and A-Ball leagues in 2013, Bryant cracked nine homers and 14 doubles and posted a gaudy .336/.390/.688 slash.

He started the 2014 season in Double-A and popped 22 homers, then went to Triple-A for the second half of the year and cranked another 21. This is a guy who has been superior to his peers for some time. In his three seasons at the University of San Diego, Bryant hit .353/.486/.702 with 54 homers in just 638 plate appearances. His freshman year, he led the team's offense with a .365/.482/.599 slash. In his final year, he broke the school record of 18 home runs—by hitting 31. The previous school record for career slugging average, .572, was eclipsed under the shadow of Bryant's .702.

In 2014, Bryant hit a homer in 7.2 percent of his plate appearances. Among minor leaguers with at least 400 PA, only three bested Bryant, and none of those players was in Triple-A. When Bryant won *Baseball America's* 2014 Minor League Player of the Year award in September, he joined an exceptionally elite roster of Hall-of-Famers and All-Stars. And even in that special fraternity, Bryant had a slugging average better than all but Ron Kittle (1982), Mike Marshall (1981) and Tim Salmon (1992). He slugged and OPS'd better than Mike Trout, Frank Thomas, Jason Heyward, José Canseco and Manny Ramirez. Granted, park and league adjustments could render the differences moot, but the point is still the same: Kris Bryant hits. Everyone and everything confirms this. Said *Baseball America's* J.J. Cooper: "A plot of Bryant's home runs looks like the spray from a sprinkler."

All signs point to Bryant joining the Baby Bears in 2015. That being said, the Cubs may choose to delay his service clock a bit and start him in the minors. This would also give third baseman Luis Valbuena or left fielder Chris Coghlan a chance to terrible their ways out of their newly acquired starting jobs. The first of those veterans to falter—or the one doing less amazing than the other when Bryant's Super Two window has closed—will land in the dugout or on the waiver wire.

Will Bryant have more contact ability than Castro? No, but he'll walk more than Rizzo. Will he have more raw power than Baez? Maybe not, but he'll connect for more homers and strike out much less frequently.

The Cubs' horizon shows signs of daylight. Rizzo and Castro are the morning stars. Alcantara, Baez, Russell and Soler are the orange-pink glow along the eastern edge. And Bryant is the sun. There will be no mistaking him when he arrives.

The NL Central better find some sunglasses.

The Descension of Baby Jesus

by David G. Temple

Ronald Tobias wrote a book titled *20 Master Plots and How to Build Them*, in which he outlines and elucidates various plot points—right around 20 of them, if I had to guess off the top of my head—and what purpose they serve and how best to employ them in writing. Oddly enough—or perhaps not, given our infatuation with grafting narrative to sports—many of these plots can be assigned to individuals within baseball. Players, managers, fans, and even entire teams can slot nicely into these predetermined tracks. Round pegs find snug homes in round holes.

But what Tobias writes about aren't his inventions. He is merely explaining tropes that had existed in nature since we started drawing on cave walls. Everything has a beginning somewhere, certainly, but it's not as if the revenge plot began in Tobias' brain. He wasn't creating the ideas, merely acting as a vehicle for their explanation and interpretation. Whether they know it or not, anyone who has had exposure to any kind of fiction—books, movies, television—has worked his or her mind through these round holes. Even nonfiction is often scraped over at least one of these treatments. It's how our brains mold our existence, how everything isn't spun into chaos. Humans need order. We need compartments. It's the way of the world, and it's okay.

The most likely plot to snake itself into sports is that of the underdog. The underdog idea plays nicely with things that have clear winners and losers. If winning is harder to define, it becomes more difficult to realize if the underdog had indeed succeeded. Baseball has clear winners and losers, bests and worsts, champions and everyone else. And because baseball also lends itself well to forecasting, it becomes quite easy to identify favorites—those who should win—and, conversely, the underdog. The 2003 Red Sox, at least at the time, were the underdogs. As were the 1960 Pittsburgh Pirates. The 1951 Giants. The 1969 Mets. How can any player born into poverty on a Latin American island and make his way to the Show not be considered an underdog story? The sport is lousy with these stories, to be honest.

Not all of Tobias' 20 plots apply. Save for Mike Kekich and Fritz Peterson, perhaps, there aren't a whole lot of Forbidden Love stories to be found in baseball. I suppose the cocaine and PED scandals could fall under the Temptation umbrella, but there isn't a great deal of applicability to be found elsewhere. Nor are there a lot of Riddle challenges involved in the national pastime, outside of how to build the best defensive metric, perhaps. But Revenge? Rivalry? How many times are those words used in columns and pre-game shows? Hell, there's an actual play in baseball named after the Sacrifice. And there's always room for a good Descension plot.

We may joyously revel in the Descension of certain teams, but that often clings to feelings of Rivalry. We loathe the Descension of our favorite teams or players. We might use it to dig into deeper analysis—the fall of the 2014 Oakland Athletics is both a very good and very recent example of this. Descension is often met with feelings of happiness or sadness, depending on the moral compass and team loyalty of the reader. But there's a third response that can accompany this classic storyline; anger.

It's an odd response because—perhaps more than any of Tobias' offerings—Descension is inherent in the basic fabric of being human. We all fall prey to pressure, to stress, to adverse situations. Our mere biology is rife with Descension. Decay and death is waiting for us all. Being angry about our own Descension can be seen as very normal. But to feel anger about someone else's? How is this a reasonable response? In baseball, which the editors insist should be the subject of this essay, it is often centrifugally tied to one thing; money.

In 1976, the United States celebrated the 200th anniversary of its independence, a noble and hard-fought Quest, to be certain. Conversely, as the Messersmith decision granted baseball players their own form of independence, baseball fans, writers, and certainly team owners lamented the perceived death of the game. These players—those who played to the best of their abilities toward a common goal when they were indentured to their teams—would now certainly become corrupt and lazy with their new-found wealth. The boy's game was now a business—destined to be brought to ruin by greed and sloth.

This ideology, this exacerbation and resentment surrounding players' salaries, still is tethered to baseball. Furthermore, it fuels the anger at a player's or team's Descension. Many Cardinals fans still harbor ill will toward Albert Pujols, who left their blue-collar team (and already-high salary) for the riches of Los Angeles, a city already ruined by its lust for money. But a player need not leave a team seeking his paycheck to be looked down upon by fans. Even those who stayed, or those who came in thanks to that very same search for a big payday, can bring rolled eyes, hack-job columns, and emphatic boos from those who once cheered.

We do not boo the Underdog, for certain. A player who does not command a large salary often is deemed less capable. If he struggles, we show empathy. We, like him, are not the champions of our field. We, like him, are simply trying our best. Assuredly, we can dislike these players who don't perform, but that ties deeper to our confusion with why the front offices signed them in the first place. We don't hate the no-hit shortstop or the ineffective reliever because he is bad. We hate the fact that our team is tasked with trying to win with him on the roster.

But that relationship between winning and money is what this is all about. If a team doesn't spend enough money in the eyes of the fans, the lack of winning is expected. *How can this team win if it never spends any money?!?* If a team manages to be successful with low payrolls, we cast it into the Underdog role. It has been one of the central points of our narrative in baseball since Messersmith, if not before. We root for the poor. We jeer the rich. That is, unless the rich are bringing trophies.

If those trophies are not obtained, if those banners are not hung even though the payroll warrants it, who is to blame? Perhaps the manager. Maybe the front office still gets a smattering of disdain. Inevitably, however, heads turn toward the highest-paid player. Anointed the de facto champion of the team based solely on their tax returns, these players are expected to shuttle in success. They are the ones who should be bearing down, lifting up the team, and moving them forward. They are one of a possible 12 or 13 players to take the field for a team in any given game, but no matter. We're not socialists. The big earners should be the big performers.

I moved to the Twin Cities of Minnesota in 2005, the same year Joe Mauer had his first full season with the Minnesota Twins. Mauer was deemed the Next Big Thing from the start. Drafted first overall in the 2001 draft, his quick rise through the minors is what allowed the Twins to trade their then-current catcher A.J. Pierzynski to the Giants for Francisco Liriano and Joe Nathan, two players who would help solidify the Twins' run of success in the mid-to-late 2000s (and yes, Boof Bonser, too—can't forget about him). Mauer was worth 3.4 wins above replacement in his first full year. He was worth 6.2 wins the next. The Mauer Years had begun.

It's tough to say who started calling Joe Mauer "Baby Jesus" first. Did the talk radio guys influence the fans, or did the fans come up with the moniker? It probably doesn't matter. The point is, the fans were all in on their hometown boy. The local ads started pouring in. Mauer's face was on everything. Still shots of his pretty swing seemed to don every program, every billboard, every banner. He was pimping everything from scratch-off tickets to milk. The only thing that could make Joe Mauer promoting milk more Minnesotan would be if he did it while tooling around on hockey skates draped in blaze orange.

But things haven't really panned out for Mauer and the Twins. Justin Morneau did win the American League MVP Award in 2006, even if it was to a bit of controversy, but the Twins were bounced from the ALDS in three games. Mauer lost some of 2007 to leg injuries, and Morneau and Michael Cuddyer fell off the table. Liriano went down at the end of 2008 needing Tommy John surgery, and the Twins lost a one-game playoff for the division. Johan Santana was traded in the offseason. Minnesota won a game 163 of its own in 2009, but was once again swept in the playoffs. Still, Mauer was performing very well and even grabbed an MVP Award in 2009. Then, as they tend to do when big money is involved, things got real.

Yes, 10 years is a long contract for a catcher coming into his age-27 season. Yes, $183 million is a lot of money for a mid-market team to commit to one player.

Yes, a no-trade clause probably wasn't a great idea, either. But, at least at the time, Twins Territory was pretty overjoyed. The sting of the Santana trade still lingered. Locking down an MVP and preventing him from getting poached by the Yankees or Red Sox was a big deal, especially since it was a local boy. The Twins had a shiny new ballpark, and hometown hero Joe Mauer was staying there. All was right in the world. Mauer responded by, once again, leading the team in WAR. The Twins won 94 games that year. They used that momentum to—you guessed it—get swept in the ALDS.

The 2010 season was really the start of what would become a fan base's love-hate relationship with a team's best player. In 2009, Mauer's MVP year, he posted career highs in average, slugging, and on-base percentage. This doesn't seem that abnormal given his age and prior track record. But he also posted his highest career BABIP that season, .373. That was good for fourth-best among qualified hitters that season behind a trio of speedy players in David Wright, Hanley Ramirez and Ichiro Suzuki. And even if Twins fans knew he wouldn't hit .365 in 2010, there was another stat they were less happy about seeing regress—the homers.

The Twins played their last season in the Metrodome in 2009. In that final season, fans saw Mauer—whose home run total usually didn't reach double digits—blast 28 bombs. Fans may not have noticed that his home run-to-fly ball ratio, which had hovered at 10 percent or below in all prior seasons, spiked to over 20 percent that year. What, in hindsight, was a statistical aberration became a point of hope for onlookers, and soon, a point of contention.

Target Field may not be the best place for left-handed batters to hit dingers, but 2010 saw Justin Morneau and Jason Kubel knock 18 and 21 of them, respectively. A 39-year-old Jim Thome smashed 25. And Joe Mauer, a year after hitting 28 home runs, a year after his MVP season and the first year of his big-time contract, logged all of nine home runs. His HR/FB percentage falling right back down to his career norm coupled with regression in his average and OBP makes sense in the aggregate, but it left fans wondering just what their team had paid so much for.

And then Mauer had the audacity to get injured. He had knee surgery following the 2010 campaign and had a fair number of complications leading into spring training and the beginning of the 2011 season. What began as an unfortunate situation turned into a point of dissidence for fans. It didn't help that he was suffering from a condition known as bilateral leg weakness, which totally sounds made up. I mean, I'm surprised my word processor didn't put a squiggly line under that phrase, to be honest. His suffering from a condition that should have been featured in an episode of *House* if it didn't sound so lame, along with a sprinkle of pneumonia at the end of the season, led Mauer to start only 82 games in 2011. When he was on the active roster, he wasn't himself at the plate. The Twins were paying Joe Mauer $23 million to miss half the season and hit .287 when he was able to hoist his carcass into the batters box.

Mauer's issues weren't the sole reason for the Twins going from 94 wins in 2010 to 63 in 2011. Numerous front-office moves—signing Tsuyoshi Nishioka and trading J.J. Hardy for what amounted to two ham sandwiches, for instance—were put under the microscope. (The Hardy deal would only sting more in later years when the player sent away to net him in the first place, Carlos Gomez, became a bona fide superstar.) Morneau's ongoing concussion problems kept him off the field, too. Liriano was not rebounding from his injury very well. Somebody named Nick Blackburn got 26 starts that season. It was a pretty terrible year all around.

That last sentence was in reference to the 2011 Twins season. It is also applicable to the 2012 Twins season. That same sentence—the one about the Twins having a terrible year—could also be in reference to their 2013 season. The Twins totaled a combined 195 wins and 291 losses between 2011 and 2013. As people were getting fired, team philosophies were changing, and players were getting traded, Mauer quietly averaged around five Wins Above Replacement between 2012 and 2014. The crap sandwich that made up the '11-'13 seasons shaded that fact, as everyone who wasn't focused on the future of the team had stopped caring already.

Mauer was the AL's seventh-best hitter, according to weighted runs created plus (wRC+), in a 2013 season that included the three-headed monster of Miguel Cabrera, Mike Trout and Chris Davis. To say that fact went unnoticed in the Twin Cities would be unfair, but the focus was clearly on the rebuilding process. Nobody looks at the cute kitten when there's a tire fire right next to it.

Ever since Mauer started cultivating a bit of an injury history, rumors and speculation started to swirl as to whether he should continue playing the catcher position. Front-office types always denied the allegations that Mauer was on the move, but this did not stop sports radio producers from cueing up the argument on a semi-regular basis. Nevertheless, even in his shortened seasons, Mauer played the bulk of his games as the backstop with only brief respites at first base or designated hitter.

For anyone paying attention though, it wasn't a question of "if," but "when." Yes, Mauer's bat at catcher freed up a spot for a possible slugger at first or DH, but at a certain point, keeping one of your best bats healthy is more important than him taking up a traditional power spot in the lineup. Mauer was going to move to first for good at some point.

There are millions of submicroscopic processes that determine if someone is good at baseball. Countless lines of genetic code are formed at the time of egg fertilization, and tiny fluctuations in that code create superior hand-eye coordination, decision-making skills, and bone and muscle structures that crest the curve of the human norm. Mauer had a lot of good things going for him, genetically, when it came to sports. He was a star basketball player in high school and was offered a scholarship to play quarterback at Florida State. If the rumors are to be believed, he struck out only once in his entire high school career. Certainly, there was a lot of hard work and persistence involved, but Mauer's DNA gave him a head start. But it was that same genetic makeup that was a big cause for concern when it came to his place on the diamond.

Mauer is big. He's listed at 6-foot-5, 230 pounds. That's a slightly meaty NBA point guard, for the sake of (a silly) argument. This also makes for a pretty big catcher. It's a considerable amount of weight to support in a crouch, and a fairly long distance to move up and down hundreds of times a game. Catchers just weren't made to be that big. In fact, Mauer holds the record for games caught by a catcher at least 6-foot-5. Only five other catchers of that height have caught even 200 games. If Mauer were a lowly backup who played only once or twice a week, it might not be a big issue. But Mauer should play as much as possible. The Twins want him to play as much as possible. Mauer's legs were the lynchpin. That is, until the end of the 2013 season.

In late 2013, Ike Davis fouled a fastball right off the top of Mauer's helmet. The ricochet carried enough force to send the ball clear over the backstop. Mauer was diagnosed with a concussion and lost more time. Soon thereafter, the Twins threw in the towel. It was announced after the regular season that from that point forward, Mauer would be a first baseman. In just three years, the fans saw the next coming of Johnny Bench turn into an untradeable, power-sapped first baseman who was still owed over a hundred million dollars.

An abdominal strain cost Mauer more than 30 games in 2014, and he hit just a bit better than league average when he did play. In yet another lost season for the Twins, the only guy who was supposed to be any good ended up being a first baseman with a 106 wRC+. This was not how things were supposed to go. This was not what was supposed to happen. Abandon all hope, ye who enter here.

There's a bit of a circular argument to be made when it comes to why sports columnists write what they do. Some are believed to be bringing up serious concerns and legitimate questions. Others are thought just be regurgitating the general ideas and opinions of the fan base looking to seem agreeable. Some have made a living producing counterarguments and blustery takes in hopes of attracting readers on both sides of the arguments. Some are obviously just cashing checks, all semblance of reason and critical thinking absent in their writing.

But the local columns truly had started to reflect a paradigm shift in the city's attitude toward Mauer: He was an overpaid baby who spent too much time on the disabled list and not enough time knocking homers. It is fairly evident, just as an observer in the stands, that some fans have turned on Mauer. Smatterings of boos when he goes to the batters box can escalate in volume if he weakly grounds out to the infield. Their great white hope, their savior from the mire that has been Minnesota sports for the past two decades, has been whittled to a shell of himself. Their big-bopping catcher is now a powerless first baseman who hits .277. The Descension is raining blows on the heads of the masses.

Harmon Killebrew joined the Minnesota Twins in 1954. Since that year, he leads the team in career WAR. Rod Carew comes in second. Joe Mauer is third. Mauer won three batting titles as a catcher, along with three Gold Gloves and an MVP award. He has a career 131 wRC+ having logged most of his time in the most demanding defensive position on the field.

Mauer is from St. Paul. His wife is from St. Paul. They live in the area with their two daughters who are, of course, twins. Mauer could have let his contract run out. He could have bolted for a coastal city with better cities, better weather, or both. Mauer was going to get paid no matter what. He had the gall to choose to get paid by the team that drafted him, the team he watched win two World Series as a boy. He's 31, coming off a brain injury and took his position move without any reported consternation with the front office.

Mauer gets booed at a ballpark about 20 minutes away from where he grew up, a ballpark built with the promise that increased revenue meant higher-profile free agents and the ability to keep the young players they had. Target Field was built so that Johan Santana wouldn't happen again. Mauer was the next logical Santana in that respect. And he stayed. He stayed to get booed in his home town.

I'm not sure where this leaves us as far as Tobias goes. Actually, there are many possible tributaries. More Descension, Ascension, Discovery, Rescue, Escape, Revenge. Mauer could get his retribution in his later years if the Twins ever manage to get their crap together and make a respectable run in the postseason. He could get traded. He simply could have a respectable career and sort of fade away. There are lots of possible outcomes, but there don't seem to be a whole lot in which Mauer turns out to be the hero everyone thought him to be. It's a possibility, certainly. Mauer will play a position that will demand less of him physically. His plate discipline and coordination still should be with him for some time. He yet may have another batting title in him.

Baseball is a sport of patterns. We usually have a pretty good idea of what a player is going to do from one year to the next and through the end of his career. There's a large sample to draw from and make reasonable predictions with. Of course there will be outliers. It happens every year. But, generally, we can look at a player and guess to a reasonable degree of accuracy what's in store the following season.

This essay becomes difficult to wrap up because we're at such a crossroads in the narrative when it comes to Mauer. So many things can happen. But perhaps that's part of the problem. Perhaps the fans and local media are so concerned with what could happen, the focus on what has happened starts to fade. No matter where Mauer goes from here, he's still one of the five most valuable Minnesota Twins of the past 50 years. He still gave a team and a town hope. That smile and those sideburns and those doubles laced to the wall still brought joy to the fans and division titles to the team. Mauer used to be very good at baseball. He may be again. But no future acts will erase what he has done for over a decade. Mauer's current descension may cause dismay. But Descension becomes difficult without a high point from which to begin. Mauer traversed that point for a good deal of time. That might be something useful for booing fans and short-sighted columnists to remember in the future.

An Impostor's Guide to Prospect Analysis

by Carson Cistulli

For two or three years now, FanGraphs CEO David Appelman and managing editor Dave Cameron have allowed me to write at some length about prospects—in particular fringe types of prospects—despite my having little in the way of qualifications for the role besides an abiding enthusiasm for the subject and an internet connection. Perhaps accidentally, or perhaps for some other reasons, my investigations into the minor leagues occasionally have yielded positive results. The Fringe Five column at the site, for example, featured discussions about Mookie Betts and Danny Salazar before those players gained more considerable notoriety. Before that, I'd championed the case of Colorado outfielder Charlie Blackmon despite his absence from top-prospect lists. Blackmon hasn't become a star, of course, but he did just produce a league-average baseball season—a non-negligible accomplishment.

In other instances, my causes have acquitted themselves decidedly less well. A search for Chris Balcom-Miller at FanGraphs, for example, returns several articles published by the present author and then also Balcom-Miller's player page—which documents the right hander's inability to escape Double-A. (Although there's still time for him!)

Below, at the request of no one, is a collection of four principles by which I've attempted to abide while examining prospects. Perhaps they are of some use to the reader.

Believe in the Fielding-Independent Numbers—for Pitchers *and* Hitters

Anyone having found his or her way to this book likely already will feel comfortable with the concept of defense- or fielding-independent pitching (FIP), the notion that a pitcher is responsible for run prevention insofar as he can record strikeouts while limiting walks and home runs. Research shows that a pitcher's FIP at any given point is more predictive of his future ERA than his present ERA. And expected FIP (xFIP), which normalizes home runs per fly ball, is even more predictive of future ERA than either ERA or FIP in small samples. FIP, and not ERA, is also the input used at FanGraphs for calculating pitcher WAR—not because pitchers exert zero influence over opponent hits (they almost certainly do exert some influence), but because *how much* influence they exert is uncertain, and it makes sense to calculate WAR based on those aspects of the game we know a pitcher controls. This is important knowledge to have with regard to prospects, because it allows us to weigh more or less heavily certain aspects of a minor leaguer's performance.

Work by Russell Carleton at Baseball Prospectus ("Should I Worry About My Favorite Pitcher?") reveals that while strikeout and walk rates become reliable after about 70 and 170 batters faced, respectively, home-run rate stabilizes only at 1,320 batters faced. As for BABIP, that requires about 2,000 balls in play, or roughly the equivalent of 3,000 batters faced. By way of comparison, consider that David Price led all major-league pitchers in 2014 with just 1,009 batters faced. In other words, even within the context of an entire season, one still can only really "rely" on a pitcher's strikeout and walk rates as indicators of true talent.

The process of estimating a prospect's future value necessarily must begin with an understanding of his present talent. It's not unusual for a prospect to receive attention because he has limited runs in the high minors—or, alternatively, to be dismissed because he's allowed too many. For pitchers, ERA figures have the power to be very convincing, but the influence of chaining and randomness is substantial in even season-long samples. In reality, how many runs a pitcher has allowed, even over the course of an entire season or two, isn't a particularly great indicator of his actual talent.

Consider the case of Mark Appel. Selected first overall by Houston in 2013, Appel recorded strikeout and walk rates of 19.3 percent and 6.4 percent, respectively, against 140 batters at Class-A Quad Cities shortly after being drafted. In 2014, beginning the season with High-A Lancaster, he recorded strikeout and walk rates of 18.4 percent and 5.1 percent, respectively, against 217 batters. Almost identical, those strikeout and walk figures—and over samples, in both cases, that would constitute reliability or something close to it. Yet, while the former performance was generally regarded as an acceptable debut effort, there was considerably more hand-wringing about the latter. The reason: Appel recorded a 3.82 ERA in the former instance and a 9.74 ERA in the latter.

The Astros responded in curious fashion—namely, by promoting Appel to Double-A Corpus Christi. It's fair to say that the move wasn't universally heralded. Indeed, as reported by the *Houston Chronicle's* Jose de Jesus Ortiz via a series of late-July Tweets, there were multiple players within the actual Astros organization who weren't particularly happy about it. Among those who saw some logic in the promotion—like Matt Snyder of CBS Sports and Mark Townsend of Yahoo!—their arguments pointed to Appel's draft pedigree. Wrote Townsend, for instance:

> *Mark Appel is different, because he is a former No. 1 pick. There's more pressure on him to reach his potential, and there's more pressure on the Astros to develop that potential. That means he gets more attention on just about every level. That's just the way it is. It isn't necessarily fair to other players, but baseball isn't about being fair, it's about winning, even if a few feelings get hurt along the way.*

More rare than this line of reasoning, so far as I can tell—if it was extant at all—was the suggestion that Appel's numbers actually *supported* the Astros' decision to promote the right hander. Because while, yes, Appel allowed a lot of runs with Lancaster, his numbers didn't necessarily suggest that he would *continue* to allow a lot of runs. And that's really the issue.

In a piece for The Hardball Times from 2012 ("Should we be using ERA estimators during the season?"), Glenn DuPaul found that, when attempting to estimate a pitcher's second-half ERA based on his first-half numbers, it was strikeout-and-walk differential [(K-BB)/IP]—more than ERA or FIP or xFIP—that provided the most accurate results. As DuPaul notes, there's actually a metric, kwERA, popularized by Tom Tango, that utilizes merely strikeout and walk rate as the inputs. The equation in full is as follows: 5.40 - [12 * (K% - BB%)]. The constant of 5.40 changes based on run environment, but the core of the formula remains the same. And, in fact, when looking at Appel's kwERA figures from his Class-A and High-A stints, the results are almost identical: 3.85 and 3.80, respectively. Stripping away the noisier elements of run prevention (home-run rate and batting average on balls in play), one finds that Appel was almost the exact same pitcher as he'd been the summer before.

Appel's performance at Double-A after his promotion appears to support the Astros' decision, and the notion that Appel's strikeout-walk differential was likely to be the most predictive element of his High-A line. Over 39.0 innings (165 batters faced) with Corpus Christi, Appel recorded strikeout and walk rates of 23.0 percent and 7.9 percent, respectively, producing a 3.69 ERA—which is to say, much different from his California League ERA but very similar to his California League kwERA.

Here's a table of Appel's most relevant numbers from these three levels:

Mark Appel's Minor League Statistics, 2013-2014										
Season	Level	G	GS	IP	TBF	K%	BB%	ERA	FIP	kwERA
2013	A	8	8	33.0	140	19.3%	6.4%	3.82	3.40	3.85
2014	A+	12	12	44.1	217	18.4%	5.1%	9.74	5.32	3.80
2014	AA	7	6	39.0	165	23.0%	7.9%	3.69	2.99	3.59

Note that, while the ERA and FIP numbers fluctuate wildly, the kwERA figures have remained rather consistent for Appel from level to level. This doesn't negate the reality of the many hits and home runs Appel allowed in the California League. He allowed them, surely, and it's possible he really was throwing the ball poorly when he did. What the sample-size research suggests, though, is that disaster outings like those suffered by Appel—if they're due largely to BABIP and home-run concession above and beyond league averages—likely aren't predictive of future troubles in those same areas, regardless of how real they seem in the moment.

Up to this point, I've discussed the utility of fielding-independent numbers with regard to pitchers exclusively; however, the same principles apply to hitters, as well, even if the precise details are different. Just as with pitching metrics, so, too, do hitting metrics begin to stabilize in differently sized samples. Once again, Russell Carleton's work ("It's a Small Sample Size After All") is of considerable help here. Just as with pitchers, hitters' strikeout and walk rates become reliable rather quickly—in 60 and 120 plate appearances, respectively. Unlike with pitchers, however, hitters exhibit a signature home-run rate in relatively few plate appearances, as well—about 170 of them, according to Carleton's findings.

Unlike these three-true-outcome metrics, a player's traditional slash stats require quite a bit more time to become reliable, largely due to the substantial sample size required for BABIP to stabilize—roughly 820 balls in play, according to Carleton, or about 1,200 plate appearances, on average. One finds, by way of comparison, that Ian Kinsler led all major leaguers in 2014 with 726 plate appearances—so, about 400-500 short of the threshold at which BABIP becomes reliable. A season isn't enough, in other words.

This isn't to suggest players don't possess actual batted-ball skills. Indeed, there absolutely *is* such a thing as a true-talent BABIP. Research shows that athletic hitters with above-average bat speed (like Josh Hamilton and Matt Kemp, for example) are more likely to produce BABIPs better than league average. Meanwhile, slow-footed hitters with fly-ball approaches (such as Edwin Encarnacion) or those who just lack physical strength (middle infielders you've never heard of who are playing at Triple-A) produce BABIPs worse than average. All that said, detecting BABIP skill from even a full-season's worth of just quantitative data isn't really a possibility.

Trust the Projections (Mostly)

Seattle shortstop Chris Taylor was omitted from every notable top-100 prospect list (or the equivalent) entering the 2014 season. The Steamer projection system, meanwhile, rated him as a two-win player per 550 plate appearances, one of the most optimistic projections among all rookie-eligible players in baseball. Why Taylor was omitted from the aforementioned top-100 lists is a discussion for a different time. The people who compose such lists—FanGraphs' Kiley McDaniel, for example, along with the editors of *Baseball America*, Keith Law, John Sickels, etc.—are uniformly more knowledgeable than I am and (simply by publishing such lists) more courageous. It's possible Taylor's long-term outlook is a poor one. It's possible that his low-ish ceiling renders his overall future value relatively low.

That said, a 23-year-old whose most likely outcome (according to the projections) is a league-average season represents a major asset to a club. A win is worth about $6 million on the open market. A player who can account for two of them at a cost of just $500,000 represents nearly $12 million of surplus value. In short, this is a sort of prospect who deserves *some* kind of attention, insofar as he's capable of doing something (i.e. producing wins at a league-average rate) that has evaded the capabilities of decidedly more celebrated prospects like Lastings Milledge, Jesus Montero, Travis Snider, Brandon Wood and Delmon Young.

Following a late-July promotion to the Mariners, Taylor produced a 1.4 WAR in 151 plate appearances with the parent club, recording a batting line slightly better than league average while also playing average-or-better shortstop defense. Given his batting line was aided by a .398 BABIP, that's very likely a higher rate of wins than Taylor is capable of producing in the immediate future. Still, his contributions to the Mariners—in light of that club's near-success in qualifying for the postseason—were important. And anyone willing to trust the projections likely wasn't surprised by Taylor's performance.

A number of studies have been published on the efficacy of projections, but none more recent or convincing than a pair of June blog posts by Mitchel Lichtman at his blog, MGL on Baseball. The ideal thing to do would be merely to produce the entirety of them ("What can a player's season-to-date performance tell us beyond his up-to-date projection?" and "Mid-season projections part II – Pitchers") right here. In lieu of that, however, below is an excerpt that details the results of hot and cold batters after three months into the season, comparing the ability of those players' to date and projected wOBAs to predict their respective rest-of-season performances.

Lichtman writes:

> *About half into the season, around 9% of all qualified (50 PA per month) players were hitting 40 points or less than their projections in an average of 271 PA. Their collective projection was .334 and their actual performance after 3 months and 271 PA was .283. Basically, these guys, despite being supposed league-average full-time players, stunk for 3 solid months. Surely, they would stink, or at least not be up to "par," for the rest of the season. After all, wOBA at least starts to "stabilize" after almost 300 PA, right? Well, these guys, just like the "cold" players after one month, hit .335 for the remainder of the season, 1 point better than their projection. So after 1 month or 3 months, their season-to-date performance tells us nothing that our up-to-date projection doesn't tell us. A player is expected to perform at his projected level regardless of his current season performance after 3 months, at least for the "cold" players. What about the "hot" ones, you know, the ones who may be having a breakout season?*
>
> *There were also about 9% of all qualified players who were having a "hot" first half. Their collective projection was .339, and their average performance was .391 after 275 PA. How did they hit the remainder of the season? .346, 7 points better than their projection and 45 points worse than their actual performance.*

Lichtman finds that, even after three months of play, a player's projected wOBA—regardless of whether his performance to date has been wildly above or below it—remains entirely indicative of his likely performance for the rest of the season. Elsewhere over the course of the two posts, he publishes similar findings for pitchers, as well. The conclusion from Lichtman's work: Even in those cases in which a player's dismal performance might really seem to indicate he's messed up, that's probably not the case.

Of course, there's a leap involved between a projection based on a relatively robust major-league resume and one that's extrapolated from minor-league performance. In reality, it's merely a question of understanding context. In 2009, Matt Holliday moved from a huge run environment in the National League (Colorado) to a much lower run environment in the more difficult American League (Oakland) to a combination of the two (St. Louis). While his raw numbers were expected to change significantly, that sort of thing had little to no bearing on Holliday's underlying talents. He was an above-average hitter in Colorado and then remained one in Oakland and St. Louis.

Projections systems like Steamer and ZiPS are adept at translating the numbers from one park or league to another by means of calculating the changes in performances that other, earlier players have exhibited when moving between parks and leagues. The context changes; the player, not so much. In this way, producing a projection for a minor-league player is, at its core, mostly a matter of understanding the context for the minor league in question. Because a number of players have moved from Double-A or Triple-A (or Japan or even Cuba) to the majors, it's possible to make reasonable assumptions about the ways their numbers will change now.

But Don't Ignore the Scouting Reports (Obviously)

Performance in the minor leagues ought not be ignored. But it's also essential to remember what one is attempting to assess ultimately is *not* how a pitcher or hitter will perform against other Double- or Triple-A players but against major leaguers. And while it's possible, merely from the numbers, to make certain reasonable assumptions about how a player's skills will translate from the minor to major leagues, it's also essential to complement that with information about *how* he's producing the numbers he's producing.

Consider, by way of example, the case of David Hernandez. A mostly effective reliever for Arizona as a major leaguer, Hernandez was among the minor leagues' most dominant starters as a younger player. In 2007, with the Orioles' Carolina League affiliate Frederick, Hernandez led all pitchers at High-A with 168 strikeouts and was second among qualifiers with a 27.0 percent strikeout rate. The next season, he performed a nearly identical feat, once again leading his level—in this case all Double-A—with 166 strikeouts and also leading all qualified pitchers at that level with a 27.7 percent strikeout rate.

Strikeout rate, in addition to becoming reliable rather quickly, is also the metric (as compared to other defense-independent numbers like walk rate or groundball rate) that most highly correlates with run prevention. Insofar as he was leading everyone by that measurement and was about an average age for his levels (22 and 23 years old, respectively, at High- and Double-A), it would follow that Hernandez would be a favorite to prevent runs at the highest level, too.

And yet, even following consecutive seasons in which he'd led his level in strike-outs, the reports on Hernandez were lukewarm entering the 2009 season. He was ranked seventh on Kevin Goldstein's organizational prospect list for the Orioles at Baseball Prospectus, ninth on John Sickels' version of that same thing, and omitted entirely from *Baseball America's* top-10 list for the Orioles.

The reason for the disparity between the seeming dominance of Hernandez's minor-league track record and the relatively unenthusiastic outlook for him lay in the scouting reports of those who'd seen Hernandez. He was rated as possessing the best slider in the Orioles system after both the 2007 and 2008 season, but his third pitch—a change-up—was a matter of debate. Kevin Goldstein wrote that it was "a below-average pitch that scouts rarely get to see" and "he's clearly uncomfortable with the offering."

The change-up, of course, is the pitch that is most useful for neutralizing an opposite-handed batter's platoon advantage. A pitcher with a good enough slider can live off that pitch in the minor leagues. In the majors, however, having no means to counter opposite-handed hitters is a real problem, and one that will get a pitcher sent to the bullpen pretty quickly.

This was the prognosis regarding Hernandez: That he was a right-hander with a repertoire suited for dealing only with other right-handers. And following his promotion to the major leagues, the reality of that prognosis was evident. Following a series of impressive starts at Triple-A to begin the 2009 season, Hernandez was promoted to the majors, where he made 20 appearances for Baltimore, 19 of them starts. Against right-handers, he was competent, recording strikeout and walk rates of 17.3 percent and 7.9 percent, respectively—serviceable numbers, those. Against left-handers, he was less inspiring. Facing 260 left-handed batters, Hernandez produced a strikeout-walk differential of just 1.2 percentage points (12.7 percent K, 11.5 percent BB).

And Remember the Endeavor Is (Pleasantly) Futile

For anyone with aspirations to become an impostor prospect analyst, this is the essential point from which all the other ones must necessarily follow: acknowledging one's contributions to the genre will likely be ignored, or at least deserve to be. Accordingly, an awareness of one's own limitations is of some importance. In the grand scheme of things, there's little to be lost from constantly underestimating and/or playing down the extent of one's own talents. The worst-case scenario for doing so is that one is merely remembered for his humility. Or maybe the alternative seems worse: not to be remembered at all—not, in fact, to be known in the first place (making it impossible to be forgotten later on).

It's a natural but also illogical compulsion, this always wanting one's opinions to be heard and to last. And yet the effects of that compulsion are evident to anyone who's consumed more than 30 seconds of cable news television or read even one tweet ever. Hot takes, served up hot, abound.

I say it's illogical to want one's pronouncements to last, because they won't (last, that is)—even if they *are* heard in the first place. (Which, they're generally not. Generally, they serve as a pretense for an interlocutor to espouse his *own* frothing opinions).

In New Hampshire, I live near an unkempt cemetery at which the last corpse was interred probably about 100 years ago. While, at some point in the past, the sons and daughters and grandchildren of the deceased buried there must have visited this space with some regularity, the only visitors now are either those (like me) with a passing morbid curiosity or, otherwise, teenagers trying to drink and smoke in relative peace.

This cemetery provides a concise lesson on the futility of our endeavors. At some point in the past, all its current residents were living people whose efforts helped, in one way or another, to build a small New England town. Now, those same people are dead—and not just dead, but (as the absence of loving visitors suggests) forgotten. Perhaps the institutions they helped create remain intact. Even so, their specific contributions are lost.

This conversation might seem to have little bearing on an article about prospect analysis. The point I'm hoping to communicate is this, however: We're all idiots. That's not to say there aren't those among us with a certain amount of expertise. For example, my colleague at FanGraphs, Kiley McDaniel, does excellent and thorough work. That said, no one who writes about prospects is more clear about how little we can know about them. On the weekly podcast we record together, McDaniel has more than once noted that even at the very top of each club's amateur scouting departments, there's little consensus about which amateur players will and won't succeed.

What else I hope to convey is that merely because we're idiots, that's hardly a reason not to find some pleasure in the examination of baseball prospects, provided that examination—and the conclusions we reach from it—are conducted in a spirit of good-natured inquiry.

References & Resources

- Russell Carleton, Baseball Prospectus, "Baseball Therapy: Should I Worry About My Favorite Pitcher?" *baseballprospectus.com/article.php?articleid=20516*
- Mark Townsend, Yahoo! Sports Big League Stew, "Astros players upset about Mark Appel's promotion, special bullpen session," *sports.yahoo.com/blogs/big-league-stew/astros-players-react-unfavorably-to-mark-appel-s-promotion--special-bullpen-session-180526499.html*

- Glenn DuPaul, The Hardball Times, "Should we be using ERA estimators during the season?," *hardballtimes.com/should-we-be-using-era-estimators*
- Russell Carleton, Baseball Prospectus, "Baseball Therapy: It's a Small Sample Size After All," *baseballprospectus.com/article.php?articleid=17659*
- Mitchel Lichtman, MGL on Baseball, "What can a player's season-to-date performance tell us beyond his up-to-date projection?," *mglbaseball.wordpress.com/2014/06/12/what-can-a-players-season-to-date-performance-tell-us-beyond-his-up-to-date-projection*
- Mitchel Lichtman, MGL on Baseball, "Mid-season projections part II – Pitchers," *mglbaseball.wordpress.com/2014/06/13/mid-season-projections-part-ii-pitchers*

The Year The Money Stood Still

by Dave Cameron

The 2014 season will be remembered for a number of memorable events: Derek Jeter's farewell tour, the Royals' remarkable postseason run, and five months of complete domination by Clayton Kershaw stand out as stories that captured the game's attention. However, perhaps the most interesting baseball development of 2014 flew a bit under the radar. For those of us intrigued by the economics of the sport, we may remember 2014 as the year when money didn't matter at all.

Okay, that last comment is a bit of hyperbole. I want you to keep reading this article, and I'm pretty sure the word economics just threatened to scare half of you away, so forgive the blatant attempt to grab your attention with a strong opener. But even if you're not an economics nerd, and you're more into the part of baseball that involves the bat and ball than the side dealing with signing bonuses and the luxury tax, the story is still pretty interesting, because the two parts of baseball are intricately related.

Without this shift in the economic model, perhaps we don't get Kansas City's remarkable October. The basic principles of spending in the majors even five years ago might have prevented the Royals from even reaching the postseason, but the economics of the sport in 2014 were quite a bit different from what we've seen in prior seasons.

What economic shift? The one where a team's payroll and their win total stopped being related to each other. The most common way to measure the relationship of two variables is to run a correlation between them. When discussing the relationship between wins and salaries in the majors, the easiest calculation is found by running a correlation between team winning percentage and team payroll, and for 2014, the correlation between those two numbers was 0.27, a relationship much closer to the point where the data sets had nothing to do with each other than the point at which the two variables moved in perfect unison. Historically speaking, this number is quite low.

In a fantastic 2012 piece on the website that shares a name with the book you currently are reading, entitled "Money and Wins," Dave Studeman plotted the history of this correlation since the beginning of free agency in 1976. In the early days of free agency, the Phillies and Yankees exploited their new-found ability to buy up the league's best players, building very strong rosters in the process. The correlation between winning percentage and team payroll jumped up to 0.7 in 1977 and climbed to nearly 0.8 the following year. Here is the chart Studes used in his piece a couple of years ago.

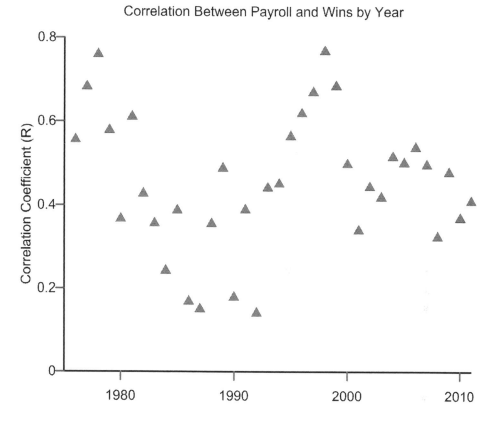

Correlation Between Payroll and Wins by Year

The late '70s and late '90s saw remarkably strong relationships between wins and dollars spent, and not surprisingly, these were eras when the Yankees padded their championship totals. The mid-'80s and early '90s saw a downturn for the Bronx Bombers, and not coincidentally, the lowest correlations between wins and payroll we've seen in the free-agent era. You know what also happened in the mid-1980s? Baseball owners colluded to drive salaries down by agreeing not to sign other teams' free agents, an anti-trust violation that eventually would see them settle for $280 million after the Player's Association filed multiple grievances over their actions.

In other words, since free agency began, we've only ever seen this low of a relationship between wins and dollars in the days when owners were actively agreeing not to sign each other's free agents. Given the amount of free agent spending we saw last winter—headlined by the Mariners giving Robinson Cano $240 million to lure him out of New York—we can say with some confidence that we haven't entered another era of collusion, or at the very least, if teams are conspiring to drive down player salaries, they're being a lot less obvious about it this time.

After nearly 30 years, we've seen that a normal non-collusive environment has a correlation between wins and payroll of around 0.4 to 0.5 in most seasons, with occasional spikes when the Yankees' spending sprees go well. This year, the Yankees' spending spree did not go well, and they were joined by high-priced failures in Boston, Philadelphia, Texas and Toronto. The inability of these teams to win with top-10 payrolls was the primary driver of the 0.27 correlation we saw this year.

The average winning percentage for a team in the top 10 in payroll this year was just .521, which translates to 84 wins over a 162-game season. In 2004, to pick a year that represented something like a normal historical relationship, the average winning percentage for a team in the top 10 in payroll was .569, or 92 wins per 162 games. Nine of the top 10 teams in 2004 spending finished with winning records. In fact, every big-spending team except the Mets finished with at least 86 wins that year. Spending a lot of money never has guaranteed a championship, but it used to provide a pretty solid foundation on which to stand.

So what changed? Well, for starters, the big dogs aren't spending as much as they used to. The biggest spenders of 2014, the Los Angeles Dodgers, had a payroll of $236 million, up about $53 million over the largest payroll in our example year of 2004. However, the average payroll has risen much faster than the top payrolls, so the spread in spending actually has been shrinking.

In every year from 2004 to 2010, the Yankees not only had the highest payroll in baseball in each season, but their budget was always at least three standard deviations above the mean; in 2005, it was nearly four standard deviations above the league average. Here is a table of the last decade for the top spender in the majors, and its number of standard deviations from the mean.

Top MLB Payroll Compared to Mean, 2005-2014		
Year	Team	Standard Deviations
2005	Yankees	3.94
2006	Yankees	3.63
2007	Yankees	3.15
2008	Yankees	3.15
2009	Yankees	3.41
2010	Yankees	3.01
2011	Yankees	2.67
2012	Yankees	2.71
2013	Yankees	2.71
2014	Dodgers	2.76

Put simply, the top teams just aren't outspending the rest of the league like they used to. The Dodgers' jump to the top spot actually hides the massive year-to-year drop by the Yankees, as their payroll was 2.04 standard deviations above the mean, a shockingly low number given their recent history.

Certainly, there's still a gap between the haves and have-lesses, but it's not as large as it used to be. And it very well might shrink again next year, as the Dodgers' hiring of Andrew Friedman—who made his bones running a lean and mean payroll for the have-less Tampa Bay Rays—suggests they might be more interested in pursuing an efficient spending path rather than continuing to pay significant luxury tax penalties going forward. Reckless spending is going out of style in major league baseball.

And perhaps this shouldn't be a huge surprise, given that it just hasn't worked lately. The Yankees' championship in 2009 wasn't just their only World Series title in the last decade; it was their only appearance in the Fall Classic since the start of the 2004 season. That's one World Series appearance in an 11-year window for a team that went six times in the eight-year span from 1996 to 2003, winning four championships in the process.

Major League Baseball is a copycat league, and the classic Yankees model hasn't resulted in many parades lately. Even Boston's 2013 World Series championship came in a season in which it slashed their Opening Day payroll by over $20 million, spending only $47 million more than the average payroll in the process. Even the most recent example of a rich team winning came in the year in which they acted the least like a rich team.

Perhaps just as notable, however, are the structural changes to the playoff system that MLB introduced in 2012. The addition of a second wild card immediately devalued a fourth-place finish, essentially halving the odds of the best division losers winning the championship, forcing them to play an extra elimination game in order to run the table. The second wild card incentivizes teams to stay in the race and make a run at a playoff spot that didn't exist before, but it also removed a safety net for a big spender, changing the value proposition associated with spending more money.

The randomness of the postseason rarely has been on display as much as it was in 2014, and playoff expansion only serves to make it less likely that a top-spending team will walk away with a World Series title in a given year. As recently as 1993, only four of the 28 major league franchises qualified for the postseason; now, we are up to 10 out of 30. Growing the postseason not only increases motivation for middle-tier teams to continue contending, it reduces the motivation for the top-tier teams to improve their rosters. With a more random postseason, building a behemoth just isn't as likely to result in a parade, and the expanded playoffs have shifted the goal toward being decent more frequently rather than cycling between greatness and rebuilding.

Of course, these aren't the only explanations that have been put forward for the decrease in correlation between wins and payroll. Brian McPherson of the *Providence Journal* explored this issue in August, hypothesizing that in addition to flattened spending, PED testing also removed many of the old-but-remarkably-productive veterans from the game, shifting the emphasis back towards younger talent.

Because young talent isn't available in free agency, high-revenue teams can't buy it up as easily—especially with the new limitations on spending in the draft and for international signings—and eliminating an entire class of market-priced producers is more likely to harm big spenders than teams that couldn't afford many free agents to begin with.

There is some evidence to support this idea. In 2001, generally considered to be something close to the peak of the "Steroid Era," players age 36 and older combined to produce 85 wins above replacement (WAR), with a 45/40 split among position players and pitchers. In 2014, this same age group combined for 19 WAR, with a -1.5/20 split between batters and pitchers.

In 2001, batters age 36 or older combined for 15,329 plate appearances and produced a combined weighted runs created plus (wRC+) of 102, making them slightly above average at the plate. In 2014, batters age 36 or older combined for 8,162 plate appearances and produced a combined wRC+ of 80, making them the offensive equivalent of a decent backup shortstop. Not only do we have roughly half as many plate appearances going to older hitters, the ones that are left can't hit anymore.

However, before we entirely accept this theory, we should note that baseball's Joint Drug Agreement was put in place in 2006, but older hitters were still roughly as effective in 2010 as they were in 2001; just five years ago, hitters 36 and older combined for a 99 wRC+ and 33 WAR in 13,054 plate appearances. If we're going to accept that the decrease in old-hitter production is due to PED testing, we have to explain why it took nearly a decade to weed these players out of the league.

I do think PED testing has had a disproportionately negative effect on older players, and perhaps the removal of those players from the sport has made it more difficult to buy wins in free agency. However, compared to the tightening gap in team spending and the structural changes in the sport designed to increase league parity, I would guess that PED testing has played a more minor role in this shift.

Bud Selig made competitive balance a primary point of his reign as commissioner and spent the better part of two decades talking about baseball's need to level the playing field between teams. In his final year in office, after years of tinkering with different mechanics designed to deflate the advantages of the richest teams, Major League Baseball saw the fulfillment of these hopes, at least for a year.

The Yankees, Dodgers, and other big-market teams still have dramatic advantages, but at least for this year, these advantages didn't seem to matter all that much. If these results really were the product of the expanded postseason, increased television revenues for all teams, and PED testing, then Selig may very well have capped off his tenure by helping to create the most level playing field baseball has seen in a very long time.

References & Resources

- Dave Studeman, The Hardball Times, "Money and Wins," *hardballtimes.com/money-and-wins*
- Brian MacPherson, *Providence Journal*, "Money can't buy success for MLB teams anymore," *providencejournal.com/sports/red-sox/content/20140825-money-can-t-buy-success-for-mlb-teams-anymore.ece*
- Phil Birnbaum, Phil Birnbaum Sabermetric Research Blog, "Is MLB team payroll less important than it used to be?," *blog.philbirnbaum.com/2014/08/is-mlb-team-payroll-less-important-than.html*

History

The Strikeout Ascendant (and What Should Be Done About It)

by Steve Treder

Major league baseball fans in 2014 witnessed something historic: A batter was more likely to strike out this year than in any other season in the long history of the sport, at a rate of 7.70 times per team per game.

Now, before we congratulate ourselves on having been present at some particularly rare event, let's bear in mind that the whiff rate of 2014 broke the previous record that had been set way back in…2013. And the 2013 record broke the all-time high-water mark achieved in 2012. Which had smashed the standard set in, yes, 2011…and so on. Indeed, an all-time strikeout frequency record has been set in *every* major league season since 2008.

That 2008 rate (6.77) eclipsed the record that had stood for an epoch of… seven years. The 2001 mark (6.67) beat the record set in 1997 (6.60), which was the culmination of another little stretch of year-in-and-year-out strikeout record-setting that encompassed 1994, 1995 and 1996 as well as '97. It isn't until we get back to that 1994 record (6.18) that we finally find one breaking a previous record that had stood for a long time: since 1967, when batters whiffed at a rate of 5.99 per team per game.

Thus, what we've seen in 2014 isn't something unique to this year; rather it's the continuation (though, perhaps also the acceleration) of a historic trend that's been rolling along for two decades.

Why is this happening? And what would the (apparently likely) extension of this tidal wave of Ks into the future mean for the sport? To answer these questions, we need to understand how it is that we got here. So let's embark on a little history of strike three.

For comparative purposes, it makes sense to begin our tour not in the dim original mists of 1869 or 1876, but rather at the point of physical placement of the key protagonists (batter and pitcher) that still abides: 1893, when the distance between home plate and the pitching rubber was set at 60 feet, six inches.

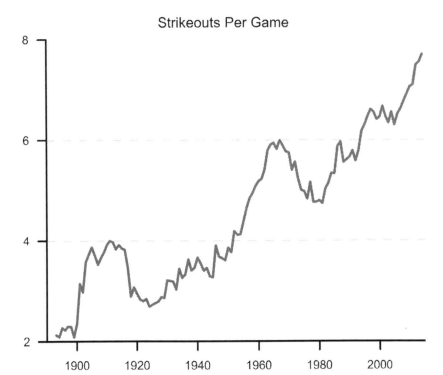

Strikeouts Per Game

In Figure 1, we see the annual rate of major league strikeouts per team/game from 1893 through the present day. What becomes clear right away is that the long-term trend is distinctly upward. Thus, the first conclusion we can draw is that whatever fundamental structural push that's currently driving strike three to become more commonplace isn't new, but is instead something of an eternal fact of baseball life.

But that isn't all we see. It's also clear that this long-scale effect hasn't held a constant pace. In addition to minor year-to-year up-and-down fluctuation, history has presented a couple of fairly long periods in which the strikeout rate stabilized at nearly imperceptible incremental growth. And, most interestingly, we see that in opposition to the overall rise, there have been two episodes of distinct decrease in K rate, the first occurring in the late 1910s/early 1920s, and the second from the late 1960s to the mid-1980s.

We know, of course, that in baseball (as in all the rest of the world), change is the only constant. Changes in playing conditions, rules, tactics and strategies have always been afoot. Let's examine the strikeout rate through the various eras within the context of particular conditions, rules, tactics and strategies, as well as within the context of the other key outcomes to which strikeouts relate: runs, hits, home runs and bases on balls.

1893-1919: The K Rises, then Falls

The term "Dead Ball Era" is generally meant to describe the period from 1901 through 1919. While mostly correct in associating a light-hitting, low-scoring mode of play with the softer rubber-centered baseball, in fact, the cork-centered "lively" baseball was introduced in 1911, and moreover, the rubber-centered "dead" ball was in use during the very high-scoring 1890s. So it's clear that while the resilience of the ball itself was a factor in determining the way the game was played, other issues were important, as well.

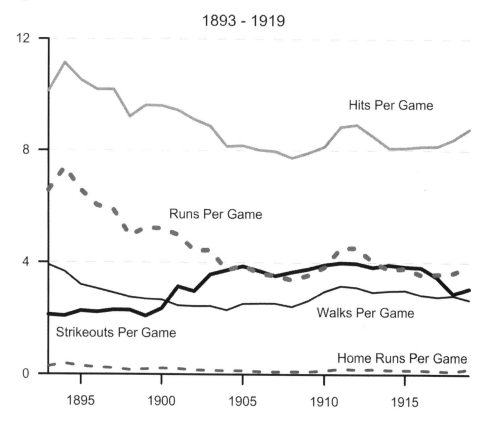

1893 - 1919

The major factor causing the drop in hitting and scoring and the sudden rise in strikeouts that took place in the earliest years of the 1900s was the adoption of the foul-strike rule (in 1901 in the National League, and 1903 in the American). But we see that following the stratospheric peak of 1894, hitting and scoring had been in decline across the 1890s, while strikeouts had been holding steady at the very low rate of just over two per game. So it's evident that general improvement in pitching technique (as pitchers adapted to the 60-foot, six-inch distance) as well as, especially, fielding (including gloves and positioning/relay tactics, reacting to the harder-hit-ball environment) were already underway before scoring fully hit bottom.

But one thing held steady through this entire era: home runs were extremely rare. The heavy hitting of the 1890s was contact-oriented, with lots of singles, doubles and triples, but few homers; through the entire decade only one batter hit as many as 20 in a season (Buck Freeman with 25 in 1899). The intermittent bump in hitting and scoring that accompanied the arrival of the cork-centered ball in 1911-12 was propelled by line drives, not big flies, and as pitchers re-established dominance across the 1910s (by ardently exploiting the spitball and other foreign substances, and also by more liberal deployment of relievers) the home run remained an extremely infrequent outcome.

And neither did the strikeout become common. After the big jump in the early 1900s, strikeouts stabilized at just under four per game and held steady until the late 1910s; interestingly, through those years a strikeout was just about exactly as likely (or unlikely) an occurrence as a run. For all its turbulence, from the beginning of this period through its end, one batting ethos remained dominant: to strike out was to utterly fail. Putting the ball in play was always the primary objective.

Fielding, despite its improvements, remained difficult, with bumpy fields and rudimentary gloves, so to fail to challenge fielders was to give the defense just what it wanted. And, in a circumstance with the home run nearly absent, long-sequence offense was the only way to generate runs, so the cost of a strikeout was additionally magnified. All of the most celebrated star hitters of this period, from Billy Hamilton and Ed Delahanty, to Nap Lajoie and Honus Wagner, to Ty Cobb and Joe Jackson and so on, shared a single characteristic: They almost never struck out. A very small number of hapless early 1900s batters struck out as many as 100 times in a season; they were the furthest thing from hitting stars, and most soon washed out of the majors.

At the very end of this era, a curious thing happened. In 1918-19, the strikeout rate suddenly dropped. There is no ready explanation for it, as the big rules/conditions changes that would begin in 1920 hadn't yet occurred. Perhaps in some mysterious way it had to do with the shortened season schedules caused by World War I, or perhaps it was just a bizarre fluke, or perhaps the boom in hitting success that we always consider as having begun in 1920 was actually somehow getting a head start. For whatever reason, batters struck out more rarely in 1918 and 1919 than they had since 1902.

1920-1945: The K at Rest

Starting in 1920, of course, the baseball world fundamentally changed. The causes began with the ball itself, in two definite ways, and perhaps a third. First, the spitball and all other ball-doctoring techniques were outlawed. Second (as a means of enforcing the first, and also as a means of making the game safer following the beaning death of Ray Chapman), any scratched or stained ball was removed from the game and a fresh white replacement introduced. And third, new ball-stitching yarn was introduced in 1920, and this (though it's debated) in combination with more modern manufacturing methods yielded a more tightly-wound, and thus harder, ball.

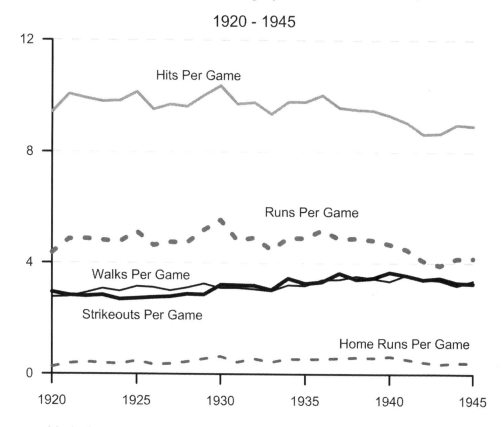

With the baseball easier to see and to hit hard, batters went to town. Leading the charge, as everyone knows, was the spectacular Babe Ruth. His towering success is often said to have convinced everyone else to eschew the traditional choke-up-and-put-it-in-play approach and swing for the fences, and while there's some truth to that, in fact, the freewheeling slugger remained a rarity through the 1920s and '30s. The great majority of hitters maintained a contact-focused approach. The main difference from the pre-1920 period is that with that the ball more readily squared up, batters just generally found more success.

The Babe never struck out as many as 100 times (his high was 93), but he fanned a lot relative to his peers, leading the league in strikeouts five times and finishing second in seven additional seasons. Several other prominent power hitters, following Ruth's lead, belted lots of home runs while striking out far more than any star before 1920. These included Hack Wilson, Jimmie Foxx, Hank Greenberg and Dolph Camilli; the latter three all tallied seasons exceeding 100 Ks yet were celebrated nonetheless.

Still, though the long ball was far more frequent than before 1920, the typical team was hitting a home run only about once every two games. This era's high scoring was mostly a product of lots of singles, doubles and triples. Strikeouts were down from their 1905-1917 peak, but they bottomed out in the mid-1920s and rose only slightly thereafter. Through this entire period of remarkable overall stability, strikeouts were always just about exactly as common as walks and never approached as many as four per game.

As the 1930s gave way to the 1940s, hitting and scoring declined. This was mostly a function of the inferior-quality baseball being used during World War II (effectively, a return to the "dead" ball), but the fact that the decline started before 1942 indicates it was more than that. Probably the major cause was the introduction of night baseball beginning in 1935; though night games were still rare, primitive lighting systems provided poor visibility and clearly favored pitchers.

An interesting figure in these years was Vince DiMaggio. Like his superstar brother, Vince was a top-notch defensive center fielder, but that's where the similarities ended. Joltin' Joe DiMaggio, though he hit with terrific power, was extremely old-school in that he practically never struck out. Vince, on the other hand, fanned with great regularity: He reached the century mark in Ks four times, and his 1938 total of 134 set a record that would stand for nearly 20 years.

Vince DiMaggio was no superstar. He had good power, but his batting average was poor. Yet unlike earlier journeymen with high strikeout totals, Vince D. was allowed to stay in the majors (perhaps because of his last name) and was deployed as a regular in eight seasons, while leading the league in Ks six times. He may be seen as an indicator of a new tolerance for the strikeout. Putting up stat lines that were strange at the time but would be considered normal today, he was a harbinger.

1946-1972: The K Comes of Age

The 1947 season is often described as the beginning of modern major league baseball, because racial integration began then. Certainly that's a valid point. But beyond the issue of who was allowed to play, the period beginning in the late 1940s—and most definitely, the decade of the 1950s—also can be properly comprehended as the beginning of the modern *style* of major league baseball.

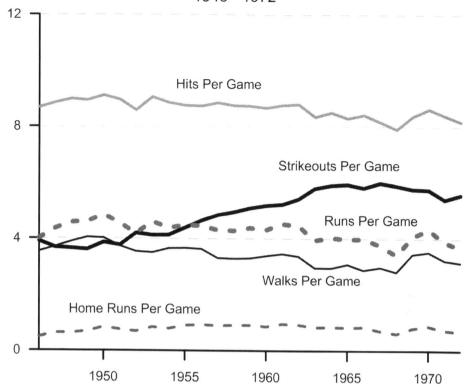

1946 - 1972

Hits Per Game

Strikeouts Per Game

Runs Per Game

Walks Per Game

Home Runs Per Game

No statistic better illuminates the changing mode of play than the strikeout. The new style was power-centered, a game of heightened reward and heightened risk. In 1948 and 1949, the record home run rate was threatened, and then it was shattered in 1950. Newer still home runs-per-game records were established in 1955, 1956, and 1961. In the wake of all this swinging from the heels, batting averages declined, and strikeouts flourished as never before. The strikeouts-per-game record that had stood since 1911 was overtaken in 1952 and then broken again every year from 1955 to 1962. Vince DiMaggio's individual record of 134 strikeouts in a season was broken by Jim Lemon in 1956 (138), and that was eclipsed by Jake Wood in 1961 (141), and that by Harmon Killebrew in 1962 (142).

The causes of this dramatic new phenomenon were several. Fielding efficiency was steadily improving, and hitters were plainly dispensing with the traditional put-it-in-play approach. Pitching staffs were making ever-more sophisticated use of the bullpen, and pitchers working shorter stints worried less about pacing themselves and instead just threw harder. Team management advanced the dynamic, as field managers filled lineups and general managers stocked rosters with more power-oriented hitters, and owners, sensing that fans did indeed dig the long ball, frequently moved outfield fences inward to stimulate home run totals.

Another factor was the changing nature of the athletes themselves. Particularly by the 1960s, arriving on the scene was a generation of young men who'd been raised amid unprecedented abundance, with better nutrition and health than ever before, and they were taller, bigger and stronger than ever before. Stronger hitters were prone to go for the bomb, and stronger, harder-throwing pitchers were prone to exploit this tendency and pitch for the strikeout.

And with all this going on, the Lords of Baseball threw gasoline on the flames with an ill-advised rule change prior to the 1963 season: enlarging the strike zone. The motivation was a desire to shorten the length of games, whose pace had been slowed by deeper counts and more frequent pitching changes. The bigger strike zone succeeded in speeding up the game, but it did so at the expense of batting averages and long-sequence innings. Scoring plummeted and strikeouts soared, with the 1962 K record rate being obliterated in 1963, and that record was surpassed again in 1964, '65 and '67.

The poster player for this era was Dave Nicholson. A big, strong (6-foot-2, 215-pound) right-handed-batting outfielder, Nicholson was signed out of high school in 1958 to a big-bonus contract by the Baltimore Orioles. Confident he would emerge as a slugging star, first the Orioles and then the White Sox gave Nicholson opportunities at the major league level, in which the youngster did indeed deliver home runs, but he was unable to hit for any kind of average, as he struck out at appalling rates. In two trials with Baltimore, Nicholson struck out 131 times in 286 at-bats, and in his one mostly-regular season for the White Sox in 1963, he blew away the record by fanning 175 times in 449 at-bats.

League-wide, by 1968 the shrinking run totals were agreed by all to have reached a crisis. For 1969, the strike zone was returned to its previous dimensions, and the height of the pitching mound was lowered. This yielded immediate scoring improvement along with strikeout reduction. However, the run-production effect was short-lived, as scoring declined from 1970 heights in 1971 and '72, prompting the American League to enact the extreme measure of the designated hitter rule beginning in 1973.

1973-1992: The K Meets Resistance

Removing pitchers from the batters' box in one of the leagues was bound to decrease strikeouts, but it wasn't the only way in which teams endeavored (wittingly or not) to reverse the trend of fewer balls in play. The wave of new ballparks arriving in the 1960s and early '70s tended to have larger outfield dimensions than those they replaced. Moreover, many parks (new and old) deployed artificial turf in this era. The combined effect was to make home runs more difficult to hit and to place a new premium on speed and defensive range. Teams responded by turning back the clock in roster and lineup-management choices, deploying fewer slow-footed sluggers than had become the norm in the 1950s and '60s, and finding more room for faster, slimmer athletes who tended to focus on old-school contact hitting.

The erosion in batting averages was arrested, and despite fewer home runs, scoring stabilized. Not only was the 1967 strikeout peak never approached in the 1970s, strikeout rates following 1972 were similar to those of the late 1950s and very early '60s.

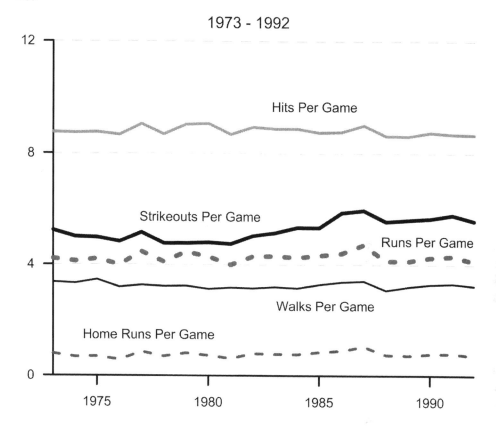

1973 - 1992

But as the 1980s unfolded, very gradually things began to change again. Artificial turf had proven unpopular with players and fans alike, and it was phased out of all but a few stadiums. Playing on grass, teams again felt safe deploying bigger and slower fielders, and hitters, seeing the advantage of upper-body strength, began to favor weight training as never before (and, of course, more than a few sought to optimize the weight training with the use of steroids).

The overall effect was incremental, essentially imperceptible at first, but by the mid-1980s it was apparent that the game was different than it had been in the '70s. Scoring was up only slightly, but the construction of runs was resembling that of the 1950s, as the 1985 home run rate (0.86 per game) had been exceeded only twice since 1962. The revived power game was coming at a price of revived strikeouts, as the rate in both 1984 and '85 was the highest since 1972.

Then in 1986, and especially in 1987, these trends rapidly accelerated. Power hitting and scoring jumped (indeed, in '87 an all-time rate of home runs was achieved, surpassing one per game for the first time), and at the same time strikeouts spiked, very nearly matching the peak rates of the mid-1960s.

It was commonly observed that hitters were achieving their newly shaped success with the apparently inadvertent assistance of umpires, who appeared ever-less willing to call the strike zone as defined in the rule book. Nearly nothing above the belt was a strike (though, curiously, pitches several inches off the plate low and away frequently were).

MLB cracked down prior to the 1988 season, issuing an edict to umpires to enforce the strike zone as the rule book intended or face replacement. Umpires complied, and the result was a sudden return to early-'80s levels of power hitting and scoring. Unable to take and rake with the confidence they'd gained mid-decade, batters struck out slightly less often, though the rate stabilized at a level distinctly higher than that of the 1970s.

Then, suddenly and dramatically, new changes arrived.

1993-2014: The K Triumphant

Exactly why the nature of the game transformed so rapidly beginning in 1993 was hotly debated at the time and has remained so ever since. What's certain is that it was not a single factor but the combination of many.

Hitters suddenly enjoyed success they hadn't known for decades. Scoring reached heights not seen since the 1930s, and the rate of home runs was unprecedented, with new league-wide records being set in 1996, 1999 and 2000. Yet all this raucous bashing was not accompanied by a decline in strikeouts: Instead, as we know, season after season, strike three was occurring at rates never seen before.

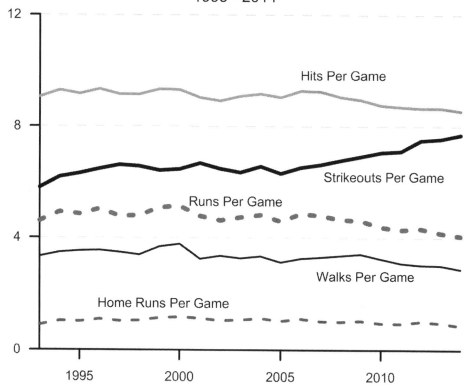

1993 - 2014

Hits Per Game

Strikeouts Per Game

Runs Per Game

Walks Per Game

Home Runs Per Game

It was an altogether new form of baseball. To what degree it was purposefully engineered by MLB (presumably as a means of pleasing fans with an action-packed brand to counteract the depressing effects of the mid-1990s labor strife) is anything but clear. But in any case, the wave of new ballparks coming online as the decade advanced was distinctly hitter-friendly (and significantly, one was at mile-high altitude). And, though it's never been proven, much less admitted as a conscious decision by MLB, it seems nearly obvious that the liveliness of the ball increased beginning in 1993.

It's plainly obvious players were bigger and stronger than ever before, to whatever extent enhanced by steroid use. Added strength helps pitchers at least as much as it does hitters (as it had done in the 1950s and '60s), and the overall effect is more strikeouts along with more power.

Though it didn't capture nearly as much media and fan attention at the time, a key factor fueling the run explosion of the 1990s was a boom in the rate of walks. After having held fairly steady since the re-imposition of the traditional strike zone in 1969, the rate of bases on balls climbed in the 1990s, until in 1999 and 2000 it was approaching an all-time high.

Clearly, this particular phenomenon was not something desired by MLB's brain trust, as following the 2000 season, baseball cracked down on umpires again (as in 1988) to call the strike zone articulated in the rule book. And this time, MLB enforced the edict by introducing an automated system (often referred to as QuesTec, for the company supplying the technology) to measure umpires' strike-calling accuracy and provide objective feedback to them.

The impact of the new strike-calling protocol was immediate and significant. In 2001, the walk rate dropped back to historically normal territory. Though home runs remained at very high levels through the 2000s, and scoring remained quite healthy, the "silly ball" heights of 1999-2000 have never again been reached.

As for the strikeout rate: In 2001, it peaked, and then it dropped a bit and stabilized. But beginning in 2006, it began to climb again and has been climbing ever since into ever-higher record territory.

Significantly, beginning in 2010, the high rates of power hitting and scoring that had been sustained since 1993 began to wane, and walk rates also—gradually but steadily—have dropped. Through 2010, historically high strikeout rates were a feature of a high-scoring environment, but increasingly that's no longer the case. The dynamic currently underway bears more than a little resemblance to that of the mid-1960s.

Yet the shape of the game today is somewhat different from the '60s. Even with the recent decline, today's scoring is slightly higher than it was then, and so is the rate of home runs. But in the mid-'60s, when for the first time strikeouts far surpassed the frequency of runs, they never approached the rate of hits. In the 2010s, strikeouts are not just far more common than runs, they are now approaching the frequency of hits. We're nearing a point at which batters will be more likely to strike out than to reach base with a hit, a situation quite unlike anything ever imagined in history.

And today's strikeouts don't occur evenly throughout the game. Modern starting pitchers, though they fan more batters than they used to, are the least likely on the staff to rack up strike three, so hitters manage to put the ball in play with something comparable to historically normal frequency through the fifth or sixth inning. But once the starter is out (which he almost always is, rarely later than the seventh), a parade of relievers marches in, each working an extremely short stint. Most throw extremely hard (virtually every bullpen now includes multiple relievers who routinely exceed 95 mph), and produce strikeout rates never seen before.

For many decades, relievers have produced greater strikeout rates than starters, and in the modern era, relievers' increasing share of the innings load increases the impact of this effect. To illustrate: In 1954, relief pitchers worked 26.8 percent of the innings and contributed 28 percent of all strikeouts. By 1984, they were up to 30.1 percent of the innings and 32.7 percent of the Ks. And in 2014, relievers handled 33.5 percent of the innings and produced 36.7 percent of the strikeouts. Thus, today's strike threes are rarely achieved by heroic stars along the lines of Bob Feller, Nolan

Ryan or Randy Johnson, and instead are commonly recorded by essentially anonymous, replaceable relief pitchers who come and go from team to team and rarely sustain a long major league career.

The K Lessons Presented

The tendency toward increasing rates of strikeouts, while certainly accelerating in the present day, is not uniquely modern but is instead an elemental function of the eternal battle between hitter and pitcher. While the dynamic has been interrupted from time to time, the default condition is weighted toward ever-more frequent strike threes. The factors favoring growth in strikeouts include a willingness of batters to swing for power at the expense of contact, but are mostly driven by the willingness—and, most significantly, by the ability—of pitchers to pitch for strikeouts at the expense of in-game endurance, as they are deployed in ever-shorter stints. The persistent decade-upon-decade increase in the size and strength of baseball players feeds both of these tendencies.

In discussions about this issue (and/or the issue of declining scoring rates in general), one often encounters an assertion to the effect of, "These things are cyclical. Left alone, current trends will revert toward historical equilibrium." However, baseball history provides no evidence to support such an assertion. Indeed, the historical record indicates that reversal of long-scale dynamics occurs only through imposition (whether intentionally or not) of significantly new conditions. Therefore:

If no changes are undertaken, *we will see ever-greater rates of strikeouts.* As the rate of strikeouts overtakes the rate of hits, batting averages, base runners, long-sequence innings, *and scoring will continue to decline.*

So What?

There is no objective "good" or "bad" to any of this. One's preferred style of play is entirely a matter of aesthetics. If you're a fan who loves strikeouts and isn't so crazy about ground balls or singles, then bully for you. Baseball has never been better, and will only improve.

But for many fans—especially, it must be admitted, those of us who've been privileged to closely observe the game for many decades—the baseball we're watching today is distinctly suboptimal, and increasingly so. Today's game presents ever-fewer balls batted into the field of play, and therefore ever-fewer challenges to fielders to catch and throw the ball, as well as ever-fewer base runners facing the split-second decision to stay put or attempt to advance, to force a throw and risk a tag play. For fans like us, today's baseball is therefore less interesting than it once was, and can be. Make no mistake, it's still baseball, and we love it, but we know it can be better than this.

Therefore, fans like us aren't content to let the present dynamic roll along. We advocate the imposition of thoughtful and careful changes in rules/conditions, to do what can be responsibly done to push against the inescapable and enduring pressure for ever-more strikeouts.

Theoretical, But Not Practical

One thing that would reduce the ability of batters to hit home runs, while simultaneously increasing the value of speed, would be to move outfield fences outward. This generally happened in the 1970s, and the impact of increased contact-hitting was significant. However, given modern stadium configurations, this simply can't happen. Outfields are almost never bounded by easily-movable chain-link fencing these days, but are instead limited by permanent grandstand structures. Until a new stock of ballparks is constructed, the only direction fences can be moved practically is inward, and that would be precisely the wrong direction.

Another idea, definitely more radical, would be to move the pitchers' rubber backward from the longstanding 60-foot, six-inch distance. Even a modest increase, say six inches or a foot, would have the effect of reducing pitch velocity and increasing batter response time. The evidence from 1892 to 1893 is that the result would be a dramatic increase in hitting and scoring (though the evidence from the 1890s suggests it might not be enduring, as pitching technique adapted). However, stadium configuration again presents a practical obstacle: While it's easy to move the pitchers' mound in the middle of the diamond, bullpens in most stadiums (major and minor league) are frequently hemmed in to accommodate the traditional dimension. The difficulty and expense of remodeling bullpens (not just in professional baseball, but in all the amateur levels across the United States and in so many other countries, where every aspiring pitcher develops) would likely prove prohibitive.

What Can Be Done

Fortunately, several practically implementable options could be enacted by themselves or in some combination. These include:

1. *Reduction in the size of the strike zone.* The evidence from 1963 and 1969 strongly suggests this can have a dramatic effect. The downside risk is that along with stimulating hits, it would significantly increase the rate of walks (and long counts in general), and just about no one finds the base on balls to be an exciting play. Still, this obvious option merits serious consideration.

2. *Reduction in the size of fielders' gloves.* Today's players are better athletes than ever before, and year after year, decade after decade, they commit ever-fewer fielding errors. Steady improvement in fielding equipment has only aided this dynamic. Imposing incremental reductions in the size/efficacy of gloves would make fielding more difficult, increasing the value of balls batted into play, and increasing the value of fielding aptitude at the expense of power-hitting ability.

3. *Increase in the thickness of bat handles.* Bill James suggested this more than a decade ago, and it continues to be sensible. An increase in the minimum circumference

of the handle of the bat would render the lightning-quick "buggy whip" power swing less effective for all but the biggest and strongest of batters and thus would motivate a revival of old-school contact-first approaches, especially if fielding the ball were slightly more challenging than it is today. (Another method of rendering swinging for the fences less productive—and thus potentially motivating swinging for contact—would be to deaden the baseball. Simply doing this might have a similar effect as thickening the bat handle. However, the World War II "balata ball" experience indicates that a deader ball works entirely in favor of pitchers and offers nothing advantageous to hitters, and in itself provides no motivation for pitchers not to pitch for strikeouts. Even with a deader ball, a strikeout is safer for pitchers than a ball hit into play.)

4. *Increase in the typical length of pitchers' stints.* Of all the factors stimulating the historic increase in strikeout rates over the decades, the more frequent deployment of relief pitchers into shorter stints appears to be the most significant. (Ever-more frequent mid-inning pitching changes are also a major element disrupting the pace and flow of games.) There are two obvious ways this trend could be reversed: a limitation on the number of pitching changes per inning/game, and/or a reduction of the number of pitchers included on the 25-man roster. (The latter would have to be enforced by a requirement that a pitcher demoted to the minor leagues could not return for a significant time, such as 30 days.) Making it necessary for teams to deploy fewer pitchers per game would require pitchers to work longer stints, thus requiring them to pace themselves and more readily pitch to contact than simply overpower hitters.

Every change in rules and regulations brings risk of unintended and possibly negative consequences. Certainly that's true of each of these suggestions. But to enact no change, and to expect current (and long-term historical) trends to slow or reverse themselves, is the height of folly.

If MLB does nothing, we will continue to see the rate of strikeouts climb to ever-unprecedented levels, and therefore continue to see ever-fewer plays in the field and ever-fewer runners on the bases. Here is one voice raised in favor of striving to act to improve the quality of the game we love.

References & Resources

- A great resource for an historical essay on the ever-changing nature of baseball rules, equipment, conditions, and techniques is reliably found in any edition of the iconic baseball resource *Total Baseball*. The first (and perhaps still the best) is "The Changing Game," by Bill Felber (*Total Baseball*, edited by John Thorn and Pete Palmer with David Ruether, Warner Books, New York, 1989, pp. 259-277). Another would be "Our Game," by John Thorn (*Total Baseball Fifth Edition*, edited by John Thorn, Pete Palmer, Michael Gershman, and David Pietrusza, Viking, New York, 1997, pp. 3-12).

- The overarching historical text in *The Ultimate Baseball Book* is organized into decade-by-decade examinations of the peculiarities of each succeeding era through the 1970s (*The Ultimate Baseball Book*, edited by Daniel Okrent and Harris Lewine, with Historical Text by David Nemec, Houghton Mifflin, Boston, 1979).
- An unsurpassed contemporary observation of the state of baseball scoring in the 1960s, originally published in 1968, is Roger Angell's "A Little Noise at Twilight," found in *The Summer Game*, by Roger Angell, Popular Library, New York, 1972, pp. 195-210.

The Power Pitcher Championship Belt

by Tony Blengino

Much of baseball's majesty lies in its detailed historical record, unparalleled among the major sports. The rules have been essentially unchanged since 1894, enabling us to at least go through the motions of comparing players across eras. Sure, hitters and pitchers are bigger and stronger today, and the game was not always open to players of all races, so inherent limitations exist. Still, I'd venture to say that many of us acquired our love for the game at least in part due to discussions with older family members, when names like Steve Carlton and Lefty Grove might come up in the same conversation.

While the introduction of power hitting, pioneered by Babe Ruth, might rank as the single biggest change in the on-field character of the game in the modern era, the role of its natural counterpart—power pitching—has also evolved over the decades. No matter the era—from Dead Ball to Steroid—there have been overpowering hurlers who have captivated the masses. In this piece, we'll revisit the game's most overpowering starting pitchers, going back to 1901, awarding a Championship Belt for each season, because let's face it, championship belts are awesome. The holder will not necessarily be the game's best pitcher at any given time—just the most overpowering, the one who made batters miss most at that moment in time. In the process, we'll learn a little bit about not only the pitchers, but the eras in which they thrived.

Throughout this article we will often refer to the pitchers' number of standard deviations above league average strikeouts per nine innings pitched (K/9 IP) rate. Each pitcher's K STD+ for each season of his reign, and his all-time single season K STD+ rank, if in the Top 100, will be presented next to his name (a list of the top 100 also appears at the end of the article). Though selection of the "belt holder" will not solely be determined by this stat, it is a primary factor. Volume of innings pitched and a general perception of dominance also apply.

Let's start with a graph, as it may be more helpful to be able to refer back to this as we go along. In this graph, I've put together the timeline of strikeouts per nine innings (you saw a similar graph in Steve Treder's article), with significant seasons sprinkled in for context. We'll talk about the seasons above the line from Rube Waddell, Dazzy Vance, Nolan Ryan and Pedro Martinez throughout the article, but I did want to call attention to the data point below the line. In 1940, Dick Errickson—pitching for the Boston Bees—put together the worst K/9 STD+ of all-time, though in 2003 Nate Cornejo did his darndest to "beat" him.

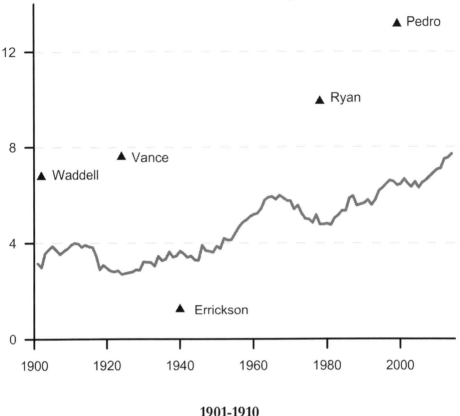

Strikeouts Per Game and Some Significant Seasons

1901-1910

This decade was a low-scoring one, with the major league average ERA peaking at 3.49 in 1901 and trending downward to 2.37 by 1908. The average K/9 rate was low, bottoming at 2.98 in 1902 and trending upward to 3.92 in 1905, regaining that level by 1910.

1901: Cy Young (1.72)

At age 34, Young didn't have the highest K STD+, but he was among the leaders, and with 371.1 IP, pitched by far the most innings. Young still had 192 of his 511 career wins ahead of him, and posted his best season ever, leading the AL in wins (33), ERA (1.62) and Ks (158). His fastball velocity and command set him apart.

1902-04: Rube Waddell ('02: 4.17, #5; '03: 4.00, #6; '04: 3.73, #14)

Our first truly elite power pitcher. Aged 25 in 1902, Waddell led the AL in Ks the next six seasons, and in K/9 the next seven, ranging from 6.5 to 8.4 while the league averaged about half as many. Waddell relied on an overpowering fastball and a hammer curve. It could easily be argued that Waddell was every bit the power pioneer among pitchers that Ruth was among hitters. Waddell had more than his share of off-field issues, and like many pure power pitchers, lacked a decline phase, so is largely forgotten in discussions of the game's greats.

1905-07: Red Ames ('05: 3.11, #53; '06: 2.77, #91; '07: 2.34)

Who? Ames and his power curveball turned up at age 22 in 1905, and he brought the power pitching that Waddell had delivered to the brand new AL to the senior circuit. He led in K/9 all three years, but his only other black ink in the record book is for wild pitches—30 in 1905 and 20 in 1907. He never logged the innings totals of his teammate, Christy Mathewson, and his K rate dropped sharply after age 26.

1908-09: Christy Mathewson ('08: 2.38; '09: 1.15)

The New York Giants rode the dominance of Mathewson, Ames and Rube Marquard to sustained excellence during this time frame. While his most overpowering season might have been at age 22 in 1903, Mathewson utilized his screwball, extreme fastball command and exceptional durability to a long run of success. He led the NL in Ks for the last of five times in 1908, and though his K rate dropped quite a bit in 1909, he did post a 25-6, 1.14 mark in a year that lacked a drop-dead power pitching standout.

1910: Walter Johnson (2.73, #98)

At age 22, he struck out a career high 313 batters, leading his league in Ks for the first of an incredible 12 times. We'll talk about this guy quite a bit more in the next section.

1911-1920

Run-scoring declined through most of the decade, with the major league ERA bottoming at 2.68 in 1917 before shooting up to 3.46 in 1920, as the reign of some guy named Babe Ruth began in earnest. Meanwhile, the average K/9 moved in the opposite direction, peaking at 4.00 in 1911 and bottoming out at 2.89 in 1918. Through all of those ebbs and flows, two power pitchers dominated the decade, though a distinct pecking order was in place.

1911: Rube Marquard (3.39, #37)

At 24, Marquard was essentially a one-season power pitcher, leading the NL in Ks for the only time with 237. He had 7.7 K/9, then plunged to 5.3 in 1912, though he won even more games (26) than he had in 1911. His fastball velocity faded early in his career, but he managed to get into the Hall of Fame despite a rather pedestrian 201-177 career record—and 4.3 career K/9.

1912-13: Walter Johnson ('12: 2.82, #85; '13: 2.19)

Here we go—this was the apex of arguably the greatest pitching career ever. How's 69-19, 1.27, with a 545/114 K/BB—he was striking out seven batters per nine in a league that averaged under four. He had an overpowering fastball and the best curve of his generation, and at age 25, he still had a lot of dominance ahead of him.

1914-15: Pete Alexander ('14: 1.77; '15: 2.14)

Johnson's rival for contemporary power pitching supremacy dominated with his screwball from the beginning of his career in 1911, but in 1914, at age 27, his command caught up with his stuff. His 241 Ks in 1915 was a career high, and he led his league in the category six times. He was on the losing end of the World Series with the Phils that season, and didn't return until 1926—when he closed out the Cards' victory as Babe Ruth was caught stealing to end it.

1916-19: Walter Johnson ('16: 1.77; '17: 2.43; '18: 1.92; '19: 1.55)

He's back, as the most dominant pitcher in the game—while in his decline phase. He led the AL in Ks all four years, though his raw total dropped from 228 to 147. He would be similarly dominant well into the 1920s, leading in Ks three more times.

1920: Pete Alexander (1.70)

Alexander's last truly great season happened to coincide with an injury-shortened campaign by Johnson. Alexander led the NL in wins (27), ERA (1.91), Ks (173), innings pitched (363.1) and complete games (33)—all for the last time.

1921-1930

This truly was the decade of the hitter—the major league ERA spiked from 3.46 in 1920 to 3.92 in 1921, and that was the decade's low, as it rose all the way to 4.81 by 1930. The average strikeout rate bottomed out at an all-time low of 2.69 in 1924, and rose slightly to 3.21 by 1930. Despite all of this, some of the most dominating pitching performances of all time occurred in this decade.

1921: Walter Johnson (2.22)

This wraps up a solid decade of belt-holding for Johnson and Alexander. This was a tough year to pick a winner, with Bob Shawkey and Urban Shocker coming close. In fact, no pitcher had posted a Top 100 K STD+ figure since Johnson in 1912. That was about to change.

1922-28: Dazzy Vance ('22: 2.79, #88; '23: 4.23, #4; '24: 4.86, #1; '25: 4.39, #2; '26: 3.99, #7; '27: 3.23, #45; '28: 3.47, #30)

Vance was a long-time minor leaguer who featured an overpowering fastball, but was oft-injured and had subpar control. Legend has it that he slammed his pitching hand on a table after losing a card game, hurting his elbow and necessitating an operation to remove bone chips. Then at age 31 in 1922, it all came together, and he began his reign of unparalleled dominance. He led the NL in Ks in all seven of these seasons by insane margins. His peak was 1924, when he struck out 262 batters to lead the NL—second-place Burleigh Grimes whiffed only 135. No one else topped 86. Vance accounted for 7.7 percent of his league's strikeouts. For context, 2014's K leader, David Price, accounted for just 1.5 percent of the American League's strikeouts. Soak that one in for a second. The Phils as a team struck out only 102 more hitters than Dazzy. Because of his late start, Vance won only 197 games for his career, but to the BBWAA's credit, he was elected to the Hall in his 16th year of eligibility in 1955.

1929-31: Lefty Grove ('29: 2.55; '30: 2.40; '31: 1.81)

Grove led the AL in Ks in his first seven major league seasons, beginning in 1925 at age 25, but he couldn't out-dominate Vance until his fifth season. He reached his peak in 1930-31, when he went 59-9, 2.30, with a 384/122 K/BB in arguably the most hitter-friendly context in modern history. He made a strong bid to keep the belt in 1932, but it wasn't to be.

1932-1940

The '30s were a decade of relative stability, especially compared to the explosive changes of the Babe Ruth Era. The major league average ERA bottomed at 3.81 in 1933—an odd, one-year blip—and peaked at 4.52 in 1936, while K/9 bottomed at 3.04 in 1933 and peaked at 3.63 in 1937. Like Johnson/Alexander in the aughts and Vance/Grove in the '20s, there were two hurlers leading the pack in this decade.

1932-35: Dizzy Dean ('32: 2.38; '33: 2.95, #64; '34: 1.78; '35: 1.68)

Dean reached the Show at age 22 in 1932, and quickly dominated the NL, leading in Ks his first four seasons with totals in a narrow band between 190 and 199. He averaged over 300 innings per season, often pitching in relief between starts. Injuries essentially ruined his career by age 28, opening things up for a couple of fresh names.

1936: Van Lingle Mungo (3.63, #18)

How's that for a fresh name. He was arguably more dominant than Dean in 1935, but over significantly fewer innings. He led the NL in Ks for the only time at age 25 with 238—but also led in walks for the third time. He struck out 6.9 batters per nine innings compared to a major league average of 3.33. His strikeout rate plunged after a late-1937 injury, and he was never the same again.

1937: Lefty Gomez (2.45)

Gomez led the AL in Ks for the last of three times in 1937, and was Dean's closest competitor for the 1933 belt. He led the AL in wins, ERA and Ks in both 1934 and 1937, and was an astounding 6-0 in seven career World Series starts.

1938-40: Bob Feller ('38: 3.05, #56; '39: 3.14, #49; '40: 2.96, #61)

A 17-year-old Feller debuted in the majors in 1936, boasting the most overpowering fastball of his generation. He led the AL in Ks in all three of these seasons, but also walked an amazing 468 batters in 894 innings. His K/9 rates ranged from 7.3 to 7.8, while the major league average ranged from 3.4 to 3.7. Feller lost a tight battle for the belt in 1941, then went off to serve his country for three years.

1941-1950

World War II was the single most impactful event upon both run-scoring and K rate trends during the 1940s (and, you know, the planet). The major league average ERA bottomed out at 3.33 in 1943 but steadily rose to 4.36 by 1950, while the K rate bounced from its low for the decade (3.27 in 1945) to its high (3.89 in 1946) in just a single year. This also marked the beginning of a 20-year period in which the belt changed hands much more frequently than in the past. Save for the war years, there were no historic power pitchers in sight.

1941-42: Johnny Vander Meer ('41: 3.82, #10; '42: 3.08, #54)

As it turns out, this guy is about more than just back-to-back no hitters. He led the NL in Ks three straight years beginning in 1941 at age 26, when his 8.0 K/9 dwarfed the major league average of 3.55. He had an overpowering fastball, and struggled with his command, walking 162 in 1943. His K/9 declined to 5.4 by 1943, and after serving in the military the next two years, he never had a K/9 of over 4.7 again.

1943-46: Hal Newhouser ('43: 2.54; '44: 2.13; '45: 2.72; '46: 2.67)

Newhouser is often pegged as a wartime pitcher, taking advantage of the watered down level of competition. He kept right on rolling after war's end, with his K total (275) and K/9 (8.5) reaching career peaks—by far—in 1946, at age 25. Within two years, his K/9 had plunged to 4.7, and his days as an effective starter were numbered.

1947: Ewell Blackwell (3.23, #44)

"The Whip" and his blazing, sidearm fastball emanating from a lean 6'6", 195 lb. frame, unfortunately had a short shelf life. He led the NL in wins (22), complete games (23) and strikeouts (193) for the only time, and was then injured for much of the next two seasons before once again winning the belt in 1950.

1948: Harry Brecheen (2.40)

This was arguably the toughest year to identify a belt-holder. It ultimately fell to the 5-foot-10, 160-pound, lefty who relied on a screwball—he's likely the softest tosser among these pitchers. He exceeded 100 strikeouts in only two seasons—but led the NL with 149 and a 2.24 ERA in 1948, at age 33. Notably, Brecheen had a career 4-1, 0.83 mark in 32.1 World Series innings.

1949: Don Newcombe (2.32)

In only the second season after the breaking of the race barrier, Newcombe seized the belt in his rookie year at age 23. His career was interrupted by two years of military service during the Korean War, and his strikeout rate, though quite stable, never rose higher. Newcombe was one of the finest hitting pitchers of all time too, batting .271/.338/.367 for his career.

1950: Ewell Blackwell (2.28)

In this era, having almost as many strikeouts (188) as hits allowed (203) was a pretty amazing feat. Alas, Blackwell could not stay healthy, and his K/9 plunged from 6.5 in 1950 to 4.6 in 1951, and he was basically done afterward. The two-time belt holder had only 82 career wins.

1951-1960

The run-scoring environment was quite stagnant during this decade, with the ERA trough (3.70 in 1952) and peak (4.14 in 1953) not all that far apart, and occurring within a single year. How those runs were scored, however, changed quite a bit, as the homer and K/9 rates steadily trended upward—the latter went from 3.77 in 1951 to 5.18 in 1960. Despite the upward strikeout trend, the group of power pitchers lacked star power compared to other decades.

1951-52: Mickey McDermott ('51: 2.63; '52: 2.32)

McDermott was a young left-handed flamethrower who whiffed 6.6 and 6.5 batters per nine innings pitched in his first two seasons as an ERA qualifier at ages 22 and 23. His innings load is far below every other hurler on this list, and his K/9 plunged to 4.0 the very next season thanks to diminished stuff and some off-field issues. McDermott wound up with a pedestrian career record of 69-69, and reached 100 strikeouts only in these two seasons.

1953-54: Billy Pierce ('53: 2.25; '54: 2.19)

Here's a truly underrated hurler. His power peak occurred here, the only two years in which he led the AL in K/9—at 6.2 and 7.1, respectively. The lefty featured a fastball and slider, and these two years set the stage for his 1955 career season, when he led the league with a 1.97 ERA. Aged 26 and 27 at this stage, Pierce went on to quietly rack up 211 wins, though the power-pitching bar was about to be raised.

1955-56: Herb Score ('55: 3.48, #28; '56: 2.91, #68)

Not since Bob Feller had a young power pitcher dominated with such a flourish—and now the two were Indians teammates. Score used an overpowering fastball/curveball combination to dominate the AL at ages 22-23, whiffing 9.7 and 9.5 batters per nine innings. He was at it again in early 1957, when a Gil McDougald liner hit him in the face, destroying his career. He would actually make another run at the belt in 1959, but continued control issues and a lack of innings caused him to fall short.

1957-58: Sam Jones ('57: 2.18; '58: 2.53)

Here's a largely forgotten outlier. Jones led the NL in strikeouts three times between 1955 and 1958 at ages 29-32, fresh off of two years of war service. He led in K/9 all of those years, with his ratios ranging from 7.4 to 8.4. Like many of the hurlers on this list, he endured significant control problems, leading the NL in walks four times from 1955-59, peaking at 185. He still had a couple of productive years left with the Giants, and finished with a 102-101 career record.

1959: Don Drysdale (2.59)

This was a tough year to pick a winner—it came down to two guys with powerful careers, who would at no other time be a clear choice to hold the belt—Drysdale and Jim Bunning. Big D gets the nod. At age 22, he led the NL in Ks (242) for the first of three times, and would pace the NL in K/9 (8.0) for the only time. He had a teammate who was about to come of age and make the first half of the next decade his own.

1960-1970

Pitchers seized control of the game in the '60s, with the major league average ERA trending down from a peak of 4.03 in 1961 to 2.98 in 1968, while K/9 ramped up from 5.23 in 1961 to 5.99 in 1967. The mound was lowered and both leagues expanded by two clubs in 1969, sending run scoring sharply upward. Only two pitchers held the belt during the '60s—one is obvious, the other perhaps not as much so.

1960-65: Sandy Koufax ('60: 2.96, #63; '61: 2.85, #79; '62: 3.53, #25; '63: 2.29; '64: 2.22; '65: 2.54)

Koufax evolved a great deal during his six-year reign—in 1960, he went 8-13 and walked 100 batters in only 175 innings pitched, while in 1965, he whiffed an amazing 382 batters while walking only 71 in 335.1 innings pitched. He possessed a knockout fastball/curve combo, and averaged between 8.9 and 10.5 K/9 over this span. He had one more massive year left in him before his early retirement in 1966 at age 30, but in a controversial decision, he lost the belt that year.

1966-69: Sam McDowell ('66: 3.18, #47; '67: 1.98; '68: 2.57; '69: 2.52)

McDowell pitched far fewer innings than Koufax did in 1966, and was by far the lesser pitcher overall, but Sudden Sam posted a much higher K/9 (10.4) and managed to lead the AL in Ks despite making only 28 starts. Just 23 in 1966, he led the AL in strikeouts five times between 1965 and 1970, overwhelming hitters with his fastball/curve combination. He never did lick his control issues—he also led the AL in walks five times—and off-field issues also contributed to his relatively early demise.

Hitters continued to gradually get the better of it in the '70s, with the major league average ERA trending up from a low of 3.26 in 1972 to 4.00 in both 1977 and 1979, while the average K/9 trended down from a peak of 5.57 in 1972 to a low of 4.77 at decade's end in 1978-79. This decade also saw the coming of age of the game's foremost strikeout artist.

1970-71: Tom Seaver ('70: 2.55; '71: 2.97, #60)

Moving forward, one no longer sees the likes of Mickey McDermott or Sam Jones—to wear the belt from 1970 on, you have to be a great pitcher, not just a live arm. After a 25-win season and an unlikely World Series win in 1969, Seaver's K rate took off the next year, to 8.8 and 9.1 respectively in his age 25 and 26 seasons. He led the NL in strikeouts in five of seven seasons beginning in 1970, copping three ERA titles along the way. His command was better, and his repertoire more diverse than most of the pitchers on this list.

1972-74: Nolan Ryan ('72: 3.40, #36; '73: 3.30, #41; '74: 3.80, #11)

Ryan and Seaver were teammates on the 1969 Miracle Mets, but it took a trade to the Angels for Ryan to get a chance to truly shine. He led the AL in both strikeouts and walks from 1972-74, averaging 314 innings per season and throwing about three billion pitches in the process. His K/9 was in the stratosphere, ranging from 9.9 to 10.6. Like Seaver, he broke through power-wise at age 25. Little did he or anyone else know at the time that Ryan would win the power pitching belt a few more times— and as late as age 42.

1975: Frank Tanana (3.14, #51)

Chances are that you remember Tanana as a soft-tossing lefty, which he was for the majority of his career. The young Frank Tanana though, with the high-octane heater, was something to behold. He led the AL—including teammate Ryan—in Ks with 269 (9.4 K/9) in 1975, and walked only 73. At age 21, his future was incredibly bright. In 1977, however, he was allowed to complete 14 consecutive games—you read that right—and his K/9 plunged from 7.6 that year to 5.2 in 1978. He pitched forever and won 240 games, but oh, what could have been.

1976-77: Nolan Ryan ('76: 3.67, #17; '77: 3.38, #39)

He's back…again leading the AL in strikeouts and walks both years, with amazing cumulative totals of 668 and 387. Another billion pitches put on his arm. He would never again put up such raw strikeout and innings totals, but Ryan still had six more K titles and an amazing five more seasons of striking out at least 10 batters per nine innings.

1978-79: J.R. Richard ('78: 3.47, #29; '79: 3.43, #34)

Ryan was a prime contender in both of these seasons, but Richard pitched many more innings. At ages 28-29, Richard exceeded 300 strikeouts in both seasons, and in 1979, had apparently conquered his career-long battle with his command, walking only 98 in 292.1 innings. He was even better in 1980, only to be felled by a stroke, depriving all of us from witnessing what a Richard-Joe Niekro-Ryan rotation could do to opposing hitters in a postseason series.

1980-1990

Run scoring bounced around in a narrow band for most of the decade, with the major league average ERA bottoming out at 3.58 in 1981, and spiking upward for a single season only to 4.29 in 1987. Strikeouts trended up throughout the decade, with the average K/9 increasing from 4.75 in 1981 to 5.69 in 1990. The steroid era is beckoning. The '80s beltholders were a unique mix of the old and new.

1980-81: Steve Carlton ('80: 2.67; '81: 2.26)

Carlton's best season was in 1972, but in terms of pure power, Ryan's breakthrough that season trumped Lefty. In 1980, Carlton paced the NL in wins (24), innings pitched (304) and strikeouts (286), and in 1981 he finally led the NL for the first time in K/9 (8.5) at age 36. Carlton's fastball and slider were both at the top of the scale, and despite his advancing years, he wasn't quite done yet.

1982: Mario Soto (2.94, #65)

Soto was brilliant in 1982 at age 25, transcending his 14-13 record. He struck out 9.6 per nine innings pitched to pace the NL, posting a stellar 275/71 K/BB in 257.2 innings. He was basically a two-pitch guy, combining a fastball with a devastating change-up. Soto was solid but not as dominant through 1985, only to be felled by shoulder injuries. He was last seen as the pitcher Pete Rose wouldn't bet on when managing the Reds.

1983: Steve Carlton (2.28)

One last hurrah for Lefty at age 38. Though his record was an ordinary 15-16, Carlton led the NL in innings (283.2) and strikeouts (275), both for the fifth and final time. His K/9 reached a career peak of 8.7, only to irreversibly crater to 6.4 in 1984.

1984-85: Dwight Gooden ('84: 3.52, #26; '85: 2.06)

How's this for generational change. Gooden jumped from High-A ball to the bigs in 1984 at age 19, posting an insane 276/73 K/BB in 218 innings pitched (11.4 K/9). His heater reached the upper 90s, and his 12/6 curveball was lethal. He peaked as an all-around pitcher in 1985, going 24-4 with a 1.53 ERA, while carrying a much heavier workload. His decline was rather swift, due both to off-field transgressions and a silly—for a guy with his stuff—focus on pitching to contact.

1986: Mike Scott (2.55)

Following the 1984 season, Scott had a moribund 29-44 career record, with barely four strikeouts per nine innings pitched. Then he learned the split-fingered fastball (as Eno Sarris detailed earlier in this book), and in 1986, at age 31, more than doubled his career high in strikeouts to 306, good for a 10.0 K/9. The league adjusted to him fairly quickly—he only exceeded 200 Ks once more—but the sight of Mets' hitters shaking their heads leaving the batters' box in the 1986 NLCS lingers to this day.

1987: Nolan Ryan (3.88, #9)

Look who's back, at age 40, with a career high 11.5 K/9, leading the NL in ERA and Ks. Oh, did I mention that he somehow went 8-16? Amazingly, he still had three league-leading strikeout seasons ahead of him.

1988: Roger Clemens (3.55, #55)

What a decade. Carlton to Gooden, then Ryan to Clemens. At age 25, Clemens led the AL in Ks (291) and K/9 (9.9) for the first time, coming off of his first two 20-win seasons. Clemens always was way more than pure power—he walked only 62 batters in 264 innings, and featured a more diverse repertoire than most of his fellow beltholders, alternately dominating with his fastball, curve and splitter. He didn't hold the belt all that often, but was always in the hunt.

1989: Nolan Ryan (3.42, #35)

One more, for old time's sake. He reached 300 Ks for the first time in 12 years, and for the first time, walked under 100 hitters when reaching that mark. His 11.3 K/9 was also the second-best mark of his career.

1990-2000

This would be the heart of the vaunted steroid era. The major league average ERA soared from a low of 3.75 in 1992 to a high of 4.77 in 2000. Pitchers also got into the act, with the average K/9 rising from 5.59 in 1992 to 6.61 in 1997. This decade was home to some of the most dominant power-pitching performances of all time.

1990-91: David Cone ('90: 2.70; '91: 3.16, #48)

People seem to forget how good this guy was. He very quietly led the NL in Ks (for the only two times in his career) and in K/9 (he would also lead in 1992) in both seasons. His K/9 ranged from 9.3 to 9.9 from 1990-92, but like many other pitchers on this list, Cone wasn't a big winner (28-24) in his belt-winning years.

1992-95: Randy Johnson ('92: 3.46, #31; '93: 3.30, #40; '94: 3.14, #50; '95: 3.54, #22)

Johnson had shown flashes of brilliance early in his major league career, but it all came together during this four-year span. He won the first four of his nine overall strikeout totals, and cut his walk total by more than half, from 144 in 1992 to 65 in 1995. He was among the handful of players whose defining seasons were impacted by the 1994-95 work stoppages—his 18-2, 2.48 ERA, 294 K in 214 IP 1995 performance would have been even more imposing over 162 games.

1996: Roger Clemens (2.77)

Kind of a weird season, as Johnson missed almost all of it due to injury. The Rocket gets the nod in his age-33 season, his last in Boston. He had a subpar 10-13 record, fooling some into thinking he was done. His 257 Ks and 9.5 K/9—both AL-leading marks, said otherwise.

1997-98: Randy Johnson ('97: 3.61, #19; '98: didn't qualify in either league)

He didn't miss a beat after his shortened 1996 season, continuing his streak of recording at least 12 K/9 in every season between 1995 and 2001. He was traded from the Mariners to Astros during the 1998 season, and didn't qualify for the ERA title in either league. Oddly, he was 9-10, 4.33, in Seattle, and 10-1, 1.28, in Houston —with at least 12 K/9 for both clubs.

1999-2000: Pedro Martinez ('99: 4.26, #3; 2000: 3.39, #38)

All the stars came into alignment, and in 1999, Pedro Martinez was as dominant as any pitcher has ever been, in an extremely hitter-friendly environment. He posted a cumulative 597/69 K/BB in 430 innings pitched, with ERAs of 2.07 and 1.74, while the major league average ERA reached 4.77 in 2000. Oh, and he did it in a DH league, in a hitter-friendly park. His fastball, curve, change, control and command were all top of the scale.

2001-2010

Pitchers began to gain the upper hand midway through this century's first decade, with the major league average ERA peaking at 4.53 in 2006 and trending down to 4.08 by 2010. The average K/9 continued its steady climb, bottoming at 6.30 in 2005 and rising to 7.06 by 2010. The decade saw another generational shift, as Martinez, Johnson and Clemens gave way to some kids who wouldn't have as much staying power.

2001-02: Randy Johnson ('01: 3.61, #20; '02: 2.82, #84)

This represented Johnson's last stretch of overwhelming dominance, at ages 37 and 38. He posted an incredible 706/142 K/BB in 509.2 innings, and his 13.4 K/9 in

2001 represented a career high. He won the Cy Young Award in both years, capping an incredible string of four in a row.

2003: Kerry Wood (2.89, #73)

Wood made a strong run at the belt as a 21-year-old rookie in 1998, but pitched only 166.2 innings. He bounced back to lead the NL in Ks (266) in 2003 for the only time in his career. Wood combined a blazing fastball with a power curve, but along with Cubs teammate Mark Prior, was never the same after their taxing, disappointing end to the campaign. Wood never again qualified for an ERA title.

2004-06: Johan Santana ('04: 2.73; '05: 2.50; '06: 2.02)

A humble Rule 5 pick, Santana dominated the AL from ages 25-27, leading the league in Ks each season and posting a cumulative 748/146 K/BB ratio. His fastball was solid, and his change-up was unhittable in his prime. He was an above-average starter, but was never quite the same after these, his first three seasons as an ERA qualifier.

2007: Jake Peavy (2.11)

Tough call; as there was no clear choice in 2007. Peavy reached his career high in innings (223.1), and paced the NL in wins (19), ERA (2.54) and Ks (240). This was his fourth straight year with between 9.4 and 9.7 K/9. It was also his last fully healthy season for a long time. Peavy's fastball/slider combo was deadly in his prime.

2008-10: Tim Lincecum ('08: 2.41; '09: 1.91; '10: 1.79)

As the strikeout rate increased, league leaders' number of standard deviations above the major league average began to shrink around this time. It seems long ago that Lincecum paced the NL in Ks in his first three years in the majors, at ages 24-26. After a while, hitters began to adjust to his delivery, his power curve receded in effectiveness (though his change temporarily replaced it as an out pitch), and the slightly built righty is now battling to keep his rotation slot.

2011-14

Pitchers have continued to hold sway in the current decade, with the major league average ERA peaking at 4.01 in 2012 and trending down to 3.75 in 2014. Strikeout rate continues to steadily climb, from 7.10 in 2011 to 7.70 in 2014. If this continues, it's just a matter of time before a rule change is enacted to inject offense into the game. Expansion isn't an option this time around.

2011: Clayton Kershaw (1.73)

Kershaw took his first major step forward at age 23, leading the NL in wins (21), ERA (2.28) and Ks (248), while cutting his walk rate dramatically. Kershaw has still not abdicated the ERA title. The big lefty's lethal fastball/slider combination gets better and better each year. Zack Greinke was a worthy contender this season.

2012-13: Yu Darvish ('12: 2.06, '13: 2.82, #83)

Darvish was exceptional in his first two seasons after a stellar career in Japan—his K STD+ was the first in a decade to rank in the all-time top 100. He has a diverse array of pitches, but his slider and fastball are the primary bat-missers. He is a product of his era in some ways—he's pitched many fewer innings than most belt-holders, and was still looking for his first career complete game at the end of 2013.

2014: Clayton Kershaw (2.45)

He's back, and better than ever. His 2014 K STD+ was the best since Randy Johnson for a lefty, and he's just as good at avoiding walks as he is at amassing strikeouts. As a bonus, he has evolved into an extreme ground ball generator. He's approaching a Pedro level of greatness.

We've awarded the Power Pitching Championship Belt for every single year going back to 1901, so it's only natural that we cap things off by declaring an all-time Belt awardee. The table below shows the all-time top 10 power pitchers—not overall pitchers, mind you; we're lasering in on the power aspect of their respective games. Listed next to each pitcher is his career cumulative K STD+ and the number of years he won the Belt.

All-Time Power Pitching Belt Top 10		
Pitcher	Career K STD+	# Belts
Nolan Ryan	58.3	7
Randy Johnson	41.0	8
Dazzy Vance	35.4	7
Walter Johnson	32.6	8
Roger Clemens	34.1	2
Pedro Martinez	27.6	2
Lefty Grove	25.8	3
Sandy Koufax	20.4	6
Rube Waddell	28.1	3
Steve Carlton	24.6	3

I know, I know—it may not pass strict statistical muster to sum together standard deviations—but doing so gives us a better feel for the statistical weight of each pitcher's entire career. The top nine career K STD+ scores are in the top 10 list, along with Sandy Koufax, whose six belts outweigh the relative brevity of his career, earning him the number eight spot on the list. Interestingly, the number 10 all-time career K STD+ guy is Bert Blyleven—who didn't really come close to winning an individual belt. Three four-time belt winners—Sam McDowell, Hal Newhouser and Dizzy Dean—don't make the all-time top 10. McDowell likely would rank 11th or 12th, along with two-time winner Tom Seaver.

The first four spots are quite easy—they each won seven or eight belts, and are ranked in declining order of career K STD+. Dazzy Vance over Walter Johnson is a tough call, but Dazzy's power so exceeded his generation's norm that he deserves the nod. Roger Clemens won only two belts, but was a power-pitching force for two decades, and while Pedro Martinez's career wasn't nearly as long, the sheer dominance of his peak period must be recognized. I dropped Rube Waddell behind Lefty Grove and Koufax, as Waddell's era lacked true power pitching competition. Steve Carlton nosed out contemporary Seaver for the last slot.

So there you have it—114 years, and 42 pitchers who at one time held the Power Pitching Championship Belt. Thirty righties, and 12 lefties, from a couple teenagers to a 40-year-old. A solid percentage of the game's all-time greats are represented, with the obvious notable absence of some inner-circle greats such as Greg Maddux and Warren Spahn who didn't rely on missing bats. There were many close calls—the guys who came closest to winning the Belt without doing so were Jim Bunning, Allie Reynolds, Justin Verlander, Zack Greinke, Max Scherzer, and of course, Floyd Bannister.

Times and eras will change, but the lure of power—both in the form of home runs at the plate, and of strikeouts on the mound—will endure. For pitchers, missing bats creates a sizeable margin for error that is the simplest path to excellence. Some of the pitchers mentioned here flamed out early, but they definitely had their moments. Others defied age and retained their power, or adapted to a loss of raw physical ability and became something totally different. They each captivated in their own way, and have their own story to tell.

References & Resources

- Rob Neyer and Bill James, *The Neyer/James Guide to Pitchers: An Historical Compendium of Pitching, Pitchers, and Pitches*
- The Society for American Baseball Research (SABR) Baseball Biography Project, *sabr.org/bioproject*

All-Time Power Pitching Belt Top 100 Individual Seasons

Rank	Pitcher	Year	Age	K/9 STD+	Rank	Pitcher	Year	Age	K/9 STD+
1	Vance	1924	33	4.86	51	Tanana	1975	22	3.14
2	Vance	1925	34	4.39	52	Ryan	1991	44	3.12
3	Martinez, P.	1999	27	4.26	53	Ames	1905	22	3.11
4	Vance	1923	32	4.23	54	Vandermeer	1942	27	3.08
5	Waddell	1902	25	4.17	55	Clemens	1988	25	3.06
6	Waddell	1903	26	4.00	56	Feller	1938	19	3.05
7	Vance	1926	35	3.99	57	Overall	1908	27	3.03
8	Ryan	1978	31	3.95	58	Hallahan	1930	27	2.98
9	Ryan	1987	40	3.88	59	Clemens	1998	35	2.97
10	Vandermeer	1941	26	3.82	60	Seaver	1971	26	2.97
11	Ryan	1974	27	3.80	61	Feller	1940	21	2.96
12	Wood, K.	1998	21	3.80	62	Grove, L.	1925	25	2.96
13	Johnson, R.	1999	35	3.79	63	Koufax	1960	24	2.96
14	Waddell	1907	30	3.77	64	Dean, D.	1933	23	2.95
15	Martinez, P.	2002	30	3.74	65	Soto	1982	25	2.94
16	Waddell	1904	27	3.73	66	Turley	1957	26	2.93
17	Ryan	1976	29	3.67	67	Johnson, W.	1924	36	2.91
18	Mungo	1936	25	3.63	68	Score	1956	23	2.91
19	Johnson, R.	1997	33	3.61	69	Bannister, F.	1985	30	2.90
20	Johnson, R.	2001	37	3.61	70	Earnshaw	1928	28	2.89
21	Ryan	1979	32	3.58	71	Johnson, R.	1991	27	2.89
22	Johnson, R.	1995	31	3.54	72	Pizarro	1961	24	2.89
23	Johnson, R.	2000	36	3.54	73	Wood, K.	2003	26	2.89
24	Grove, L.	1926	26	3.53	74	Feller	1941	22	2.88
25	Koufax	1962	26	3.53	75	Cooper, M.	1939	26	2.86
26	Gooden	1984	19	3.52	76	Grove, L.	1927	27	2.86
27	Mathewson	1903	22	3.50	77	Score	1959	26	2.86
28	Score	1955	22	3.48	78	Vaughn	1917	29	2.86
29	Richard, JR	1978	28	3.47	79	Koufax	1961	25	2.85
30	Vance	1928	37	3.47	80	Malone, P.	1929	26	2.85
31	Johnson, R.	1992	28	3.46	81	Eckersley	1976	21	2.83
32	Nomo	1995	26	3.46	82	Waddell	1908	31	2.83
33	Jones, Sa.	1956	30	3.44	83	Darvish	2013	26	2.82
34	Richard, JR	1979	29	3.43	84	Johnson, R.	2002	38	2.82
35	Ryan	1989	42	3.42	85	Johnson, W.	2012	24	2.82
36	Ryan	1972	25	3.40	86	Martinez, P.	1997	25	2.82
37	Marquard	1911	24	3.39	87	Maloney, J.	1963	23	2.81
38	Martinez, P.	2000	28	3.39	88	Vance	1922	31	2.79
39	Ryan	1977	30	3.38	89	Clemens	2002	39	2.78
40	Johnson, R.	1993	29	3.30	90	Soto	1980	23	2.78
41	Ryan	1973	26	3.30	91	Ames	1906	23	2.77
42	McDowell, S.	1965	22	3.25	92	Clemens	1996	33	2.77
43	Waddell	1905	28	3.25	93	Schilling	1997	30	2.76
44	Blackwell	1947	24	3.23	94	Erickson	1919	24	2.75
45	Vance	1927	36	3.23	95	Leonard, Du.	1914	22	2.74
46	Cone	1992	29	3.19	96	Morton, G.	1918	25	2.74
47	McDowell, S.	1966	23	3.18	97	Queen	1951	33	2.74
48	Cone	1991	28	3.16	98	Johnson, W.	1910	22	2.73
49	Feller	1939	20	3.14	99	Martinez, P.	2003	31	2.73
50	Johnson, R.	1994	30	3.14	100	Reynolds, A.	1943	28	2.73

A Place in the Sun for the Sun Devils

by Frank Jackson

On the night of Feb. 13, 2015, Arizona State University will begin a new chapter in its storied baseball history, shifting from on-campus Packard Stadium to near-campus (2.5 miles away) Phoenix Municipal Stadium, where the university has a 25-year lease. The new venue isn't exactly virgin territory, since the Sun Devils have played occasional games there over the years—in fact, ASU's Reggie Jackson hit the ballpark's first-ever college home run way back in 1966.

After an off year in 2014, the Sun Devils could benefit from a fresh start at a new home. As it turns out, 2015 also marks the golden anniversary of another notable season: 1965 was the year ASU first won the College World Series.

Hard to believe, but there was a time when Arizona State was not a perennial power. It had the perfect excuse, however: ASU did not field a varsity baseball team until 1959. This, despite the fact that the school dated back to 1885 (founded under the daunting name of Territorial Normal School at Tempe), and spring weather in the Valley of the Sun is ideal for baseball—as the influx of major league teams for spring training has verified.

Of course, college baseball wasn't exactly packing 'em in a half a century ago, even though it was older than college football. In fact, college baseball was at least 100 years old when ASU initiated its program (the first game in the official record was an 1859 contest between Amherst and Williams played in Pittsfield, Mass.) and a number of outstanding players (e.g., Eddie Collins, Lou Gehrig, Eddie Plank) came from college teams at a time when high school was the end of the line for most amateur players. By 1965, even basketball, which wasn't invented until 1891, attracted more interest than baseball at the collegiate level.

Of course, college baseball had to contend with the major leagues, the minor leagues, semi-pro leagues, American Legion ball and industrial leagues. Back in the days when fewer young men pursued formal education beyond high school, the talent pool was pretty shallow at the college level. Consequently, determining a Division I national college champion wasn't a priority. A team could have a very good season, a team could win its conference easily, a team could even go undefeated...but they were all dressed up with no place to go. If there was a champion of champions out there, there was no way to determine it on the field—until 1947.

The NCAA could hardly have failed to note the post-war baseball boom that featured record crowds at the major league level and renewed interest in the minor leagues. Perhaps some of that enthusiasm would spill over to college ball. The first

Little League World Series was also held in 1947, so the folks in charge of that organization might have been thinking along the same lines.

So the NCAA staged its first postseason tournaments in June 1947. Four teams from the east were whittled down to one (Clemson, Illinois and New York University bowed to Yale) while a bracket of four western teams duked it out (Denver, Oklahoma, Texas and Cal-Berkeley, the eventual winner). Cal-Berkeley featured Jackie Jensen, at that time better known as an All-American halfback than a baseball player. Texas boasted Bobby Layne, Mr. All-Everything in football, who eventually landed in both the College and Pro Football Halls of Fame.

One might suspect that the football players were there simply to stay in shape in the offseason…or perhaps to avoid spring football practice. (Believe it or not, Reggie Jackson entered ASU on a football scholarship in the fall of 1965 and was a baseball walk-on the following spring.) But Jensen eventually chose baseball when he turned pro, while Layne stuck with football. He had a couple of no-hitters to his credit at Texas, so it's obvious he wasn't just taking up space on the baseball roster. Either way, during their college years, their gridiron exploits inspired far more column inches in the sports pages than their diamond deeds.

The best-of-three finals (it was known as the College World Series right from the start) in 1947 was played at Hyames Field on the campus of Western Michigan College in Kalamazoo, Mich. Cal-Berkeley swept Yale (captained by war hero and future President George H.W. Bush, who went 0-for-7) by scores of 17-4 and 8-7.

The CWS (and Yale with Captain Bush) returned to Kalamazoo in 1948, but this time were defeated by another California school, Southern Cal, at that time co-coached by Rod Dedeaux, a college baseball legend (perhaps the ultimate legend; he was named "College Coach of the Century" by *Collegiate Baseball Magazine* in 1999). He would win 10 more titles with the Trojans, including five in a row from 1970-1974.

In 1948, Yale was not held winless (and Bush was not held hitless), but Southern Cal prevailed in three games. Yale never returned to the CWS, and the self-proclaimed good-field, no-hit Bush went into the oil business in Midland, Texas. Fittingly, his trusty first baseman's mitt, not his bat, is on display at his Presidential library on the Texas A&M campus in College Station, Texas. Without doing any research, I think it's safe to say he was the only man to play in the College World Series whose son went on to own a major league team. If he is not alone, then the list would be very short.

In 1949, the tournament was played in Wichita, now with four teams instead of two. The University of Texas won its first championship (another would come in 1950). The coach was former Longhorn Bibb Falk, a 12-year major league veteran who got his main chance after the White Sox roster was depleted by the Black Sox scandal. Falk reigned over the UT program through the 1967 season; like Dedeaux at USC, he turned the Longhorns into perennial contenders.

In 1950, the CWS final field widened to eight teams—which is where it stands today—but Wichita was not able to host the tournament. So the CWS shifted to Omaha, where a new minor league ballpark had opened less than two years before. At the time, it probably didn't seem like a big deal, but the CWS has been played in Omaha ever since, though the original park, Rosenblatt Stadium (named after a prominent local businessman, former mayor and semi-pro ballplayer), was supplanted by TD Ameritrade Park in 2011.

Eventually, Omaha became synonymous with the CWS. The first baseball game ever played at Rosenblatt, then a 10,000-seat facility known as Omaha Municipal Stadium, was on Oct. 17, 1948. It featured a team of barnstorming major leaguers led by Nebraska's own Richie Ashburn.

The ballpark also hosted minor league ball—Omaha has been the only Triple-A affiliate the Kansas City Royals have ever had—but Rosenblatt was better known as a neutral site for college teams than as a home park for Omaha minor league teams. By 2001, after the stadium's capacity had been enlarged to 23,145 to accommodate growing CWS crowds, the Omaha Royals found themselves playing in the largest minor league park in the country. Rosenblatt had become a unique facility, as it was bigger than any minor league ballpark, but smaller than any major league ballpark.

That first CWS year in Omaha, total attendance was only 17,805 for 10 games and the books reflected a loss of $7,500. Nevertheless, local businessmen wanted to keep the CWS in Omaha and vowed to underwrite any losses in the future. Attendance varied from year to year, depending on the total number of games played, the teams involved, and the weather, but by and large the trend was upward. During the first decade in Omaha, the peak attendance was 38,731 in 1952, but most of the fans were locals, not road-trippers.

By the end of the 1950s, the CWS was an established tournament and Omaha appeared to be its permanent home, but if there'd been one of those "100 Baseball Experiences You Absolutely, Positively Gotta Have Before You Croak" lists back then, the CWS probably wouldn't have been on it. Such was the status of "big-time" college baseball and the CWS itself on the eve of Arizona State's inaugural program.

In 1959, the State of Arizona was not exactly a desert when it came to college baseball. One Arizona college could lay claim to elite status. The University of Arizona was a regular visitor to Omaha. It must have irked the ASU brass that the university's downstate rival in Tucson had played in the CWS in 1954, 1955, 1956 and 1958 before NCAA umpires ever shouted "Play ball!" in Tempe.

Arizona also went to Omaha in 1959 and 1960, albeit without winning a title. Like ASU, AU was founded in 1885, but got in under the wire ahead of ASU, so they could lay claim to being the oldest university in Arizona. That too might have stuck in the craw of the ASU faithful.

So the mission in Tempe was obvious. Initiate a college baseball program and get it up to elite status as soon as possible. Talk about a ground-floor opportunity...

the university had no field, no scholarships…nada, nada, nada. Coincidentally, the program was launched just as the institution was changing its name from Arizona State College to Arizona State University, so it was a turning point in more ways than one. (At the time, the student body was around 17,000; today it is more than three times that number.)

Looking at the college teams that had been successful, it was obvious that the choice of a coach (for whatever reason, the term "manager" has never taken hold in college ball) was key. But starting a program from scratch was a long way from taking over an established program. One might think that ASU would have chosen a former major leaguer just for the sake of PR. Instead, it chose a no-name coach.

It was not necessary to be a former big league star (Dedeaux had just four at-bats with the Cubs in 1935) to be a successful college coach, but clearly it would take a very special person to kick-start a baseball program. And ASU found such a person: It hired Bobby Brooks Winkles of Swifton, Ark.

In 1959, that name would hardly have caused a glimmer of recognition among ASU sports fans. A 28-year-old career minor leaguer who got as high as Triple-A twice (Charleston, W.V. in the American Association and Indianapolis of the International League), Winkles was hardly a household name, even in the cities where he had played.

His prospects for promotion to the major leagues were dim. His career batting average was .270, but it was trending downward—he hit .292 in Single-A ball, then .249 in Double-A ball and then .234 in Triple-A. If Winkles had any illusions about his talents, Walker Cooper, his manager at Indianapolis, set him straight, declaring that there was only one thing keeping him out of the major leagues…his ability.

But Winkles had turned some heads while coaching American Legion ball, and the fact that he was working on a master's degree probably didn't hurt his chances at landing a college coaching gig. ASU athletic director Clyde Smith had heard about Winkles through back channels and offered him the job. He never had cause to regret that decision.

The results on the field were obvious. The Sun Devils sported a winning record right off the bat, going 28-18 in 1959. They followed this with 32-13 in 1960, 36-13 in 1961 and 27-18 in 1962.

In 1963, ASU joined the newly-created Western Athletic Conference, whose other members included Arizona, Brigham Young, New Mexico, Utah and Wyoming. Immediately, the Sun Devils made their presence known: They went 34-17, including 7-5 in conference play.

Then in 1964 came the breakthrough: a 44-7 record with a gaudy 11-1 conference record, and the team's first appearance in Omaha. It was also the first of two Omaha appearances for Sal Bando, the team's first "name" player. Many more would follow.

For a six-year-old team making its first appearance in the CWS, the results were not bad. On June 9, ASU lost 7-0 to Missouri, but the next day they beat Mississippi (who had Don Kessinger at shortstop), 5-0. On June 12, the Sun Devils were eliminated when they lost to Maine, 4-2. ASU, the fourth team eliminated, did not play the eventual winner, Minnesota—which was something of a powerhouse in those days, as they had won titles in 1956 and 1960.

That first trip to Omaha surely whetted the players' appetites, but it was time to go beyond the "just glad to be here" mode. Of course, to return to Omaha, they would have to have another outstanding season in 1965. They did, as they posted a 43-7 record during the regular season, and then went undefeated in the postseason, as they blitzed Utah and Colorado State in three games each. So the Sun Devils went back to Omaha with a 49-7 record. This was the year the park's name was changed from Municipal Stadium to Rosenblatt Stadium.

In addition to ASU, the CWS participants in 1965 consisted of Connecticut, Florida State, Lafayette, Ohio State, St. Louis, Texas and Washington State.

The 1965 CWS boiled down to a tussle between Ohio State and Arizona State. At the outset of the series, ASU continued its winning streak, while OSU lost one game, 9-4, in its first match-up with the Sun Devils on June 9. When the two teams met for the second time two days later, OSU won by a 7-3 score. With each team having lost once, they would have to play one more time for the title. The final game was a squeaker, and ASU triumphed by a narrow 2-1 score. Ohio State would go all the way in 1966, but 1965 belonged to ASU.

The ASU-OSU showdown was a fitting one, as the All-Tournament Team was dominated by OSU players (pitcher Steve Arlin, catcher Chuck Brinkman, first baseman Arnold Chonko and shortstop Bo Rein) and ASU players (pitcher Doug Numberg, second baseman Luis Lagunas, outfielder Rick Monday, and third baseman Sal Bando, who was also named the "Most Outstanding Player").

Bando, of course, was drafted by the Athletics—then still in Kansas City—in the sixth round of the very first major league draft in 1965. He would go on to be team captain of the A's during the 1972-1974 World Series championship seasons, as well as the general manager for the Brewers when he finished his playing career.

In a sense, Bando's presence in the 1965 CWS was also something of a turning point. No disrespect to the previous winners of the MOP award (from 1949 through 1964: Tom Hamilton, Ray Van Cleef, Sidney Hatfield, Jim O'Neill, J.C. Smith, Tom Yewcic, Tom Borland, Jerry Thomas, Cal Emery, Bill Thom, Jim Dobson, John Erickson, Littleton Fowler, Bob Garibaldi, Bud Hollowell, and Joe Ferris), but none of them enjoys anything close to Bando's stature.

Bando was the first MOP to be an impact player in the big leagues. Bando showed that success at the highest level of college ball could translate to the same in the major leagues—and not necessarily after a long apprenticeship in the minor leagues, as Bando made his major league debut just a year later, in 1966. Today the debate continues as to whether it is better for a talented high school player to sign a pro contract or go to college. Of course, it all depends on the player, the offers on the table, and other variables, but in 1965, going directly to minor league ball from high school was more common.

The arrival of Rick Monday (like Winkles, he was a native of Arkansas, which probably gave ASU a leg up in recruiting) during the 1965 season also elevated the status of the ASU program. Monday was the 1965 College Player of the Year and the first player taken in that first-ever 1965 draft. Like Bando, Monday enjoyed a long, productive career as a major league player and beyond. Since 1985, he has been a broadcaster for the Dodgers.

Unfortunately for ASU, neither Bando nor Monday was around in 1966, but Duffy Dyer returned, and Reggie Jackson made his debut. Even so, ASU did not make the CWS that year. But it was obvious the 1965 title was no fluke after Winkles took the Sun Devils back to the CWS in 1967 and 1969, bringing home titles both years.

While Winkles racked up more titles, Bando, Monday and Jackson were plying their trade for the Kansas City/Oakland Athletics (Bando and Monday starting in 1966, Jackson in 1967). They were, in effect, walking testimonials for the ASU baseball program. Bando and Jackson were still there for Oakland's 1972-1974 World Series championships, though Monday was traded to the Cubs after the 1971 season.

High school baseball stars weighing offers from colleges couldn't help but notice how far ASU had come in such a short time. If they visited the campus, they could hardly fail to notice that weather-wise it was quite salubrious during the school year (if not the summer) and off-campus entertainment in Tempe and Phoenix was abundant. Thus a powerhouse, once established, sold itself.

Bobby Winkles and ASU parted ways after the 1971 season. Of course, the job he had done with ASU was well known (524 wins against just 173 losses), so he was not unemployed for long (as he once noted, he never had to apply for a job in baseball). Fittingly, his success at the college level enabled him to finally crack the major leagues while his three prize pupils were enhancing their big league resumes.

After a 76-86 season in 1971, Angels owner Gene Autry cleaned house. The 1971 brain trust (manager Lefty Philips and coaches Rocky Bridges, Fred Koenig, Pete Reiser and Norm Sherry) were all canned. Sadly, Phillips passed away less than a year later after a severe asthma attack.

The Angels manager for the 1972 season was Del Rice, who had been named 1971 minor league manager of the year by *The Sporting News*. Rice was promoted from the Angels' Triple-A affiliate in Salt Lake City. His coaches were Peanuts Lowrey, Tom Morgan, John Roseboro—and Bobby Winkles.

When Rice's efforts produced scant improvement in 1972 (75-80), Autry promoted Winkles to manager in 1973. So two years after he had coached his final college game, Winkles was at the helm of a major league club. Unfortunately, the results under Winkles were also sub-.500, as the Angels went 79-83 in 1973. A few games shy of the midpoint of the 1974 season, Winkles was fired with the Angels at 30-44.

In 1976, Winkles went to work as a coach for the Giants, but across the bay, Charlie Finley saw something he liked in Winkles, and offered him the job of managing the A's in 1977. It was a rather thankless job, as the great A's teams of the early 1970s had been all but disbanded (or one might say dis-Bandoed—Sal Bando had signed with the Brewers after the 1976 season).

After taking over from Jack McKeon on June 10, Winkles went 37-71 the rest of the way in 1977. Such a result was pretty much a given, considering the roster turnover, dismal attendance and speculation that the team was going to be sold and moved. The result was a last-place finish in the AL West, as even the expansion Mariners finished ahead of the A's. Nevertheless, Winkles led the A's to a 24-15 start in 1978 before deciding that putting up with Finley was too much. (As unpredictable as ever, Finley responded to Winkles' resignation by bringing back McKeon.)

But Winkles wasn't through with Major League Baseball. After quitting Finley, he was hired by Tony La Russa (then managing the White Sox) as a coach. Later he went to Montreal, where he oversaw player development, and even logged several seasons as a broadcaster. Now 84, Winkles is retired and living in La Quinta, Calif.

Winkles' cumulative record as a major league manager was a lackluster 170-213. Of course, there is a world of difference between coaching amateurs in their late teens and early 20s for, say, 50-60 games a year, and managing a band of more mature (theoretically anyway) professionals for 162 games, plus spring training (and possibly a postseason). It is still unusual for a successful college coach to move to pro ball. As with college professors, the privileges of tenure (even if unofficial) bind college coaches to their institutions.

Winkles probably could have had lifetime employment at ASU if he'd wanted it. At any rate, the foundation he had built at ASU was sound. The baseball program kept rolling. When the university built a new ballpark in 1974, it was bankrolled by a prominent family named Packard—hence the name Packard Stadium. But it wouldn't do to exclude the man who built the program from the ground up, so the facility was officially known as Bobby Winkles Field at Packard Stadium.

When Jim Brock took over as head coach in 1972, the transition was seamless. The Sun Devils appeared in the CWS in 1972, 1973, 1975, 1976, 1977, 1978 (by then Arizona State and Arizona had joined the PAC-8, which thus became the PAC-10), 1981, 1983, 1984, 1987, 1988, 1993 and 1994, with titles in 1977 and 1981. Sadly, coach Brock died of cancer during the 1994 CWS. As a result, the formal name of the ASU ballpark became Winkles Field-Packard Stadium at Brock Ballpark, creating something of a challenge for radio announcers.

Like the New York Yankees, the Sun Devils have a lengthy list of retired numbers—0 - Oddibe McDowell; 1 - Bobby Winkles; 5 - Bob Horner; 6 - Sal Bando; 7 - Alan Bannister and Hubie Brooks; 9 - Alvin Davis; 12 - Kevin Romine; 14 - Larry

Gura; 16 - Paul Lo Duca; 19 - Floyd Bannister; 21 - Eddie Bane; 24 - Barry Bonds; 27 - Rick Monday; 33 - Jim Brock; and 44 - Reggie Jackson. Those numbers were prominently displayed at Packard Stadium, and will likely find a home at Phoenix Muni as well. McDowell, Winkles, Horner, Bando, the two Bannisters, Bane and Brock are also in the College Baseball Hall of Fame.

Today college baseball gets far more attention—from fans and scouts both—than it did when ASU won its first CWS. Though high school players are more likely to go to college today than 50 years ago, the competition for players has also intensified, even though some schools have ended their baseball programs, either to cut costs or to comply with Title IX. Consequently, in 2015, it would be much more difficult for a university to start from scratch and end up with a title after just seven seasons.

Considering the success Arizona State enjoyed in the early going, it is a bit surprising to learn that it has not won a title since 1981. The Sun Devils have played postseason ball 26 times since then, and have been to the CWS 11 times since '81.

The CWS has changed a lot since ASU won that last title. In 1981, total attendance hit six figures (120,456) for the first time. The all-time high-water mark in 2013 was almost triple that number (341,483).

Today, the CWS is a big deal. Today, it would be on a baseball buff's bucket list—even if no alma mater is involved. Walk into any sports bar during mid-June and you will likely encounter a telecast of a CWS game. In fact, thanks to the assortment of sports networks out there, even regular season college telecasts are not unusual any more.

Over the past half-century, Arizona State has played a big part in the growth of college baseball and the CWS, but after a 34-23 season in 2014, it seems unlikely that another title will occur in 2015, the 50th anniversary year of that first championship.

There is cause for optimism, however. Tracy Smith, the new coach (only the fifth in ASU history), won plaudits in 2013 when he took Indiana University to the CWS for the first time ever and was voted not only Big 10 Coach of the Year—Indiana was the first Big Ten team in Omaha since Michigan in 1984—but also National Coach of the Year.

Bobby Winkles, of course, won the CWS in his second trip to Omaha in 1965. The ASU faithful are hoping that Smith will duplicate Winkles' feat—sooner rather than later.

References & Resources

- Steven Pivovar, *Rosenblatt Stadium: Omaha's Diamond on the Hill*, Omaha World-Herald Co. (Omaha, 2010)
- The always indispensable Baseball-Reference, Baseball Almanac and Wikipedia

Marathon Men

by Warren Corbett

Joe Oeschger and Leon Cadore each pitched 26 innings in a single game. Their arms didn't fall off.

The May 1, 1920, marathon between the Boston Braves and Brooklyn Dodgers—the longest in major league history—illuminates how the game was played in the final season of the Deadball Era and how drastically it has changed.

The full story of baseball's longest game is told here for the first time, assembled from Retrosheet's unpublished play-by-play data, accounts in contemporary newspapers, and reminiscences of the two pitchers and other players.

The Dodgers, under manager Wilbert Robinson, were on their way to the National League pennant for the second time in five seasons. (The team was called Dodgers, Robins, and Superbas by various newspapers. Let's stick with Dodgers.) The Braves finished seventh that year, losing 90 games under manager George Stallings. His Miracle Braves had won the 1914 World Series championship, but this would be his fourth straight losing season and his last as a manager.

Saturday, May 1, was raw and rainy in Boston, with an official high of just 54 degrees, and the lousy weather held down the crowd at Braves Field. The *Brooklyn Eagle* said "about 2,500 frostbitten and damp fans" attended; other papers' estimates ranged from 2,000 to 4,500. Oeschger (pronounced ESH-gur) was happy to get the start. Twelve days earlier, he had lost an 11-inning, 1-0 decision to Brooklyn and Cadore, and he wanted payback.

Right-handers Oeschger and Cadore were middling big league pitchers. Both were born in Chicago, just five months apart (Oeschger, the younger, was not quite 28), but grew up in the West—Oeschger on a dairy farm in northern California, Cadore in an Idaho mining town. They were college men; Oeschger earned an engineering degree from St. Mary's in Oakland, a baseball powerhouse that has produced more than 60 major leaguers, while Cadore attended Stanford and Gonzaga.

The historian Lee Allen said Wilbert Robinson "liked his pitchers big and strong." Cadore qualified at 6'1" and 190 pounds, but he was a curveball specialist rather than a flamethrower. He had turned in two outstanding seasons sandwiched around World War I service as an infantry lieutenant. Cadore was popular with his teammates, a cut-up and amateur magician. He had been Casey Stengel's roommate. When a sparrow flew out from under Casey's cap, it was Cadore who had given him the bird.

Oeschger, an inch shorter and also 190 pounds, was a power pitcher with a skimpy resume, a 31-44 record in six seasons with mostly weak clubs. A year earlier, he had endured a 20-inning complete game on April 30 and had been practically useless for the next two months. He was traded from the Phillies to the Giants to the Braves during the 1919 season.

The rain stopped in time for the first pitch at 3 p.m., although it would return for several encores as afternoon turned to evening. Oeschger retired Brooklyn's leadoff man in the top of the first, but the next batter, right fielder Bernie Neis, reached on an error by the Braves second baseman, Charlie Pick. Pick's day would get much worse. Oeschger's catcher, Mickey O'Neil, bailed him out by picking Neis off first. After Jimmy Johnston singled, Oeschger escaped unharmed when the Dodgers' most dangerous hitter, Zack Wheat, popped out. In the bottom of the inning, Cadore set the tone for his day by walking the first man he faced, but he then set down the next three.

The Dodgers center fielder, Hi Myers, led off the second with a single. When he tried to steal second, catcher O'Neil's throw had him nailed, but Charlie Pick dropped it for his second error. Oeschger stiffened to retire the side.

Pick was at the center of the action again in the Dodgers' fourth. With Wheat on first, Myers slapped a roller toward the second baseman, a double-play ball. Wheat ran into Pick before he could field the ball and was called out. At the time, there was no rule allowing umpires to call the double play in case of interference, so the Braves got one out instead of two. Myers stole second but left the game, probably injured, and was replaced by a pinch runner. That eliminated one of the Dodgers' best hitters. Oeschger restored order, and stranded the two runners.

The Dodgers scratched out their only run in the fifth, and Oeschger blamed himself. He walked Brooklyn catcher Ernie Krueger leading off the inning. Cadore smacked a hard one-hopper back to the mound. Oeschger, rushing to turn a double play, fumbled the ball and had to settle for the out at first, while Krueger moved up. The Boston pitcher got two strikes on Brooklyn second baseman Ivy Olson, but Olson punched a broken-bat humpbacked liner over shortstop Rabbit Maranville's head—Oeschger called it "a dinky single"—to score Krueger. Brooklyn led, 1-0. After that, Oeschger held the Dodgers scoreless for 21 innings.

The Braves nearly got the run back in their half of the fifth when a single and an error put men on first and third, but Pick flied out to kill the rally.

Cadore let at least one Braves hitter reach base in every inning, but clung to his shutout until the sixth. With one out, the Braves' cleanup hitter, right fielder Walt Cruise, caught up with a fastball on the outside corner and hammered a drive to the scoreboard in left. The ball dug a divot in the soggy grass while Cruise cruised all the way to third. Next, first baseman Walter Holke sliced a blooper into short left field as Cruise headed home. When the sprinting Wheat plucked the sinking liner off his shoe tops, Cruise, already near the plate, was the deadest of ducks—but nobody was covering third. The Brooklyn third baseman and shortstop had chased after Holke's little flare. Wheat did the only thing he could do: He ran like hell for third base, but not fast enough to beat the retreating Cruise.

That reprieve cost Brooklyn the win. Tony Boeckel, the Boston third baseman, made the Dodgers pay with an RBI single to tie the score. Maranville followed with a double to center, and Boeckel raced around toward the plate. Brooklyn's replacement center fielder, Wally Hood, threw wildly, but Cadore intercepted the ball near the first-base line and relayed to Ernie Krueger. As Boeckel slammed into Krueger, the Dodgers catcher held on for the third out. He preserved the tie, but had to leave the game with a spike wound to his leg.

Oeschger's teammates had gotten him off the hook. He recalled that he set down the Dodgers on three pitches in the seventh, getting three groundouts. Boston mounted a bid for victory in the bottom of the ninth. After Maranville led off with a single, pinch hitter Lloyd Christenbury put down a sacrifice bunt. Cadore fielded the ball, but his throw to first hit Christenbury in the back, and both runners were safe. Oeschger's sacrifice moved them up to second and third. Brooklyn manager Robinson waddled out to confer with Cadore and ordered an intentional pass to Boston's leadoff batter, Ray Powell. That loaded the bases with one out, bringing up Pick. With the infield pinched in for a double play, Pick smashed a hard grounder to second baseman Olson, who made a "spectacular stop," in the opinion of one reporter. Olson tagged Powell running from first, then threw out Pick to complete the double play and quash the threat.

Cadore had allowed at least one baserunner in each of the first nine innings, giving up 11 hits and walking two. "Time and again it looked as if Cadore would fall," *The Sun and New York Herald* writer commented, "but time and again the Brooklyn men behind him rose to heights of superefficiency as they converted seeming hits into outs and lifted their pitcher out of many a tight situation."

With the shivering spectators treated to free baseball in the 10th, Cadore set down the Braves in order for the first time. Oeschger was rolling. Beginning in the eighth, he retired 18 in a row before Wheat singled in the 14th.

"I think the most critical inning for me was the 17th," Oeschger said later. Wheat led off with another single and was sacrificed to second. The Dodgers first baseman, Big Ed Konetchy, drilled a hot shot to Maranville at short. The Rabbit managed to knock it down, stopping Wheat at third, saving a run. Chuck Ward hit another grounder to short, and Maranville snapped a throw to third trying to catch Wheat off base, but third baseman Boeckel was not on the bag, either.

The bases were full with one out, setting up the play that saved the game. Brooklyn's backup catcher, Rowdy Elliott, hit a comebacker, and Oeschger threw home for the force out. Catcher Hank Gowdy, who had entered the game in the 10th, fired to first, but his throw was low and wide. Walter Holke stretched to knock it down as Konetchy, a lead-footed runner, rounded third. Seeing the ball loose, he kept chugging. Holke's frantic throw home was off line. Gowdy snared it and dived across the plate, tagging Konetchy with the ball clutched in his bare fist. Inning over. Oeschger said, "A great play by Hank Gowdy saved my neck." The *Boston Herald's* Ed Cunningham called it the "greatest play ever staged on a Boston diamond, and probably on any hearthstone of the grand old game." If not for Gowdy's dive, the game would have ended in the 17th, and we never would have heard of it.

Instead, they played on. Drizzle was falling again. Oeschger kept throwing fastballs and didn't allow another hit. Cadore kept throwing "curves and slow stuff," and set down 15 straight through the 19th. Oeschger admitted he was getting tired. He limited himself to just a couple of warmup tosses before each inning. His teammates pumped him up: "Just one more inning, Joe. We'll get a run for you." In the Brooklyn dugout, somewhere around the 20th, Robinson asked his pitcher if he wanted to come out. Cadore replied, "If that fellow can go another inning, I can, too." Cadore was feeling sleepy—he thought the tension was grinding him down.

The rest of the game could have put everybody to sleep. There was little action to warm the fans. Brooklyn right fielder Neis recorded all three putouts in the bottom of the 19th. The Braves' Leslie Mann led off the home half of the 20th with a single, but was picked off first when the next batter whiffed on a bunt attempt. In the 22nd, Oeschger walked Wally Hood, the only Brooklyn baserunner in the final nine innings. From the bench, Dodgers pitcher Burleigh Grimes observed that the hitters appeared more arm-weary than the pitchers: "You never saw so many lazy bats; they couldn't get a ball out of the infield. Oeschger and Cadore were just throwing that thing right in there." (Grimes had pitched the 20-inning game against Oeschger in 1919.)

If the game had been played the day before in the same weather conditions, it would have ended by now. But May 1 was the first day of Daylight Saving Time, which pushed sunset an hour later and made the record marathon game possible.

In the 23rd, it became the longest game in National League history; Brooklyn and Pittsburgh had played 22 innings in 1917. (Cadore started but pitched only seven innings.) In the 24th, it equaled the longest ever in the majors, between the Philadelphia Athletics and Boston Americans in 1906. (Jack Coombs—the winner—and Joe Harris went all the way.)

The hapless Pick popped out to end the record-breaking 25th. That made him 0-for-11, a day of futility that has never been matched in at least 100 years. His batting average dropped from .324 to .250. He also grounded into a double play and committed two errors.

When Oeschger retired the Dodgers in order in the top of the 26th, he completed a nine-inning no-hitter, setting down the last 13 in a row. In the bottom half, Cadore disposed of the first two batters, having retired 19 straight and allowed only one baserunner in 10 innings. But the Braves weren't quite done. Holke's nubber off his bat handle dribbled past Cadore for Boston's 15th hit. Cadore recorded his 78th out when Boeckel tapped a grounder to Konetchy at first.

And it was over. The umpire in chief, Barry McCormick, consulted both managers then called the game. It was still daylight at 6:50 p.m., nearly an hour before sundown, but heavily overcast. Several batters had complained that they couldn't see the ball. The *Brooklyn Eagle's* Thomas S. Rice thought, "If it had been a cloudless day the athletes might well have gone thirty innings or more." The Dodgers' Ivy Olson ran up to McCormick wagging one finger and begged him to play one more so they could tell their grandchildren they had completed three games in a day, but McCormick brushed him off. One writer suggested the umpire had a date with a steak.

"It was the hitters who were squawking to end it," Oeschger remembered. "I certainly didn't want it to stop, and I don't think Cadore did." Cadore said, "[T]he chief thing that was bothering me was the fact that after working all those hours we still failed to win the game."

The longest game took three hours, 50 minutes. To reel off 26 innings in under four hours, teams had to play at a radically different pace than we see today. On Sept. 11, 1974, the Mets and Cardinals played 25 innings in a game that lasted seven hours, four minutes. On May 8-9, 1984, the White Sox and Brewers played 25, spread over two days because of a curfew, in 8:06. The two teams used 14 pitchers. A 36-year-old Carlton Fisk caught the entire game for Chicago; of course, he had a short night's sleep in the middle of it.

In 1920, nobody was dawdling. From the available evidence, we can make some confident assumptions about how the game was played. Pitchers delivered at a steady pace, and batters didn't step out of the box between pitches (they had no batting gloves to adjust). Batters generally didn't go deep in the count. The two pitchers faced 186 men. That's an average of about 74 seconds per plate appearance, even less after subtracting the down time between innings. With no radio or TV commercials to accommodate, the break between half-innings was likely about half as long as today's two to two-and-a-half minutes.

The 1920 season is usually cited as the beginning of the lively ball, or long ball, era, because Babe Ruth stunned the world when he slugged 54 home runs, but most of baseball was still playing John McGraw's "scientific" game. Other than the Yankees, just one entire team, the Philadelphia Phillies in the ridiculous Baker Bowl, hit more homers than Ruth. The longest game featured six sacrifices and three more attempts. The Dodgers' nine hits were all singles. Oeschger said pitchers didn't have to try to be perfect, because they had little reason to fear the long ball, so they went after the hitters.

Oeschger thought he threw around 250 pitches, an average of fewer than 10 per inning. Cadore, who allowed 15 hits and five walks, estimated his total was "closer to 300." It's significant that they provided those numbers in interviews more than three decades after the game. Nobody even thought to ask about pitch counts in 1920.

Cadore, for the first time in his career, got a rubdown from the trainer at the end of his workday. Then he returned to his hotel room and went to bed. He said he couldn't lift his arm to comb his hair for three days. Oeschger, however, said his elbow didn't hurt any worse than after a normal start. The next day, the *Boston Globe's*

James C. O'Leary found him "as chipper as ever, and showing no signs of the extra exertion or the physical and mental wear and tear of his remarkable performance." The paper also ran an elaborate cartoon commemorating the game:

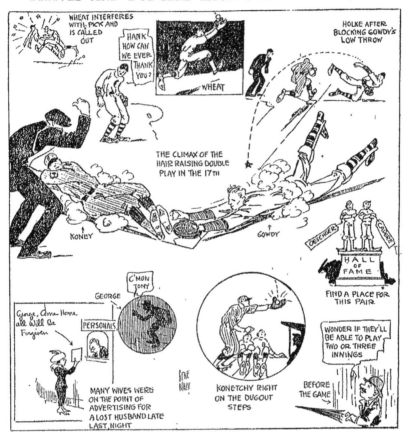

SOME GAME! THAT 26 INNING BATTLE IN WHICH BRAVES AND DODGERS EACH SCORED ONE LONE RUN

Oeschger may have been chipper, but he was not unharmed. Trying to stretch his weary body between starts, Oeschger strained a leg muscle running in the outfield and didn't pitch again for 11 days. He was pummeled in his next three outings, but righted himself to finish 15-13 for a 90-loss team, with a 3.46 ERA in 299 innings. The next year was his best: 20-14, 3.52. His big league career lasted until 1925, and then he pitched for two more years in the minors.

Cadore took seven days off before his next start, when he didn't finish the fifth inning. After another 11 days' rest, he shut out the defending champion Cincinnati Reds. By season's end, his 2.62 ERA was tenth-best in the league, and his record was 15-14. For the next two years, he was a below-average pitcher, though he hung on until 1924. "I think the game definitely did something to my arm," he said decades later. "I don't think I ever had the same stuff again."

Cadore became a stockbroker in New York after he retired. In 1931, he married Maie Ebbets, a daughter of the late Brooklyn owner. His life soon turned sour. He was arrested in 1935, accused of stealing from two clients. The disposition of the case could not be found, but the next year he was working as a pharmaceutical salesman and reported to be nearly destitute. The multimillion-dollar Ebbets estate was tied up in court for more than two decades. It was not settled until a few months before Maie Cadore died in 1950. Her husband moved back to Idaho to live with a friend, a former minor league catcher. He and Oeschger met again only once, at a San Francisco Seals old-timers game in 1957. The next year, Cadore died of stomach cancer at age 66.

Oeschger enjoyed a long and apparently happy life after baseball. He taught physical education at a San Francisco junior high school for 27 years, picking up a master's degree from Stanford along the way. He said, "My compensation was that I might have helped, in a small way, to help some of these boys out." Oeschger and his wife, Ivy, retired to the family farm near Ferndale, Calif., where he lived to be 94. Almost until the end, he was still fulfilling autograph requests and retelling the story of the longest game.

Pitchers have worked 20 or more innings in a major league game at least 20 times, according to research by Retrosheet, Philip J. Lowry and the author. The most recent, and surely the last, were Ted Lyons, who started and lost a 21-inning complete game in 1929, and George Uhle, who pitched 20 in the same game before he was relieved. Joe Oeschger is the only man who did it twice.

References & Resources

- Play-by-play is copyrighted by Retrosheet and provided free of charge.
- Newspaper sources: Associated Press, *Boston Globe*, *Boston Herald*, *Brooklyn Eagle*, *Chicago Tribune*, *New York Times*, *New York Tribune*, *New York World-Telegram and Sun*, *The Sun and New York Herald*.
- Lee Allen, *The National League Story*. New York: Hill & Wang, 1961.
- *Baseball Magazine*
- Lynwood Carranco, "Joe Oeschger Remembers," *Baseball Research Journal*, Vol. 9. SABR, 1980.
- Donald Honig, *A Donald Honig Reader*. New York: Fireside/Simon & Schuster, 1988.
- Philip J. Lowry
- National Weather Service
- *The Sporting News*

The Winning Combination

by Bill James

The following is a reprint of an article that first appeared at Bill James Online (billjamesonline. com) on Sept. 25, 2013. You can subscribe to Bill James Online for $3 a month.

On July 1, 1956, Don Blasingame, leading off for the St. Louis Cardinals, had four hits in the game. Stan Musial also had four hits in the game for the Cardinals, while Wally Moon and catcher Hal Smith had three hits each. The other five spots in the batting order collected nine more hits, for a total of 23. One of Moon's hits was a Grand Slam. Stan Musial also homered in the game, as did left fielder Rip Repulski

In spite of all this hittin', the Cardinals lost the game, 19 to 15. The Cardinal starting pitcher, Willard Schmidt, pitched 2 innings, giving up 6 hits and 5 runs. It was all downhill from there.

On June 27, 2007, the Kansas City Royals scored only one run in a game in which their starting pitcher, Jorge De La Rosa, gave up 10 hits in 6 innings of work. In spite of that, the Royals won the game, 1-0.

On May 18, 1955, the Cleveland Indians scored 19 runs in a game in which their starting pitcher, Herb Score, pitched a 3-hit shutout, striking out nine batters. Obviously, the Indians won the game.

On August 13, 2006, the Kansas City Royals were shut out in a game in which their starting pitcher, Luke Hudson, gave up 11 runs while retiring only one batter. Hudson's game score, on what is normally a zero-to-one-hundred scale, was minus nine.

If your offense is shut out and your starting pitcher has a Game Score of -9, I would generalize, your team has little chance to win the game. Actually, we don't need to generalize, because it doesn't really happen very often; that's actually the worst or second-worst combination of runs scored and starting pitcher performance in any game in the last 60 years.

I got into this by asking this question: What is a winning combination of Runs Scored and Starting Pitcher performance? Obviously if you score ten runs and your starting pitcher has a Game Score of 80, you're likely to win the game. (More than "likely", as it turns out. There is no game on record in which a combination of ten runs and a starting pitcher Game Score of 80 did not result in a victory.)

Suppose that you take the number of runs scored in the game by the offense, multiply by 10, and add to that the starting pitcher Game Score. What is a Winning Combination of those two numbers?

90. Let us suppose that you predict:

a. That if the "Winning Combination Score" is 90 or more, the team will win, whereas,

b. If the Winning Combination Score is 89 or less, the team will lose.

The Winning Combination Score being 10 * Runs Scored, plus the Game Score of the Starting Pitcher. If you make those that prediction, you will be correct 88 percent of the time…actually 87.6 percent, so let's say seven times in eight.

These numbers are (this formula is) essentially impervious to changes in Run Scoring Levels. 1968, as most of you know, was the deepest point of the run-scoring drought of the 1960s. But if, in 1968, you had predicted that every team that had a Winning Combination Score of 90 or higher would win and every team that did not would lose, you would have been right 90 percent of the time…actually, 89.97 percent.

2004 was more or less the heart of the steroid era, when many runs were scored. If, in 2004, you had predicted that every team with a Winning Combination of 90 or more would win and every team at 89 or below would lose, you would have been correct 87 percent of the time.

The formula "balances" across time, of course, because it has both a run-scoring and a run-prevention component. Let us say that your "90" is a combination of 3 runs scored by the offense (30 win points) and a starting pitcher Game Score of 60. Three runs scored by the offense are a "better" total in 1968 than they are in 2004, of course—but a Game Score of 60 is a better total in 2004 than in 1968. As one number gets "better" compared to the league, the other gets worse, so that the balance point stays about the same. Actually, the balance point goes to about 88 in 1968 and 91 in 2004, but…it doesn't move very much.

If your Winning Combination Score is 120, what is your chance of winning the game? 91 percent…actually, .913.

If your Winning Combination is 60, what is your chance of winning the game? It is essentially zero. In my data, the won-lost record of teams with a Winning Combination Score of 60 was 1 and 2,304, which figures out to .000 even though there is a win in there.

This chart gives the winning percentage, in the data, at every Winning Combination Score up to 180:

	0	1	2	3	4	5	6	7	8	9
	Winning Combination Winning Percentages									
18-	1.000									
17-	1.000	.997	.989	1.000	1.000	.996	.992	.995	.995	1.000
16-	.991	.993	.995	.995	.992	1.000	.995	.997	.997	.987
15-	.989	.985	.983	.985	.988	.989	.988	.992	.985	.996
14-	.972	.983	.984	.974	.980	.983	.984	.986	.986	.984
13-	.952	.963	.953	.967	.969	.969	.970	.967	.970	.972
12-	.913	.921	.940	.924	.930	.935	.947	.949	.935	.956
11-	.875	.871	.880	.890	.899	.884	.896	.916	.911	.921
10-	.760	.783	.789	.815	.798	.825	.845	.847	.862	.854
9-	.531	.559	.587	.623	.648	.674	.696	.716	.726	.746
8-	.176	.208	.232	.257	.316	.352	.373	.422	.453	.481
7-	.015	.026	.031	.042	.049	.060	.080	.090	.127	.143
6-	.000	.001	.004	.002	.003	.004	.006	.008	.010	.011
5-	.000	.000	.000	.000	.000	.000	.000	.001	.000	.000
4-	.000	.000	.000	.000	.000	.000	.000	.000	.000	.000
3-	.000	.000	.000	.000	.000	.000	.000	.000	.000	.000
2-	.000	.000	.000	.000	.000	.000	.000	.000	.000	.000
1-	.000	.000	.000	.000	.000	.000	.000	.000	.000	.000
0-	.000	.000	.000	.000	.000	.000	.000	.000	.000	.000

The chart, as you can see, goes from near-zero to near-one very rapidly. At a Combination Score of 75, your winning percentage if .049. At 105, it's .798. Around 90, the numbers move upward very rapidly. But when you're not near 90, each point has very little impact.

The point of that is, most games are not in the "close call" range. About one-third of all team games have Winning Combination Scores of 106 or higher, about one-third are 74 and below, and about one-third are in the "competitive" range of 75 to 105.

I'm not trying to make this sound like something profound. It's basically a truism, stated in numbers, the truism being that if you score more runs than you allow, you are likely to win. The games I started with at the top of the article were all extremely unusual games, from this standpoint. The Cardinals in the 1956 game had a Winning Combination Score of 176 (15 runs scored and a Game Score of 26), but failed to win—one of very few times, in the data, when a Combination Score that high did not yield a win. The Royals in the 2007 game had a Combination Score of just 62, which has a winning expectation of .004, but they were able to win that game, due to the unusual fact that De La Rosa gave up 10 hits in six innings, but no runs. (The "winning" games that score lower than 62 are almost all games in which the starting pitcher was injured and left the game in the first inning.)

The Indians in the 1955 game started by Herb Score had a Combination Score of 277 (19 runs and a Game Score of 87)—one of the better Combination Scores on record. And the Royals in the 2006 game had a Combination Score of negative nine, which narrowly misses being the worst combination on record. The one worse was an Oakland/New York game in 1998, in which Mike Oquist gave up 16 hits and 14 runs in a 14-1 loss, and I didn't highlight that game here because I've written about the Oquist game before.

Picky, Picky, Picky

Of course some of you, who should be tortured before you are shot, are no doubt thinking that having a Combination Score of 115 based on 7 runs and a Game Score of 45 is different than having 4 runs of support and a Game Score of 75, and might yield a different win expectation for the team.

This is true, but not very true. If you think about it, if a system is 87.6 percent accurate at predicting whether a team will win or lose, there can't be very much room to improve it by making simple adjustments. That's why I didn't experiment with 9 * runs and 8 * runs and 11 * runs. It's just a back-of-the-envelope calculation. How much better than 88% do you think we're going to get?

Just Didn't Pitch Well

It occurred to me that, with the Winning Combination Score, one could very easily estimate to what extent each pitcher was responsible for the games he didn't win. If it takes a combination of 90 to win a game and each run is 10 points, then it could be said that:

a. The offense has entirely won the game if they score 9 runs or more, and
b. The starting pitcher has entirely won the game if he has a Game Score of 90 or higher.

Take, for example, the five losses of Justin Verlander in 2011, which was the year Verlander went 24-5. On April 11, Verlander pitched a six-hit complete game, losing to Texas 2-0. Obviously that's not really his fault. His Game Score was 70. Verlander fell short of perfection by 20—two runs—whereas the offense fell short of perfection by 90, or nine runs. The offense was 82 percent responsible for that defeat (90/110), whereas Verlander was 18 percent responsible for it.

Verlander dropped his next start as well, losing to Oakland 6-2 on April 16. That one was more on Verlander's shoulders than the Texas game, and that one is probably the reason Kate Upton didn't like him at first. His Game Score was just 45, which is 45 short of guaranteeing a win; still, the offense fell short by seven runs, so that one is still 61 percent the responsibility of the offense (70/115), and 39 percent the responsibility of Verlander (45/115).

Verlander won one game and then lost again, dropping him to 2-3. He lost to Seattle 10 to 1, the bullpen giving up 7 of the 10 runs. Verlander had the oft-questioned Quality Start, 3 runs in 6 innings, a Game Score of 53. Again, the offense fell short of the Win Standard by 80 points (8 runs); Verlander fell short by 37 points. The offense is 68 percent responsible for that loss (80 of 117); Verlander is 32 percent responsible.

Verlander ripped off a string of wins then, lifting him to 11-3, finally losing to the Angels and Danny the Rabbit (Haren), 1-0 on July 5. This one was almost entirely on the offense, which did nothing, which is 90 points short of the Winning Standard. Verlander gave up 7 hits and one run in 7 and two-thirds innings, striking out 8, Game Score of 67. Verlander was 20 percent responsible for that defeat, the offense 80 percent responsible (90/113).

Verlander Just Didn't Pitch Well, didn't pitch up to the standard of the rest of the season, in his final loss of the year, July 15 against the White Sox. In that one he gave up five runs in six innings, Game Score of 44, losing the game 8-2. That one is 46 points on the shoulders of the 'lander (90 - 44), and 70 points on the shoulder of the team (9 - 2, times 10). So even that loss is 60 percent the responsibility of the team, 40 percent Verlander. There actually aren't any games in 2011 that Verlander Just Didn't Pitch Well.

You are probably thinking, at this point, that the system gives most of the blame for defeats to the offense, which is not really true; Verlander isn't a typical pitcher, and he actually pitched pretty well even in the games that he lost. My system does hold the offense responsible for 54 percent of games that starting pitchers don't win and for 52 percent of their losses. I had a more complicated version worked out in which the most important runs scored were the first runs scored, and this gave most of the responsibility to the starting pitcher, but…it's just a little messing-around toy, as opposed to a serious analytical tool. I liked the simple version that was easy to explain better, but the more complicated version did hold pitchers 60% responsible for the games they didn't win.

I figured the "Didn't Pitch Well Percentage" for every pitcher in my data…basically everybody in the last 60 years. I figured the Didn't Pitch Well Percentage both for losses and for no-decisions, but weighted each Loss at twice the impact of a no-decision. These are the ten "most innocent" pitcher/seasons in my data:

1) **Greg Maddux, 1992.** Maddux won his first Cy Young Award in 1992, going 20-11 with a 2.18 ERA, four no-decisions. But the 20-11 record significantly understates how well Maddux pitched. Maddux lost 1-0 to the Pirates (April 25), 4-0 to the Reds (May 1), 2-0 to the Giants (May 16; one of the two runs in that game was allowed by the bullpen), 2-0 to the Padres (May 22; complete game), 6-2 to the Giants (May 27; Maddux pitched great but the bullpen was hammered), and 4-0 to Atlanta (July 10; Maddux gave up two runs in eight innings). He gave up four hits and one run in nine innings to Houston on May 11, but the team lost the game in

extra innings. Maddux pitched 108.2 innings in the 15 games that he didn't win that year—more than seven innings per start—and posted a 2.90 ERA in those games.

Maddux was 27.6 percent responsible for the games he didn't win that year; the offense, 72.4 percent. No pitcher in the last 60 years has been less responsible for the games he didn't win.

I should explain...Justin Verlander isn't eligible for this category, because there weren't enough games that he didn't win. To be eligible for this list, a pitcher to have 25 "points" worth of games that he didn't win, with a Loss being two points and a No Decision being one. Basically, it takes about 8 to 10 losses to qualify for the list.

2) Gaylord Perry, 1972. A moderately famous season, and another Cy Young Award. Perry went 24-16 with a 1.92 ERA in 342.2 innings. Perry was only 28.5% responsible for the games that he didn't win that year.

3) Roger Clemens, 2005. Clemens went 13-8 with a 1.87 ERA for Houston.

4) Sam McDowell, 1968. 15-14, 1.81 ERA. This system, if you are trying to decode this, discriminates slightly in favor of a pitcher in a low-run context (1968), and against a pitcher in a high-run environment (2003). But only slightly.

5) Randy Johnson, 2004. 16-14, 2.60 ERA. 290 strikeouts and 44 walks. Johnson, Clemens and McDowell are each 29% responsible for the games they didn't win, with their offenses being 71%.

6) Tom Seaver, 1967. 16-12, 2.20 ERA.

7) Tom Seaver, 1973. 19-10, 2.08 ERA.

8) Mike Scott, 1986. 18-10, 2.22 ERA, 306 strikeouts. Scott won the Cy Young Award despite poor offensive support, as did Seaver in '73.

9) Joel Horlen, 1964. 13-9, 1.88 ERA.

10) Steve Carlton, 1969. 17-11, 2.17 ERA.

If you focus on other famous tough-luck seasons—Dave Roberts in 1971, Nolan Ryan in 1987, Bert Blyleven in 1985—they all show up ON the list of pitchers least responsible for their losses, but just not at the top of the list. Nolan Ryan was actually less responsible for the games he didn't win in 1972, 1973 and 1974 than he was in 1987, although the offense was still 66% responsible for Ryan's defeats and no-decisions in 1987.

Bob Gibson in 1968 lost 9 games despite a 1.12 ERA. That season doesn't show up on our list, because Gibson didn't lose enough games (9 losses, 3 no-decisions equals 21 points; list requires 25), but the offense was 75% responsible for the games Gibby didn't win that year, even higher than the number for Maddux. If I had used 20 points as the qualifying standard, Gibson—and only Gibson—would have ranked ahead of Maddux in '92. Other than Gibson, no one with more than two losses would rank ahead of Maddux. Luis Tiant in '68 would have been very close to the top of the list, had he qualified, and the Deaf Frenchman, Kevin Appier in 1992, would have been on the list, had he qualified. Appier was 15-8 with a 2.46 ERA.

Now, the other end of the scale. The head of the Just Didn't Pitch Well Brigade was Mark Hendrickson in 2003 (9-9, 5.51 ERA). Hendrickson was 63% responsible for the games that he didn't win.

Second on the list was Rich Gale in 1979, with regard to which I have a personal memory. Gale was 9-10, 5.65 ERA—but Gale always insisted, more than any other pitcher I ever knew, that he was not responsible for the games that he didn't win. No matter how badly he had been pitching, Gale would tell you "well, of my last seven games I lost four and had two no-decisions, but I pitched very well in four of those, and gave up only 4 runs in one of the other ones." He was actually famous for doing this, and the people in the press box used to joke about it; you can go back to the Kansas City newspapers at that time, and find places where Gale picks through his losses and writes them all off to bad luck. It turns out that he was near the top of the list of pitchers MOST responsible for his own troubles.

Third, Casey Fossum, 2006 (6-6, 5.33 ERA, 13 no-decisions), fourth, Luis Tiant, 1977, fifth, Doug Drabek, 1998, sixth, Jeff Fassero, 1999, eighth, Colby Lewis, 2003. Colby Lewis in 2003 was 10-9 with a 7.30 ERA. After that he went to Japan for a couple of years, and returned a better man for it, or at least a better pitcher. Ninth, John Doherty, 1993, and 10th, Darren Oliver, 2000.

Career leaders and trailers…in their careers, the pitchers LEAST responsible for the games they didn't win were:

Lowest DPW%, Career					
Rank	Pitcher	DPW%	Rank	Pitcher	DPW%
1	Tom Seaver	38.7%	11	Matt Cain	40.3%
2	Nolan Ryan	38.9%	12	Pedro Martinez	40.3%
3	Bob Gibson	38.9%	13	Jose RIjo	40.3%
4	Andy Messersmith	39.1%	14	Don Wilson	40.3%
5	Mel Stottlemyre	39.8%	15	Gaylord Perry	40.4%
6	Joe Horlen	39.9%	16	Gary Nolan	40.4%
7	Jose DeLeon	40.0%	17	Larry Dierker	40.5%
8	Sam McDowell	40.0%	18	Don Drysdale	40.5%
9	Ken Johnson	40.0%	19	Felix Hernandez	40.8%
10	Steve Rogers	40.0%	20	Jon Matlack	40.8%

The most interesting name there being, perhaps, Jose DeLeon, in that you don't expect to see Jose DeLeon's name on a list with Tom Seaver, Nolan Ryan, Bob Gibson and Pedro Martinez.

DPW Pct stands for "Didn't Pitch Well Percentage". The other extreme, the pitchers most responsible for the games they didn't win, minimum 200 points:

Rank	Pitcher	DPW%	Rank	Pitcher	DPW%
	Highest DPW%, Career				
1	Darren Oliver	52.7%	11	Brian Anderson	50.2%
2	Aaron Sele	51.7%	12	Sidney Ponson	50.0%
3	Kirk Reuter	51.0%	13	Tom Brewer	49.9%
4	Bill Swift	50.9%	14	Jose Lima	49.9%
5	Steve Avery	50.9%	15	Jaime Navarro	49.7%
6	Kenny Rogers	50.8%	16	David Wells	49.7%
7	Russ Ortiz	50.6%	17	Pedro Astacio	49.5%
8	Jamey Wright	50.6%	18	Scott Erickson	49.5%
9	Jeff Francis	50.2%	19	Mike Hampton	49.5%
10	Jimmy Haynes	50.2%	20	John Thomson	49.4%

About Game Score

Game Score is a metric devised by Bill James to determine the performance of a pitcher in any particular baseball game on a scale of one to 100. As introduced in the *1988 Baseball Abstract*, the goal of the Game Score is to "create a way to scan a pitcher's line from a game…and give it its proper rank along the continuum." A great game approaches 100, an average game is about 50 and a terrible game approaches zero.

To determine a starting pitcher's game score:

1. Start with 50 points.
2. Add one point for each out recorded, so three points for every complete inning pitched.
3. Add two points for each inning completed after the fourth.
4. Add one point for each strikeout.
5. Subtract two points for each hit allowed.
6. Subtract four points for each earned run allowed.
7. Subtract two points for each unearned run allowed.
8. Subtract one point for each walk.

Analysis

The Other Shifts

by Jeff Zimmerman

Infield shifts have been on the increase over the past few seasons. As you might already know, this really is a landmark change in how the gane is played. Just a few seasons ago, they were so rare that they were not even tracked. Now every team implements them to differing extents. While regular use of the extreme infield shifts seems to be a recent phenomenon, teams have been slightly repositioning their players on the field in various ways for decades. Play the infield in to get a runner out at home. Position the first and third basemen on the line to prevent extra-base hits. And so on. Each of these finite adjustments have been used for decades, but do they really work? I looked at several common fielding adjustments to see when they are used, how effective they are and if a better approach could be used in the future.

First off, a little background on the data. I would like to thank Inside Edge for collecting most of the data. All the information was taken from the 2013 and 2014 seasons unless stated otherwise.

Infield Up On, Or Near, Grass

This infield position was made infamous in 2001 when the Yankees and Diamondbacks were down to the final inning in Game Seven of the World Series. Arizona had the bases loaded with one out and Luis Gonzalez up against Mariano Rivera. The Yankees pulled the infield in for a play at the plate. Gonzalez, of course, blooped the game-winning single to where Derek Jeter was normally positioned at shortstop.

The preceding memorable moment is a perfect example of when teams bring in the infield. Late in the game when each run is critical. The infield moves up so they can make a quick, easy throw to home plate. This positioning is different than when a team rushes in from the corners to field a bunt attempt (more on this later).

In 2013 and 2014 combined, teams shifted the infield up 4,061 times. So how successful was the ploy? To find this answer, I broke down first when teams normally moved the entire infield up. Then I looked at situations when it commonly occurred and the results.

Here is a breakdown of when teams shift up the entire infield:

Infield Up Shifts, by Outs	
Outs	Times Shifted
0	1,046
1	2,975
2	40

Infield Up Shifts, By Inning			
Inning	Times Shifted	Inning	Times Shifted
1	192	6	482
2	297	7	630
3	381	8	635
4	399	9	354
5	476	Extras	215

Infield Up Shifts, By Score			
Score	Times Shifted	Score	Times Shifted
Down 7 or more	54	Down 2	612
Down 6	84	Down 1	732
Down 5	166	Tied	1,092
Down 4	324	Up 1	418
Down 3	498	Up 2 or more	81

Infield Up Shifts, By Baserunners			
Runners On	Times Shifted	Runners On	Times Shifted
Nobody on	71	First & Second	80
First	96	First & Third	352
Second	60	Second & Third	942
Third	1,992	Bases Loaded	468

Examining all the info, the most typical times a team implements this shift is:

1. Later in the game, with the peak starting in the 7th inning.
2. Less than two outs.
3. A close game, with the trailing team being more likely to use it.
4. A runner on third base.

To get a sense of when teams are expected to shift up, I will use in the 5th inning or later, zero or one outs, with the shifting team behind by three to ahead by one, and of course there is a runner at third base.

This specific situation occured 2,092 times with the shift and 3,822 times with no shift, so teams employed this shift 35.4% of the time.

Overall, when teams are in the preceding situation, they hit .354/.363/.523 overall. Teams who don't move up allowed a .339/.355/.517 triple-slash line. However, when teams did move up, the numbers turn into a nearly-impossible line of .380/.347/.533. That is not a typo. When the teams shift, their batting average jumps higher than their on-base percentage.

This unique situation, where a player's average is higher than their on-base percentage, happens for two reasons. First, the players in question barely walk. The fielders are playing in for the out and want to get an out at the plate. They have no desire to walk the batter, and need the out. When teams have the shift on, hitters only walk 1.3 percent of the time. When the shift is not on, the walk rate jumps to 5.0 percent.

Second, a high number of sacrifice flies are in play. At-bats, the denominator for slugging percentage and batting average, remove sacrifice flies. In this specific situation (runner on third and zero or one out), about any well-hit fly ball will become a sacrifice fly and a run will score. The same percentage of sacrifice flies were hit with the infield in or at normal depth.

Usually, only one type of player doesn't walk and must always sacrifice and those hitters are called pitchers. Since 1955, only 10 players have posted a batting average greater than their on-base percentage, and eight were pitchers (min 100 PA). Only two position players pulled off the feat, Ernie Bowman in 1963 (.184 AVG vs. .181 OBP) and Rob Picciolo in 1984 (.202 vs. .200).

Just so we're getting a broad picture, let's look at the outcomes beyond just the triple-slash line. Here is the percentage of times when each raw event happened when compared to the overall total.

Infield Up Shift Outcomes					
Outcome	No shift	Shift	Outcome	No shift	Shift
Plate app	64%	36%	Strikeout	68%	32%
Out	64%	36%	Single	59%	41%
Sac bunt	68%	32%	Double	68%	32%
Sac FB	65%	35%	Triple	42%	58%
Intent Walk	88%	12%	Home run	71%	29%
Walk	60%	40%	Hit by pitch	60%	40%

Basically, teams who move the infield up get no more outs than those who don't. They spread around the damage a bit, they take away singles and doubles, but give up more triples. They are also far less likely to strike anyone out.

With teams getting the same number of outs is useful information, the fielding teams bring players closer to home to prevent runs because it is a close game. Teams who bring players in for the play at the plate see the other team score 1.24 runs (-0.086 WPA) on average, while teams who don't will have 1.42 runs (-.102 WPA) scored on them. A high number of runs should be expected since a runner is at third with no or one outs and a fly ball will generally score a run. When shifting in, teams don't allow a run 5.9 percent of the time and when they play a normal depth, the rate shifts down to 5.6 percent. None of the differences are significant.

It seems like shifting in doesn't really matter to help make a play at the plate. Most of the runs allowed in this situation are from balls hit to the outfield. It doesn't mean teams should or should not employ the shift. If they feel there is an advantage to gain, do it. If not, don't. It is all up to the individual manager.

So we know there is little evidence of the shift being helpful in preventing runs, some teams make use more than others. Here is how often each team has used the shift in two situations (total and late game situations).

Infield Up Shifts, Totals and Late Game Situations					
Late-Game Situations					
Team	Shift on	Shift not on	% Used	Total shifts	Rank
Cubs	104	112	48.1%	202	2
Blue Jays	89	123	42.0%	152	8
Astros	97	137	41.5%	172	3
Rockies	109	156	41.1%	213	1
Cardinals	66	104	38.8%	146	11
Reds	57	90	38.8%	122	19
Tigers	73	116	38.6%	161	4
Marlins	86	143	37.6%	161	5
Royals	65	110	37.1%	121	20
Pirates	64	113	36.2%	136	14
Giants	73	129	36.1%	137	12
Padres	69	125	35.6%	130	16
Mariners	72	131	35.5%	136	13
D-backs	68	124	35.4%	114	26
A's	68	125	35.2%	120	22
Brewers	66	122	35.1%	146	10
Rangers	71	134	34.6%	153	7
Twins	71	134	34.6%	151	9
Red Sox	61	119	33.9%	133	15
Angels	60	118	33.7%	115	25
Yankees	59	117	33.5%	121	21
Phillies	84	172	32.8%	154	6
Rays	52	107	32.7%	116	24
Nationals	57	119	32.4%	108	27
White Sox	74	160	31.6%	127	17
Mets	71	159	30.9%	123	18
Indians	55	150	26.8%	101	29
Orioles	41	124	24.8%	69	30
Braves	45	144	23.8%	103	28

I really didn't expect to see such a difference in philosophies between teams, though as you can see, there is a 24-percent gap between first and last place. Since having the infield in doesn't really help or hurt a team, how teams use it doesn't exactly matter in the aggregate, but it can still be useful info on an individual level.

Anti-bunt

I am not sure if many people remember the 1986 World Series, but in Game Seven (YouTube the 1986 World Series, Game 7: Red Sox @ Mets, 2:19:00 mark) Mets pitcher Jesse Orosco came to bat with runners on first and second and one out in the bottom of the eighth. The Red Sox thought he was going to bunt. The announcers thought he was going to bunt. Most fans sitting in the stands and at home probably expected a bunt, as well. And with good reason. It was just his second postseason plate appearance. In his first, he had bunted.

This time though, he didn't bunt. After he faked a bunt on the first pitch, Orosco pulled the bat back and slapped the ball into center field, right to the area where shortstop Ed Romero had been standing, before he had left to cover third base. Ray Knight scored from second, the Mets took an 8-5 lead and three meek outs later they were World Series champions.

The reason the hit caught the Red Sox off guard is they expected Orosco to bunt. In almost 30 years, nothing has changed. When a pitcher is up with less than two outs and a runner is on first or second, 57 percent of the time the pitcher will bunt. Teams may also have a weak-hitting position player bunt to move a runner over late in the game.

Teams have a good idea the hitter is going to bunt, so they bring up just the first and third baseman to help the pitcher field the bunt. The fielder is trying to either get to the ball in time to at least get the batter out, be lucky enough to catch the bunt in the air for an out or perhaps even gun down the lead runner.

I will break the examination into two groups, pitchers, as ugly as it is sometimes, and position players hitting.

Pitchers Bunting

Starting with pitchers, here is the breakdown of when teams bring the first baseman and third baseman crashing in to field the bunt.

Pitcher Bunting Shifts, by Outs	
Outs	Times Shifted
0	662
1	717
2	17

Pitcher Bunting Shifts, By Inning			
Inning	Times Shifted	Inning	Times Shifted
1	2	6	119
2	278	7	74
3	339	8	19
4	197	9	4
5	351	Extras	13

Pitcher Bunting Shifts, By Score			
Score	Times Shifted	Score	Times Shifted
Down 5 or more	62	Up 1	197
Down 4	75	Up 2	101
Down 3	100	Up 3	68
Down 2	163	Up 4	30
Down 1	225	Up 5 or more	24
Tied	351		

Pitcher Bunting Shifts, By Baserunners			
Runners On	Times Shifted	Runners On	Times Shifted
Nobody on	22	First & Second	285
First	882	First & Third	88
Second	106	Second & Third	6
Third	5	Bases Loaded	2

So teams anticipate the bunt with zero or one out; runners on only first or second, first and second, or first and third; with the innings and score not mattering.

Beyond this data, I also found that the biggest change happens with two strikes. If a batter bunts a pitch foul with two strikes, they are out. Here is how often teams shifted in with zero or one strike, or two strikes with the other conditions set.

Shifts, by # Strikes			
# Strikes	Shift On	Shift Not On	Percentage
< Two Strikes	969	771	56%
Two	382	391	49%

Teams don't completely back off preparing for the bunt with two strikes. They may back off a bit, but around half the time they have the corners charging in.

So now we know when teams bring in the infield. Let's see how they perform in those situations with fielders charging in.

Pitcher Bunt Outcomes, Corners Charging vs. Not Charging							
Stat	All	Charging	Not Charging	Stat	All	Charging	Not Charging
AVG	.085	.050	.116	BB%	0.8%	0.4%	1.2%
OBP	.103	.070	.148	K%	16.7%	15.3%	18.4%
SLG	.113	.053	.167	Sac bunt rate	.51	.58	.42
ISO	.029	.004	.051				

The pitchers who are getting charged in get a hit one out of 20 times and on top of that, strike out 15 percent of the time (or, about one in six times).

Now, how successful was bringing in the infielders to stop the bunt compared to when they backed off? The WPA was -.064 when teams charged for the bunt. When teams back off, it is -.060. In other words, charging in with a pitcher at bat didn't make much of a difference.

Now, how do different teams differ in their approach attacking pitchers? Here is all 30 teams, though I also grouped together all the AL teams as well.

Charging Pitcher Shifts Per Team							
Team	Shift	No Shift	% Shifted	Team	Shift	No Shift	% Shifted
Reds	103	63	62.0%	A's	8	3	72.7%
Padres	102	69	59.6%	Rangers	6	6	50.0%
D-backs	97	63	60.6%	Astros	5	7	41.7%
Cardinals	95	78	54.9%	Mariners	5	6	45.5%
Pirates	90	69	56.6%	Blue Jays	5	6	45.5%
Mets	89	67	57.1%	Rays	5	5	50.0%
Braves	86	65	57.0%	Angels	5	2	71.4%
Marlins	84	72	53.8%	Yankees	4	5	44.4%
Cubs	84	70	54.5%	Orioles	3	8	27.3%
Phillies	83	99	45.6%	Indians	3	6	33.3%
Rockies	81	90	47.4%	Red Sox	3	4	42.9%
Brewers	79	83	48.8%	White Sox	2	8	20.0%
Dodgers	78	54	59.1%	Twins	2	5	28.6%
Giants	75	70	51.7%	Tigers	1	5	16.7%
Nationals	67	69	49.3%	Royals	1	5	16.7%
All AL Teams	58	81	41.7%				

Not a huge amount of difference with the NL teams—the spread is just 15 percent. The value I find most interesting is the low amount of AL teams bringing in the corners. I wonder whether a NL manager herd mentality exists. They see the opposing team bring the corners in all the time, so they have to do the same thing. Or perhaps AL teams didn't waste time looking at pitcher tendencies and just decided to be safe and play back? It is not for a lack of unfamiliarity for the AL teams. As we will see in the next section, the leaders and laggards are a mix of teams from each league.

Position Players Bunting

With position players—or hitters to save on words—bunting, the occurrences happen less frequently then with pitchers. At least as a percentage of total plays. There are more overall shifts, but then, position players hit far more frequently. Here is the breakdown of when the fielders are positioned for a hitter to bunt.

Hitter Bunting Shifts, by Outs	
Outs	Times Shifted
0	4,749
1	1,804
2	993

Hitter Bunting Shifts, By Inning			
Inning	Times Shifted	Inning	Times Shifted
1	1,300	6	735
2	497	7	842
3	1,052	8	799
4	511	9	585
5	921	Extras	304

Hitter Bunting Shifts, By Score			
Score	Times Shifted	Score	Times Shifted
Down 5 or more	96	Up 1	1,087
Down 4	140	Up 2	636
Down 3	356	Up 3	354
Down 2	644	Up 4	194
Down 1	871	Up 5 or more	162
Tied	3,006		

Hitter Bunting Shifts, By Baserunners			
Runners On	Times Shifted	Runners On	Times Shifted
Nobody on	4,515	First & Second	558
First	1,588	First & Third	126
Second	516	Second & Third	71
Third	117	Bases Loaded	55

So we now know when a hitter bunts—zero or one out and the following runners on base combinations: XXX, 1XX, X2X and 12X—but what type of hitters get extra attention? Teams aren't going to expect the best hitters to bunt. Often, it is a player with some speed but who is a poor hitter. In the 5,879 instances when the corner fielders were positioned in for a bunt, the hitter had an average 5.7 Speed Score but just a .301 wOBA. When teams didn't rush in for the bunt, those numbers were 3.8 and .316, respectively, in 230,599 occurrences.

Teams shift in by just using the out and base runner state 2.5 percent of the time. I wanted to run a comparison of the success for the highest percentage of players shifted in, and I had a decent comparable sample. I ended up focusing on players with a 4.4 Speed Score or better and a wOBA under .340 to compare.

The non-shifted group was a bit slower (5.7 Speed Score vs 6.3 Speed Score) and hit better (.301 wOBA vs .297 wOBA). Also, I could only get the group who shift up the most to being just over six percent of the total sample. Still though, the results are pretty staggering:

Hitter Bunt Outcomes								
Stat	All	Charging	Not Charging	Stat	All	Charging	Not Charging
AB	52,602	3,270	49,332	ISO	.132	.116	.133
AVG	.282	.324	.279	BB%	4.8%	2.3%	5.0%
OBP	.319	.343	.318	K%	14.3%	5.2%	14.9%
SLG	.414	.440	.412	Sac bunt rate	1.1%	8.1%	0.7%

The players, who historically hit worse, performed significantly better when the opponent crashed their first and third baseman towards home plate instead of playing each back. The differences in on-base and slugging percentage can point back to a near 40-point gain in batting average. This adjustment is not surprising, because the hitter can swing away and the corner infielders are completely out of position. If a team is known for bringing in their corners, the hitting may act like they are going to bunt and then swing away. Why not swing away and have the entire infield out of position?

So, which teams are most worried about the bunt when looking at different scenarios?

Hitter Bunting Shifts, By Team					
	All Hitters			Near Hitter Ability	
Team	Total	Total Opp	Chance	Total	Total Opp	Chance
Giants	295	7,242	4.07%	217	1,998	10.9%
D-backs	286	7,525	3.80%	195	1,919	10.2%
Tigers	286	7,834	3.65%	196	2,386	8.2%
Red Sox	235	7,800	3.01%	176	2,183	8.1%
Brewers	229	7,686	2.98%	156	1,712	9.1%
Twins	225	7,873	2.86%	156	2,453	6.4%
Rangers	223	7,829	2.85%	154	2,184	7.1%
White Sox	223	8,004	2.79%	143	2,396	6.0%
Padres	213	7,525	2.83%	142	1,912	7.4%
Yankees	212	7,958	2.66%	164	2,146	7.6%
Braves	209	7,410	2.82%	155	1,934	8.0%
Marlins	202	7,350	2.75%	136	2,044	6.7%
Orioles	200	7,770	2.57%	135	2,249	6.0%
Angels	197	7,931	2.48%	137	2,384	5.7%
Cubs	197	7,712	2.55%	157	1,797	8.7%
Reds	197	7,305	2.70%	127	1,649	7.7%
Dodgers	194	7,441	2.61%	131	1,974	6.6%
Pirates	194	7,664	2.53%	135	1,932	7.0%
Phillies	189	7,609	2.48%	121	1,921	6.3%
Royals	181	8,003	2.26%	120	2,280	5.3%
Indians	176	7,726	2.28%	119	2,379	5.0%
Rockies	172	7,569	2.27%	134	2,014	6.7%
Cardinals	166	7,375	2.25%	118	1,924	6.1%
Astros	165	8,090	2.04%	108	2,495	4.3%
Athletics	164	7,862	2.09%	119	2,245	5.3%
Mariners	154	8,023	1.92%	106	2,553	4.2%
Nationals	139	7,267	1.91%	100	2,015	5.0%
Mets	138	7,458	1.85%	91	2,012	4.5%
Blue Jays	134	7,820	1.71%	92	2,165	4.2%
Rays	84	7,938	1.06%	69	2,111	3.3%

Here, we see huge differences in the numbers, as some teams charged in four times more frequently than others. The value does drop to only 2.5 times when bunt candidates are up (more speed, less hitting ability). The Rays just refuse to charge in the corners. The next team (Blue Jays) brought in their corners in over 50 percent more often than did the Rays. The Rays may have figured out they were putting their players out of position with this shift and limited its usage.

No-Doubles Defense

The no-doubles defense is used to prevent a team from hitting a double or triple. It positions the first and third baseman on the lines and all the outfielders play back near the wall as well. The team is hoping to prevent balls hit down the line or all the way to the fence. By doing this, the teams open up holes on each side of the infield and allow weakly-hit fly balls to fall in the shallow outfield. I have always considered this the prevent defense for baseball, as in it prevented a team from winning. Is that really the case?

Teams felt they needed to shift in this fashion 355 times during these past two seasons. Here is a breakdown of when teams employed it.

No Doubles Shifts, by Outs	
Outs	Times Shifted
0	117
1	111
2	127

No Doubles Shifts, By Inning			
Inning	Times Shifted	Inning	Times Shifted
1	0	6	4
2	2	7	3
3	0	8	52
4	1	9	150
5	1	Extras	142

No Doubles Shifts, By Score			
Score	Times Shifted	Score	Times Shifted
Down 5	1	Up 1	94
Down 4	0	Up 2	38
Down 3	3	Up 3	12
Down 2	2	Up 4	1
Down 1	5	Up 5	3
Tied	196		

No Doubles Shifts, By Baserunners			
Runners On	Times Shifted	Runners On	Times Shifted
Nobody on	213	First & Second	15
First	101	First & Third	4
Second	11	Second & Third	3
Third	3	Bases Loaded	5

As you can see, this shift was most heavily implemented in the eighth inning or later, when tied or ahead by one run and with no runners on or a runner on first.

Looking at just those instances, looking at just those situations, the league moves into the setup 277 times in 18,084 chances. This works out to only 1.5 percent, so I tried to look for a situation that would raise the percentage, but I didn't find any. Maybe against a unique hitter (a top echelon hitter or one fast enough to take an extra base) teams will concede the single, but you don't want to give up the extra base.

The hitters who got shifted against here had an average wOBA of .319 and 3.7 Speed Score, while those not shifted against posted a .314 wOBA and 3.8 Speed Score. The hitters who are shifted on are a bit better, but not enough to make a difference.

So were these shifts effective? Let's take a look.

No Doubles Outcomes			
Stat	All	Normal	No Doubles
AVG	.257	.256	.370
OBP	.306	.304	.393
SLG	.392	.389	.538
ISO	.134	.134	.168
BB%	5.9%	6.0%	3.7%
K%	19.0%	19.1%	9.9%

The implementation of the no-doubles defense on this small sample turns average hitters into monsters. Normally, these hitters have a .693 OPS, but against this shift they morph into beasts, as their .931 OPS shows. When putting this shift on, the pitchers seem to bring in meatballs right across the plate for the batters. We can't tell that conclusively of course, but the drop in walks and strikeouts certainly is a strong indicator. Normally, there is a walk or strikeout 27 percent of the time, but against this shift, the total drops to under 14 percent. Pipe shots for everyone!

The goal though is to prevent doubles and triples. Unfortunately, this goal is not being achieved. In general, teams hit a double or triple 4.3 percent of the time, but when against this shift, the value increased to 5.2 percent. When just looking at balls in play, the difference lessens, but the shift didn't prevent doubles and triples (6.2 percent) as well as not shifting did (6.0 percent).

With the success rate known, which teams implement this unsuccessful strategy? I sorted by the overall count, but also totaled up the shifts during common shift times.

Team	Shifts Against Pitchers			
	All No Doubles Shift	Common Shift Times	No Shifts, Common Occurence	Rate for Common Occurence
Mets	41	36	514	6.5%
Nationals	29	26	428	5.7%
Pirates	26	19	503	3.6%
Rangers	21	17	364	4.5%
Phillies	19	19	480	3.8%
Royals	16	13	370	3.4%
Braves	15	9	428	2.1%
Giants	15	10	401	2.4%
Padres	15	15	433	3.3%
Athletics	14	10	453	2.2%
Marlins	14	10	536	1.8%
Tigers	13	9	410	2.1%
D-backs	12	9	550	1.6%
Cardinals	11	6	442	1.3%
Rays	11	11	456	2.4%
Brewers	10	6	386	1.5%
Mariners	10	6	444	1.3%
Dodgers	8	7	451	1.5%
Angels	7	5	474	1.0%
Rockies	7	6	383	1.5%
Twins	7	5	372	1.3%
Cubs	6	4	448	0.9%
Orioles	6	5	483	1.0%
Astros	5	3	401	0.7%
Yankees	5	4	446	0.9%
Reds	4	3	538	0.6%
White Sox	4	3	495	0.6%
Red Sox	3	1	479	0.2%
Indians	1	0	484	0.0%
Blue Jays	0	0	385	0.0%

The Mets put on the no-doubles defense more than any other team in the league—12 more times than the next-highest team. If you want to make a case for manager group think, the NL East is ripe for that—five of the top 11 teams here are

NL East squads. Additionally, we find that American League teams shy away from this shift. On the extreme end, the Indians implemented it only once, and the Blue Jays never did. It is almost like some teams know it is an ineffective strategy.

Conclusions

Major infield shifts with three players on one side of the infield have taken over the headlines in recent seasons, as more and more teams implement them. And, as I detailed in these pages last year and has been shown elsewhere, those shifts are on the whole very effective. But teams have been moving players around the field for decades in search of an advantage. With the help of the Inside Edge data, I was able to look at how three different shifts played out and the effectiveness of the shift. But ultimately, what I found is that in the aggregate, these shifts don't really provide said advantage.

- When teams brought in their infield in hopes of cutting down a runner at the plate, the shift didn't matter much. Outs happen at the same rate, and most of the damage is done via outfield fly balls.
- Data for shifting in the corner infielders for bunts against pitchers showed mixed data and no ideal way to implement it.
- For position players, teams shouldn't crash the corners unless they like giving the batter an additional 40 points of batting average.
- The no-doubles defense with the corner infielders guarding the line and the outfielders playing back was possibly the worst of the bunch. This shift simply doesn't work at all. When it is implemented, teams hit for more average and power. It accomplishs nothing except making the manager feel like he is in charge.

While the human element should never be stripped from the game, and managers and coaches should play their hunch when the situation feels right, on the whole, managers would be better off sticking their hands in their pockets than employing these shifts the majority of the time.

References & Resources
- All statistics courtesy of Inside Edge and FanGraphs
- 1986 World Series, Game 7: Red Sox @ Mets, MLB Classics on YouTube, *youtube. com/watch?v=ZmODgrzd_b8*

Hitting the Wall: Do Overused Catchers Fade Late?

by Shane Tourtellotte

It plays almost as a morality tale. In 1969, manager Leo Durocher had the Chicago Cubs well out in front in the newly created National League East. Up eight and a half games in mid-August, it seemed he could cruise to victory against the St. Louis Cardinals and the fluky New York Mets.

He did not. Durocher and his Cubs suffered a historic collapse, going 17-26 to close the season, the cornerstone on which the Mets built their miracle. It is perhaps to that failure, 24 years since the last time the team had reached the World Series, the belief that the Cubs are cursed can trace its origin.

What caused the collapse? Blame largely has fallen on Durocher for overworking his front-line players, running them onto the field constantly when some scattered days off would have restored their stamina in the race. Even among late swoons by the hard-ridden Ron Santo, Ernie Banks and Don Kessinger, Exhibit A in that case is Durocher's handling of catcher Randy Hundley.

The particular physical demands of the catching position mean that nobody can work behind the plate every day, or even all that close to it. Durocher ignored this received wisdom, starting Hundley at catcher in 145 games that season, plus six more where he put on the mask mid-game. Unsurprisingly, Hundley crumbled down the stretch. Against a .255/.334/.391 batting line for the full season, Hundley hit a miserable .151/.240/.221 for September and two October games.

The most shocking part is that this was standard procedure for Hundley. From 1966 to 1969, Durocher had Hundley play a total of 612 games. They were all at catcher: no pinch-hitting cameos, no easier days playing first or third. The peak of the abuse came in 1968, when he was behind the plate for 160 games. Yes, he got exactly three days off (the Cubs had one tie). His 1969 Atlas impersonation actually fell below the four-year average.

Hundley did not sustain the brutal workload. Injuries to his left knee in 1970 and his right knee in 1971 undermined his career, and he would start 100 games at catcher only one more time. Cause and effect cannot be proven—the 1970 injury came from a nasty home-plate collision—but one can definitely posit that the wear on his knees made him more susceptible.

Leo Durocher obviously leaned too hard on Randy Hundley. But how obvious is the abuse in less extreme circumstances? Do catchers noticeably wilt in the late stages of a season when they are being overworked? And how much playing constitutes overwork? This article will scout out some of the borders of catcher endurance.

Defining Usage

How do we measure catcher usage? Games played at catcher, games started at catcher, and complete games catching are all fairly imprecise. Innings caught is better but can be deceptive due to the offensive environment. In a high-scoring league, or on a team that gives up more runs than the norm, there will be more batters coming to the plate for every three outs recorded.

Plate appearances against catchers promises the greatest precision of statistics readily available. Ideally, we would use total pitches thrown to catchers, but that is taking the completism of stat-keeping a step too far, for now.

An added factor to consider is that catchers don't necessarily play just that one position. They'll sometimes perform duty in the field, though this is less tiring than their work behind the plate. To reflect this, for every defensive inning not at catcher, I credit players with two plate appearances against. This approximates the lesser but still real demands on stamina we would expect. Pinch-hitting counts for zero and will happen seldom enough not to distort the figures too far.

Going by opponent's plate appearances—I will start calling them OPA for brevity's sake—means we can expect more fatigued catchers in high-run years, as there will be more OPA for the catchers on a team to share. Tracking runs per game against the number of catchers facing at least 4,500 batters (or their equivalent) in a season generally bears this out. The parallel is by no means exact: correlation coefficient $r=0.371$. (Runs per game does track very closely with plate appearances per season.)

Managers may have noticed the heavier demands of the high-run "Steroid Era" and shifted some innings to backup catchers, switching back when the offensive tide ebbed. That could explain the fairly gentle changes in numbers, but as those numbers do still change, they clearly aren't holding catchers to pitch counts and inning limits the way they often do for pitchers.

The question thus becomes, should they?

The General Case: Position Players

Before examining catcher fatigue, it's a good idea to draw a baseline from other position players. If playing constantly or near-constantly grinds down shortstops and right fielders near season's end, it means the fatigue effects on catchers aren't due so much to the particular exigencies of that position.

I took a 10-year sample (2004 to 2013) of players who appeared in at least 160 games in a season, netting 136 player-years matching the criterion. I then set a lower bound of eight defensive innings played per team game, to exclude designated hitters and others not handling a full defensive load. This trimmed 10 player-seasons from the sample, including Billy Butler and Carlos Lee twice each.

I then looked at their tOPS+ ratings per month. tOPS+ measures a subset of a player's offensive performance against his full season, with 100 as the average. I adjusted the ratings for how the league-wide tOPS+ fluctuated month to month, so overall shifts in the offensive environment wouldn't warp the individual stats.

Averaged all together, this is how everyday players' adjusted tOPS+ figures looked by month and for the year as a whole. (April includes any games played in March; September includes regular-season games that spill into October.)

tOPS+, Non-Catcher Position Players	
Month	tOPS+
April	100.83
May	100.70
June	97.97
July	100.33
August	100.08
September	99.34
Season	99.88

The full-year undershooting of the average by an eighth of a point comes from several factors. The tOPS+ ratings are all rounded to the nearest full point, so slight inaccuracies can accumulate. Also, there are differences in how many games are played each month. Lines that would average out when weighted by games played won't when one month is assumed to be just as long as all the others.

The underlying pattern is still pretty clear. Iron-man position players are not wilting in the stretch. Two-thirds of an OPS+ point works out to roughly three points of OPS: say, one point off on-base, two off slugging. That will not ruin anybody's season.

Taking the year as a whole, one can almost see an overall pattern. Players start well, sag in June, are rejuvenated by the All-Star Break and its days off, catch a second wind in July and August, and start losing steam again in the final weeks.

There are two problems with this interpretation. First, the variations are not big enough to be confident they aren't random. Second, players who go out there every day tend to be highly productive, otherwise their managers would have more leeway to replace them on the lineup card. Highly productive players often don't get a full rest from the All-Star Break, because they're going to the All-Star Game. The rationale for the June-to-July uptick loses some force.

So for players at seven positions, constant play exerts no meaningful drag on their performance. If catchers suffer such a penalty, it points to something special in the demands of their position.

The Specific Case

I cast a wider net for catchers, looking at seasons from 1996 to 2013. The 1994-95 strike meant nobody played full seasons those years, setting a natural boundary for the survey. Finding the right workload boundaries was a trickier matter.

The average OPA for teams has fluctuated in the study period from a high of 6,342 (in 2000) to a low of 6,139 (in 2012). I rejected using a percentage of each year's figure as too unsteady: fatigue is more absolute than that. I went with round-numbered markers, starting at 5,000 (which is semi-coincidentally almost exactly 80 percent of average plate appearances per team in the 18-year sample) and going up and down in increments of 250.

This gave me a broad pool of catchers at the lowest level of 4,500 OPA, 139 total or more than seven per season. (4,500 OPA equates roughly to playing 117 full games at catcher, a heavy but not overwhelming load.) It further allowed me to track how increasing levels of use affected late-term fatigue at the plate, with the hitch of a shrinking sample size.

Looking at the adjusted tOPS+ patterns for the main group, the general theory seems to be borne out.

tOPS+, Catchers	
Month	tOPS+
April	105.24
May	99.68
June	98.81
July	100.90
August	100.17
September	94.88
Season	99.95

There is a definite tailing off in offensive performance during the final month of the season for "iron-man" (4,500+ OPA) catchers. That fade closely matches the hot start catchers have in April. Indeed, the pattern seen with position players repeats itself, only with greater magnitude. The notion that the All-Star break gives players a second wind gets a little more support.

This is a good time to note a confounding factor in the data. It's intuitive that players who have a cold April are likelier to get some bench time. This would drastically cut one's chances of a 160-game season, while having a lesser but significant effect on a catcher reaching arbitrary OPA milestones.

This means the data sets are going to lean toward players who do well in April, also tipping the other months toward negative territory. That could account for a good portion of the position players' relative success in April and fading in September. With catchers, it would have a smaller absolute effect on much larger swings, so it means much less toward the pattern we see.

With meaningful fatigue effects established at the 4,500 OPA level, we might expect that those effects would strengthen as the workload grew heavier. This turns out not to be so. Raising the threshold lessens the September swoon, until the sample size becomes so small as to be useless.

tOPS+, Catchers, by OPA level								
Min. OPA	Seasons	April	May	June	July	Aug.	Sept.	Season
4,500	139	105.24	99.68	98.81	100.90	100.17	94.88	99.95
4,750	85	103.86	100.88	98.43	96.73	100.31	97.75	99.66
5,000	38	104.76	95.11	100.39	100.74	96.26	100.89	99.68
5,250	20	107.15	105.60	92.30	96.60	98.95	96.90	99.58
5,500	4	117.00	86.00	100.25	91.50	118.50	84.50	99.62

Note that the All-Star hypothesis loses the support it had once we go to higher OPA numbers. Those are also smaller sample sizes, so the counter-example isn't a full disproof, but it does deflate the balloon a good deal.

It may be easier to show how the fatigue patterns change by separating the sample buckets, so one does not contain the others. For the sake of uncluttering the table, I will leave out the middle months of the season this time.

tOPS+, Catchers, by OPA buckets				
OPA	Seasons	April	Sept.	Season
4,500-4,749	54	107.30	89.46	100.37
4,750-4,999	47	103.26	96.23	99.67
5,000+	38	104.76	100.89	99.68

The September penalty for moderately heavy use rises past 10 points of tOPS+, shrinking to three for the next level then becoming a tiny bonus for the most over-worked catchers. I can see two possible factors that would create the overall pattern, plus a third that would help explain the seeming invulnerability of the 5,000+ OPA catchers. That third I will save for later.

The first factor is Darwinian selection. Catchers whose batting holds up well to season's end may be more resistant to the types of nagging injuries that can degrade physical performance. This strongly implies resistance to more serious injuries that can lead to a few weeks on the disabled list, knocking one's workload from Herculean to merely heavy (or from heavy to off the lists). Only the strongest survive to put up seasons with 4,750 OPA, or 5,000, or more.

The second factor is intelligent design. Managers, and analytics offices, can see how front-line catchers bear up during the long season. Those who weaken in the final months may have their workloads trimmed back in later seasons so they don't run out of gas. Those who finish strong even under punishing schedules will get the chance to do it again, to pile up added value for their teams.

If these factors are operating, we should see signs of it in the data. Catchers with a lot of high-work seasons under their belts would show less propensity to melt in September than those with just a few, or one. I looked for that pattern next.

The Winnowing

There are 48 separate catchers in the survey with at least one season of 4,500 OPA or more. Of those, 19 have accumulated three or more such seasons; 14 have at least four. I split the set into two groups two ways, using three or four seasons as the cut-off, and totalled up how they fared in the Septembers of all their iron-man years. The numbers were pretty clear.

Adjusted Sept. tOPS+ by Iron-Man Seasons					
Iron-Man Seasons	Seasons	Adj. Sept. tOPS+	Iron-Man Seasons	Seasons	Adj. Sept. tOPS+
1 or 2	40	88.3	1 to 3	55	88.9
3 or more	99	97.5	4 or more	84	98.8

One caveat: some surveyed catchers are still in mid-career, eligible to play more iron-man seasons. Likewise, some earlier catchers have only the tail ends of their careers covered, meaning they may have played some overwork seasons that aren't tallied. These factors potentially warp the numbers, but with a margin as strong as this, wider error bars do not really change the conclusion.

That margin remains strong and constant through several other ways of interpreting the data. Among them:

- Catchers with one hard-use year had an average 83.39 September tOPS+ (adjusted), those with two came out at 80.21, those with three had a 90.4 average, and those with four or more heavy-load seasons averaged a 98.81.

- Catchers' first "iron" seasons had an 83.39 tOPS+ average for catchers with one such season. For those with two, it took a flukish jump to 109.09 (but you'll see just below how that balanced out). That fell back to 80.4 for those with three "iron" seasons, and for catchers with four or more, rose to 100.57. Those who had long futures as heavy-use catchers showed it early.

- Catchers' final "iron" seasons came in at (again) a 83.39 tOPS+ for those with just one, 75.00 for those with two (told you), 91.68 at three seasons, and 95.43 at four or more. This suggests that older backstops do start feeling late energy depletion in their final iron-man go-rounds as age catches up, but not as much as those combed out earlier through injury or managerial discretion.

I came up with several other breakdowns, but none of them contradicts the consensus. Catchers who pile up more heavy-duty seasons have a clear track record of holding up better at the end of the year than those with few such years.

It's fair at this point to insert a reminder. This is measuring performance compared to the player's whole year, not to the whole league. A mediocre hitter who maintains his baseline in September will score well; a powerhouse batter who fades in the stretch to a batting line still a little better than the first catcher's will score badly. Holding up well during one month is not the decisive criterion for a catcher's worth, but it does matter, especially to fans watching their hometown team get passed in the final weeks.

I mentioned three possible causes for the fatigue penalty fading away with extreme use, deferring the third until now. That third possible cause is the effect one player has on the data set I chose, and it may not be an obvious candidate for such a role.

Steel Mask, Iron Man

In the 1996-2013 period, just five catchers had six seasons or more with at least 4,500 OPA. Ramon Hernandez recorded six, while A.J. Pierzynski, Jorge Posada, and Ivan Rodriguez each logged eight. (Rodriguez had two before the cutoff year, lifting him to 10 total.) But leaving them all in the dust is Jason Kendall with 13—and all but two of those seasons had him above 5,000 OPA, without needing to adjust for positional play. Three of the four heaviest workloads in the 1996-2013 study period are Kendall's.

Among other interesting traits, Kendall was notable for strength in the stretch. In his 13 iron seasons, he averaged a September adjusted tOPS+ of 103.31. In case one suspects a fluke, his August numbers came in at 121.85. He did not just hold up late, he flourished. All by himself, he bends the trajectory of the numbers in this survey.

One might argue that this undermines my conclusions, but I disagree. Kendall's highest September tOPS+ in those dozen seasons was 137, and his lowest was 63. That range is lower than for the other four catchers anywhere near his seasons measured. Also, the standard deviation for his seasons comes in just above 22 points, his closest competitor among the four being Hernandez at 33.8. Kendall's results don't reflect random fluctuations, they resist them.

Kendall's career, running from 1996 to 2010, was remarkably free of injury for a catcher. His worst one by far came in 1999, unrelated to his defensive work. He dislocated an ankle trying to beat out a bunt and lost half the season. He invited, and shrugged off, abuse in other ways, his aggressive crowding of the plate piling up 254 career hit-by-pitches, the fifth-highest total ever.

A record like Kendall's suggests that there really are iron-man catchers who can shoulder a workload that would pulverize many of their brethren, emerge little the worse, and earn as their reward the chance to do it again next year, and next. This is no surprise probabilistically: there has to be someone on the far end of the bell curve. Jason Kendall, though, was proof of concept.

This isn't to say that he was Superman. Both FanGraphs and Baseball-Reference measure him as just below average offensively—and roughly average defensively for a catcher—over his career. He was no Mike Trout (sabermetric by-laws require acknowledging him as the standard for superstardom), but a mid-range backstop with a bat almost at average produces a good deal of value per game. Kendall's prime virtue was that you could squeeze so many games of that good value into one season.

Endurance within the season did not quite add up to endurance over his career. His last good offensive year was 2004, his ninth season out of 15, and the modest power he possessed had vanished back in 2001. His in-season steadiness may have earned him a benefit of the doubt that his weakening bat did not. Then again, he had a solid-average two-to-three WAR season as late as 2008, so he could still be worthwhile without the offense.

Kendall amassed over 40 WAR during his career. That's not a Hall of Fame level, but the Hall of Pretty Darn Good will welcome him gladly. That he maintained his production late in the season likely made it easier for managers to keep putting him behind the plate at exhausting rates. That workload might have used him up a little early by years, but with the density of value he packed into his good seasons, it probably evened out.

So maintaining one's pace through the whole season may come naturally to good catchers, indeed being part of what makes them good. Pittsburgh Pirates manager Clint Hurdle has said, "To be great, you just have to be good for a long time." Change "great/good" to "good/average" and you have Kendall's career to a T. Is it something that comes naturally to great catchers?

Saving the Best for Last

I did not intend to measure the greatness of catchers against their late-season stamina in this article, but the matter deserves at least a quick peek. Kendall's example helps to show that part of excellence lies in how often you're playing, so your value can accumulate. To borrow from Woody Allen, a big part of success is just showing up.

I picked a handful of post-war Hall of Fame-caliber catchers, looking at their heavy-use seasons and their overall September numbers in those years. All five put up high numbers of years over 4,500 OPA, though Kendall need not fear for his mark. Their performance in September varies, naturally, but overall comes out gratifyingly strong, better than the average.

Sept. tOPS+, Select Catchers		
Catcher	Seasons	Sept. tOPS+
Yogi Berra	6	102.67
Johnny Bench	11	94.45
Carlton Fisk	7	87.29
Gary Carter	10	113.80
Mike Piazza	6	113.17

This is, again, adjusted for the league's tOPS+ for September. Berra, for example, put up a 97.5 tOPS+ in his hard-use Septembers, but offense in the 1950s reliably cooled off in that month, more steadily than these days. Yogi's adjusted figures thus wind up above the average.

Berra's relatively few hard-use years must be seen in the context of a season eight games shorter, with less opportunity to pile up OPA. He had a reputation as a catcher you could run out nearly every day. His iron-man years came in a compact group from 1950 to 1956, closing with his age-31 season. Just four years later, he was a left fielder and backup catcher, though maybe less from physical breakdown than for giving Elston Howard the shot he deserved.

Bench got the rented-mule treatment early in his career. In his second full season, 1969, he had the exact same OPA as Randy Hundley, who is so bemoaned for having been overworked. The previous year, Bench had over 100 OPA more than that. He never took abuse like that again, but many hard seasons remained ahead. One could point to that as why he had to spend the last three years of his career playing the infield. Not to belittle, but his replacement was no Elston Howard.

The image of Gary Carter is not usually of someone gritty and rock-hard, but his numbers say otherwise. He had eight seasons with an adjusted OPA of 5,000 or higher, and five past 5,250, sometimes getting over the top with additional play in the field. Combined with how he finished those seasons, his stamina is up there with Jason Kendall—and he didn't exactly settle for average performance, at or behind the plate.

Piazza's number of iron-man seasons isn't as surprising as it might be. His outstanding bat insured that he'd almost never be lifted for a pinch-hitter, but you can say the same for everyone else in this section for most of their careers. He was getting lifted for defensive replacements often: he failed to finish almost a quarter of his starts at catcher, a very high total for a star. (If you really want to traumatize New York Mets fans, remind them of his experiment at first base in 2004.) Still, he had four years over 5,000 OPA, and that use did not weaken his greatest weapon.

Lastly, Carlton Fisk may not have been able to go reliably full-tilt for six months, but he compensated in longevity, lasting long enough to strap on the tools of ignorance for 106 games at the age of 43. Those seven seasons I credit him with include two consecutive years when he faced 5,580 and 5,774 OPA, utterly terrifying numbers, the latter one worse than anything Randy Hundley ever endured.

One could well argue that 5,774 OPA represents a managerial failure even worse than Durocher's. It came in 1978, the year Fisk's Boston Red Sox frittered away a 14-game margin against the New York Yankees to lose the division in an epic one-game playoff. Fisk, playing constantly, crashed to a 58 tOPS+ in the crucial final month. Of all the managerial missteps laid at the feet of Don Zimmer, could this have been the back-breaker?

Perhaps not. Zimmer took Boston's reins midway through 1976. Fisk had a heavy season that year, his third such, and finished it with a 114 tOPS+ in September. He was used massively in '77 and finished that season with a 130 tOPS+ September. Zimmer had some cause to believe Fisk would be strong in the homestretch. He would have been less confident if he'd looked up Fisk's earlier heavy seasons in 1972 and '73, when Fisk posted September tOPS+ marks of 83 and 42. Over-valuing experiences closer to us is a common failing, so I will let the shade of Zim rest a bit on this.

Leo the Lip has no excuse, though. He drove Randy Hundley through all four of his meat-grinder years and saw him crack like balsa wood each September, with tOPS+ marks of 24, 51, 44 and 28. The man could not take a hint if it was dropped on his head.

So while Hundley's late buckling was surely less decisive in the Cubs' playoff dreams vanishing than Fisk's was for the BoSox, my scorn goes not to Zimmer but to Durocher. Leo kept doing the same thing and expecting different results, which Albert Einstein is attributed as calling the definition of insanity.

And Einstein thought he couldn't understand baseball.

References & Resources
- Baseball-Reference and FanGraphs were their normal indispensible selves.
- Wikipedia provided information/sources about Randy Hundley's injuries.

Not All Fly Balls Are Created Equal

by Chris St. John

It is a typical May evening in Boston. The air is chilly and a light breeze blows through Fenway Park. Koji Uehara stands on the mound for the Red Sox in the top of the ninth inning with the score knotted at three. Zack Cozart leads off the inning with a tapper to Mike Napoli. No one covers first, allowing Cozart to reach. The speedy Billy Hamilton pinch hits, lays down a sacrifice bunt, and pushes Cozart to second. In steps Tucker Barnhart, a switch-hitting defensive-focused catcher who is a much tougher out from this, the left side. The first pitch is an 88-mph fastball, low and inside. Then comes another fastball, this one a strike low and away. Uehara toes the rubber. Barnhart readies himself as the pitch comes in low and over the plate. With all the strength he can muster, Barnhart launches the ball deep down the right field line. At the crack of the bat Shane Victorino sprints to the corner and as he stumbles at the wall, the ball drops into his glove. Out.

Fast forward a few months. It's July 26, 2014—a clear Texas summer night. The pitcher—Nate Adcock. The hitter—Josh Reddick. The first pitch is a ball low and away. Reddick then hits the next pitch—a 93 mile per hour fastball—foul. The third offering is a slider, but is thrown to the same spot, middle-in. Reddick jumps on the pitch and blasts it into the second deck at Globe Life Park. Home run.

What is the connection between these two completely separate events? The path the ball took off the bat. Both hits traveled 380 feet from home plate to their eventual landing spot. Both were hit near the right field line. Both were in the air for about six seconds. The difference? The distance from home plate to the fence. The result? A possible game-winning home run turned into a harmless fly ball.

Introduction

These variable outcomes intrigue me to no end. No other major American sport has such variability of outcomes due to the shape of the playing field. The same exact batted ball can be either the worst outcome (an out) or the best (a home run) based on the stadium in which it is hit.

Comparing these hits is possible using MLB's Gameday data. However, the location data there are calculated by fielding, not landing, location. It is also missing one important column: how long the ball was in the air. A 350-foot fly ball is not the same as a 350-foot line drive.

Thankfully, Inside Edge solves both of these problems and was used as the underlying data in this analysis. I obtained the landing point and hang time for all fly balls, line drives and pop-ups from 2012 through a majority of the 2014 season. I also used data from Baseball Savant's PITCHf/x database, ESPN Home Run Tracker and FanGraphs.

Before I continue, I must take a detour to speak about my favorite data set: the ESPN Home Run Tracker. Greg Rybarczyk created a system to find how far a home run "really went." He uses hang time and location data to recreate the path of a home run and calculate how far it would have traveled if it had dropped all the way to the ground. This system was the inspiration behind this analysis. If I were as capable as Mr. Rybarczyk, I would use the hang time data from Inside Edge to estimate the speed off the bat, apex, and launch angles of each hit, effectively creating a mini-HITf/x.

I spoke with Dr. Alan Nathan about this and he is skeptical about the accuracy of this process. At the 2013 SABR Analytics Conference, he compared actual speed off the bat data to landing point and hang time and found very large discrepancies even for stringently filtered data. Due to these limitations and skepticisms, I have instead created a comparison system using similar trajectories to find the average expected run value.

Method

As stated previously, the underlying data came from Inside Edge. Each pop-up, fly ball and line drive has an x/y coordinate that shows where the ball lands on the field. Using these coordinates, I calculated the distance and spray angle each ball in play traveled. For home runs, I used ESPN Home Run Tracker's "True Distance" variable instead, which calculates how far the ball would have traveled if it had fallen all the way to the ground. This places home runs that land high in the stands on the same landing plane as fly balls that drop in the field of play or are caught by fielders.

However, distances calculated from Inside Edge data for balls that hit high off the wall may be miscalculated by a few feet since they are still traveling horizontally and landing height is not a known variable. In general this isn't a big issue, as the added distance is most likely only a few feet. Fenway, AT&T Park and other very high-walled stadiums will have much larger errors, though.

With the data in hand—distance, spray angle, and hang time—I put similar trajectories in buckets with which to compare each hit. These buckets were plus-or-minus 10 feet, ±2.5 degrees, and ± 0.1 seconds of hang time. The average number of similarly batted balls is 76.

The data are fuzziest in terms of distance, since every field is a different size and shape. This makes plotting the exact point a ball lands in the outfield somewhat difficult. However, an approximately 450-square foot landing area is enough range. Hang time can be calculated with much better precision, and a spread of almost a quarter of a second should be enough. Just to see how these ranges affected the overall results, I used different values and gained similar conclusions.

Then, using these same buckets and the Fangraphs wOBA constant for each result, I found the average run value of each trajectory. For example, say a ball is hit 400 feet to straight center and hangs in the air for 5.3 seconds. Of the balls hit with this trajectory and using the ranges given above, there were one error, 46 fly outs, 16 doubles, nine triples and 12 home runs. Using the run value for each, the expected run value (xRV) for this trajectory is 0.72.

Now we have the expected run value of every hit in the air, regardless of outcome. Instead of a results-based calculation, we have a process-based calculation and can dive into the data and compare the process with the results.

Expected Run Value Analysis

At first, it may help to visualize the data. What is the expected run value for various locations on the baseball field?

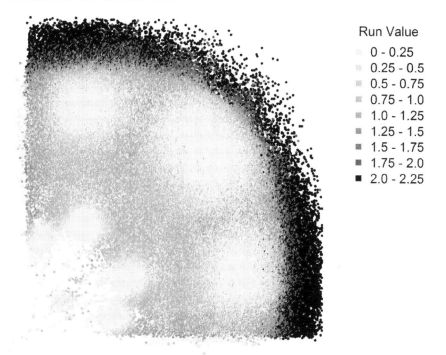

Run Value
0 - 0.25
0.25 - 0.5
0.5 - 0.75
0.75 - 1.0
1.0 - 1.25
1.25 - 1.5
1.5 - 1.75
1.75 - 2.0
2.0 - 2.25

This is to be expected. Run value is highest at greater distances from home plate. Center field is the hardest place to hit a home run. There are large swaths of low run value in the outfield where the fielders stand, with a bigger hole in center field than in right and left, since the fielders who patrol there have more range. There are also places of low run value behind the infielders' typical areas, especially shortstop and second base. The large gathering of hits in the center of the diamond is those pesky line drives that land behind the pitcher's mound and skip out toward center field. However, that covers only two dimensions. How does run value increase as the distance and hang time increase?

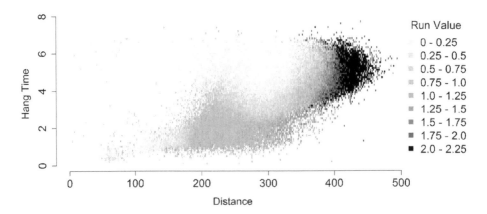

In general, if a ball goes more than 150 feet and is in the air for fewer than 2.5 seconds, it lands as a hit. As distance and hang time increase, so does run value. There is a large spread of hang time possibilities between 200 and 250 feet; the longer these balls are in the air, the more likely they are to be caught. But the most interesting area of the chart is the intersection of landing points over 350 feet. This is where doubles become triples, triples become singles, singles become home runs, and home runs become outs. This subsection of batted ball trajectories is absolutely bananas, and much of it happens due to the arbitrary shape of the playing field.

Unfortunately, this does not take every variable into account. Wind and temperature are two big variables that affect the ball flight path. Temperature is a somewhat easy correction, but wind is difficult to apply to every batted ball. The only currently easily attainable data are the initial weather conditions for each game, but the value of these data are limited on its own, as wind changes abruptly moment by moment and can vary by location within the stadium as well as by altitude.

Another missing variable is the position of the fielder. Improved positioning has grown exponentially in the major leagues due to the realization that hitters can't control exactly where the ball goes. Hitters put the ball in similar areas on average and it is very difficult for them to adjust on the fly. But are some hitters better at this than others? What if the hitter gets a pitch that he can put in a gap? Regardless, the position and quality of the fielder definitely impact whether a ball lands for a hit.

With those caveats out of the way, let's move on to anecdotal results. The home run with the lowest expected run value during this period was hit by Dustin Pedroia on June 5, 2013. In any other park, it would have been a can of corn, a pop-up to the left fielder. But in Fenway it was a home run just over the Green Monster. The out with the highest run expectancy was also at Fenway Park, this one to right field.

On Aug. 19, 2014, Brock Holt hit an impressive shot that flew over 380 feet into the bullpen, but Kole Calhoun leaned over the fence to pull it back.

Expected Run Average Overall

What happens if we add up all of these trajectories from 2012 through 2014? Which players hit the ball in the air with the highest expected run value trajectory, regardless of outcome?

xRV Top 10			
Hitter	Chances	xRV	xRV AVG
Chris Davis	621	420.5	0.677
Giancarlo Stanton	540	364.0	0.674
Carlos Gonzalez	461	307.5	0.667
Pedro Alvarez	535	344.3	0.644
Paul Goldschmidt	662	420.2	0.635
Matt Kemp	458	289.8	0.633
Joey Votto	538	337.2	0.627
Adam Dunn	550	344.0	0.626
Miguel Cabrera	824	502.2	0.609
Michael Morse	426	258.5	0.607

The order is interesting, but this is a list of well-known power hitters. Chris Davis had a down 2014, but his expected run value is tops in baseball over the past three years on the strength of his monster 2013 season. Giancarlo Stanton has been much more consistent even as he battled through injuries in both 2012 and 2013. Carlos Gonzalez and Paul Goldschmidt almost certainly benefit from their home parks, but they would be elite power hitters even in different areas of the country.

By total expected run value added, Miguel Cabrera is number one since he has hit the ball in the air more often than other top hitters. This may be because of his ability to follow through on his approach. He likely knows that a ground ball may not be the best result for him and is capable of putting the ball in the air when he desires.

Jose Abreu vs. George Springer			
Hitter	Chances	xRV	xRV AVG
Jose Abreu	182	133.5	0.733
George Springer	98	65.0	0.663

Two players who don't have enough chances yet but are worth mentioning are Jose Abreu and George Springer. Their current xRV averages are high enough to be on this list, and I would expect them to get there eventually. In fact, Abreu's 2014 numbers were the best in baseball by a wide margin.

xRV Bottom Five			
Hitter	Chances	xRV	xRV AVG
Kurt Suzuki	539	187.9	0.349
Darwin Barney	594	213.2	0.359
Clint Barmes	403	145.5	0.361
Ruben Tejada	464	171.7	0.370
Alberto Callaspo	642	240.0	0.374

The hitters with the lowest expected run value are a bunch of light hitters. Many of their fly balls end up going right to the area where the outfielders generally stand.

The Mike Trout Differential

Finding which players hit the ball with the best trajectory is a non-trivial pursuit, but I want to look even deeper. What happens when we compare the expected with the actual run value? Then we have differential run value (dRV). These are plays that "should have" been an out but were actually not and vice versa.

If we add up all of the dRV values for each hitter, some definite separation occurs. Here are the best and worst hitters at getting a higher run value than expected from the trajectory of their batted balls:

Player dRV		
Hitter	Chances	dRV
Mike Trout	722	42.7
Cody Ross	438	26.4
Yoenis Cespedes	723	26.2
Mike Napoli	472	25.4
Seth Smith	476	21.6
Jarrod Saltalamacchia	486	20.9
Carlos Gomez	630	20.5
Alex Gordon	771	20.2
Starling Marte	350	18.9
Ryan Braun	523	18.2
David Wright	701	-18.8
Victor Martinez	557	-20.3
Matt Holliday	683	-20.4
A.J. Ellis	442	-21.2
Daniel Murphy	812	-24.3

Here we go again. Mike Trout or Miguel Cabrera? Cabrera hits the ball with the best trajectory, but Trout gets more value out of where he hits it. Out of the 24 parks in which he has qualifying hits, only seven have a total negative dRV. The places he has performed the worst are Baltimore's Camden Yards, Turner Field in Atlanta and Minute Maid Park. At this point the samples are very small, but it does appear Trout has been trying for right field in Camden and has been a bit unlucky (or perhaps Nick Markakis is Trout's kryptonite). The stadiums he performs best in are Angel Stadium, Fenway Park and O.co Coliseum. He actually has a slightly higher dRV on the road than he does at home.

Where do these hits land? Trout takes advantage of right center and center the most, but has a positive value everywhere except down the right field line. This may be due to his ability to place the ball with authority over the center fielder's head.

Mike Trout dRV by Hit Location			
Field	Chances	dRV	dRV Rate
Right Center	73	13.4	0.183
Center Field	160	8.3	0.052
Left Field Line	43	5.3	0.123
Left Field	42	4.5	0.107
Right Field	91	4.1	0.045
Left Center	65	3.7	0.058
Right Field Line	92	-0.4	-0.005

What are the results of these extra hits and what did we expect them to be based on their trajectory?

Mike Trout dRV by Outcome							
Outcome	Chances	dRV	xOut%	x1B%	x2B%	x3B%	xHR%
Out	390	-40.6	90.9%	3.8%	4.4%	0.7%	0.2%
1B	135	16.4	16.8%	76.5%	6.0%	0.7%	0.0%
2B	88	31.8	24.6%	19.1%	51.1%	4.0%	1.2%
3B	24	20.1	42.9%	3.3%	42.1%	6.9%	4.8%
HR	85	15.0	6.4%	0.0%	4.0%	1.8%	87.6%

Trout gets most of his extra runs from doubles, but he truly separates himself from the league with extra singles and triples. Seventeen percent of his singles and 43 percent of his triples were expected to be outs. The extra singles are mostly weakly hit to routine or shallow right field. On average, they are easy outs but in this situation they had a very low likelihood of being caught according to Inside Edge, probably since the outfielder was playing in a different area. Most of the triples were well-hit to right center field, perfectly placed in the gap between outfielders.

One particularly interesting hit was a triple to right center. Out of the 386 similar trajectories there was one single, 61 doubles, and 18 triples. The other 306 were outs. Typically well-regarded center fielder Austin Jackson took a strange route to the ball, which then spun in an abnormal way after hitting the ground. One hypothesis I have in terms of why Trout so outperforms the expected run value is that he hits the ball with an extreme amount of spin. There were many plays that should have been outs where Trout hit the ball and the outfielder stumbled over his feet and misplayed the ball.

Alan Nathan thought the idea that sidespin added to Trout's ability in this area was intriguing and would be easily testable with launch angle, landing angle and hang time. So I used ESPN Home Run Tracker's initial launch angle and Inside Edge's landing angle and calculated the sidespin for each of his home runs.

For home runs hit to right field, Trout actually has a sidespin closer to zero than average. Many of the hitters with less sidespin are left-handed or switch-hitters. Trout has the 15th highest spin of right-handed hitters with at least five home runs to right field since 2012. This is not exactly a smoking gun; however, there may be other factors here such as discrepancies between the two data sets and the fact that home runs hit farther away from center have more spin regardless of who hits them. A more thorough analysis may prove fruitful.

Trout is obviously an outlier here, but what do we make of the rest of the results? Are the hitters with high dRV lucky due to their ballpark or are they skilled at missing the fielders? What about hitters with low dRV? Which ones are hitting in a bad stadium for their skills? Which ones lack bat control? A study that included fielder positioning data might provide answers to those questions.

Best I can tell, Trout combines a mixture of a great eye, elite bat control, impressive power, and blinding speed. The combination of all of these skills puts him on a level far beyond anyone else in the major leagues.

Home Field Advantage

While studying Trout's dominance in this area, I started poking into how well teams take advantage of their own ballpark. I calculated the dRV for home and away teams at each park per chance. Then I found the difference between these rates and scaled back up to the season level (approximately 2,400 chances). The result is a factor of home-field advantage (listed as HFA).

Team	xRV Home	xRV Away	HFA	Team	xRV Home	xRV Away	HFA
Red Sox	214.4	59.8	147.4	Padres	56.4	52.3	8.9
Angels	101.6	36.2	70.7	Astros	63.9	70.4	4.0
Marlins	-18.8	-87.6	64.5	Rockies	9.2	6.5	2.7
Braves	24.3	-36.0	63.8	Nationals	49.7	47.1	2.4
Cubs	67.8	8.2	63.2	Rangers	-63.7	-62.5	-4.2
Pirates	-7.6	-54.6	53.0	White Sox	-15.5	-8.7	-6.8
Reds	43.8	13.7	31.7	Yankees	36.6	44.8	-7.0
Brewers	45.4	17.3	29.3	Blue Jays	50.9	64.8	-11.6
Royals	23.2	-5.5	28.8	Cardinals	-18.1	-4.9	-13.1
A's	81.1	50.2	26.6	Phillies	82.7	101.0	-13.4
D-backs	3.3	-17.1	20.4	Tigers	-26.6	-9.2	-15.6
Rays	26.0	5.8	19.8	Mariners	-14.2	6.0	-20.4
Indians	17.5	3.1	14.9	Dodgers	-101.5	-59.2	-43.0
Orioles	40.4	26.3	14.8	Twins	63.8	126.9	-48.5
Giants	-29.8	-39.9	9.9	Mets	-110.3	-69.8	-48.6

The Boston Red Sox gain 150 runs more than their opponents from the difference between the expected and the actual run value of their hits, which is a direct result of the Green Monster. Since these balls are not calculated exactly due to hitting high off the wall, this number may be slightly inaccurate. But the fact that the Red Sox take advantage of the Green Monster more than their opponents is definitely true. This may have to do both with the fielders not playing the ball off the wall properly and hitters aiming that way more often. The most successful hitters at Fenway are Dustin Pedroia and David Ortiz.

In addition to playing the Green Monster better, the Red Sox are much better than their opponents at avoiding the depths of right field. Those two fields—Fenway right and left—are the top two fields in baseball in terms of home field advantage. The away players to get the most out of Fenway Park are Nick Swisher and...Mike Trout.

Which brings us back to the Angels. Not only is Mike Trout tops in baseball by far, but the Angels are second only to the Red Sox in terms of dRV home field advantage. Angel Stadium is shaped in a fairly normal way, but it is asymmetrical. The deepest area in the ballpark is slightly to the right of center, which is the third highest location in terms of home field advantage in baseball. However, the Angels' extra hits are spread all around the park, unlike the Red Sox who have a large concentration of unlikely hits to the Monster.

I found that the Angels hit the ball with a slightly lower hang time at home than their opponents, so perhaps they are more line-drive friendly. However, as a team, the Angels have a higher hang time at Angel Stadium than away from it. Maybe the wind whips around the ballpark and the home team knows how to play into it. Maybe visiting outfielders have poor positioning due to the park being asymmetrical. Maybe the Angels in the outfield can cover more ground and take away the gap in deep right center. Whatever the case, Trout, Albert Pujols, Erick Aybar, Mark Trumbo and Howie Kendrick in particular have taken advantage of it.

Ballparks

We touched on it in the team analysis, but which stadium locations affect the result of hits the most? Again, this does not take environmental impacts into account. For instance, some parks are known to be windier, which may impact how hard it is to get the ball to a certain trajectory. This simply states that once the ball reaches a certain trajectory, how likely is it to land for a hit?

Stadium	Field	Feature	HFA/season	dRV
Fenway Park	Left	Green Monster	46.9	392.5
Minute Maid Park	Left	Crawford Boxes	10.3	175.9
Target Field	Right	Overhang	-33.9	142.5
Yankee Stadium	Right	Short Porch	-15.2	112.6
Comerica Park	Left	Unknown	0.6	-143.5
AT&T Park	Right	Triples' Alley	-12.1	-152.9
Fenway Park	Right	Deep	49.8	-165.5

The four-easiest ballpark locations for extra-base hits are all well known and directly connected to peculiar ballpark features. As stated before, the Red Sox are the best team at taking advantage of their ballpark. Conversely, the Twins have actually been outperformed by their opponents in right field. It may be that their regular right fielder, Oswaldo Arcia, is not good at reading the overhang and does not have the speed to make up for the mistakes. Another possibility is that the Twins have not had the left-handed power hitters that their opponents have had. Maybe as Arcia and Kennys Vargas continue to mature as hitters they can pelt right field together.

Detroit's Comerica Park confuses me. I looked at many of the surprising results there and still cannot place my finger on why there are so many. My only guess is that the wall is at a perfect angle, distance and height, creating a perfect storm where most potential home runs land either just short of the wall or close enough to it and are easier to rob. Many of the underperforming trajectories were home runs pulled back over the wall for an out.

Center field is harder to hit a home run to in general, so it does not appear in a counting stat such as this. The hardest center field by far is Minute Maid in Houston, with Marlins Park and Tropicana Field in St. Petersburg distant seconds. Comerica, even with its deep 420-foot dimension, shows up as nearly average. The easiest center fields are Milwaukee's Miller Park and O.co Coliseum.

Conclusions

We covered more area in this research than Willie Mays at the Polo Grounds, but what did we learn? Miguel Cabrera has the best quality and quantity of fly balls while Mike Trout gets more value from the trajectory of his than anyone else by a large margin.

Similarly, the Red Sox have a massive home field advantage due to the dimensions of their park. Whether this comes from a superior offensive approach of wearing out the Monster, defensive familiarity with the ballpark or a mixture of both, Fenway is indeed friendly, at least to the home team.

In addition to the two positive and negative outliers at Fenway, many of the easiest and hardest places to get the appropriate run value from a fly ball are linked to well-known ballpark features. Left field at Comerica is the only unknown.

In the end, this study produced more questions than answers, the first question being how the elements affect the actual flight of the ball. A more exhaustive wind, temperature and altitude model may help create better comparisons among the trajectories, as would the HITf/x data that we don't have to access to in the public sphere. With it, we could compare batted balls based on bat speed and vertical and horizontal launch angles, giving the results much more accuracy and precision.

Secondly and finally, how does fielder positioning play into this? The new StatCast system could be combined with hit location to find hitters who avoid fielders better. Are teams better at positioning their fielders at home? As I said at the outset, this area of research fascinates me, and while it's great to have a baseline of information, said baseline has only further stoked my curiousity.

References & Resources

- My thanks to Jeff Zimmerman, Alan Nathan, Bill Petti, Daren Willman, Stephen Loftus, Matthew Yaspan, the ESPN Home Run Tracker and the folks at Inside Edge for their assistance in this project.

Will Insurance or Long-Term Deals Dominate?

by Matt Swartz

Young baseball players have signed long-term deals with gradually less service time in recent years. This came to a head during the 2014 season, when Jonathan Singleton signed a guaranteed $10 million deal with the Houston Astros before making his major league debut in June. On the other extreme, Max Scherzer turned down a $144 million deal from the Tigers just a year away from free agency, instead opting to reach an agreement with an insurance company to hedge against the risk of injury before becoming a free agent at the end of 2014 campaign.

Both of these agreements reflect the reality that players are reluctant to take on risk and would prefer a guaranteed sum of money. Dave Cameron wrote about this in an excellent and insightful piece at FanGraphs, in which he discussed the fact that although players are eager to transfer the risk of their future earnings to another entity, teams do not have a monopsony on purchasing this risk. Although the other 29 teams are unable to negotiate with a player until he hits the open market, there is no such rule for insurance companies.

While insurance companies forays into baseball have traditionally focused on providing insurance to teams that have guaranteed money to players, the example of Scherzer clearly shows that there are now four possibilities:

1. Player signs extension with no insurance involvement
2. Player signs extension and team purchases insurance
3. Player does not sign extension and purchases insurance himself
4. No extension or insurance contract is signed

The fundamental reason why any of these deals exist is that a player's utility of the expected earnings is greater than the expected utility of earnings. A guaranteed $15 million is a lot more attractive than a 50/50 shot at $30 million or $0, and it is so much more attractive that most people would happily take a guaranteed $10 million rather than the 50/50 gamble for $30 million. A team or an insurance company, by making many of these $10 million dollars deals, can get $15 million on average and make a profit. This is because of the well-known diminishing marginal utility for money, i.e. $20 million is nowhere near twice as good as $10 million. Each dollar you receive is less valuable than the next. This is the reason why insurance exists, and Cameron is correct when he writes that teams are not the only entity capable of buying risk from a player.

This obviously piqued my curiosity, as I have the (probably) unique position of working full-time for an insurance company (whose views I do not speak for in this article), and moonlighting for a baseball team (whose views I also do not speak for in this article). This is a market that has yet to settle, and forecasting where these types of deals will go requires an understanding of the market forces behind them. In this article, I will discuss these forces and explain where I believe the market is headed over the next few years.

Why do multi-year deals exist in the first place?

The first question to ask is why any multi-year deals exist at all. Why would a team and a player on the free-agent market prefer to reach a long-term deal instead of a short deal for more money annually? Teams obviously prefer to avoid commitment where possible, and players obviously prefer longer deals at the same annual value, but why do teams instead choose to offer lower annual rates for longer instead of simply increasing the salary on a one-year deal? There are many factors afoot.

Diminishing marginal utility

As explained above, players are happy to take less money on a long-term deal than they would expect to make being a free agent every season because it provides them with financial security. They sell risk to a team.

Cost certainty for teams

Rather than engage in many different negotiations with players for every roster spot each offseason, teams would prefer knowing that they have given players under control, and they are willing to trade flexibility for knowing their costs and the players they have.

Lowering negotiating costs

Reaching a new agreement with each player every year requires more work by agents, more work by lawyers, and more front-office work. Negotiating several years of salaries in one stage can lower these costs.

Lowering moving costs

Moving a player's family to another team every year is not free. Not only is it an expensive process, but it adds stress for the player and his family.

Increasing the cost of separating

People often are willing to increase their own cost of severing an agreement in the future. They do so to increase the cost to the other party of severing that agreement if the other person later so desires. That's part of what marriage contracts ("in sickness or in health") are all about.

Creating a loan from the player to the team

Although players want to transfer risk of not having money later in life to a team or insurance company once they reach a certain threshold, they should need only a fraction of their current salaries in the year that they earn them. Teams, on the other hand, are constantly focused on cash flow and would prefer to have spending money on hand. By creating a contract that pays the player the same amount each year (or more) as their production declines, the team gets added production in the early years of a long-term deal, which can be used for other investments or players. The player gets slightly more money to spend later by agreeing to this contract structure than they would if they insisted on a contract that paid them their value each year.

Brand value

If players switched teams every year upon reaching free agency, it would be harder for teams to market their players to fans. By providing continuity to the makeup of its team, an organization can sell tickets more easily than generating the same number of wins with different players each year.

––––––––––––––

Ironically, many of the above reasons why long-term deals exist are more applicable to free agent signings than to younger players. That is why young players often get one-year contracts each year and free agents often get multi-year deals. This is why I believe that young players like Singleton, rather than established stars like Scherzer, may be more likely to contract directly with insurance companies in the future, while established stars may be more likely to sign extensions.

Which players will most desire financial security?

Players will always want their money to be guaranteed, but they will vary greatly in what they consider an acceptable discount. Players who are more risk-averse are naturally going to be inclined to take a discount, but "risk-averse" is not a personality trait as much as it is determined by a player's situation. Mathematically, risk-averse means that the second derivative of a player's utility function for money is negative. Verbally, even though every dollar adds something, the steeper the decline in the value of an additional dollar, the more likely a player will be to take a deal. There are several groups of players who will be more likely to have very negative second derivatives for money.

Young players

The first $10 million is worth a lot more than the second $10 million. The first $10 million establishes a comfortable lifestyle for the rest of your life and any opportunities for your children you could realistically imagine. The second $10 million is for yachts and bling. However, the difference between the second $10 million and the third $10 million is nowhere near as large. The third $10 million is also for yachts and bling, just bigger and shinier, respectively. (At the risk of drowning the reader in math, this means that the third derivative of utility for money is positive.) Players with established wealth are far less likely to take extreme discounts to get guarantees.

Foreign players, particularly from Latin America

Baseball players are not going to make anywhere near as much money in other industries as they would in baseball, Bo Jackson and Deion Sanders notwithstanding. However, the prospects are far more lucrative for players born in the United States than in countries with fewer economic opportunities. The average income per person in the United States is about $52,000. Other countries that produce a lot of ballplayers earn far less. In terms of purchasing power parity, the Dominican Republic only averages about $11,000 per person, Mexico only averages about $16,000 per person, and Venezuela only averages about $18,000 per person, as does Argentina.

A player whose alternative is working in a country with fewer opportunities than the United States, especially a young player without established wealth, will be more inclined to take a discount on average. (I noted this in an August piece at THT's website.)

Players without college educations, incomplete college educations, or with less lucrative degrees in terms of school or major

Although the average income in the United States is about $52,000, there is a pretty wide distribution around this. A player coming out of an Ivy League school with an engineering degree probably has a lot more opportunity to make a living after his baseball career and would be less likely to take a sure thing, while a player without similar alternatives might jump at the security of a discounted long-term deal.

Pitchers

Although pitchers do not quite fit the criteria of having different economic opportunities outside of baseball, they do have more variance when it comes to their future earnings within baseball. A pitcher knows he has a higher chance of getting injured than a hitter and may be more likely to accept guaranteed money early on in his career to insure against this.

Risk factors for player value

Of course, most players are not on multi-year deals. There are several risk factors that would deter teams or insurers from wanting to guarantee money to a player. Each of these can make either contract extensions and/or insurance agreements less likely to happen.

Uncertainty of production even if healthy

This actually may be the most important reason. Even most free-agent contracts are one-year deals, and the reason is that most players may not be worth their roster spot the following season. A player who is more likely to get injured but will otherwise play well will receive less money in a multi-year deal than otherwise, but a player who may decline below replacement level is unlikely to get a multi-year deal. The uncertainty of production from a healthy player is also something a team cannot obtain insurance for easily, because it is difficult to contract hypotheticals—you cannot ask an insurance company to give up the value of a player's salary because your coaches have determined in spring training that he wouldn't outplay the young rookie the team has been grooming.

Injury due to a publicly predictable cause

Purely public knowledge of injury risk actually opens the door to insurance. If the team, the player, and the insurer are all aware that a player has a history of injuries, but none of them is any better able to predict the injury than any other, the team can sign the player to the extension and purchase insurance, or the player can purchase insurance directly. Which path will be taken will rest on whether the team values the player more highly than other teams, in which case the insurer would not have an incentive to outbid the team when deciding how much to guarantee the player. In that case, the team and insurer can still reach a deal to reduce the uncertainty for the team. If the player would be valued more elsewhere, the insurer can purchase the risk directly at a price the team would pass up.

Injury due to a privately predictable cause

If teams and insurers have asymmetric information about the medical history and injury risk of a player, the insurer is unlikely to want to contract with the team if it extends the player. If the team does not extend the player, the insurer surely would become aware that the team has avoided this for a reason and would be unlikely to contract with the player himself. In this case, the team may still decide to extend the player if the player is willing to take a sufficient discount—which he often would if he possesses the same information as the team about his health.

Injury due to a random cause

Fluke injuries happen. Like the publicly predictable cause, as long as the team, the insurer, and the player do not have differing information about the probability of the injury occurring (or re-occuring), this can be a fertile ground for insurance for either the team or the player.

Uncertainty of the value of wins to the team

Even if we knew that a given player will add exactly three wins relative to his replacement, a team may not know how to value that. This is especially true several years in the future. For some teams, like the Yankees, Dodgers, or Red Sox, they know they will add a large sum of revenue for wins in any environment as they attempt to compete every year. However, for teams that are only competitive some of the time, such as the Diamondbacks, Mariners or Twins, they may have a very high value for a win if they are on the cusp of the playoffs or a low value if they are rebuilding. This can deter teams from signing extensions because even sustained high levels of production may not generate the revenue necessary to warrant the large salary. These cases are fertile grounds for players to contract with insurers directly.

Uncertainty of player effort

This can deter either insurers or teams from wanting to guarantee money for players. Knowing that the guarantee could change the player's behavior can kill any potential deal.

Overall, when all known information is publicly agreed upon and when expectations of behavior are known, insurance can add value. However, the economic value generated may vary depending on whether the insurer contracts with the team or with the player directly. The very existence of insurance may be enough to remove the team's monopsony on purchasing a player's services, but in some cases, a looming insurer may only function to drive up salaries for long-term deals that would happen whether insurance existed or not. However, if a player's current team values his performance less than another team would, an insurer is more likely to contract with the player directly.

Adverse Selection

One of the greatest dangers to insurance is adverse selection, the corrosive market process that transpires if buyers and sellers have asymmetric information. Based on my research, this is definitely most likely to be the case for pitchers. Consider the following table from my article in March at The Hardball Times website on the methodology and calculations of how I compute the cost per WAR on the free-agent market. Hitters who sign with new teams ("Other People's Players" or "OPP") have almost no difference between their performances on a per-dollar basis relative to hitters who re-sign. However, pitchers produce far less per dollar when they sign with new teams. To wit:

Revised OPP Premium						
Group	$/fWAR, re-signed	$/fWAR, OPP	fWAR OPP Premium	$/rWAR, re-signed	$rWAR, OPP	rWAR OPP Premium
Hitters	5.8	5.8	0%	5.7	6.0	5%
Pitchers	6.2	7.7	25%	6.2	8.5	36%

As I explained in more detail in *The 2012 Hardball Times Annual*, this is primarily because teams know more about their own pitchers than other teams. This same market failure easily could wound the insurance market as well. Just as other teams who scout a player over a long period of time cannot gather the same information as a team with inside information about a pitcher (his current team), neither can the insurance company.

As a result, I expect insurance companies will be more likely to eschew insuring pitchers whose teams will not sign them to extensions and probably will offer less generous coverage (e.g. higher deductibles and longer elimination periods) for pitchers in general. Hitters may be more likely to be insured directly or have more thorough insurance agreements with teams who have extended hitters. However, there is some tendency for OPP bias among hitters, too (particularly with longer-term deals), so any other players whose teams have potential inside information may be less likely to be extended.

Moral Hazard

Another common foil to any type of contract is moral hazard, in which a party is likely to take risks after a contract is reached that it would not otherwise take. For instance, some players with guaranteed contracts may be less likely to stay in shape. This could lead to shorter deals than would be possible otherwise. On the other hand, teams could be more likely to work a pitcher harder if they know that the insurer will pick up the cost of an injury. This could lead to fewer insurance contracts, as well.

A more subtle example of moral hazard comes from playing time. A team could be more likely to promote a player or give him more playing time if they do not believe it will hurt them in arbitration. This actually could encourage players to sign contracts in an effort to avoid this situation. Such was the case with Singleton. Although moral hazard is less likely to become an issue than adverse selection, it is still an important topic to keep in mind.

Partial Insurance

Just because a fully insured contract could run the risks of adverse selection or moral hazard, this need not preclude partial insurance. This could take the form of higher deductibles or longer elimination periods (time a player needs to miss before the insurance kicks in). Either way, keep in mind that when I say insurance is less likely in one case or another, this is really a continuum.

Forecasting Results

Now that I've laid out the particulars, let's dive into some explicit predictions of how the market will play out over the next several years. Before I start to forecast where I think the market is going, let's recap who and what the decision-makers and categories of outcomes are:

Decision-makers
- Players
- Teams with rights to a player
- Teams without rights to a player
- Insurers

Categories of outcomes
- Player signs extension and team doesn't get insurance
- Player signs extension and team gets insurance
- Player gets insurance directly and doesn't sign extension
- Player doesn't reach agreement with insurer or team

Predicted trends
- Young players will prefer to sell risk away, and when they can achieve an agreement large enough to provide some long-term stability, they usually will do so. Young players with the most incentives to reduce their risk, typically those with the least lucrative economic alternatives to baseball (e.g. those who are foreign, those with low education levels, or those with less lucrative degrees), will be more likely to settle for a guarantee from a team or insurer.
- Young players with enough upside that teams will fear large arbitration settlements will be more successful at receiving extensions from their teams. Hitters will be more likely to reach agreements with insurers than pitchers will, because of the adverse selection issue discussed above.
- Older players also will sign extensions or receive insurance in many cases, but those who have achieved a secure level of wealth will be less likely to settle for a discounted extension or insurance.
- Unhealthy pitchers, both young and old, will be less likely to be insured or extended, but many young pitchers may be willing to take steep enough discounts that an agreement with their team (if not an insurer) can be reached. However, this will be more likely to occur with teams that are perennial contenders.
- Healthy pitchers on perennial contenders may find it difficult to obtain a fair price from an insurer because they could be difficult to distinguish from players whose teams would avoid signing for fear of injury. Even healthy pitchers could look like lemons. As a result, perennial contenders will be able to receive discounts that other teams might not.
- Although players who sign extensions very early in their careers typically take major discounts, these discounts will become smaller, particularly for hitters.

Insurers will drive up these prices since teams no longer will have the same monopsony power they have enjoyed in recent years.

- Players who uniquely value their current home will be more likely to be extended rather than insured. Teams still may be able to obtain insurance in these cases.

- Teams and insurers both will be more likely to provide a guaranteed sum to a player with a stronger work ethic than they would otherwise, because they will be less afraid of the moral hazard a guarantee could create.

- Teams that want to increase playing time for a player (or perhaps even move a reliever into a closer role) will be more inclined to guarantee money up front.

- Teams who know that they will have high values for wins (again, teams like the Dodgers and Yankees, who always have the payrolls to be competitive) often will end up seeking insurance so they can spend money elsewhere in the event of an injury. Since such teams are unlikely to avoid signing players because of their certainty about their own place on the win curve, they will be the most likely to end up going through with extensions and getting insurance. On the other hand, players on teams with less certainty about their future winning potential will be more likely to get insured directly and avoid signing extensions.

- Older hitters (post-free-agent-eligibility years) on teams with more uncertainty about their future competitiveness will be the most likely to contract with insurers directly. Since they are not bound to their teams by the rules of free agency, insurers often will realize they have more value to other teams than their own teams and will outbid their current teams accordingly.

Wrapping Up

Max Scherzer's deal with an insurance company last winter has shined a light on a whole new market for baseball player value that few had considered. The typical analysis of player extensions in advance of free agency entails considering the potential value of a contract signed at a specific time in the future, and adjusting for potential risk of what could happen before then. The risk of forgoing a long-term deal that is not available later has been teams' main source of leverage in these negotiations. Now, insurance companies can provide the players with leverage.

However, that does not mean that players will ultimately sign with insurance companies in lieu of extensions, or even that the potential threat of an insurance company will drive up the extension value a team ultimately gives to a player. This will depend on a variety of circumstances, and ultimately will center on differences in information between teams and insurers, and to a lesser extent, on differences between how a player's current team values him and how other teams value him.

Ironically, it seems that, over time, young hitters like Singleton may be more likely to reach an agreement with insurance companies because of the uncertainty of their teams' future position on the win curve and the relative lack of asymmetric information between team and insurer, while insurers may be likely to avoid pitchers like Scherzer whose teams have opted not to outbid the insurer.

However, the players who are most likely to get extended are young pitchers from foreign countries who are very talented but inherently risky due to their position. The players most likely to get insured directly are older hitters on teams with uncertain future competitiveness.

References & Resources

- Dave Cameron, FanGraphs, "Max Scherzer and the Incentives to Self Insure," *fangraphs.com/blogs/max-scherzer-and-the-incentives-to-self-insure/*
- Matt Swartz, The Hardball Times, "Methodology and Calculations of Dollars per WAR," *hardballtimes.com/methodology-and-calculations-of-dollars-per-war/*
- Matt Swartz, The Hardball Times, "Searching for Racial Earnings Differentials in Major League Baseball," *hardballtimes.com/searching-for-racial-earnings-differentials-in-major-league-baseball*
- *The Hardball Times Baseball Annual 2012*
- Wikipedia, "List of Latin American and Caribbean Countries by GDP (PPP)," *en.wikipedia.org/wiki/List_of_Latin_American_and_Caribbean_countries_by_GDP_%28PPP%29*
- Wikipedia, "Adverse Selection," *en.wikipedia.org/wiki/Adverse_selection*
- Wikipedia, "Moral Hazard," *http://en.wikipedia.org/wiki/Moral_hazard*

Teams Capitalize on Antiquated Arbitration System

by Matthew Murphy

There are a number of different ways to build a winning team. The most obvious way is to spend a lot of money. Outbid your opponents for the best available players, and watch high-priced free agents carry your team to victory. Of course, it doesn't always work this way, but having extra money to throw around is always desirable. Teams without a big checkbook might have to resort to finding under-valued assets on the free agent market. They will search for players who, for one reason or another, are overlooked by other teams. The other way to build a winner is by acquiring cost-controlled players. Invest heavily in drafting, scouting, and player development. Build the farm system, and reap massive rewards when you produce cheap, major league-quality players.

The reality is that every team employs some combination of these strategies. Even teams with monster payrolls will need contributions from cost-controlled youngsters or bargain-bin veterans if they want to contend. While most estimates put the cost of a win on the open market around $6-8 million, players are paid only a fraction of their market value before they hit free agency. For teams on the lower end of the payroll spectrum, these discounted players are critical for success, especially as analytics departments grow and it becomes increasingly difficult to find true bargains in free agency. In 2014, three teams reached the playoffs despite being in the bottom half of payroll, and each relied heavily on cost-controlled talent.

The Kansas City Royals regular starting lineup featured only one player who had hit free agency. Key contributors such as Lorenzo Cain and Jarrod Dyson have yet to reach arbitration, while Alex Gordon and Salvador Perez are playing out team-friendly contracts they signed before they hit the open market. The story is similar with the Pittsburgh Pirates, who are getting huge contributions from Neil Walker (in his second arbitration year) and Josh Harrison (playing for the league minimum), while cheap extensions for Starling Marte and Andrew McCutchen continue to pay dividends.

Of the seven Oakland Athletics with the highest wins above replacement (WAR) totals in 2014, only pitcher Scott Kazmir had reached free agency. The other six players combined for just under 20 WAR—a value of nearly $150 million, depending on whose $/WAR figure you use—but earned under $10 million.

While this talent comes at a huge discount, arbitration costs can still add up. The Athletics' Opening Day roster featured 10 arbitration-eligible players who earned over $33 million, more than 40 percent of the team's payroll, a figure that is the highest in baseball. Here are the 10 teams who had the highest percentage of their Opening Day payroll dedicated to arbitration-eligible players:

Teams Most Reliant on Arbitration-Eligible Players		
Team	Arbitration ($M)	Payroll ($M)	Arbitration, as % of Payroll
A's	$33.2	$79.0	42.0%
Padres	$34.3	$86.0	39.9%
Rays	$25.9	$75.5	34.4%
Orioles	$31.8	$105.0	30.2%
Cubs	$25.3	$89.0	28.4%
Marlins	$11.7	$42.5	27.5%
Mets	$21.1	$82.0	25.7%
Tigers	$40.5	$161.0	25.1%
Pirates	$17.6	$71.5	24.6%
Royals	$21.8	$91.0	24.0%

Ten teams coughed up more than $20 million in arbitration, and eight teams committed over a quarter of their payroll for arbitration salaries. This doesn't even count any money from contract extensions signed before free agency, which would drive up these numbers further.

The key takeaway here is that while arbitration-eligible players are paid at a discounted rate, many teams are paying out large sums of money in arbitration. With so much money on the line, teams have a big incentive to identify ways they can save money in the arbitration process.

The Disconnect Between Arbitration and the Open Market

The free agent market has evolved quite a bit over the past decade, especially in the past few years. Position players who generate much of their value through their defense, baserunning, or on-base percentage, aren't going overlooked anymore.

Of all the recent changes in values on the free agent market, perhaps no position has been affected more than the relief pitcher. Between 2008 and 2011, eight multi-year contracts went to relief pitchers with an average annual value (AAV) of more than $10 million. After seeing players like Brad Lidge and Heath Bell completely fall apart after signing multi-year contracts, the market for Proven Closers began to (or continued to) soften.

In the past two years, only Jonathan Papelbon and Rafael Soriano received multi-year contracts with an AAV of over $10 million, despite the continued increase in the cost of a win. Meanwhile, in the 2014 offseason, set-up men Boone Logan and Joe Smith received more guaranteed money (albeit with a slightly lower AAV) than Grant Balfour, Fernando Rodney and Joaquin Benoit, who had all just closed for a team in the playoffs.

While the free agent market may have been slow to catch up to advances in baseball analytics, the arbitration process has been completely stagnant. Arbitration salaries are determined by several key factors that don't always reflect a player's true talent level. Matt Swartz has researched this in depth for MLB Trade Rumors, finding that position players are awarded mainly on playing time, home runs and RBI, while innings pitched and wins are weighted heavily for starting pitchers. Meanwhile, the most important factor for relief pitchers is saves.

The problem isn't just that saves play a big role in arbitration, but how disproportionately they are weighed relative to everything else. Here are the stat lines for three current relievers from when they first became arbitration eligible:

Blind RP Comparison, Career Stats, First Time Arbitration Eligible						
Player	IP	K	ERA	FIP	WAR	Arb. Salary ($M)
Player A	231.1	315	2.76	3.44	2.1	$3.80
Player B	277.0	309	2.96	3.91	3.0	$1.65
Player C	202.0	270	3.03	2.88	4.2	$1.60

While the 2.76 ERA of "Player A" is the best in the group, is it enough to justify more than double the pay of the other two relievers? No, because the driving force in the salary here is saves. While Ernesto Frieri (Player A) entered arbitration with 60 saves, Tyler Clippard (B) and David Robertson (C) only had four saves combined when they became arbitration eligible.

What makes this disconnect so important is that the primary factor driving relievers' salaries is completely determined by the manager and the team. While you could try to manipulate certain factors for position players and starting pitchers, doing so could be costly in terms of that player's production. For example, a team could bat its young star in the leadoff position to try to limit his RBI opportunities—but then he will accumulate more plate appearances. If you bat him at the bottom of the order to reduce both plate appearances and RBI, his ability to contribute to the team is reduced.

With save opportunities under the control of the team, and plenty of high-leverage opportunities elsewhere in the late innings, teams have a large incentive to limit the save totals of their cost-controlled relievers. Unsurprisingly, this past season, that's exactly what happened.

The Hidden Benefit of Signing a Free Agent Closer

Heading into the 2014 offseason, a number of teams had young, high-quality relief pitchers who appeared poised to take over as closer. The following five pitchers all had solid seasons in 2013 (by ERA and/or WAR), with quality strikeout rates, and appeared more than capable of handling the ninth inning.

2013 Statistics, Potential 2014 Closers					
Team	Player	'13 WAR	'13 ERA	K%	SV
Indians	Cody Allen	1.0	2.43	29.2%	2
Rockies	Rex Brothers	1.1	1.74	27.1%	19
Athletics	Sean Doolittle	1.7	3.13	22.6%	3
Mariners	Danny Farquhar	1.9	4.20	34.7%	16
Rays	Jake McGee	0.6	4.02	28.9%	1

Importantly, none of these relievers had more than three years of service time. Only McGee had gone through arbitration as a Super Two (earning $1.45 million). Why does this matter? Arbitration salaries build on each other from one year to the next, and players almost never see their salary decrease. The earlier arbitration salaries set the baseline for the later years of team control, so any increase in pay the first time through arbitration will be amplified threefold or more.

Also importantly, these five teams all ranked in the bottom half of the majors in Opening Day payroll; three were in the bottom six. Most of these teams have a reputation as being fairly cost conscious, and several of them are commonly praised as having some of the brightest front offices in the game. So why did all of these teams sign free agent closers when they had a perfectly capable in-house option?

I explored this question for The Hardball Times in February 2014, focusing on the Athletics' trade for Jim Johnson, and my conclusion tied back to arbitration. All of these young relievers would be in line to get huge arbitration raises if they started racking up saves. By reducing the save totals of their cost-controlled relievers, these teams could cut millions in future arbitration costs. Exactly how much could they save? I estimated that by signing Jim Johnson, the A's could have saved $7-8 million in future payroll. That was just one example, but the same principle applies to the other teams.

When a reliever reaches arbitration for the first time as a "full-time closer," he usually earns around $3.5 to $5 million, depending on how good he is and how many saves he accumulated. Meanwhile, a set-up man with comparable numbers will receive only $1.5-$2 million. If that pitcher remains in a set-up role, he may earn around $10 million in three trips through arbitration, if he remains remain productive. A closer with the same numbers could earn twice that number, if not more. So while signing an aging reliever to pitch the ninth inning may seem risky, if a team can sign him at market value and get the added benefit of saving future payroll, then why not do it? It's pretty much a win-win. That is, unless the free agent completely collapses, which can always happen to a reliever (especially an older one).

With all this in mind, let's see how these five signings ended up playing out, and whether they paid off for the team. To aid in my evaluation of these transactions, I constructed a simple model to project first-time arbitration salaries based on four parameters: innings pitched, ERA, saves and holds. Looking at 33 first-time arbitration-eligible relievers who earned at least $1 million from 2012-2014, this model came within 15 percent of the awarded salary for all but one pitcher, with a mean absolute error of $150,000.

Oakland Athletics acquire Jim Johnson: One year, $10 million

The A's didn't sign Johnson as a free agent. Rather, they acquired him via trade (giving up very little) and agreed to pay his arbitration salary, which came in at $10 million. At the time of the trade, Johnson wasn't a typical closer, but was extremely durable and coming off back-to-back seasons with 50+ saves and an ERA under 3.00. While he was turning 31, he looked like a safe bet to provide some quality innings in the back end of the bullpen. The real question was whether he would be worth his $10 million salary.

Of course, we all know how this trade worked out for the A's. Johnson completely fell apart; he couldn't find the zone, and walked nearly as many batters as he struck out, while his ERA ballooned to 7.14. After posting -0.6 WAR and -1.49 win probability added (WPA), the A's released him.

As Johnson was removed from the ninth inning early in the season, he was replaced by a committee, featuring two very different pitchers: right-handed slider monster Luke Gregerson, and left-handed thrower-of-almost-nothing-but-fastballs Sean Doolittle. Gregerson was also acquired via trade and was a pending free agent, while Doolittle was still likely two years from reaching arbitration (depending on the Super Two cutoff).

Doolittle was clearly the best option, but the team was reluctant to make him the full-time closer. That is, of course, until he signed a very team-friendly extension with the club—five years, $10.5 million, with two option years that could bring the full value of the contract to $23 million. The A's willingness to let Gregerson pick up saves, along with their alleged desire to move Johnson back into the ninth once he figured things out, and Ryan Cook's return from injury likely played a role in the low cost of the extension.

It looked like Doolittle would miss the Super Two cutoff going into 2015, meaning he was still a couple years from a big payoff in arbitration. Doolittle knew that the A's could keep him from being a full-time closer if they wanted, so he accepted set-up man type money. Doolittle secured his financial future, and the A's secured their closer without paying him like one. While it's hard (okay, impossible) to call the Johnson trade a win for the A's, having him and Gregerson, and showing a willingness to share save opportunities, definitely gave them leverage in signing Doolittle to a long-term contract, which should pay dividends for years to come.

What does the model say?

In a hypothetical world where Doolittle didn't sign an extension and made the Super Two cutoff, he would be in line for a $1.7 million salary in 2015. If, in this same hypothetical world, the A's committed to Doolittle as closer from Opening Day and he picked up all of the A's 31 saves this season (as opposed to 22), that number would jump to $2.1 million.

Now let's imagine a second hypothetical world where Doolittle didn't sign an extension and didn't make the Super Two, but the A's still used him as their primary closer in 2014. Adding his 2015 Steamer projection to his career line, he would be projected to earn $4.3 million in 2016—not far off from the $3.9 million Andrew Bailey was in line for when he was traded to Boston in 2012. Under his current extension, Doolittle will make just $1.55 million in 2016, and won't reach $4.3 million until 2018. This is all to say, the A's made a very smart move in locking up Doolittle long term.

Tampa Bay Rays sign Grant Balfour: Two years, $12 million

Another ugly one. Balfour saw his strikeout rate collapse and his walk rate skyrocket en route to a replacement-level season. Just like Johnson, he was coming off three straight years of at least 60 innings and an ERA below 3.00, although Balfour's age (36) and contract debacle with the Orioles (they backed out of a deal after he allegedly failed his physical) might have made this collapse a bit more predictable.

One main reason the club signed Balfour may have been to keep lefty Jake McGee from getting too expensive down the road. McGee just barely made the Super Two cutoff (by six days) going into 2014, and earned a $1.45 million salary for his 3.28 career ERA along with one save and 50 holds.

McGee ultimately led the team in saves, which might lead you to believe that the Rays' strategy failed, if one of their goals was indeed to save on future payroll. However, Balfour's presence, along with manager Joe Maddon's willingness to share save opportunities (sound familiar?), meant that McGee picked up only 19 saves on the season. Balfour did manage 12 saves in 15 opportunities, despite his terrible numbers elsewhere, while Joel Peralta and Brad Boxberger received an additional seven save chances between them.

As McGee enters arbitration for the second time, he'll be in line for a significant raise (thanks in large part to a sparkling 1.89 ERA), but his lack of saves (20 for his career) means that he won't be paid like a true closer and should remain affordable for the cost-conscious Rays as they look to bounce back in 2015 and beyond.

The arbitration model doesn't apply directly to McGee, as 2015 won't be his first trip through arbitration, However, we can use the saves variable in the equation to predict the value of the dozen saves McGee may have picked up in the absence of Balfour, and estimate that the Rays will save around $500,000 off of McGee's arbitration salary in 2015.

Cleveland Indians sign John Axford: One year, $4.5 million

Maybe the real lesson here should be "don't count on free-agent relievers." After a three-year run as one of the most-feared relievers in the National League, Axford struggled in 2013 with a 4.02 ERA. However, a brief stint with the Cardinals at the end of the season (1.74 ERA in 10.1 innings pitched) led to optimism for a turnaround in 2014. That optimism turned out to be unfounded, as Axford's control issues (10 walks and three home runs in 13 innings) led to his removal from the Indians' closer role in early May. Right-hander Cody Allen emerged from the ensuing committee and never looked back, posting a 2.07 ERA with 24 saves on the season.

While Axford may have delayed Allen's ascension to closer and suppressed his save totals (getting 13 opportunities early in the season), Allen has another full year before hitting arbitration for the first time and will likely get paid "closer" money assuming he keeps his role in 2015.

What does the model say?

Allen is still a full year away from arbitration, so we'll have to include his 2015 Steamer projection to estimate his career numbers heading into 2016. As things stand, Allen will be looking at a $4 million salary in 2016. With an extra 13 saves that went to Axford and other closer-by-committee members, that number jumps to $4.5 million. If Axford had succeeded in the ninth and Allen took over as closer in 2015? His projected 2016 salary drops to $3.1 million. So, while limiting Allen's save chances in 2014 may save the Indians a bit of money down the road, it won't make up for the money they spent on Axford, let alone the -0.5 WAR he posted in his time in Cleveland.

Colorado Rockies sign LaTroy Hawkins: One year, $2.5 million

Despite failing to top 1.0 WAR since his 2004 season with the Cubs, Hawkins' solid 2013 with the Mets (2.93 ERA) earned him a chance to close games in Colorado. While Hawkins' peripherals weren't impressive, his 3.31 ERA in the hitter-friendly Coors Field was one of the better performances in the Rockies bullpen.

The man he supplanted was Rex Brothers, who had long been Colorado's "closer of the future." Brothers had a shiny 1.74 ERA in 2013 and earned 19 saves after the team lost Rafael Betancourt for the season in late August. After he dominated as a closer in 2013, why didn't the Rockies front office trust Brothers to handle the ninth inning the following season? Maybe they knew something we didn't. While Brothers was projected for another solid season, his strikeout rate fell, his walk rate rose, and he posted a disappointing 5.59 ERA.

Or maybe the Rockies were keeping an eye on their future payroll. The projected gap between Hawkins and Brothers was pretty small, and Brothers was in line for a big raise if he completed another year as closer. While Brothers probably wouldn't have made it through the year in the ninth given his struggles, he probably would

---

have picked up his fair share of saves. His 2.49 ERA through May 25 may have earned him a bit of extra leash, and with 20 career saves coming into the season, it may not have taken much for him to get paid like a closer in arbitration.

In the end, this worked out quite well for the Rockies. Hawkins outperformed Brothers and converted 23 of 26 save opportunities with a 3.31 ERA and 0.8 WAR—the Rockies even picked up his $2.25 million option for his age-42 season! Meanwhile, Brothers didn't pick up a single save in 2014 and should only see a modest raise in his first trip through arbitration. If he manages to figure things out, he should remain cheap as the Rockies evaluate their plans for 2015 and beyond.

What does the model say?

Heading into his first trip through arbitration, my model projects $1.8 million for Brothers. This number is largely driven by his 20 career saves, but given his all-around terrible 2014 season, I expect the actual number to be significantly lower. As mentioned earlier, Brothers would not have lasted the whole season as closer, but he still may have picked up saves through June. If we turn his 11 holds from the first three months of the season into saves, his projected salary rises by $400,000.

Seattle Mariners sign Fernando Rodney: Two years, $14 million

If all you saw of Danny Farquhar's 2013 stat line was his 4.20 ERA, you might not be particularly impressed. However, his 1.86 fielding independent pitching (FIP) was fourth-best in baseball, and only seven relievers surpassed his 34.7 percent strikeout rate. Despite the short track record (before 2013, he had thrown just two major league innings), the Mariners trusted Farquhar with the ninth inning when incumbent Tom Wilhelmsen faltered in 2013. He thrived, with 16 saves in 18 opportunities to go along with a 2.38 ERA in August and September, and appeared poised to keep the closer role going into 2014. The Mariners had other plans.

After committing nearly a quarter-of-a-billion dollars to bring in superstar Robinson Cano, the team saw an opportunity to bring in a Proven Closer for their playoff push without paying the usual premium. And so, Seattle came to know the Fernando Rodney Experience.

Despite his tendency for the occasional erratic outing, Rodney proved a valuable asset, posting a 2.85 ERA and finishing a third consecutive season with a sub-3.00 FIP. More importantly, the combination of Seattle's sluggish offense and an excellent rotation led to a huge number of save opportunities for the Mariners, with Rodney converting 48—tops in baseball.

While Rodney's performance may not have been enough to carry the Mariners to the postseason, his signing was not in vain. Farquhar posted an excellent year as a set-up man, with a 2.66 ERA and 2.86 FIP. Were it not for the presence of Rodney, Farquhar likely would have picked up the vast majority of those 48 saves.

What does the model say?

Farquhar is another reliever who still has a full season left before reaching arbitration. As it stands, he is projected to make $1.7 million in 2016—pretty standard for a set-up man. If, on the other hand, he had picked up both Rodney's 48 saves in 2014 and his projected 28 saves in 2015, he would be in line for $3.8 million. Given that his career ERA is inflated a bit by his 2011 season, which will be a distant memory in 2016, I wouldn't be surprised if the projection were on the low side. This means a savings of over $2 million in 2016 alone. When you include the cumulative effect this will have on Farquhar's salary in 2017 and 2018, the Mariners will end up making back a big chunk of the $12 million they spent to sign Rodney for 2014-2015.

Closing thoughts

While it can be tempting to think of players under team control as "cheap talent," it's important to remember that arbitration costs can add up quickly. As it becomes more difficult to find excess value on the free agent market, some teams—especially those with financial restrictions—may be looking elsewhere to get an edge.

In most scenarios, while arbitration salaries may not perfectly reflect a player's market value, they do a good enough job of measuring talent and contribution. While the system may be skewed towards certain types of players, it's almost always in the best interest of the team to maximize the production of its young players. Plus, some of the same skills that are overvalued in arbitration (namely power) are also overvalued in free agency.

The biggest exception here is relief pitchers and saves. Save totals tell you almost nothing about a player's actual performance, just in which situations he pitched and whether he was adequate. However, a closer will make more than twice as much money as a set-up man with identical numbers. As long as this discrepancy exists, there will be incentive for teams to keep young pitchers out of the ninth inning.

Despite this incentive, we still see plenty of teams with young closers. Some, such as the Dodgers, can clearly afford to pay for saves in arbitration. With other teams it might be a matter of communication. How do you tell a manager that his job is to win as many possible games with the roster he has, but maybe try not to give the team's best reliever too many save chances?

Saberists are often critical of managers' bullpen decisions, and this frustration was highlighted in several high-profile 2014 playoff games. This could be an extra point in favor of progressive managers who are open minded and may understand that limiting a young reliever's save opportunities means that the team will be able to invest elsewhere on the roster in subsequent years. Sometimes, the best form of communication is action. Rather than tell a manager not to use a young reliever, give him a Proven Closer he can trust in the ninth. However, as we saw when we looked back at 2014, this is much easier said than done.

Is this a growing trend? Is the arbitration system broken? Given how this played out this season and the teams that are involved, it's tough to argue that this is purely a coincidence. While the teams may not sign a free agent closer for the sole purpose of saving money in the future, they are certainly taking this potential savings into account when they make decisions.

While the arbitration system is flawed, I wouldn't say it is broken. Arbitration is one of the things that makes baseball so unique and interesting. Teams get incentive to develop young players, who, in turn, play at a discount but still earn a salary that reflects their talent to a certain degree. The system doesn't need an overhaul, but I could see a push to take some emphasis away from saves and close the salary gap between closers and set-up men. Until that day comes, young relievers will just have to hope that their team has enough money that it doesn't have to worry about paying for saves in arbitration—or that the Proven Closer blocking their way turns out to be the next Jim Johnson or Grant Balfour.

References & Resources

- Special thanks to Matt Swartz, whose extensive research on MLB salary arbitration that is published each year at MLB Trade Rumors laid the foundation for this article.
- All statistics from FanGraphs
- Additional salary information from Cot's Baseball Contracts

Mind the Gap

by Matthew Carruth

An 0-2 slider is thrown. It starts out looking like it's headed for the edge of the strike zone. The hitter commits to protecting. It ends up in the dirt, chased after and badly missed. It was a woeful attempt, but an understandable one given the hitter has to hedge against a third strike and breaking pitches are designed to elicit just such a foolish swing.

Contrast that to an 0-2 fastball thrown seemingly in the hitter's wheelhouse but instead calmly taken for strike three. The hitter almost serenely turns and heads immediately back toward the dugout with nary a protest. He knows it was a strike. He knows he was fooled. How? Why? "Just swing!" we exclaim.

However, the reality is that these two outcomes are borne from the same skill, the pitcher deceiving the hitter as to the end location of the forthcoming pitch. We track the first set of outcomes, swings and misses, as contact rate or swinging-strike rate (depending on the denominator used) and have exalted its importance for seemingly a decade now. True enough, it tells us the most about a pitcher's most important job—getting strikeouts. A high strikeout rate without a correspondingly high swing-and-miss rate tells us to be wary of that's pitcher's success level going forward.

And we have a plainspoken way of communicating that, too. "He has great stuff," a broadcaster might explain. "He's unhittable." It's the skill of having a pitch that even if the hitter knows is coming, is still missed. Mariano Rivera's cutter was unhittable. There wasn't anything deceptive, per se, about it. The hitter, the catcher, the umpire, the fan, the ball boy, even blind dogs knew Rivera was going to throw a cutter. It didn't matter.

The other set of outcomes, freezing a hitter, is important, too. If you think about a pitcher's motivation on a very basic level, it would be to get hitters to swing at pitches the hitter cannot hit well, if at all (typically those outside the strike zone), and also to get hitters to not swing at pitches that will otherwise be called a strike.

We sometimes track this in the form of called-strike percentage, but rarely is anything done with it. And I bet if you asked someone versed in that number to give you a brief description of what it's measuring—something akin to contact rate and measuring a pitcher's "stuff"—they'd struggle to find a clear answer.

I propose that with a slight shift in how we approach this, we can find a good analogy to more common language and actually build a statistic that is interesting to consider in its own right. To begin, let me go back to the start of the 2014 season.

Felix Hernandez is an incredible pitcher, no doubt. And he began the 2014 season in particularly wonderful fashion. After his first four starts, Hernandez had faced 110 batters, struck out 39, walked three, and allowed two home runs. He was piping almost 70 percent of his pitches for strikes, and a piece deep inside those strike zone numbers caught my eye. Hitters stepping in against him thus far had swung just as often at pitches marked inside the strike zone as they had at pitches outside the strike zone.

That probably sounds trivial, but it got me thinking. I began contemplating how one might quantify the amorphous scouting term 'deception.' The notion of mapping qualitative terms to quantitative ones isn't new, as described earlier with stuff, but it is useful.

The label of deceptive is used in two main ways. Perhaps the more common meaning refers to the pitcher's throwing mechanics and how well he hides the ball from the hitter. In other words, how close to the plate can the pitcher get before the hitter gets his first look at the actual ball? In a way, we have an avenue for pursuing that now with advances in measuring arm angles, release points, and their effect on perceived velocity.

A broader view, though, and one focused on a measurable end result would be to look holistically at the pitcher's mechanics and also his pitches and his sequencing and ask the question: **How often does a pitcher confuse a hitter?**

To answer such a question, it's best to go back to those primary goals I mentioned earlier. Of course, for the hitter the main goal is to put the ball over the fence. For the pitcher, it's to get a strikeout. But more basically, I think a good description of the battle between the two is that the pitcher wants to get the hitter to take strikes and swing at balls while the hitter wants to do the opposite. That then leads to a possible measurement by examining the swing rates on pitches inside versus outside the strike zone.

This isn't exactly new; we've talked about that many times with hitters and cited large gaps between the two measurements as examples of a hitter's skill at 'discipline' or 'patience.' (For example, not Josh Hamilton.) But I find it interesting for pitchers as well, with the inverse, a small gap, being desired.

Wanting a hitter not to swing at pitches inside the strike zone carries an obvious benefit for the pitcher; usually they are called a strike and there's very little risk to the pitcher. Wanting a hitter to swing is trickier because it involves the risk of the hitter making contact. As an offset, getting a hitter to swing at pitches outside the strike zone carries three benefits to balance some of that risk.

The first, obviously, is that the pitch would likely otherwise be a ball, and balls typically are bad for the pitcher. So getting a swing instead eliminates the risk of the count advancing in the hitter's favor. The second is that contact rates on those pitches naturally are lower. These pitches are further from the natural contact zone for hitters and for pitchers, so a swing and a miss is a great result, provided that his catcher hangs onto the ball. Finally, even if the hitter makes contact with the swing, it's in the pitcher's favor if it's on a pitch outside the strike zone.

Using data from 2010 to now, I grouped all batted balls based on MLB's classification of type and whether the pitcher was in or outside the strike zone. Then I examined how often the hitter successfully reached base in each group.

For instance, in 2013, left-handed hitters put a little over 25,000 ground balls into play. They reached base about 27 percent of the time if contact came off a pitch classified as inside the strike zone. That rate dropped to 21 percent on pitches outside the zone. Right-handed hitters saw a similar drop of roughly six percentage points.

And that's not isolated to 2013. Grouped together over the past five seasons, it's a persistent trend that ground balls experienced that six-point drop. Line drives see about a two percentage point drop. Fly balls are nearly neutral but are still a shade better when hit off pitches in the zone.

RBBIP, 2010-Present			
Type	Bat Handed	Sample	RBBIP in zone minus out zone
Grounder	R	162,708	.059
Grounder	L	122,335	.057
Fly ball	R	96,618	.003
Fly ball	L	72,474	.009
Line drive	R	73,654	.024
Line drive	L	58,140	.019

RBBIP, by the way, stands for reached base on ball in play. It is the same as the more commonly used batting average version (BABIP), but it also includes reaching via error. Since I'm not a huge fan of the subjective nature of assigning errors, I prefer to look at RBBIP as a way of differentiating whether or not the defense actually made a successful play or not.

While fly balls don't exhibit much difference, that is a massive difference when it comes to ground balls. Put in batting average terms, it's 58 points. Not that anyone comes close to having all his at-bats end in ground balls in play, but laying off pitches outside the zone and getting to a baseline average of nearly .270 instead of around .210 on those batted balls is a huge improvement for hitters.

Line drives, too, though about one-third of the magnitude of ground balls, are noteworthy, since line drives are far more likely than ground balls to go for extrabase hits when not turned into outs.

Hooray, so pitchers will definitely prefer hitters to swing at those out-of-zone offerings and not swing at pitches inside the zone. There are a couple ways of thinking about combining those two outcomes into one metric. They both end up with the same rankings, but perhaps one clicks more with you than the other.

First, you could examine the gap between the in-zone and out-of-zone swing rates. As mentioned before, the smaller that gap, the more deceptive I would label the pitcher. Or, somewhat more intuitively, you could add the percentage of pitches that got a swing while outside the zone to the percentage of pitches that got a take inside the zone to get an overall percentage of pitches that were advantageous to the pitcher, for lack of a more precise term.

More mathematically, in the first case we look at swing (in zone) − swing (out of zone), and in the second we look at take (in zone) + swing (out of zone). These two spit out the same ordering of pitchers because swing or take is a binary event, and the second formula is essentially just the inverse of the first formula.

One quick tangential note, for either measurement: It is best to exclude pitches on 3-0 counts. Too often in those counts the hitter is acting in a separate manner than in other counts, taking a vast majority of the time. Take a look at data from 2014.

Take Percentage by Count, 2014				
Balls	Strikes	Sample	Takes	Take%
3	0	7,108	6,439	91%
0	0	183,407	132,872	72%
1	0	71,577	41,375	58%
2	0	23,751	13,525	57%
0	1	91,231	47,867	52%
0	2	45,438	22,320	49%
1	1	72,343	32,924	46%
3	1	14,913	6,533	44%
1	2	66,505	27,933	42%
2	1	36,495	14,861	41%
2	2	55,725	19,025	34%
3	2	32,584	8,533	26%

I'm half-tempted to exclude first pitches as well based on that chart, but unlike with 3-0, there's no clear narrative reason to do so. Still, I'm intrigued by how often first pitches are taken these days. Curious if it was just a recent development, I repeated the same query for 2009.

Take Percentage by Count, 2009				
Balls	Strikes	Sample	Takes	Take%
3	0	8,573	8,065	94%
0	0	186,401	136,948	73%
2	0	26,834	16,133	60%
1	0	77,140	45,876	59%
0	1	88,237	47,871	54%
0	2	41,690	20,943	50%
1	1	74,090	34,755	47%
3	1	17,002	7,840	46%
1	2	63,866	26,929	42%
2	1	39,659	16,478	42%
2	2	55,217	19,208	35%
3	2	33,761	9,039	27%

Nope, the rates are remarkably similar given five years of separation.

Moving back to measuring the swing rate gaps based on strike zone, here are some of the best performers at having the smallest gap between swing rates over the past five seasons—from when we have more reliable PITCHf/x data—with a minimum of 500 pitches in the season.

Smallest Gap, 2010-2014					
Pitcher	Year	Sample	zSw	oSw	Gap
Sergio Romo	2012	797	56.5%	37.4%	19.2%
Sean Burnett	2012	938	60.5%	41.2%	19.3%
Joe Paterson	2011	583	52.0%	32.4%	19.6%
Al Alburquerque	2011	741	51.0%	31.2%	19.8%
Luke Gregerson	2013	944	58.9%	38.7%	20.2%

Unsurprisingly, all five are relievers who had very fine seasons in question. Interestingly, it was in 2011 and not 2012 that Sergio Romo had his dominant strikeout season, knocking out over 40 percent of the batters he faced in 2011.

However, that year, hitters were more clued in to swinging at his pitches inside the strike zone (61 percent versus the 56 percent here). They just couldn't hit them, as the contact rate against Romo on those pitches was a paltry 74 percent versus 79 percent in 2012, and the league average was around 85 percent.

Sean Burnett leveraged his great 2012 season into a two-year, $8-million contract with the Angels. He threw 10.1 innings for them. Total.

Joe Paterson may not be a name you're instantly familiar with. The 2011 campaign was his rookie season, and he did fine over 28 innings in Arizona's bullpen, with a superficially low 2.91 ERA. He's only thrown six major league innings since then, spending almost all of 2012-14 with Triple-A Reno. It's somewhat curious given that he hasn't been struggling down there. A 22 percent strikeout rate coupled with a nine percent walk rate is fine enough. Ten home runs total allowed isn't many over 138 innings spent with Reno as your home park. Granted, Arizona hasn't hurt for relievers over the past three seasons, but Paterson does seem like an asset not being used at the moment.

Alburquerque and Gregerson are more obviously two of the games better relievers, both for many years now.

Moving on to the biggest gaps over the same period.

Largest Gap, 2010-2014					
Pitcher	Year	Sample	zSw	oSw	Gap
Bob Howry	2010	627	75.3%	24.7%	50.6%
Paul Clemens	2013	1,139	72.6%	22.1%	50.4%
Rob Scahill	2013	500	72.4%	22.9%	49.6%
Jim Henderson	2013	1,019	73.2%	23.8%	49.5%
Edgmer Escalona	2013	786	72.0%	23.0%	49.0%

Poor Bob Howry; he was a perfectly fine relief pitcher for many years, but his final season in 2010 was abysmal, and he gets caught up here. Paul Clemens pitched for the Astros. I'm unsure if I need to write any more to explain that he was not effective. He was even worse this past season, but didn't reach my playing time cutoff. Scahill and Escalona were, and continue to be, mediocre relievers for the Rockies. Henderson is a more interesting player. He was a journeyman who actually delivered good numbers for the Brewers in 2012 and in 2013, despite the above rates.

One helpful factor for Henderson in 2013 was an artificially low .261 BABIP and a correspondingly unsustainable strand rate of over 88 percent. It will be worth tracking Henderson next season, as hopefully he is able to return from this summer's shoulder surgery.

Despite Henderson, the overall picture is pretty clear. The better pitchers tend to find themselves with lower gaps, while the lesser pitchers tend to have higher gaps. That's intuitive given the components we're dealing with.

Also, relievers dominate the crop above as you might expect given their smaller samples. Wanting to get more of a starter-centric view, I then grouped all seasons together, weeded out pitches thrown in relief, and upped the minimum sample to 1,500 pitches.

Smallest Gap, Starting Pitchers, 2010-2014				
Pitcher	Sample	zSw	oSw	Gap
Doug Fister	14,001	57.8%	30.8%	27.0%
Chris Sale	8,877	59.9%	32.5%	27.4%
Jose Fernandez	3,328	60.2%	31.6%	28.6%
Alex Cobb	7,693	61.0%	31.0%	30.0%
Andy Pettitte	5,943	61.9%	31.6%	30.3%
Masahiro Tanaka	1,975	66.9%	36.4%	30.5%
Chris Capuano	9,173	62.1%	31.4%	30.6%
Mat Latos	13,891	63.5%	32.8%	30.7%
T.J. House	1,538	63.4%	32.7%	30.8%
Roy Halladay	10,426	64.5%	33.5%	31.1%

That's a solid crop of pitchers to have. Of note, Felix Hernandez, the inspiration for all of this, hovers near here at 23rd overall, with a 31.7 percent Gap.

Doug Fister at the top isn't a surprise to me. His success in the majors has never been based on missing a lot of bats or even on getting many strikeouts. Rather, he throws a lot of strikes in a lot of different ways and manages to get hitters to watch them go by.

In fact, Fister has the lowest in-zone swing rate of this group and actually the second lowest in the entire sample, just barely above C.J. Wilson's, who ends up not appearing here because nobody swings at anything Wilson throws. Wilson actually checks in at 36th overall, by Gap, sandwiched between Anibal Sanchez and Hishashi Iwakuma.

Masahiro Tanaka has a small sample thus far in the American major leagues, but the Japanese superstar quickly has established himself over here as a force on the mound. Nobody has a higher swing rate on out-of-zone pitches than he, and it's not particularly close, either. Tanaka outpaces second-place Scott Baker by three whole percentage points.

Be on the lookout for lefty T.J. House next season. He's showing solid core skills and a strong penchant for generating ground balls. If his bad luck on the fielding behind him—a .332 BABIP—regresses, then the rest of baseball might start taking notice when his already low ERA (3.35 in 2014) drops further.

Enough about the good pitchers. Let's examine the bottom of the barrel.

Largest Gap, Starting Pitchers, 2010-2014				
Pitcher	Sample	zSw	oSw	Gap
Aaron Laffey	1,971	67.9%	22.5%	45.5%
Chien-Ming Wang	1,620	66.7%	22.2%	44.5%
Kevin Gausman	2,349	70.7%	26.2%	44.5%
Alex White	2,506	70.0%	26.8%	43.3%
Rubby De La Rosa	2,639	68.1%	25.2%	43.0%
Brian Bannister	2,107	66.1%	23.5%	42.5%
Jonathan Pettibone	1,801	66.5%	24.1%	42.4%
Yordano Ventura	3,085	68.7%	26.4%	42.3%
Mike Pelfrey	9,893	67.1%	25.0%	42.1%
Robbie Erlin	1,715	66.7%	24.7%	42.0%

Yordano Ventura is the closest thing to a successful starter in the list above, and he remained a part of the Royals' rotation through the World Series. Where Ventura deviates from his list-mates above is in throwing quite a few of strikes, with 51 percent of pitches inside the strike zone compared to a league average of 47 percent.

Ventura also excels at getting hitters to miss on their swings inside the strike zone, as his contact rate on in-zone swings was just 84 percent, while league average was 88 percent. The combination of throwing strikes and missing bats on those strikes is enough to generate an above-average strikeout rate. The high-90s fastball certainly plays a big factor in that, and it will be worth tracking how Ventura performs as his fastball speed decreases over time.

Just looking at the top and bottom ten, the smaller the gap, the better overall a pitcher tends to be. For example, here are the average core rates for the pitchers listed.

Rate Stats, Top and Bottom 10 in SP Gap				
Group	K %	BB %	HR%	RBBIP
Top ten (smallest Gaps)	22.2%	5.6%	2.3%	.303
Bottom ten (largest Gaps)	15.5%	7.4%	2.8%	.318

The metric does appear to track to more macro levels of success, but how well? Well, it turns out, not that great. There's a lot of noise in the correlations, though they do go in the direction you'd expect.

I'd like to focus on four correlations that I ran, using the same starter-only sample. Because I thought it was more intuitive, I used the additive version of Gap, which as a reminder is taking a strike in the zone (zTake) plus swinging at a ball out of the zone (oSwing). As mentioned previously, it results in the same ranking of players.

The first correlation I want to highlight is Gap and K Rate. To date, I have seen nothing that correlates better to strikeout rate than plain old contact rate. That remains the bar to clear among simple stats for checking on the validity of a pitcher's strikeout rate. Strikeouts without missing bats don't tend to hold up over time.

A while back, I looked at trying to predict strikeout rate using a combination of swinging-strike rate and called-strike rate. At the time, I didn't find much added use from called-strike rate, and these results back up that conclusion. The R-squared here is .1109. It's a positive trend line, but not the strongest relationship by any means. There just aren't all that many called strike threes.

The main benefit in the deception skill of avoiding in-zone swings is probably to get the pitcher into more favorable counts earlier in the at-bat. Finishing off a hitter with a called third strike remains far noisier.

Next, I naturally looked at the opposite, i.e. Gap and walk rate. This is the correlation that surprised me the most because, contrary to getting a called third strike, I assumed the combination of swings on outside pitches and takes on in-zone pitchers would correlate very well with avoiding walks. There is a trend present, but with an R-squared of just .1048, it's much weaker than I hoped for.

Let's round out the three true outcomes by looking at Gap and home run rate for the third highlighted correlation. It makes sense for there to be some negative correlation here, as the more pitches swung at outside the hitter's wheelhouse lead to more contact made on such pitches, which I showed earlier tends to result in weaker contact. The R-squared here was .0384.

Speaking of weaker contact, what about straight up comparing Gap to ball in play success? That was what I looked at in the fourth correlation.

Oh, nope, ball in play success remains an enigma. Yet again we are unable to pin any blame on the pitcher himself. Despite showing early on how getting hitters to make contact on pitches out of the zone—and avoiding contact on pitches inside the zone—puts weaker contact into play, it doesn't roll up into a total BABIP or RBBIP that's demonstrably lower.

Given that Gap here looks at swing, not necessarily contact, rates and BABIP or RBBIP is predicated on contact, it is not a total surprise that little to no relationship exists between the two above. This is our flattest trendline and weakest R-squared, at just .0072.

Okay, so what is there to gain here? What Gap isn't is some gold mine secret metric to pitcher success, though it certainly tracks along those lines. What it can be, though, is a quantitative number that tracks alongside a common pitching description—that of deception.

When someone says something akin to "this guy (or pitch) is filthy," we have a tangible number with which to judge that assertion. In that case, it's contact rate. It maps intuitively that if a pitcher has filthy stuff, he should be literally hard to hit.

Despite a much weaker connection to statistical pitching success, the Gap metric, used as a numerical bridge to statements like "keeping a hitter off balance, or confused, or guessing," is equally useful. It provides a way to validate the observation, and that's never worth dismissing.

References & Resources

- Derek Carty, The Hardball Times, "Introducing plate discipline stats," *hardball-times.com/introducing-plate-discipline-stats* (For talking about hitters and citing the gap as "discipline" or "patience")
- Jeff Sullivan, Lookout Landing, "Swinging Strikes & Strikeout Rate," *lookout-landing.com/2008/9/26/622755/swinging-strikes-strikeout* (For relationship between swinging strikes/contact and strikeout rate)

Pitching in the Wind

by David Kagan

Recently, I was sitting in front of the tube watching the Giants play the Phillies at Citizens Bank Park. In the top of the fifth, Cole Hamels fired a fastball. Gregor Blanco was barely able to foul it off. It was the fastest four-seamer Hamels had thrown all day, inspiring Giants broadcaster Mike Krukow to comment:

> *"One thing pitchers like—and you don't see it very often in this ballpark—they like winds at their back. You know, wind at your back is just like a golfer with the wind at his back in the tee box. You feel like you can hit the ball farther. Well, the same thing for a pitcher. They think they can throw harder, and you can."*

Well, Kruk (rhymes with Duke), I never made it very far playing baseball, so I don't really know what pitchers think or why they think it. Some coaches even claim pitchers are better off not thinking. However, what I do have to offer is the knowledge to examine the physics of pitching in the wind. Let me start by reviewing the forces that act on the ball on its journey from pitcher to catcher.

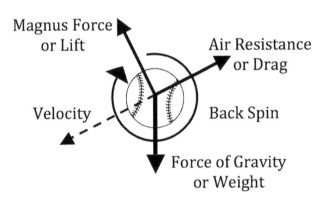

Figure 1: The forces on a ball in flight with backspin are lift, drag and weight.

There are two things that exert forces on a pitch in flight. Gravitational force is exerted by Earth. This steady downward inescapable pull is highly structured and predictable. In contrast, the forces air exert on the ball are complex and subtle. They give rise to the beauty and nuance of pitching.

If you've read my work recently at The Hardball Times website, Figure 1 may look familiar. It shows the three forces acting on a typical four-seam fastball, one from gravity and two from the air. These forces are shown as the solid straight arrows.

The velocity is represented by the dashed arrow, while the backspin on the fastball is indicated by the circular arrow.

The gravitational force, or weight, pulls the ball downward. The weight depends on the mass of the ball as well as the mass and size of Earth. Even Hall of Fame pitchers known for outstanding control have no ability to adjust these variables.

The effect air has on the ball is usually thought of as two distinct forces. Air resistance, or drag, acts opposite the velocity of the ball. Drag, as the name implies, slows the ball down. The drag grows as the square of the speed of the ball through the air. Again, pitchers really have no sway as far as the drag is concerned. If they throw it faster, there will be more drag. Try as they may, they can't change the laws of physics.

The other force exerted by the air is the Magnus force, or lift. It is always perpendicular to the velocity and is in the direction of the spinning motion of the front of the ball as it moves through the air. Due to the spin, the front of the ball in Figure 1 is moving mostly up the page and slightly to the left, matching the direction of the lift. The lift is responsible for the "hop" on a typical fastball causing the ball to drop more slowly than if gravity were acting alone.

The lift is not always upward. A curveball, for instance, has mostly topspin, opposite to the backspin in Figure 1. The result is the oxymoronic "downward lift." So, the ball falls more rapidly than gravity alone requires. In baseball speak, it "drops off the table." To avoid the confusion associated with the word "lift," I usually use the term Magnus force.

Magnus force depends upon the speed of the ball through the air and the rate the ball is spinning. Unlike gravity and drag, the pitcher can control the Magnus force. In fact, spin is the primary mechanism by which the pitcher manipulates the trajectory of the ball. The differences between a fastball, a curve, a slider, and a sinker all are due to varying the amount and direction of the spin put on the ball, linked with the speed it is thrown.

You probably will be surprised to note that for a typical Cole Hamels fastball, the drag is almost equal to the weight of the ball. The lift is about two-thirds of the weight of the ball. Now you can understand why the motion of a pitch in flight can be so dramatic. The forces on the ball are comparable to the force pulling it toward Earth!

Passing Wind

In 2007, Mike Fast wrote a brief article at his blog Fast Balls that listed average wind speeds by ballpark. He claimed the speeds range from zero in indoor parks to 17 mph at AT&T Park in San Francisco. Citizens Bank in Philly comes in a little above average at 10 mph. The box score for the game in question records the wind at 11 mph in from center field.

It is unclear where these numbers are measured exactly. While every MLB game has a wind speed listed in the box score, I've never seen anyone with an anemometer wandering around the field before or during the game. Hold on a second—I just can't let that word go by unnoticed. An anemometer is that twirling gizmo with four cups. How is it pronounced anyway? a-nemo-meter, an-emo-meter, an-e-mo-meter? Actually, nowadays they eschew the four cups and use an electronic device, though in the past, the careful observer could see them sometimes at the tops of ballparks. In any case ... back to business.

However they get the wind speed, we can rest assured it is not measured on the mound. The mound is reasonably well protected from wind by the structure of the stadium compared to center field, for example. Considering all these unknowns, it is unclear what values to use for the wind speed during a pitch. For lack of anything better, let's consider wind speeds up to 10 mph. At least it's a round number.

Now back to Hamels' fastball. It turns out that three weeks earlier he pitched in Miami with the roof closed—no wind. Using the PITCHf/x data from that day we learn he threw 47 four-seam fastballs averaging 92.2 mph. They ranged from 89.3 mph to 95.0 mph. In the matchup with the Giants, Hamels tossed 74 fastballs averaging 94.0 mph and ranging from 91.7 to 96.2 mph. So, the data would indicate he got about a 2.0 mph bump in speed due to the wind.

I can hear you howling already! That doesn't prove anything. Maybe Hamels had the flu in Miami...he is 9-13 lifetime against the Marlins ... perhaps he threw harder because he hates the Giants ... it may have just been your basic case of "home cooking" ... who knows? In fact, his manager, Ryne Sandberg, said of his performance, "He was missing off the plate and threw a lot of pitches. He wasn't the sharpest he's been." Hamels left in the fifth having given up three runs.

A Mighty Wind

Since you insist, I'll look at the question more analytically. We can use the data from the game in Miami and the laws of physics to calculate the effect of wind on the pitches. This is relatively easy to do using Alan Nathan's Trajectory Calculator. The calculator requires the initial x, y, and z-positions of the ball, as well as the initial speed and direction of the pitch. The average values of these quantities for the fastballs in the Miami game were entered into the Trajectory Calculator.

The challenge then becomes estimating the spin on the ball. The Miami data tell us the average position of the fastballs at home plate. By adjusting the values for the backspin and the sidespin until they produce the correct position at the plate, we can establish reasonable values for the spins. A backspin of 1314 rpm and a sidespin of 876 rpm seemed to do the trick, although they are smaller that the PITCHf/x estimates.

The Trajectory Calculator has a place to enter the wind speed and direction...problem solved! Figure 2 is a graph of the final speed of the ball versus the wind speed. Negative wind speeds are at the back of the pitcher while positive wind speeds are in the pitcher's face. The final speed of the ball at the front of the plate increases about two mph for every 10 mph of wind speed at the pitcher's back.

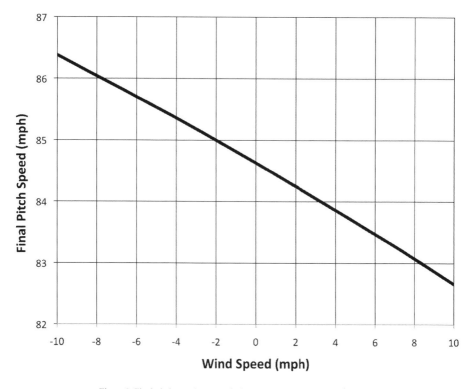

Figure 2: Final pitch speed versus wind speed. Negative wind speeds are at the pitcher's back, while positive speeds are in his face.

The drag force is proportional to the speed the ball moves through the air, *not the speed the ball moves with respect to the ground*. When the ball moves with the wind, it is moving *more slowly* with respect to the air. Therefore, the drag force is reduced. The lower drag force allows the ball to maintain its speed as it makes its way to home.

So, Kruk, it looks like you're right! The final speed of Hamels' fastball will be measurably higher with the wind at his back. It should be noted that we haven't really explained why his start speed was also higher on the day in question. This turns out to be the more likely reason his fastball was 2.0 mph quicker against the Giants.

We can go further with the Trajectory Calculator and examine the effect of the head or tail wind on the flight path of the ball. Figure 3 shows the side view of the four-seamer for wind speeds from 10 mph at the pitcher's back (-10 mph) to 10 mph in the pitcher's face (+10 mph) in 5 mph increments. The central curve is for no wind. The inset is a blow-up of the curves near home plate.

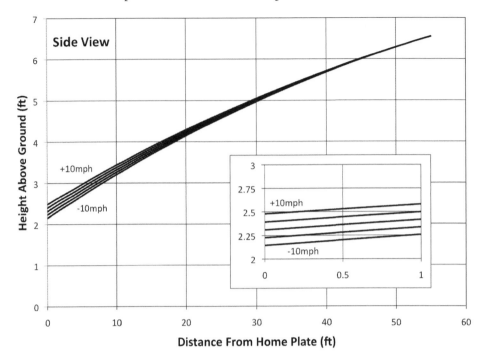

Figure 3: The side view of the trajectory by wind speed. The inset is a close-up of the path near plate.

Strangely, these fastballs have more sink with the wind at the pitcher's back. The ball will drop about two inches for every 10 mph of wind speed. You might think the opposite: since the wind carries the ball along faster, it should sink less—but that's not so, and here's why.

Just like the drag force, the lift force is proportional to the speed the ball moves through the air. The air speed will be less than in still air for a wind at the pitcher's back. With less lift, the ball drops more rapidly due to gravity. In other words, a fastball traveling downwind has less "hop" or "rise."

Figure 4 shows the top view for the same pitches. Again, 10 mph at the pitcher's back is negative, while 10 mph in the pitcher's face is positive, and the inset is a blow-up of the trajectory near home plate.

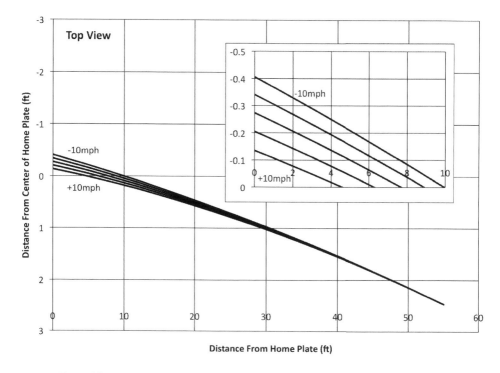

Figure 4: The top view of the trajectory by wind speed. The inset is a close-up of the path near home plate.

The data show a ball thrown downwind will have a straighter horizontal trajectory than a ball thrown into the wind. Again, we see the effect of the reduced Magnus force due to the reduced speed between the air and the ball. The net effect is a bit smaller than the vertical motion—in this case, about 1.5 inches for every 10 mph of wind speed. The horizontal change should be smaller than the vertical change since the sidespin is less than the topspin.

So, how about that, Kruk? A tailwind will speed up a pitch and give it more sink at the cost of less break. Conversely, a headwind will slow the pitch, but accentuate the "hop" and break. Your golf analogy was perfect. If you tee off with a tail wind, the ball goes faster and straighter. If you hit your drive into the wind, it goes slower, and your hook or slice is more pronounced.

It's not clear which type of wind is better for a given pitcher. My personal suspicion? Break is more important than speed, so pitching into the wind might be a better choice. In the extreme example, knuckleballers generally prefer to pitch into the wind.

Ill Wind

As mentioned earlier, the mound is reasonably well protected by the structure of the stadium from winds blowing either in from or out to center field. However, in some parks it is conceivable that a wind blowing in from left might follow the contour of the stands. It would become a crosswind between the pitcher and the plate as it makes its way around the park and out to right field.

Then again, maybe not, but the Trajectory Calculator gave us some intriguing results for pitching downwind. So, let's see if it is just as interesting to look at the effect of a crosswind on the path of a pitch.

The final speed of the pitch at home only increases by 0.4 mph as the wind switches from first to third at 10 mph to third to first at 10 mph. It is not surprising that the final speed is nearly unchanged, since the wind is blowing across the ball's path, not along it.

The question is whether that 0.4 mph change is real or just a numerical artifact from the Trajectory Calculator. The side spin of the ball should be interacting with the wind to create a small Magnus force along the line between the mound and home.

This is hard to follow, but keep in mind that Hamels is a lefty. When the wind is blowing toward third, the side of the ball facing the wind has some spin toward the mound. The Magnus force will be away from the plate, slowing the ball down. The opposite is true when the wind is blowing toward first. So, at least the 0.4 mph increase is the right direction for these pitches.

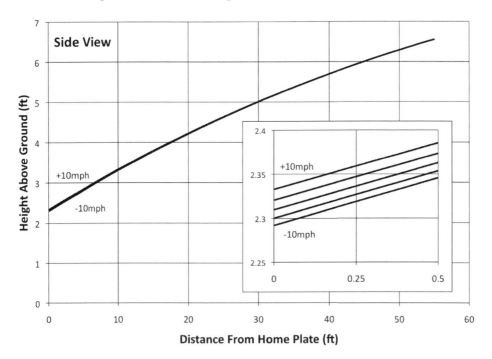

Figure 5: The side view of the crosswind trajectory by wind speed. The inset is a close-up of the path near home plate.

Figure 5 is the side view of the trajectories of the Hamels fastball with the cross-wind along the line from third to first at varying speeds. In this figure, 10 mph from first toward third is negative, while 10 mph third to first is positive. Since the wind is moving pretty much across the trajectory of the ball, the side views of all the trajectories are very close to the same.

The inset shows the difference to be about 0.04 feet (0.5 inches) over the velocity change of 20 mph. If you assume the differences between the paths are due to the 0.4 mph speed increase explained earlier, a quick estimate does produce a height difference of a fraction of an inch. Maybe the reduction in speed from the Trajectory Calculator is really due to the Magnus force.

As you probably guessed, the biggest effect of a crosswind is the horizontal position of the ball as it crosses the plate. Figure 6 shows a variation of about half a foot over the 20 mph range or three inches for every 10 mph. This is the largest change due to the wind we've seen yet.

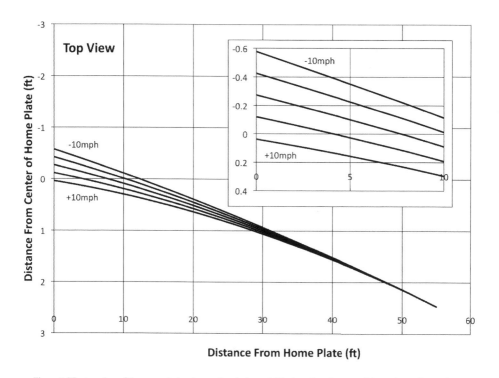

Figure 6: The top view of the crosswind trajectory by wind speed. The inset is a close-up of the path near home plate.

Usually, the horizontal break of a pitch is due to sidespin and Magnus force; here it is also due to the drag. Hamels had released the ball with a small fraction of its velocity toward third—on average six mph. When the wind blows toward third at 10 mph, the ball is only moving through the air at four mph.

On the other hand, when the wind blows toward first base, the ball is moving at 16 mph with respect to the wind. Since the drag depends upon the square of the speed, the force due to the wind will be not four times larger, but rather *16 times* larger. That's why the -10 mph trajectory is much straighter than the +10 mph variety.

The crosswind was a bit more complicated. Are you still with me, Kruk?

In summary, the crosswind hardly changes the speed to the plate or the vertical motion of the ball, but it makes relatively large changes in the horizontal break. Just as for the head or tail wind, it is not obvious which type of crosswind is better for a given pitcher.

Breaking Down Wind

Since you are one of the hearty souls still hanging in there, I thought I would provide a special treat. Figure 7 is the catcher's view of the situation. It summarizes what we've learned from the previous discussions.

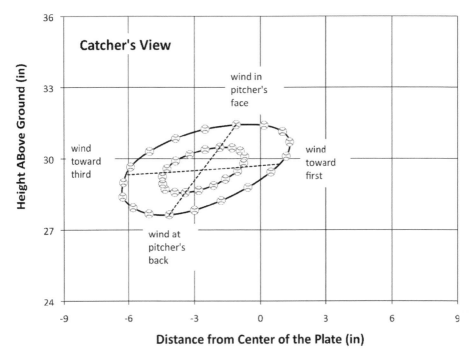

Figure 7: The catcher's view for different wind speeds and directions. The inner ring is for the 5 mph wind speed and the outer ring for 10 mph.

The location of Hamel's four-seamer with no wind is at the intersection of the dashed lines. The inner ring shows the pitch location for a five-mph wind from different directions as indicated on the plot. The outer ring is for a 10-mph wind.

The dashed lines are the two cases we've considered in detail. The more vertical dashed line is for the wind either at the pitcher's back or in his face. The more horizontal dashed line indicates the situations with crosswind.

Since home plate is 17 inches wide, the horizontal scale extends to one-half inch beyond the plate on both sides (the baseballs in Figure 7 are not to scale). The catcher's view illustrates the magnitude of the deviations in trajectory due to the wind. The horizontal variations at 10 mph are almost half the width of the plate.

The crosswind affects the horizontal location of the pitch more strongly than the vertical. The head/tail wind affects the vertical position most strongly. The crosswind has a larger overall effect on pitch location than the head/tail wind.

Perhaps these wind-driven effects are sufficiently large that you data miners out there might want to figure out which pitchers should throw which pitches on windy days. The COMMANDf/x folks might want to see if command suffers on windy days. I'm handing you the ball here because at this point I have reached the limit of my skills.

So Kruk, next time you're commenting on why the pitcher seems to be having control problems, you can just break into the old folk song…"The answer, my friend, is blowing in the wind."

References & Resources

- For a complete discussion of the forces on a baseball in flight see A. M. Nathan, "The effect of spin on the flight of a baseball," *American Journal of Physics*, vol. 76, 119 - 124 (2008).
- For a more detailed description of the drag force see D. T. Kagan and A. M. Nathan, "Simplified Models for the Drag Coefficient of a Pitched Baseball," *The Physics Teacher*, vol. 52, 278 (2014).
- Mike Fast, Fast Balls, "Average Ballpark Weather Conditions," *fastballs.wordpress. com/2007/08/06/average-ballpark-weather-conditions*
- Brooks Baseball, Cole Hamels player page, *brooksbaseball.net*
- Alan M. Nathan, University of Illinois, "Trajectory Calculator," *baseball.physics. illinois.edu/trajectory-calculator.html*
- For more on anemometers: *http://en.wikipedia.org/wiki/Anemometer*
- For more on CommandF/X: *https://www.sportvision.com/baseball/commandfx*

Regulating the Performance of Baseball Bats

by Alan M. Nathan

The game of baseball as played today at the amateur level is very different from the game I played growing up in the early 1960s. In my youth, wooden bats were the only option. Now, almost no one outside the professional level uses wooden bats, which have largely been replaced by hollow metal (usually aluminum) or composite bats.

The original reason for switching to aluminum bats was purely economic: aluminum bats don't break. However, in the more than 40 years since their introduction, they have evolved into superb hitting instruments that, left unregulated, can significantly outperform wooden bats. Indeed, they have the potential of upsetting the delicate balance between pitcher and batter that is at the heart of the game itself. This state of affairs has led various governing agencies (NCAA, Amateur Softball Association, etc.) to impose regulations that limit the performance of non-wooden bats.

The primary focus of this article is to discuss the science behind the regulation of bat performance. This will require a precise working definition of what we mean by "bat performance" as well as a consideration of the properties of a bat that determine its performance. That will lead naturally to a discussion of why aluminum is better, how to measure performance in the laboratory, and the approach used by the NCAA to regulate the performance of bats.

Qualitative Features of the Ball-Bat Collision

We start with a brief introduction to the important features of the ball-bat collision. First refer to Figure 1, which was captured from a high-speed video clip from a laboratory experiment done at the University of Massachusetts Lowell Baseball Research Center. It shows the baseball in contact with the bat at the exact moment when the ball is compressed to its maximum. Notice how distorted the ball becomes as it wraps itself around the cylindrical surface of the bat. The process of compression followed by recovery is very inefficient, as the strands of wool that make up most of the volume of the ball rub together, creating a lot of heat. That heat represents energy that is lost, or dissipated, to the kinetic energy of motion of the ball. The technical term that characterizes this dissipation of energy is the called the "coefficient of restitution," or COR, and the fraction of the initial energy that is dissipated is $1-COR^2$, or one minus the square of COR.

A less technical term for this phenomenon is the "bounciness" of the ball, which can be explored by dropping it onto a hard rigid surface, such as a thick steel plate, and observing how high it bounces. A perfectly elastic ball, such as a superball, will bounce nearly to its initial height. Such a ball would have almost no energy dissipated and a COR close to 1. A completely inelastic ball, such as one made of putty, would hit the plate and die. Such a ball would have all its energy dissipated and a COR of 0. For a baseball at typical collision speeds, about ¾ of the energy is dissipated, so the COR is about 0.5, halfway between perfectly elastic and completely inelastic.

As we will see, the COR of the ball plays a significant role in the efficiency of the ball-bat collision. (By the way, from time to time baseball pundits speculate whether the ball is "juiced", usually during periods when home run production greatly exceeds expectations. In our language, "juiced" means an elevated COR.)

Next refer to Figure 2, which shows a motion analysis experiment done at the Washington State Sports Science Laboratory. High-speed cameras were used to track the incoming slow-pitch softball and three different markers on the bat, with the different symbols showing the locations at 1/1000-second intervals. By looking at the distance between successive points, you can get some indication of the speed.

First, note the incoming pitch is moving very slowly, as is appropriate for slow-pitch softball, whereas the outgoing batted ball is moving significantly faster. From this we learn that bat speed plays a very important role in determining the batted-ball speed. Next, note the bat is moving at progressively higher speeds as one moves closer to the barrel tip, an indication the bat is being rotated. In fact, careful analysis of the video shows the bat is being rotated about a point very close to the knob of the bat. Finally, note the bat slows down significantly after making contact with the ball. This is a consequence of Newton's "action/reaction" law. The bat exerts a force on the ball, so the ball must exert an equal and opposite force on the bat, slowing it down.

Defining Bat Performance

Any discussion of bat performance needs to begin with a working definition of the word "performance." We probably have some intuitive feeling about what this means, but that is not good enough for present purposes. After all, if we want to regulate the performance of non-wood bats, then at the very least we need to quantify what we mean by performance. So, let's sharpen up the question by asking a slightly different question.

Suppose we say, "Bat A outperforms bat B." What exactly do we mean by that statement? Among people who have thought about this question, a consensus has emerged that a good working definition of performance is batted-ball speed in a typical game situation, which I will denote simply by BBS. Generally speaking, if you want to improve your chances of getting a hit, then you want to maximize BBS, regardless of whether you are swinging for the fences or just trying to hit a well-placed line drive through a hole in the infield. The faster the ball comes off the bat, the better are the chances of reaching base safely.

Figure 3

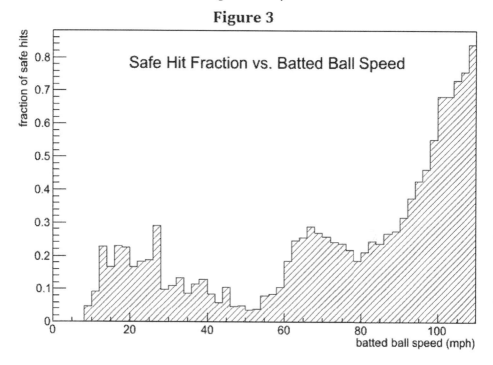

This is borne out in Figure 3, a plot of the safe-hit fraction versus BBS, as determined from the publicly available HITf/x data from April, 2009. The plot shows that a batter's chance of getting on base increases sharply from 20 percent at 80 mph to 70 percent at 100 mph. These data make it clear that BBS matters a lot and is a very good candidate for a metric of bat performance. So, we will say that bat A outperforms bat B if a generic batter can achieve higher BBS with bat A than with bat B under typical game conditions.

The Only Formula You Need to Know

Now that we have decided on BBS as our metric of bat performance, we can then ask what BBS depends on. We answer that by writing down the following formula, the only one you will see in this article:

$$BBS = q*(\text{pitch speed}) + (1+q)*(\text{bat speed}).$$

This "master formula" is remarkably simple in that it relates the BBS to the pitch speed, the bat speed, and a quantity q that I will discuss shortly. It agrees with some of our intuitions about batting. For example, we know that BBS will depend on the pitch speed, remembering the old adage that "the faster it comes in, the faster it goes out." We also know that a harder swing—i.e., a larger bat speed—will result in a larger BBS.

All the other possible things besides pitch and bat speed that BBS might depend on are lumped together in q, which I will call the "collision efficiency." As the name suggests, q is a measure of how efficient the bat is at taking the incoming pitch, turning it around, and sending it out at high speed. It is a joint property of the ball and bat and can assume values between -1 and +1. All other things equal, when q is large, BBS will be large. And of course, the opposite is also true.

Before delving into the properties of the ball and bat that determine q, let's do some numerical estimates. For a typical 34-inch, 31-ounce wood bat impacted at the "sweet spot" (about five to six inches from the tip), q is approximately 0.2, so the master formula becomes:

$$\text{BBS} \approx 0.2*(\text{pitch speed}) + 1.2*(\text{bat speed}).$$

This simple but elegant result tells us something that anyone who has played the game knows very well, at least qualitatively. Namely, bat speed is much more important than pitch speed in determining BBS. Indeed, the formula tells us that bat speed is six times more important than pitch speed, a fact that agrees with our observations from the game. For example, we know that a batter can hit a ball off a tee a long way (with the pitch speed zero) but cannot bunt the ball very far (with the bat speed zero). Plugging in some numbers, for a pitch speed of 85 mph (typical of a good MLB fastball as it crosses home plate) and a bat speed of 70 mph, we get BBS=101 mph, which is enough to get you on base about 70 percent of the time. If hitting long fly balls is your thing, a ball hit at that speed and at a launch angle of approximately 27 degrees will carry close to 400 feet. Each one mph of additional pitch speed will lead to about another one foot, whereas an extra one mph of bat speed will result in another six feet. So bat speed matters a lot. We all knew this, but it is good to be able to quantify just how important bat speed really is.

Delving Deeper: The Alphabet Soup of Bat Performance Metrics

Guided by our master formula, let's delve a little deeper to find the properties of a bat that determine bat performance. First, let's eliminate pitch speed as a factor, since it has nothing to do with the bat or the batter. That leaves bat speed and collision efficiency as the important factors. Let's simplify things further by only considering bats of a given length, eliminating that as a variable.

We now come to the following question: For bats of a given length, what properties of the bat determine BBS? And here's the answer. The only properties that matter are the ball-bat coefficient of restitution (BBCOR) and the moment of inertia

(MOI), two more additions to our alphabet soup. In the following paragraphs, I'll explain what these properties are and how they contribute to bat performance.

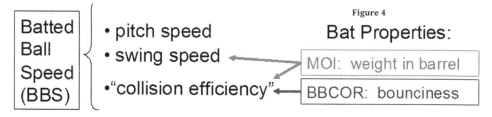

The interplay among the various quantities is shown schematically in Figure 4. For reference in the ensuing discussion, refer also to Figure 5, a plot of BBS, bat speed, BBCOR, and collision efficiency as a function of impact location along the barrel.

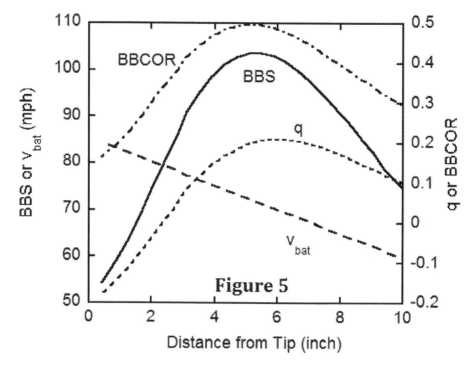

Let's start with the BBCOR. As already discussed, the COR is a measure of the bounciness of the ball collision when it collides with a rigid steel plate. But when a ball collides with a bat, the bounciness may be different, so instead one refers to the "ball-bat coefficient of restitution," or simply BBCOR. When a baseball collides with a wood bat near the sweet spot, the bat behaves very much like the steel plate, so that BBCOR=COR. However, if the ball is hit off the sweet spot, either toward the handle or the tip, some of the energy is transferred to the bat in the form of vibrations, often resulting in a stinging sensation in the hands. With less energy returned to the ball, the BBCOR is smaller than the COR.

Figure 5 shows the dependence of BBCOR on impact location for a typical wood bat. Note that it reaches a maximum of 0.5, corresponding to minimal vibrations, about five inches from the barrel tip. This is as good a definition as any of the "sweet spot", since it both minimizes vibrations and maximizes BBS. Note also that the collision efficiency, q, more or less tracks with BBCOR: A larger BBCOR leads to larger q, and vice versa. The figure also shows the importance of hitting the ball at or near the sweet spot from the rapidity with which the BBS falls from its maximum value, especially for impacts near the tip.

Before turning to the MOI, let's take a look at a simpler impact of a golf driver with a ball, where essentially all the weight of the club is concentrated in the head. For that case, it is the weight of the club head that plays a role in the collision efficiency. All other things equal, a heavier head will hit the ball harder than a lighter head.

Similar considerations hold for a baseball bat, except in that case, the weight of the bat is not concentrated in the barrel but is distributed along its length. For that reason, it is not the weight of the bat that plays a role but rather the MOI, which depends on both the weight and the weight distribution. For a given weight, the MOI is larger when a greater fraction of the weight is concentrated in the barrel end of the bat. In fact, as a rough guideline, you can think of the MOI as proportional to the weight of the bat in the barrel. A larger MOI means a larger q (and vice versa), in complete agreement with our golf analogy. And all things being equal, a batter will get a higher BBS with a larger MOI bat than with a smaller one.

However, as indicated in Figure 4, all other things are not equal in that the MOI affects bat performance in two different ways: It affects both the collision efficiency, q, and the bat speed. So while a larger MOI means a larger q, it also means a smaller swing speed. The inverse dependence of swing speed on MOI agrees with our intuition and is supported by a considerable amount of current research.

The fact that the MOI affects bat performance in two opposite ways raises an interesting question. If I have two bats with the same BBCOR but with different MOI, which one will have the larger BBS? For example, if I "cork" a wood bat, which reduces its MOI, will the resulting increase in swing speed compensate for the reduction in collision efficiency? Current research suggests that the answer is "no," and that corking a bat does not lead to a larger BBS. By the way, corking a wood bat does have some important advantages, even though higher BBS is not one of them. By reducing the MOI, the batter will have a "quicker" and more easily maneuverable bat, allowing him to wait a bit longer on the pitch and to make adjustments once the swing has begun. So, although corking a bat may not lead to higher BBS, it certainly may lead to better contact more often.

Why is Aluminum Better?

Now let's get to the heart of the matter: Why is an aluminum bat better? To sharpen up the question, let's consider two bats of the same length and weight, one made of wood, the other made of aluminum. What features of these bats will lead to a difference in performance?

First, it is very likely that the aluminum bat will have a smaller MOI. Being hollow, as opposed to a solid wood bat, a smaller fraction of its weight will be concentrated in the barrel. An interesting little experiment you can perform is to take these two bats of the same length and weight (e.g., 34 inches, 31 ounces), one wood and one aluminum, and find the point on the bat where you can balance it on the tip of your finger. You will find that the balance point is farther from the handle for the wood bat than for the aluminum bat, showing that a larger concentration of the weight is in the barrel for the wood bat. What will be the effect of the smaller MOI on BBS? The answer is not much, since there will be a cancelling effect, with the larger swing speed compensated by the smaller collision efficiency. As with the corked bat, there will be no significant change (either increase or decrease) in BBS, although the lower-MOI aluminum bat will have the "quicker bat" advantage.

So, what is the real reason why aluminum generally performs better than wood? The answer is the feature of aluminum bats popularly called the "trampoline effect," which is shown schematically in Figure 6. A hollow aluminum bat has a thin flexible wall that can "give" when the ball hits it, unlike the surface of a solid wood bat. Some of the ball's initial energy that would otherwise have gone into flattening out the ball instead goes into compressing the wall of the bat. While a large fraction of the former energy is dissipated, as we have already discussed, most of the latter energy is very effectively returned back to the ball. As a result, there is less overall energy dissipated, and the BBCOR is larger. The more flexible the wall, the larger the BBCOR.

Figure 6
Ball impacting solid bat

Ball impacting hollow bat

It is not at all atypical for a non-wood bat to have a BBCOR = 0.55, resulting in an increase in BBS of about six mph relative to an otherwise comparable wood bat. For a fly ball on a typical home run trajectory, that will increase the distance by over 30 feet! Indeed, the technology of making a modern high-performing bat is aimed primarily at improving the trampoline effect. For aluminum this is achieved by developing new high-strength alloys that can be made thinner (to increase the trampoline effect) without denting.

The past decade has seen the development of new composite materials that increase the barrel flexibility beyond that achievable with aluminum, giving rise to a new generation of high-performing bats. Left unregulated, aluminum and composite bats can greatly outperform wood bats and upset the delicate balance between pitcher and batter.

As an aside, the trampoline effect also plays a role in other sports, such as golf and tennis. A "wood" driver is no longer made of wood but rather is hollow metal with a thin plate that makes contact with the ball. The trampoline effect results from the flexing of the thin plate. In a tennis racket, the trampoline effect is a result of the stretching of the strings. It is perhaps non-intuitive but nevertheless true that a tennis ball will be hit harder with reduced string tension (as opposed to higher string tension), since the lower tension means more flexible strings, which in turn means more of a trampoline effect.

Measuring Performance in the Laboratory

When testing in the lab, the basic idea is to fire a baseball from a high-speed air cannon onto the barrel of a stationary bat that is held horizontally and supported at the handle. Both the incoming and rebounding ball pass through a series of light screens, which are used to measure its speed accurately. The collision efficiency, q, is the ratio of rebounding to incoming speed. The bat is scanned across the barrel to determine the location of the sweet spot. The MOI is measured by suspending the bat vertically and allowing it to swing freely like a pendulum while supported at the handle. The MOI is related to the period of the pendulum by a standard physics formula. Once q and the MOI are known, these can be plugged into a well-established formula to determine the BBCOR. These three quantities—q, MOI, and BBCOR—can be determined very precisely by these measurements, with no further assumptions.

To determine BBS, the master formula is used along with a prescription for specifying the pitch and bat speeds, the latter of which will depend inversely on the MOI according to some formula. Clearly, assigning a BBS value to a bat requires assumptions about pitch and bat speed, both of which can vary considerably. So it is not possible to predict BBS in any absolute sense. For example, if we are told that a particular bat is a 98-mph bat, that certainly does not imply that 98 mph is the absolute maximum BBS for that bat in the field. However, the BBS value has meaning when making comparisons among different bats. It is only in that relative sense that BBS has any meaning.

Since I am a physicist, I feel compelled to include some brief remarks about how the laboratory measurements can be used to replicate performance in a game situation. To that end, let me bring up three issues where physics plays an important role.

How do we know that measurements done by firing a ball at a stationary bat have anything to do with a game situation where the bat is swung at a moving ball? Physics tells us that the collision efficiency, q, depends only on the relative ball-bat speed. So, if the game situation one is trying to replicate has a pitch speed of 85 and a bat speed of 70, then the laboratory experiment will determine the correct q provided the impact speed is 85+70=155 mph.

The batter's grip in a game situation is not the same as the end support used in the laboratory. Doesn't the collision efficiency depend on how the bat is supported at the handle? The quick answer to that question is "no," but the physics is very subtle. The bottom line is that the ball-bat collision is so rapid that the handle end of the bat does not have time to react before the ball has already left the bat. I have written extensively about this topic, and the interested reader can find lots of information on my web site, baseball.physics.illinois.edu/grip.html.

Measuring the collision efficiency in the laboratory requires using a baseball, the properties of which can vary. In order to compare one bat to another, how do we take into account variations in the baseball itself, particularly the COR and the stiffness of the ball? As it turns out, this is not a trivial problem. However, guided by our understanding of the physics of the ball-bat collision, techniques have been developed to normalize the laboratory measurements to a baseball with "standard" properties.

The NCAA Bat Performance Protocol

Finally we come to the NCAA bat performance protocol, which has been in effect since the start of the 2011 season. The National Federation of High Schools started using the same protocol with the 2012 season. In the interest of full disclosure, I served on the NCAA Baseball Research Panel that devised the protocol in 2008 and recommended its adoption. The panel was charged by the NCAA with developing a standard that would have non-wood bats perform as close as possible to wood. That is, if we have a wood bat (A) and an aluminum bat (B) of the same length, the goal was to have a standard that would assure that the BBS of B wouldn't exceed that of A.

In order to avoid making assumptions about the pitch and swing speed scenarios, which are needed for a direct BBS comparison, it was decided instead to use BBCOR, as measured at the sweet spot, as the performance metric. BBCOR is a very good surrogate for BBS, at least for comparative purposes, because the only other property of the bat that matters, the MOI, plays a very small role in determining BBS because of the compensating effect on q and bat speed. It is for this reason that comparing the BBCOR of bat A to bat B is nearly equivalent to comparing the BBS.

Since the BBCOR of a typical wood bat is just under but very close to 0.50 and virtually independent of other construction details of the bat (e.g., the type of wood), the decision was made to set the performance limit for non-wood bats at exactly 0.500. When performing the standard test described in the preceding section, any bat having a BBCOR anywhere along the barrel exceeding this value is not certified for use in NCAA games.

So how well does the new performance protocol work? Prior to 2011, a different performance protocol was used, resulting in non-wood bats outperforming wood bats by as much as five mph. Such a difference in maximum BBS would result in about a 25-foot difference on a long fly ball. Therefore, removing that five-mph gap would be expected to result in a considerable reduction in home run production. And that is exactly what happened. In the two years prior to the new regulations, the average number of home runs per team per game in Division I play was 0.95. In the four years since then, that average has dropped to 0.45, more than a factor of two reduction. Science really does work!

People often ask me whether or not I think the decrease in home run production is a good thing for baseball. In my interactions with the NCAA and their Rules Committee, I have always been careful not to express my view on that matter. It was the job of the Rules Committee to decide how they wanted the game to be played. It was my job as a member of the Panel to provide technical advice on how to achieve their goal. So I never expressed my opinion on the subject.

However, I am no longer serving on the Panel so I am free to express my view as a fan of the game. I confess to being a traditionalist when it comes to baseball. I love the sound of the crack of a wooden bat when it makes good contact with the ball, as opposed to the annoying "ping" from an aluminum bat. Moreover, I am very much a fan of close, low-scoring games rather than the high-scoring affairs that NCAA baseball had become. So, let it be known that I very much like the new bat standards used by the NCAA and the brand of baseball that has resulted from the change.

Summary

In this article, I have presented a working definition of bat performance and discussed the features of bats that contribute. I have shown why non-wood bats generally outperform wood bats and shown how to regulate the performance of these bats to make them more wood-like in their performance. Finally, I have shown how the NCAA is currently regulating bat performance, as well as the effect their new protocol is having on home run production.

References & Resources

- At my site, under "Bat Performance Research," you can find a comprehensive list of links on bat performance and its regulation: *baseball.physics.illinois.edu/bats.html*
- The Washington State University Sport Sciences Laboratory is where all the bat certification for the NCAA is performed: *mme.wsu.edu/~ssl/index.html*

- The actual NCAA bat performance protocol: NCAA Standard for Testing Baseball Bat Peformance, "Bat-Ball Coefficient of Restitution," *fs.ncaa.org/Docs/rules/baseball/bats/NCAA%20BBCOR%20Protocol%20FINAL%205%2009.pdf*.

Trying to Quantify Recency Effect

by Jesse Wolfersberger and Matthew Yaspan

One fundamental pillar of sabermetric research is sample size. Even the least sabermetrically inclined baseball fans and analysts understand to some degree that a couple of at-bats does not a season make. By all accounts, Jose Altuve's .250 batting average in his opening three-game series against the Yankees would have been a poor barometer by which to predict the rest of his 225-hit 2014 season. On the flip side, even the most lay of laymen could tell you that Trevor Plouffe's 4-for-4 Opening Day performance was not a sign that he'd be batting 1.000 or anywhere close for the rest of the season. Those more in tune with sabermetric research of the past decade would likely put it even more bluntly: "Hotness" and "coldness" are not real, they are just an illusion created by the random nature of each individual plate appearance.

The importance of this topic is more than just what an announcer fills air time with. Batting order and playing time decisions are made every day by each major league manager, often highly influenced by the perception of hotness or coldness. Despite the years of research, the idea of streakiness is one that has persisted. You would be hard pressed to find a player or coach who thinks it does not exist. One way or the other, if the idea of hotness could be definitively found and measured, or finally put to bed, it could have a significant effect on the way baseball is managed.

There have been piles of great research done on sample sizes in baseball. Russell Carleton was a pioneer on this topic, when, in 2008 he was the first to study the points at which certain statistics stabilize. Carleton found that the more control a batter has on the statistic, the quicker it stabilizes. For example, strikeout rate stabilizes at 60 plate appearances, while the more commonly cited "triple slash" stats of batting average, on-base percentage, and slugging percentage do not stabilize until 910, 460, and 320 plate appearances, respectively.

Further replications, tweaks, and extensions of Carleton's research have been done by Derek Carty at The Hardball Times and Baseball Prospectus, Tom Tango on his blog, and Harry Pavlidis at The Hardball Times. These studies were important in cementing the concept of sample size in sabermetrics.

The common thread for each of these articles was identifying the stabilization point when a player's batting average, for example, represents his true talent batting average. One assumption in this methodology is that every plate appearance is created equal in its predictive power. In other words, each plate appearance is akin to a marble in a sack, and one can simply reach in and grab a few and expect each individual marble to be as useful as another. Carleton and Carty partitioned the plate appearances into two groups and ran correlations between the groups. When the correlations met a certain threshold value, the number of plate appearances was deemed the stabilization point.

Carleton also performed a similar method, KR-21 and Cronbach, which essentially compares the sum of the variance of each individual plate appearance to the total variance of all plate appearances, and when the total variance swallows the sum of the individual variances enough, the statistic has been deemed as stabilized.

The research presented in this article is not aimed at disproving any of the previous research, but asks a slightly different question: does the order of the plate appearances matter? Are they really like marbles in a sack, or more like the letters in your first name, which lose meaning when they are jumbled in the wrong way? For example, we know on-base percentage stabilizes at 460 plate appearances, but when a batter walks up to the plate for number 461, does his last plate appearance have any more predictive power than the one before that? Does it have any more relevance to the plate appearance at hand than when he stepped into the box on Opening Day?

The theory of recency would mean, all things being equal, if you lined up a batter's plate appearances starting from most recent to least, the more recent results may be a better predictor of the outcome of a player's next PA than the results from weeks or months ago. The last plate appearance, PA_{n-1}, would have slightly more predictive power than the one before, PA_{n-2}, which would have slightly more than the one before it, PA_{n-3}, and so on. If you could graph this effect, it should be a gently declining decay curve, which might look something like the graph to the right (which, it should be emphasized, is not real data).

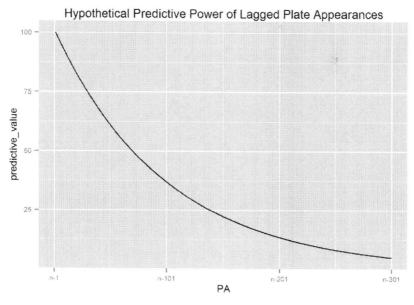

Hypothetical Predictive Power of Lagged Plate Appearances

To test this theory, we used the Retrosheet event files from 2013. We used the data from the 2013 season to create a panel data set in which each observation was a plate appearance from that season by a player who had 100 or more non-bunt plate appearances in 2013. Each observation consists of the Retrosheet ID of the player at bat, the result of the plate appearance PA_n, and each previous plate appearance from that season sorted in reverse order from the most recent, PA_{n-1}, down to PA_1. Below is a sample from this data set:

Sample from Data Set						
Description	retroID	PA_n	PA_{n-1}	PA_{n-2}	...	PA_1
"Mike Trout PA_{561}"	troum001	Double	Single	Fly out	...	Single
"Miguel Cabrera PA_{32}"	cabrm002	Strikeout	Home Run	Single	...	Flyout
"Adam Dunn PA_{417}"	dunna001	Home Run	Strikeout	Strikeout	...	Walk
"Dan Uggla PA_{353}"	uggld001	Strikeout	Strikeout	Strikeout	...	Single
.						
.				.		
.						
"Mike Trout PA_{560}"	troum001	Single	Flyout	Strikeout	...	Single
"Miguel Cabrera PA_{31}"	cabrm002	Home Run	Single	Lineout	...	Flyout
"Adam Dunn PA_{416}"	dunna001	Strikeout	Strikeout	Strikeout	...	Walk
"Dan Uggla PA_{352}"	uggld001	Strikeout	Strikeout	Error	...	Single

The first statistic we tested our theory on was on-base percentage. To start, we transformed our dataset above by turning each plate appearance value into a 1 for any value that contributes positively toward on-base percentage, such as a single, walk or home run, and 0 for any value that does not, such as reaching on an error, a strikeout or a flyout.

Because on-base percentage really serves as the probability that a batter reaches base and our only true two outcomes are 1 for "yes" and 0 for "no," a linear regression does a relatively poor job in modeling the data. If one imposed a line of best fit over a plot of PA_n against expected PA_n from a linear regression, we'd see a seemingly random line that does a poor job of fitting the data well. Additionally, the expected PA_n would occasionally exceed 1 or dip below 0, which we know is not possible.

With this in mind, we chose a logistic regression as our model. A logistic regression takes the odds a batter reaches base (the probability of the batter reaching base divided by the probability of him not reaching base), and the logit takes the natural log of these odds. The logit is used as a dependent variable in a linear regression against the previous plate appearances. For our model, we regressed the logit against the previous 200 plate appearances. Our results are displayed below:

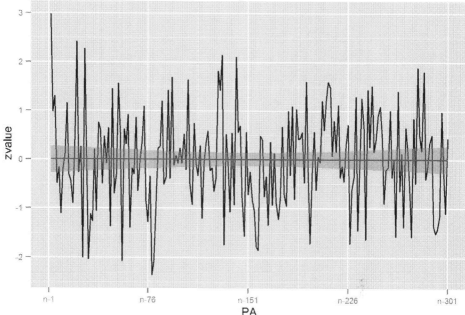

Normalized Predictive Power of previous PAs on On-Base Outcome

Our results are mixed. On one hand, we've found that PA_{n-1} is much more individually significant than any other plate appearance and has the highest coefficient. Additionally, out of all groups of 10 plate appearances, PA_{n-1} through PA_{n-10} are orders of magnitude more significant than all of the less recent plate appearances, according to the Wald test (in this case, the Wald test tests to see the probability that the actual coefficient of the given explanatory variables is zero). On the other hand, as our graph shows, the pattern is tenuous at best, especially beyond PA_{n-1}. Additionally, the likelihood ratio of the model is about 0.004. In other words, our model explains about 0.4 percent of the variation between plate appearances.

While this test yielded mixed results, the nature of the on-base dependent variable may have been causing some of the trouble. If hotness exists, it certainly means a player would hit for more power, as well as hitting singles and walking. By changing our dependent variable, it becomes possible to better capture all of the outcomes of a given plate appearance. With this in mind, we decided to test our hypothesis on wOBA, which gives more weight to better outcomes, such as doubles, triples and home runs.

In this case, we can use linear regression to model the data without the risk of wonky results. The dependent variable of the model is the outcome of the plate appearance, measured using the linear-weighted run value. The independent variables are a series of lagged plate appearances, PA_{n-1}, PA_{n-2}...down to PA_1. It is also important to include a control for pitcher quality. If the opposing starting pitcher is Clayton Kershaw, the batter has a lesser chance of getting on base in that plate appearance, and significantly so. This is one possibility why the PA_{n-1} variable had such a large effect on the first model—the batter was likely to be facing the same pitcher in consecutive plate appearances.

The sample size for this regression is again the 2013 season, including every batter who had at least 300 plate appearances in the season. Since each batter will have multiple observations in the sample, the total number of observations used is 55,000.

After running the model, each previous plate appearance is given an estimated coefficient that should characterize the average effect of that plate appearance. If the theory is correct, graphing the coefficient estimates of the lagged PAs (after normalizing them for simplicity's sake) should yield a shape resembling that theorized decay curve:

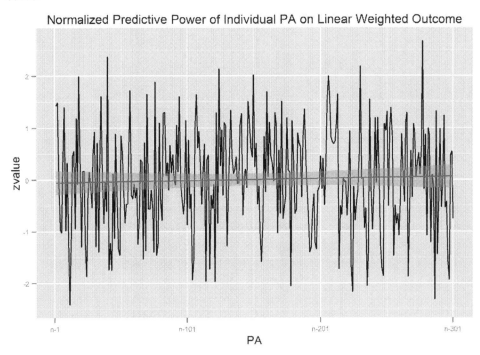

Normalized Predictive Power of Individual PA on Linear Weighted Outcome

The actual results, however, yield results that look as if they were created by a random number generator. Not only is the theorized decay curve nowhere to be found, but there is no trend at all. A line of best fit of the coefficients has essentially a slope of zero. According to the R^2 value—our coefficient of determination—even if we found a trend, our model of 301 variables could only explain around 0.1 percent of the variance of what occurs in plate appearances. From this regression, there is simply no evidence that more recent plate appearances have any more predictive power on the next PA than older ones.

Other model specifications might help further investigate the hypothesis. After all, estimating significant coefficients on hundreds of highly random variables is a tall order, even with a sample size of 55,000 observations. In an attempt to alleviate this issue, lags were grouped into pools of 10 PAs. For example, t-1 to t-10, t-11 to t-20, t-21 to t-30, etc. This reduces the number of variables by a factor of 10, plus it smooths out some of the fluctuation between the lags. The results, however, tell a similar story to the first model: no evidence that recency improves predictive power. In fact, there is a slight correlation to the opposite effect, with older PAs being more predictive, although it should be stressed that this correlation is insignificant.

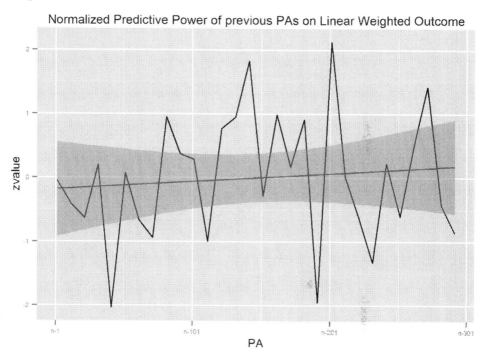

Normalized Predictive Power of previous PAs on Linear Weighted Outcome

Both previous models controlled for pitcher quality, but what about hitter quality? It was not included until this point due to the potential multicollinearity with the PA lag variables, but it is worth investigating for the chance that controlling for hitter quality could improve the coefficient estimates by separating the true talent level from the lagged terms, isolating the effect of the trailing PAs.

This approach mimics a common technique in panel data modeling known as fixed effects. Each batter's individual talent level is controlled for by including his season's wOBA in the regression, and this allows for the trend to be entirely based off a time-based (recency) effect. The results, however, are again a rather random trend. For the first time, there is a positive correlation between recency and predictive power, but it again is insignificant.

Normalized Predictive Power of previous PAs on Linear Weighted Outcome

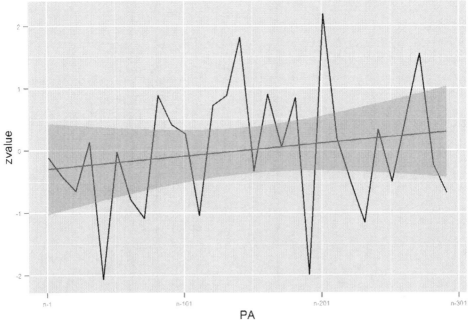

These three models (and truly many more) were unable to find the theoretical signal, so we are left empty handed. True, this is not an exhaustive process where every model specification or methodology has been attempted. Nor does it use decades worth of data, which would help the significance of the coefficient estimates. However, this initial attempt to mine for gold found no nuggets, or even specks of gold dust that would suggest that there is anything further below ground.

The results, or lack thereof, are reminiscent of the research into some of baseball's other tropes, such as clutch. It is not true that a clutch skill does not exist, but that it is so small that it is hard to find and inconsequential even if it is there. The same may be true in the case of recency. It is not necessarily true that a batter's last plate appearance has the same predictive power as one that happened months ago, but that the difference is just too small to matter. When a player walks up to the plate late in the game, what he did in the third inning doesn't mean any more or less than what he did on Opening Day. More accurately, his recent at-bat might be a slightly better predictor than Opening Day, but who is pitching, what park they are in, how many days in a row he has played, or even the temperature of the air are more important factors to consider.

We were cautiously optimistic that a new methodology would shed new light on this subject, finding a bridge between the analysts who considered hotness a dead topic for years and the fans, players and journalists who have yet to be convinced. In the end, every result, every model we ran was just another nail in the coffin. For those who believe hotness and coldness exists, one more article using more complicated mathematical methodology is unlikely to change their minds. For analysts, this is further vindication, and hopefully an enjoyable or educational read. It is often said that non-results still need to be published so that we know ground has been covered, and this is certainly an example of that.

Analysts have made amazing strides in making the baseball world smarter. Front offices are nearly all embracing sabermetrics, and coaches and players are joining the fray as well. This season, there was even a stats-centric simulcast of Game 1 of the National League Championship Series on FOX Sports 1. However, there are seemingly three traditional pieces of baseball logic sabermetricians have had the hardest time disproving to the mainstream: streakiness, clutch and batter-pitcher matchups. These concepts decide games every season, with managers playing a "hot hand" or bringing in a pitcher because of good matchup numbers. It is unlikely that one more article disproving hotness will convince someone who is convinced it exists, but let this attempt be another straw added to the back of an already encumbered camel.

References & Resources

- Tom Tango, The Book Blog, "Regression equations for pitcher events," *insidethebook.com/ee/index.php/site/article/regression_equations_for_pitcher_events*
- Harry Pavlidis, The Hardball Times, "It makes sense to me, I must regress," *hardballtimes.com/it-makes-sense-to-me-i-must-regress*
- Derek Carty, Baseball Prospectus, "Resident Fantasy Genius: When Hitters' Stats Stabilize," *baseballprospectus.com/article.php?articleid=14215*
- Russell Carleton/Pizza Cutter, FanGraphs/StatSpeak, "525,600 Minutes: How Do You Measure a Player in a Year?," *fangraphs.com/blogs/525600-minutes-how-do-you-measure-a-player-in-a-year*

Noteworthy 2014 Leaderboards of Note

by Carson Cistulli

As F. Scott Fitzgerald's widely celebrated novel *The Great Gatsby* illustrates unequivocally, there's no greater purpose in this life than to realize one's most urgent ambitions—regardless of how empty one's personal relationships or interior life might become as a result of pursuing of same.

As it has in recent previous editions, The Hardball Times presents *here* a series of four leaderboards, each featuring a collection of players who, like that sad and lonely millionaire Jay Gatsby, have distinguished themselves from the rabble by means of one extraordinary performance or another. Unlike Jay Gatsby, however, only *some* of the players invoked herein own lavish mansions in exclusive Long Island towns that are symbols of the era's corrosive decadence.

Best Pitches

There probably are multiple ways to identify what the league's "best" pitches are—and, of course, the effectiveness of one offering in a pitcher's repertoire depends on the quality of all the others, too.

One way of evaluating the quality of a pitch, using a methodology developed by Dave Allen, is to see what it's been worth in terms of linear-weight runs. What follows are the top-10 pitches by linear-weight runs (relative to league average) for every 100 thrown—with a minimum of 250 thrown for each pitch.

Best Pitches, 2014					
Name	Team	Pitch	IP	%	R/100
Carlos Carrasco	Indians	Slider	134.0	22.1%	4.48
Wade Davis	Royals	Cut Fastball	72.0	21.0%	4.13
Corey Kluber	Indians	Curveball	235.2	15.7%	3.95
Andrew Miller	---	Slider	62.1	42.0%	3.52
Ken Giles	Phillies	Slider	45.2	39.2%	3.42
Pedro Strop	Cubs	Slider	61.0	36.6%	3.35
Homer Bailey	Reds	Change-up	145.2	11.2%	3.12
Santiago Casilla	Giants	Two-seam Fastball	58.1	40.8%	2.97
Joe Smith	Angels	Slider	74.2	29.0%	2.94
Marcus Stroman	Blue Jays	Two-seam Fastball	130.2	13.1%	2.93

Notes

- Among starters in 2014, only Clayton Kershaw and victim of great misfortune Jose Fernandez recorded a park-adjusted xFIP- better than Carlos Carrasco's 67 xFIP-. Much of Carrasco's success—in terms of run prevention, at least—is due to his slider. With that pitch, Carrasco produced a swinging-strike rate of about 27-29 percent, depending on classification—better, in either case, than Craig Kimbrel's own breaking ball, itself widely celebrated.

- The only pitcher here to record more than Homer Bailey's ca. 145 innings is Cleveland right-hander Corey Kluber, who compiled nearly 100 more of those (innings, that is) than Bailey en route to producing the top WAR among all major league pitchers. Having entered the 2013 season as a 27-year-old with just 63.0 major league innings pitched, Kluber produced the highest WAR among all major league pitchers in 2014 and won the American League Cy Young Award.

- On account of he throws it at 100 mph, Philadelphia right-hander Ken Giles' fastball receives considerable attention. What most immediately facilitated his major-league success in 2014, however, was the improvement of his slider. The combination of the two allowed him to produce nearly two wins in only 45 innings of relief work. Indeed, no pitcher in baseball with fewer than 50 innings of work recorded a mark as high as Giles' 1.7 WAR.

Minor League kwERA Leaders

Work by Russell Carleton demonstrates that, while pitcher strikeout and walk rates tend to stabilize rather quickly (at about 70 and 170 batters faced, respectively), home run rates require a considerably larger sample. As such, fielding independent pitching (FIP) numbers, which include home run rate, distort what might be called a pitcher's "true-talent ERA." An alternative to FIP is kwERA, an ERA estimator developed by Tom Tango that accounts only for a pitcher's strikeout and walk rates. Below are the top 10 minor league starters by kwERA, all with a minimum of 170 batters faced so as to allow a reliable sample size for both of the relevant inputs. Only pitchers who made starts above Rookie ball have been considered.

Minor League kwERA Leaders, 2014										
Name	Org	Level	Age	G	GS	IP	K%	BB%	kwERA
Mat Batts	MIN	R, A	22	13	10	60.2	30.6%	3.2%	2.11
Mike Fiers	MIL	AAA	29	17	17	102.1	31.5%	4.1%	2.12
Brandon Leibrandt	PHI	R, A-	21	12	10	60.2	29.3%	4.4%	2.41
Marcos Molina	NYM	A-	19	12	12	76.1	30.7%	6.1%	2.44
Vincent Velasquez	HOU	R, A+	22	22	16	77.0	32.6%	8.5%	2.51
Kyle Lloyd	SD	A	23	27	21	119.2	30.6%	6.7%	2.53
Daniel Norris	TOR	A+, AA, AAA	21	26	25	124.2	32.5%	8.6%	2.53
Taylor Cole	TOR	A+, AA	24	26	25	144.1	30.3%	7.7%	2.69
Aaron Wilkerson	BOS	A-	25	8	8	50.0	28.1%	5.7%	2.71
Troy Scribner	HOU	A-, A, AA	22	18	14	81.2	30.4%	8.1%	2.71

Notes

- Selected by the Twins out of UNC-Wilmington in the 14th round of the 2014 draft, left-hander Mat Batts was old for both the rookie-level Gulf Coast and Appalachian Leagues, between which he recorded strikeout and walk rates of 28.9 percent and 3.5 percent, respectively, over 32.0 innings. He was more appropriately aged for the Class-A Midwest League, however, to which level he was promoted at the beginning of August and at which level he produced even *better* strikeout and walk rates (32.4 percent and 2.9 percent, respectively). That his fastball rarely, if ever, reaches 90 mph is a less promising sign, however, so far as his major league future is concerned.

- Milwaukee right-hander Mike Fiers represents an almost excessively neat argument on behalf of minor-league translations. After recording the numbers shown here over ca. 100 innings with Triple-A Nashville, Fiers— who possesses less than dominant stuff—proceeded to post just a slightly lower strikeout rate (27.7 percent) and slightly higher walk rate (6.2 percent) over ca. 70 innings at the major league level. The result was an 85 xFIP- and 1.5 WAR—exceptional figures, those, for a pitcher who has had some difficulties in recent seasons.

- The minor-league kwERA leaderboard isn't entirely populated by soft-tossers. Mets right-hander Marcos Molina sits at 92-95 mph with his fastball; Houston right-hander Vincent Velasquez, slightly harder than that, even.

- Toronto's Daniel Norris, meanwhile, had himself a nice little season. He began the year in the High-A Florida State League, and made the rare four-level season, ultimately ending it with the Blue Jays themselves.

Reckless Power (RECK) Leaders

While patience and power are two different skills or tools, it's also generally the case that batters who hit for power are likely to draw more walks, simply because pitchers are afraid of conceding the home run.

Certain players, however, seem to have little interest in taking the walks their power has earned for them. Reckless power is what we might say they have. RECK is a toy metric designed to identify the players who displayed the most reckless power. It's calculated by dividing Isolated Power by Isolated Patience, or, stated differently, (SLG – AVG) / (OBP – AVG). The results appear to approximate the Richter Scale, such that less than 2.0 is barely felt, 5.0 is considerable, and 9.0 and up happens less than every 10 years and is totally destructive.

Minor League kwERA Leaders, 2014						
Name	Team	PA	AVG	OBP	SLG	RECK
Adam Jones	Orioles	682	.281	.311	.469	6.3
Yan Gomes	Indians	518	.278	.313	.472	5.5
Josh Harrison	Pirates	550	.315	.347	.490	5.5
Matt Adams	Cardinals	563	.288	.321	.457	5.1
Salvador Perez	Royals	606	.260	.289	.403	4.9
Torii Hunter	Tigers	586	.286	.319	.446	4.8
Yoenis Cespedes	---	645	.260	.301	.450	4.6
Ian Kinsler	Tigers	726	.275	.307	.420	4.5
Alexei Ramirez	White Sox	657	.273	.305	.408	4.2
Nelson Cruz	Orioles	678	.271	.333	.525	4.1

Notes

- Last year, Baltimore outfielder Adam Jones appeared atop the RECK leaderboard, with a mark of 6.3. One notes that the 2014 season has yielded precisely that same arrangement, as well—and, with A.J. Pierzynski recording too few plate appearances to qualify, has given Jones a significantly greater lead over the league's second-place finisher than last year.

- Also making consecutive appearances among the top-10 hitters by this unnecessary metric are Detroit's Torii Hunter and Kansas City's Salvador Perez. As noted by Mike Petriello in FanGraphs towards the end of October, Perez was particularly reckless after the All-Star break, posting a line of .229/.236/.360 from that point till the end of the season—a line that produces an 18.7 RECK. Over those 259 plate appearances, he recorded twice as many homers (six) as he did walks (three).

- Of particular note here is the presence of Detroit second baseman Ian Kinsler. Between 2006 and 2013, Kinsler never recorded a walk rate under 7.7 percent—and, in fact, produced a double-digit walk rate on multiple occasions. In 2014, that number descended to just 4.0 percent. The results were entirely competent, nevertheless: For the ninth consecutive season—which is to say, all of the major-league seasons he's ever played—Kinsler produced an overall batting line better than league average.

Fans Scouting Report Leaders, 2012-14

Every season, noted sabermetrician and pseudonymist Tom Tango facilitates the Fan Scouting Report, a project that allows the public to rate the defensive tools—instinct, speed, hands, etc.—of major-league players on a 0-100 scale. The various ratings, when combined, produce an overall rating (denoted as **Rating** below) of the relevant player's defensive skills regardless of position.

The ratings are thereafter compiled and converted into one overall stat (**FSR** below) that measures a player's total defensive ability in runs above or below average relative to his position. This statistic is presented in the same scale as other popular defensive metrics Ultimate Zone Rating (UZR) and Defensive Runs Saved (DRS), meaning it can be compared directly with these two statistics to provide more context on a player's defense.

What follows is a leaderboard of the top FSR figures between 2012 and 2014.

Fans Scouting Report Leaders, 2012-2014					
Name	Team	Position	Inn	Rating	FSR
Yadier Molina	Cardinals	Catcher	3,244.1	76	49
Andrelton Simmons	Braves	Shortstop	3,055.1	87	47
Alex Gordon	Royals	Outfield	4,161.1	81	45
Adrian Beltre	Rangers	Third base	3,586.1	77	41
Brandon Phillips	Reds	Second base	3,652.1	77	40
Salvador Perez	Royals	Catcher	3,026.2	71	38
Dustin Pedroia	Red Sox	Second base	3,801.1	75	38
Manny Machado	Orioles	Third base	2,595.1	83	36
Matt Wieters	Orioles	Catcher	2,584.1	70	32
Evan Longoria	Rays	Third base	3,083.2	75	32

Notes

- Even though they ignore the available framing metrics (by which measure he's also well acquitted), the extant defensive figures for catchers consistently rate St. Louis's Yadier Molina as the best at his position. That he would finish first by a different measure isn't entirely surprising.

- Largely the same can be said of Atlanta's Andrelton Simmons, who, despite recording a league- and park-adjusted offensive line about 30 percent worse than league average in 2014, still managed to produce an above-average quantity of wins. The Curacao native posted 2.3 WAR in 576 plate appearances, largely on the strength of the fielding runs he saved, along with the shortstop positional adjustment.

- Royals left fielder Alex Gordon has recorded UZR and DRS figures far higher than his left-field peers in recent years, exhibiting both reasonable range and the sort of arm strength and accuracy that made him a viable third base prospect at one point.

A Theoretical Blueprint for Improving MLEs

by Dave Allen and Kevin Tenenbaum

The following article is probably different from what you would normally read in these pages. We don't analyze data to find a specific result, but we take a theoretical approach to a concept that has been around for a long time. This article is simply a plan to improve upon the current construction of Major League Equivalencies (MLEs).

The baseball analytics community has come a long way since Bill James called MLEs one of the most important ideas he ever had, but the structure of MLEs has changed little since James introduced them. MLEs are one of the most valuable and fascinating areas of baseball analytics, and there is still much work to be done before we can be satisfied with them.

Tom Tango wrote an essay titled, "Issues with MLEs: Why I hate how they are used," in which he outlines five issues he has with MLEs. He concludes the article with this summary of the current state of the adjustments:

> "MLEs, as currently published, is a first step. We have many steps to go through before we can reduce the error range. We should not treat the current-ly-published MLEs as a final product."

We agree with Tango, and we feel that we can take a few steps towards improving the adjustments that we apply to minor league performance. While our list has some ideas in common with Tango's, we expand and take our own stance on these values and provide our own propositions as to how we plan to handle the problems that we hope people will take on in the future.

What Are MLEs?

MLEs are a translation of minor league statistics to major league ones. In other words, they approximate how well a player would have done if he had been in the major leagues, based on his performance in the minor leagues. It is important to note that MLEs are *not* projections. You can think of them as exchange rates that only convert minor league statistics into a major league context.

MLEs are typically multiplicative, which means that you simply multiply minor league performance by the MLE to get the adjusted value. For example, if the MLE from Triple-A to the majors for HRs is 0.8, and Player A hits 20 HR in Triple-A, we would have expected him to hit 0.8*20=16 homers in the majors if he had played at the top level over the same time period. MLEs make no claims about how Player A will perform in any other time period in the future.

Goal of MLEs

Any time you embark upon a project, it is a good idea to take a step back and lay out the model's goals. We feel MLEs should be the best possible tool for translating a player's performance from the minor leagues to the major leagues. These translations should be the best unbiased estimator of how a player would have performed in the major leagues given his minor league performance over the same time period for every player. Therefore, the adjustments need not be identical for all players at the same level, as variation in level may affect players differently.

These MLEs can be used for a variety of work in baseball, but we feel they are most useful in player forecasting. While remembering that an MLE is not a forecast unto itself, it is an essential part of a good forecasting system that uses minor league performance. These adjustments are essential because the forecaster needs to be able to use minor league statistics in the same way he or she uses major league statistics. Therefore, he or she can use MLEs to adjust minor league statistics so they correspond to the major league context. In other words, MLEs are important, and we hope to get the ball rolling towards improving forecast accuracy for young and inexperienced players.

Current Methodology

Below, we outline the general methodology used to generate MLEs.

First, restrict the sample of players to those who played at each of the two levels being compared over a short period (i.e. less than two years) but still have a decent sample size of plate appearances or total batters faced at both levels (i.e. > 50 plate appearances or total batters faced). Next, make a few other adjustments to ensure you are using the best sample of player possible. For instance, Brian Cartwright makes sure he only uses starting players that have at least 2.5 PA/G as a hitter. Then, take each of the performance samples and divide the major league performances by the minor league performances. The average of these ratios is the calculated MLE.

The methodology becomes slightly more complicated when we examine jumps of more than one level (i.e. Double-A to MLB). In this case, the MLE can be constructed with or without a method that we call chaining. With chaining, we would calculate an MLE for both Double-A to Triple-A and Triple-A to MLB and multiply, or chain, the two together to find the MLE. The other option would be to ignore chaining and simply calculate the MLE for players that played in both Double-A and MLB within the allotted amount of time. We will discuss the merits of each of these approaches in the next section.

Existing Issues

There are several issues with the above methodology we feel have been unaddressed for too long. Below, we outline six major issues with the current implementation of MLEs we believe hinder the accuracy of major forecasting systems.

1. Minor League Over-performance

When we look at the sample of players promoted from one level to another, we need to consider the thought process of the farm directors and general managers who decide when a player will be promoted. When making these decisions, they take several pieces of information into account, including roster construction, injuries, player attitude, scouting reports and player performance stats. Because these decision makers take a player's minor league performance into account, promoted players are more likely to have been over-performing than under-performing their true talent level while in the minor leagues.

Thus, we have a bias, as our MLEs will artificially be more extreme than they should be because the denominator (i.e. minor league performance) will overestimate players' talent levels.

2. Aging Effects

A second issue is that MLEs currently ignore player age, even though players will age between the middle of their minor league stint and the middle of their major league stint used to calculate the MLEs. This age difference poses a problem, as players of different ages will experience various magnitudes of aging effects on their performance.

For instance, consider the difference between Bryce Harper and Rick Ankiel. Harper was first called up to the major leagues at the age of 19, while Ankiel was first called up as a position player at 28 years of age. If the differences between the average age in the major league and minor league stints were identical, they still would have different aging effects because Harper is at a much steeper part of the aging curve than Ankiel. Therefore, an MLE constructed from many more Bryce Harpers than Rick Ankiels would be artificially closer to one because the MLB performance would be inflated by the players who benefited from aging a year or two. These influences can be fairly large, and they might not wash out in the sample. Therefore, it is important that MLE calculations account for this bias in their calculations.

3. Skill Profile

Another major issue with the current construction of MLEs is that league changes will affect each player differently. For instance, consider two position players with average strikeout percentages at Triple-A. These two players differ in that Player A has a high walk percentage, while Player B has a low walk percentage at the Triple-A level. Currently, we assume that a change in level will affect both these player identically on average.

However, this may be a naïve assumption, as Player A could be a player who has good patience, while Player B might have a problem making contact on his swings. Therefore, we would expect these players to experience a promotion to MLB differently. We would think that Player A would have a lower strikeout percentage than Player B at the major league level because Player B strikes out from ineptitude, while Player A strikes out through strategy. Thus, the MLE process would benefit from the examination of a player's other peripheral statistics instead of creating one value that applies to every player.

4. No Error Estimate

Historically, MLEs have been treated as simple estimates of league adjustments, and researchers and forecasters have ignored their uncertainty levels. This neglect is unacceptable for MLEs. Our adjustment for a transition from High-A to the majors is much more uncertain that the corresponding adjustment from Triple-A to the bigs. This poses a major problem when we combine league-adjusted statistics for different minor league levels and regress to the mean.

The major factor in how much we regress performance to the mean is the uncertainty around our true talent level estimates. In the majors, we can express this uncertainty in terms of the number of plate appearances in our sample. However, at the minor league level, we also must embed the uncertainty in our MLE estimate into the overall model uncertainty. Thus, we need to report our MLE estimates with a standard error in addition to the expected value of our MLEs. This will allow forecasters to essentially weight performance at higher levels more than lower levels based on the uncertainty of the MLE estimates, similar to how league-average performance is combined with player performance when we regress towards the mean.

5. A Better Look at Chaining

Currently, there are two major schools of thought on MLEs. Most systems use a method called chaining. Chaining is the practice of calculating league adjustments for change of one level at a time (i.e. Double-A to Triple-A and Triple-A to MLB) and multiplying the levels a player must go through to reach the majors. For example the MLE for Double-A would be the product of an adjustment from Double-A to Triple-A and an adjustment from Triple-A to the majors.

On the contrary, Brian Cartwright does not use chaining in his forecasting system, OLIVER. In an article he wrote for Baseball Prospectus in 2009, he shows that his MLEs perform better when they are not chained. While his results are intriguing, we believe that an inherent bias in the test sample means they require further testing.

All of the players that Cartwright uses for testing are good enough to reach MLB. Therefore, the direct method, which only incorporates players that played at both levels, will be overly optimistic in its adjustments because it only includes players who are promoted very quickly. This bias could create more accurate forecasts for players that do reach the majors, but it could be detrimental for those players a team is unsure of whether to promote or not. This bias presents an inherent problem, as the MLE could see an improvement in test results while actually being a worse estimate.

6. Experience at Level

Another bias current MLEs incorporate is the experience that a player has at a given level. There is evidence that minor league players perform better as they rack up experience at that level. This means there is a subsample of minor league performance data that is used in the calculation of MLEs that is inherently inflated above the players' true talent levels. Thus, our MLE estimates would benefit from removing the effect that experience at a level has on player performance in the minor leagues.

Solutions to Problems

In this section, we will go through each of the six issues we outlined above and propose a potential change to the current MLE model that we would like to see people use to craft MLEs in the future.

1. Minor League Over-performance

Promoted players are likely to be over performing their true talent levels (think Gregory Polanco when he was promoted to the Pirates). To work towards removing this selection bias, we propose regressing minor league stats towards the mean for MLEs. This will move the population average closer to the true talent level for the player group that we want to study (i.e. minor league players who could be promoted to the major leagues).

The big question here is what value we should regress these performance statistics toward. We can think of two possible choices:

a. **Average of players within the league.** This option does a great job of removing a portion of the overperforming player bias by shifting inflated statistics from overperforming players toward the league average. This change, therefore, does exactly what we want it to. However, the main reason to regress to the league average instead of the level mean would be that there are major differences in the environment of one league to the next at the same level. These differences in league mostly can be handled with park factors. Therefore, we would hope to find a larger sample for the prior.

b. **Average of entire level.** Therefore, we propose that minor league performance statistics be regressed to the level mean. Therefore, an individual player's Triple-A strikeout percentage performance would be regressed toward the average K% for all Triple-A players. This is the best answer we could come up with because it is the largest sample of available players that does not amplify the overperforming player bias.

2. Aging Effects

Next, we will address the issue of aging. To incorporate the various magnitudes of aging effects on players in the major league and minor league samples, we propose all statistics are aged to the same year. This will essentially create age-neutral statistics for every player's performance at both the minor league and major league level.

We recommend performance be aged forward or backward to the peak age on the aging curve used. While it does not matter what age you choose, it does need to be consistent. The removal of aging bias from MLE calculations requires a different aging method than most researchers tend to use. Normally, people create aging curves using only major league performance. This method would not yield the optimal results, as you would be applying the aging effect to a sample of players that is different from the sample the curve was designed for.

MLEs do not look at players who were in the majors for all years in the sample. Rather, they use data for players who have been promoted from the minor leagues to the major leagues recently. Therefore, we believe this information should be incorporated into any aging curve used to adjust performance in MLE calculations.

3. Skill Profile

To solve the problem of level changes affecting each player differently, we propose that personalized MLEs be created for each player. Personalizing these adjustments would create a system in which every player is treated uniquely. For instance, a player who tends to strike out often would have a different MLE than a player who is able to make contact on all pitches. While we will not hypothesize on what these differences might look like, we can say that they should be treated differently when trying to predict their major league performances from their minor league performances.

We propose a solution to this issue that uses similarity scores to construct an MLE for each player. In this case, a similarity score would fall between zero and one. You can think of this as a weight. Therefore, we would create an MLE in the same way that we normally would with one small change. Rather than taking the straight average of the ratio of major league to minor league performance, the weighted average would be computed with weights proportional to the similarity scores.

Now, the most difficult part of this process actually would be to calculate the similarity scores. While it would be easy to use the simple similarity scores that Baseball-Reference publishes for all players, this would be an inappropriate measure of player similarity for MLE construction. Rather, we want to really key in on the variables that are important for successfully changing levels. To find these properties, it would be best to run a regression or other machine-learning technique to determine what variables have a lot of influence on how players adjust to new leagues. These factors would be different for each statistic we adjust and could range from biographical information like height to performance statistics like isolated power (ISO). We can calculate the difference between these values and then weight these differences to develop a similarity score to use in our weighted MLE and come up with a personalized MLE for each player to minimize our forecast errors.

4. No Error Estimate

Next, we address the question of how to measure the uncertainty surrounding our MLE estimates. To make any inferences about the MLE sampling distribution, we must generate an estimate of the actual distribution. To do so, we will use a technique called bootstrapping. To create the MLE sampling distribution, we repeatedly take the average of a random sample (with replacement) of players' ratios between their minor league and major league performance. Therefore, we have several averages of these resamples. We treat these averages as the resampling distribution of the MLE, thinking of it as representing how likely we are to draw each value of the MLE if we choose one at random.

While we could report this distribution, it makes it difficult to incorporate into the forecasting process without making any assumptions. We assume the resampling distribution is normally distributed, which is a good assumption because of the central limit theorem (which states that if we take enough independent samples from any probability distribution, the average of the samples will follow a bell curve with its average being the true mean). Therefore, we can take the standard error of the MLE estimate as the standard deviation of the resampling distribution. We then use this standard deviation to weight level-adjusted statistics by their true uncertainty in addition to understanding their uncertainty. Because of the normality assumption, knowing the expected value (i.e. the MLE) and the standard error gives us everything we need to recreate the MLE distribution.

5. A Better Look at Chaining

Chaining presents an issue we have found very difficult to solve. The biased data makes it almost impossible to objectively compare the two methods (i.e., chaining or not). With that said, we believe it to be important that we can confidently say which method we prefer, or that either method works just fine. Therefore, we propose a Bayesian framework to test the utility of each method. Rather than testing the MLEs in a simple forecast and choosing the model with the smaller error, we suggest that the errors are compared while holding onto a prior belief that chaining is the better method. This Bayesian procedure will allow for a comparison of the accuracy of the two methods with the understanding that the test data are biased in favor of not chaining. This is admittedly an imperfect solution and an area for further brainstorming.

6. Experience at Level

Incorporating experience at level will prove to be a difficult task going forward. To make this happen, we must quantify the effect of playing another game at the same level. While it would be easy to assume this phenomenon is a linear effect (i.e. the performance boost from game one to game two is identical to the boost from game 1,000 to game 1,001), we cannot do that because we expect there to be diminishing marginal returns for the effect. Therefore, you would gain a larger boost for games earlier in your career at that level than you would for later games.

What's needed is a slightly more complicated model that does a good job handling diminishing marginal returns. We believe the best model for this would be logarithmic. Therefore, we want to approximate the effect the log (games played at level) has on the player's performance. As always, we need to fit separate models for each statistic.

While we would like to solve this issue with a simple linear regression, there will be issues here because of a sampling bias. Players who play more games at a certain level are probably performing worse than players who play fewer games. To counteract this bias, we assume that, on average, an extra game will affect all players identically. We understand this may not be a good assumption, as we treat it as a flaw for current MLEs, but we do not have a better solution at this time. Therefore, if we take a subset of players who have played at least n games, we can run a linear regression that uses the log (games played at level) to predict player performance at a given level based on the number of games played at that level. Then, we can actually adjust the performance statistics that go into the MLE model for the effect that experience at that level would have on each player.

Summing Up

MLEs can be improved upon, and here we have a blueprint for doing so. Some of these changes may not help the process, but we believe they are all worth at least testing and seeing if they lead to any measurable improvements in forecast accuracy. Improving them will be a complicated process, but we believe that the framework here will reap benefits for those who have the time to act upon them.

References & Resources

- Tom Tango, Tangotiger, "Issues with MLEs: Why I hate how they are used," *tangotiger.net/hateMLEs.html*

- Brian Cartwright, Baseball Prospectus, "Prospectus Idol Entry: Brian Cartwright's Initial Entry," *baseballprospectus.com/article.php?articleid=8887*

- Brian Cartwright, The Hardball Times, "Oliver, smarter than your average monkey," *hardballtimes.com/oliver-smarter-than-your-average-monkey*

Et Cetera

Glossary

BABIP: Batting Average on Balls in Play. This is a measure of the number of batted balls that safely fall in for hits (not including home runs). The exact formula we use is (H-HR)/(AB-K-HR+SF).

Batted ball statistics: When a batter hits a ball, he hits either a ground ball, fly ball or line drive. The resulting ground ball, fly ball and line drive percentages make up a player's mix of statistics, with infield fly balls, or pop-ups, being tracked as a percentage of a player's total number of fly balls.

BB%: Walk rate measures how often a position player walks—or how often a pitcher walks a batter—per plate appearance. It is measured in percentage form.

BB/9: Walks allowed per nine innings

BsR: UBR+wSB. UBR, or Ultimate Base Running, accounts for the value a player adds to his team via baserunning. It is determined using linear weights, with each baserunning event receiving a specific run value. wSB, or Weighted Stolen Base runs, estimates the number of runs a player contributes by stealing bases, as compared to the average player.

ChampAdded: The proportion of a World Series championship contributed by a player or team, based on the impact of a play on a team's winning a game, and the value of that game within the context of winning the World Series. Please refer to "A Bumgarner for all (Post)Seasons," for more information.

Defensive Efficiency: The percentage of balls in play converted into outs. It can be approximated by 1-BABIP.

DRS: Defensive Runs Saved. DRS rates players as above or below average based on "runs," with data from Baseball Info Solutions used as an input. It tracks a number of different aspects of defensive play, including stolen bases, double plays, outfield arms, robbing home runs and range.

ERA: A pitcher's total number of earned runs allowed divided by his total number of innings pitched, multiplied by nine.

ERA-: A pitching version of OPS+ and wRC+: 100 represents a league-average ERA, and a smaller ERA- is better.

ERA+: ERA measured against the league average and adjusted for ballpark factors. An ERA+ over 100 is better than average, less than 100 is below average.

FIP: Fielding Independent Pitching, a measure of all things for which a pitcher is specifically responsible. The formula is (HR*13+(BB+HBP)*3-K*2)/IP, plus a league-specific factor (usually around 3.2) to round out the number to an equivalent ERA number. FIP helps you understand how well a pitcher pitched, regardless of how well his fielders fielded.

FIP-: A pitching version of OPS+ and wRC+: 100 represents a league-average FIP, and a smaller FIP- is better.

ISO: Isolated power. This is a measure of a hitter's raw power, or how good they are at hitting for extra bases. Most simply, the formula is SLG-AVG, but you can also calculate it as such: $((2B)+(2*3B)+(3*HR))/AB$.

K%: Strikeout rate measures how often a position player strikes out—or how often a pitcher strikes out a batter—per plate appearance. It is measured in percentage form.

K/9: Strikeouts per nine innings

kwERA: An ERA estimator that works similar to FIP, but takes home runs out of the equation. The formula is: $5.40-12*(K-BB)/PA$.

LI: Leverage Index. LI measures the criticality of a play or plate appearance. It is based on the range of potential WPA outcomes of a play, compared to all other plays. 1.0 is an average Index.

Linear Weights: The historical average runs scored for each event in a baseball game.

OBP: On-base percentage, an essential tool, measures how frequently a batter reaches base safely. The formula is: (hits+walks+hit-by-pitch) divided by (at-bats+walks+hit-by-pitch+sacrifice flies).

OPS: On Base plus Slugging Percentage, a crude but quick measure of a batter's true contribution to his team's offense. See wOBA for a better approach.

OPS+: A normalized version of OPS that adjusts for small variables such as park effects and puts OPS on a scale where 100 is league average, and each point above or below is one percent above or below league average.

PITCHf/x: Sportvision's pitch tracking system that has been installed in every major league stadium since at least the start of the 2007 season. It tracks several aspects of every pitch thrown in a major league game, including velocity, movement, release point, spin and pitch location.

Pythagorean Formula: A formula for converting a team's Run Differential into a projected win-loss record. The formula is $RS^2/(RS^2+RA^2)$. Teams' actual win-loss records tend to mirror their Pythagorean records, and variances usually can be attributed to luck.

You can improve the accuracy of the Pythagorean formula by using a different exponent (the 2 in the formula). The best exponent can be calculated this way: $(RS/G+RA/G)^.285$, where RS/G is Runs Scored per Game and RA/G is Runs Allowed per Game. This is called the PythagoPat formula.

SIERA: Skill-Interactive Earned Run Average estimates ERA through walk rate, strikeout rate and ground ball rate, eliminating the effects of park, defense and luck.

Slash Line: At times, writers may refer to a batter's "slash line," or "triple-slash line." They mean something like this: .287/.345/.443. The numbers between those slashes are the batter's batting average, on-base percentage and slugging percentage.

Total Zone: The lone defensive stat calculated exclusively from Retrosheet play-by-play data. It is the defensive stat used in both WAR calculations for games played prior to the UZR era (2002-present).

UZR: A fielding system similar to Defensive Runs Saved. Both systems calculate a fielder's range by comparing his plays made in various "vectors" across the baseball diamond to the major league average rate of plays made in those vectors. Both systems also look at other factors such as the effectiveness of outfield throwing, handling bunts and turning double plays.

WAR: Wins Above Replacement. A "win stat" that calculates the number of wins a player contributed to his team above a certain replacement level. WAR is calculated at FanGraphs and Baseball Reference. Though the two implementations vary a bit, they share a common framework that includes a linear weights approach to runs created, advanced fielding metrics, leverage for relievers and replacement levels that vary by position. In addition, beginning in 2013, both versions unified their definition of replacement level, making the two versions more directly comparable.

Win Shares: An all-encompassing look at a player's value. Each team win is made up of three win shares, though the calculation for deriving each player's Win Shares is complex and based on the defensive position they play, among other things.

wOBA: A linear weights offensive rating system that is similar to OPS, except that it's set to the scale of on-base percentage.

WPA: Win Probability Added is a system in which each player is given credit toward helping his team win, based on play-by-play data and the impact each specific play has on the team's probability of winning.

wRC+: Like OPS+ and ERA+, wRC+ is scaled so that 100 is average and a higher number is positive. The "RC" stands for Runs Created, but it's not Bill James' Runs Created. It's a "linear weights" version derived from wOBA.

xFIP: Expected Fielding Independent Pitching. This is an experimental stat that adjusts FIP and "normalizes" the home run component according to the number of fly balls a pitcher allowed.

For more information on these and other statistics, visit: *hardballtimes.com/tools/glossary* or *fangraphs.com/library*.

Who Was That?

To commemorate Dave Studenmund's last year producing the *Annual*, we asked that writers, in addition to their biographies, offer an anecdote about what Studes and/or The Hardball Times has meant to them over the years. As with the letter from David Appelman in the front of the book, this happened unbeknownest to Studes.

Dave Allen is a visiting assistant professor of biology at Middlebury College. He studies forest succession and ecology. In his spare time—between his biology teaching and research—he still does some baseball analysis, but not as much as he would like.

I first met Dave Studenmund at a SABR meeting in Atlanta. Obviously, I knew who he was from his writing and the Hardball Times Annual *and website. So it was a real thrill to meet him. But more than that initial thrill, what really struck me was what a friendly, down-to-earth person Dave was (and still is!). He came up and introduced himself, had kind words for my baseball writing and SABR presentation, and then we just had a really nice chat about baseball analysis. Since then it has always been very nice to check in with him when we are at the same conferences, or through quick emails.*

Tony Blengino has worked 11 years in major league baseball, most recently spending five seasons as special assistant to the GM with the Seattle Mariners. Previously, he spent six years with the Milwaukee Brewers, three as their area scout in the northeastern US, and three as assistant scouting director. Prior to his baseball career, he was a CPA, primarily in the healthcare and non-profit industries. He has been writing for FanGraphs since November, 2013. Tony graduated from Saint Joseph's University in Philadelphia—where he was a classmate of Jamie Moyer—in 1985. He and Kathy, his wife of 28 years, live in Waukesha, Wis. They have two grown children, Jessica and Anthony.

A word of thanks to Dave Studenmund, the driving force behind The Hardball Times for many years. The rise of sabermetrics in the last decade plus has on balance been an extremely positive development for those who love the game, but one of its unattractive byproducts has been a tide of animosity between traditionalists and the more analytically inclined, a situation that really doesn't need to exist.

Above the fray for the duration of this era, The Hardball Times sits. You want cutting-edge analysis, you get it. You want storytelling, you want to learn more about the players of the past and present who put up those numbers, you get that too. I recall a time when FanGraphs was a fairly new endeavor, and I had only recently become acquainted with Dave Cameron. In what might have been our first discussion ever, he asked what other data I would like to see on the site. "How about Hardball Times' RZR and Out Of Zone Plays data," I replied. THT gives both sides of your brain some exercise, and for that I say thanks, Studes.

Dave Cameron is the managing editor of FanGraphs, and he also contributes regularly to Fox Sports and the *Wall Street Journal*. More importantly, he's a leukemia survivor, and will take any opportunity given to shamelessly suggest that you donate both blood and platelets. He's happy to still be writing about trivial things like baseball.

I don't know that there's ever been a recurring column I enjoyed as much as Dave Studenmund's brilliant "10 Things I Didn't Know..." pieces. Studes certainly didn't invent the notes format, but few have been able to weave cohesion through a series of often unrelated tidbits, and fewer still have been able to do so while actually educating their readers about complex topics. Within one article, he could write intelligently about win probability, ERA estimators, and the distance traveled by astronauts walking on the moon. No, really, those were all in the same piece, published on March 27, 2008.

Studes wrote well enough that you knew he was intelligent, but he didn't write like he was talking down at his readers. He has been perhaps the most humble educator in the sabermetric community, pushing forward overall knowledge without promoting his own agenda. And as I was lucky enough to get to spend some time with him the last few years, I've come to realize that his writing was simply an extension of who he is as a person: a genuine, kind, humble man who gave far more than he ever asked for in return. Thank you for giving so much, Studes, and for giving us all something to aspire to.

Matthew Carruth: I think third person biographical blurbs always sound awkward. I joined The Hardball Times way back in 2007. It was an incredible opportunity for me as a raw near-college-graduate and I thank all, especially Studes, for bestowing that. I hope, over the years I was active here and on FanGraphs and while still running Statcorner, that I contributed something in the way of baseball knowledge while at the same time putting a premium on cordiality and humor. I failed many times and those were personal failures. I succeeded many times and those were team successes. I wouldn't be who or where I am today without the people I worked with. I'm grateful to all and implore everyone to apply the same critical thinking we use herein to more places than just baseball or sports.

Carson Cistulli lives in New Hampshire with his wife and dog.

Of Dave Studenmund, I have only the warmest associations. Having known him for years merely by way of occasional correspondence, I finally met him at a Neapolitan pizzeria in Phoenix in March of 2014. At the conclusion of our meal, the restaurant's proprietor brought out multiple servings of complimentary cream limoncello, a beverage I enjoy more than considerably and which I drank with enthusiasm. Whether it was because of Studenmund that the owner looked upon us so favorably, I can't say. Perhaps not. But the facts of the matter are immutable: 100 percent of meals I've eaten with Studes have ended in one or more servings of free and delicious liqueur.

Warren Corbett has contributed to more than a dozen other books, and is the author of *The Wizard of Waxahachie: Paul Richards and the End of Baseball as We Knew It*. He lives in Bethesda, Md.

Karl de Vries is a writer and journalist who lives in Astoria, N.Y. Aside from THT and FanGraphs, his work has appeared in *The Star-Ledger* of Newark, *Newsday* and FoxNews.com, as well as the official *2008 Major League Baseball All-Star Game* program. A long-suffering Mets fan, Karl still maintains that "Ken Griffey Jr. Presents Major League Baseball" for Super Nintendo is the best baseball video game ever made.

Studes gave me a shot writing for THT several years ago when I had virtually no baseball writing experience, and it's been an honor to have been a part of his team. It's been especially gratifying to have worked with him on two THT Annuals, contributing alongside an all-star team of baseball writers and analysts.

Joe Distelheim, The Hardball Times' chief copy editor, is a lifelong Cubs fan and a lifelong newspaperman. Despite overwhelming evidence that both institutions are in decline, he continues to believe in them.

As my wife will tell you—she tells everyone—I never throw anything away. So it didn't take long for me to find, among old emails, my first correspondence with Dave Studenmund. I'd accepted a "job" as copy editor for The Hardball Times; he, the big boss, was writing to welcome me.

That was in January of 2007. Bruce Markusen was already writing for the Web site. Otherwise, I seem to be the longest-tenured staffer here. How can that be? It's Dave's outfit.

I put "job" in quote marks above. I'm retired. I had jobs in real life. This is not that. I don't go to an office. This is, if not a labor of love, a labor of like very much. I met Dave once, over lunch, when I was in the Chicago area. No face time ever with anyone else at THT. But Dave somehow fostered an organizational culture, an espirit, an easy camaraderie among the troops, that any company would envy.

He's been an ideal boss, one who never felt compelled to say "I'm the boss." He gave people jobs to do, and let them do those jobs. I was assigned to police THT writing—style, grammar, readability, all that. He was the big picture guy.

And so, for years, he wrote about ten fascinating baseball things he—and we—didn't know last week. And I reminded him that Hardball Times style was "10 things." I leave it to you to decide whose contribution was more important.

August Fagerstrom covers the Cleveland Indians and their Double-A affiliate, the Akron RubberDucks, as well as the Cleveland Browns, for ohio.com and the *Akron Beacon Journal*.

I've never met Dave Studenmund. Never talked to him. Not even sure if he knows who I am. But I extend to him a gigantic thank you for the work he's done in the baseball community and at The Hardball Times. His work has allowed me the opportunity to do something I never thought I'd do: be published in a book. A book that I read and enjoy every year. The fact that my name appears alongside many of my favorite authors, as well as the legendary Bill James, is surreal.

Frank Jackson was born in Philadelphia in 1950, the year of the Whiz Kids, but by the time he was introduced to Connie Mack Stadium, the Phillies were perennial tail-enders. Subsequently living in Illinois and Maryland, he also followed the White Sox, Cubs and Orioles, but his longest tenure as a fan has been with the Rangers, as he has lived in Dallas since 1976. In recent years, he has written articles for the Rangers program magazine.

Frank has visited 48 major league ballparks, including all but five of the current parks, and has visited all of the current Texas League parks, as well as some that are no longer in use. Altogether, he has visited 78 minor league parks and 39 college parks. Also, he has visited all the Arizona spring training ballparks and all but one in Florida.

I can't remember when I first stumbled upon The Hardball Times (shameful self-disclosure: I'm always behind the curve) but it's been a bit more than three years since I started writing there. There are plenty of baseball-oriented Web sites out there, some more statistics-oriented, some more history-oriented; many are informative, some are insightful, but few are also entertaining. The Hardball Times was the exception. I actually enjoyed reading the articles. Figured I'd enjoy writing some myself.

I work in an office where legal jargon had all but numbed the verbal area of my brain. Legal documents are lifeless; you can't call legalspeak dead prose because that would imply it was once alive. But after years of dealing with dreary documents, one learns to appreciate, even relish good writing all the more. So kudos to Studes for keeping it lively.

Bill James lives in Lawrence, Kan., and has no grandchildren or felony convictions.

Brad Johnson is a baseball addict and a statistics junkie who currently resides in Atlanta, Ga. He played four seasons of injury-plagued baseball at Macalester College from 2006 through 2009, and has since made the transition to a purely off-the-field existence. You can find his work on The Hardball Times and FanGraphs.

I "met" Studes back in 2010 on Tom Tango's website. I had been talking with Tom about the best ways to break into baseball professionally. He suggested the easiest way would be to become established as a writer. Perhaps some work in PITCHf/x would open doors. Our conversation turned into a post on his site, and Dave reached out to offer me a slot with THT. At the time, I had recently graduated college, was writing irregularly for a now-defunct Phillies fan blog, and generally had no idea what I wanted to do with myself.

I credit the opportunity Dave gave me with everything I've become. While my initial goal of working for an major league franchise dissolved—turns out I have no interest in working 80-hour weeks for little pay—I learned to love conducting player analyses and puzzling through major league decisions. Without Dave, there's no question I wouldn't be where I am today.

David Kagan earned his Ph.D. in physics from the University of California, Berkeley. He has been a faculty member at California State University, Chico since 1981. He has served as the chair of the Department of Physics and as the founding Chair of the Department of Science Education. Dr. Kagan is a regular contributor to *The Physics Teacher* as well as THT. All the while, he has remained true to his lifelong obsession with baseball by using the national pastime to enhance the teaching and learning of physics.

The first article I submitted to THT, I had prepared in the more technical style required for academic publication. Dave was so polite and delicate when he said he thought it was interesting, but could I "rewrite it with less math." I have taken this to heart and not only did it improve all my writing overall, it has made me think harder about explaining physics in less mathematical terms. Thanks Studes!

Jason Linden teaches English and creative writing in Kentucky. His debut novel, *When the Sparrow Sings*, may be out by the time you read this. He writes and edits at The Hardball Times and also contributes to the Reds blog Redleg Nation.

Studes can be...intimidating. The first time I worked with him, I almost ran away screaming. He didn't like my idea. He didn't think it was well thought out, and he let me know it. I won't lie, it stung a little. But he was right, of course. Studes has a habit of being right, I have found.

I didn't run screaming. I stuck around for a bit. As an editor, I pitched an idea for someone else and ended up writing a column because of it. It wasn't serious. Just a fun compiling of numbers. Studes liked it. And when I had fun with the writing, he really liked it. And so that made me feel really good when he liked the novel pitch I gave him at the beginning of the year. You see, the thing about Studes telling you—very honestly—when he doesn't like something, is you never have to doubt him when he does. We all need people like that. Too many people tell you what you want to hear. Studes tells you the truth. When he liked my first pages, I knew I probably had something. Studes is responsible for publishing my first novel. That's a big debt, and while I'll always be grateful, I'll never doubt why he published it. Because he believed in it. It's nice to be believed in. Thanks, Studes.

Jack Moore is a freelance writer based in Minneapolis writing about sports, history, mythology, and the intersection of the trio. He is not looking forward to Bud Selig Bobblehead Day.

Since I first started writing about baseball in 2008, The Hardball Times has consistently been a top producer of interesting and illuminating work about baseball, its statistics and its history. My job and my career wouldn't exist without spaces like THT, and I am thankful for the writers like Studes who constantly found new and interesting ways to view the game and inspired readers like me to do the same.

Matthew Murphy lives in New York City, and when he isn't reading or writing about baseball, he studies cancer and stem cell biology at the New York University Medical Center. He has also written about the analytics of beer at BeerGraphs.com.

Since I started reading FanGraphs a few years ago, I've looked forward to reading the Annual *each offseason. Last year there was a profile on St. Louis Cardinals GM John Mozeliak and how the team utilizes sabermetrics. At the end of the article they noted a copy of* The Hardball Times Annual 2013 *on his desk, which he referred to as "my geeky reading." I remember seeing that and thinking about how cool it would be to be a part of the book. Almost two years later, what I thought was a pipe dream has turned into reality. I've had so much fun writing for THT and couldn't be more excited and honored to be a part of the* Annual *and the great group of writers and editors that make it possible every year.*

Alan M. Nathan is professor emeritus of physics at the University of Illinois. After a long career investigating the collisions of subatomic particles, he now devotes his efforts to the study of the physics of baseball in general and the collisions between a baseball with a bat in particular. For over a decade he served on the NCAA Baseball Research Panel, providing scientific advice on issues related to bat performance.

What's a guy to do on those long cold winter days with no baseball? Here's what I do. I sit by the fireplace with the latest edition of The Hardball Times Annual *and work my way through it, cover to cover. So, many thanks, Studes, for making my winter far more enjoyable.*

Dustin Nosler is a writer at Dodgers Digest, co-host of the Dugout Blues podcast, and wears a number of hats for FanGraphs and The Hardball Times.

Writers are basically professional BSers, but I'm not going to try to BS my way through this anecdote. I've been associated with The Hardball Times for just a few months and haven't had much interaction with Studes. But he gave me the opportunity to contribute to this publication, and I couldn't be happier.

A former river guide, ranch hand, farm hand, oyster shucker and, most unlikely of all, editor-in-chief of a magazine, **John Paschal** has written sports and opinion for *The Dallas Morning News*, *The (Memphis) Commercial Appeal*, the *Corpus Christi Caller-Times* and other dead-tree publications. Online, he has contributed to The Hardball Times, NotGraphs, Baseball Prospectus, Deadspin and The Good Men Project.

I used to be a writer. Then, for a long time, I wasn't. Wanderlust held me captive for years. Then one day I wrote a story, a baseball story, but I had nowhere to put the thing. My hard drive held it captive for months. Later, while exploring, I discovered a Web site full of good baseball writing. "Hmm," I said. Sometimes you just have to take a chance. You never know where that first step will lead. So I contacted someone at that website. And in what might have been an Internet first, he responded promptly and amiably. Now here I am, with dozens of THT stories to my credit, writing a sincere note of gratitude to Studes.

Mike Petriello writes for FanGraphs, ESPN and Dodgers Digest, and also built the TechGraphs and Hardball Times Web sites. He lives in New York City with one wife and two cats.

When we embarked on the redesign of THT in late 2013, Studes was understandably very attached to everything it had been, and at first I wondered if some of our mild disagreements would make the project harder than anticipated. But I quickly learned that every comment and opinion Studes had on the site came from a place of great passion, the site having been his for a decade, and maintaining the reputation THT had worked hard to build was extremely important to him. It's that passion that has made the site so strong for so many years, and ultimately made the redesign project a fully enjoyable experience.

Alex Remington writes for The Hardball Times and manages Braves Journal. He is a product manager at *The Washington Post* and a fellow at the Reynolds Journalism Institute.

I started reading The Hardball Times in the mid-2000s, when Carlos Gomez pioneered the usage of animated GIFs on the internet as he broke down pitching mechanics. (He wasn't the first to use GIFs, of course, but he was definitely the first one I ever saw who knew how to use them well.) The whole staff was fantastic, with great work from Studes, Carlos, Chris Jaffe, Josh Kalk, John Beamer, Victor Wang, Craig Calcaterra, and of course the late John Brattain. The Hardball Times was also the only place that you could go to get updated Win Shares counts for players. After Rob Neyer's columns got me into sabermetrics in the first place, THT was where I really fell down the rabbit hole. It's an honor to add my name to the author roll, next to so many of the greatest names in baseball writing. Thanks for everything, Dave.

Chris St. John earned a degree in chemical engineering, but that did not satisfy his intellectual curiosity. Instead he found his solace studying baseball statistics, writing his first article in 2010. His analyses focus on minor league statistics and home runs, because what is more exciting than that? His work has appeared at Beyond the Boxscore, Baseball Prospectus and ESPN.

Dave Studenmund and THT have been around for longer than I've been following baseball stats, and the quality of the work speaks for itself. During my research on this topic for the Annual, I used a few articles on THT from years ago that still hold as relevant resources. Regardless of the subject, Dave or THT has an article on it, usually done far more thoroughly than I could hope to do myself. Thank you to Dave for holding the reins to such an incredible resource.

Eno Sarris once asked Daniel Straily to show him all 17 change-up grips the pitcher had used in his career. Since then he's been taking pictures of pitchers' fingers for a living. He writes for FanGraphs and runs BeerGraphs and doesn't think deep dives ruin the fun of either baseball or beer.

I love to link to other people's work because it's usually better than mine. And if you look through my links, there's probably no site that has been linked to as often as The Hardball Times. Aaron Gleeman. Carlos Gomez. Josh Kalk. Mike Fast. Colin Wyers. Harry Pavlidis. Max Marchi. I name all these names because in a way they all point back to one name: Dave Studenmund. His affability, passion, energy, and open-mindedness—along with his own obvious dedication to the site and the Annual—were the magnet that drew this great research together. And so let's salute him! Thank you for being the engine behind such a great site over the years! Thank you for being Studes!

Greg Simons has been writing about baseball in various formats since the last millennium. He has been part of The Hardball Times since 2010, serving as both an editor and writer. When he's not thinking about baseball, he's playing it, participating in 1860s-era vintage base ball (yep, it was two words back then) matches around the Midwest. While he is an avid St. Louis Cardinals fan, he never has claimed to be one of "the best fans in baseball."

I've yet to have the pleasure of meeting Dave Studenmund in person, though I hope to remedy that situation at some point. What I have been able to do is work with one of the brightest and most dedicated baseball minds around. Without Studes, you wouldn't be reading this book, and The Hardball Times Web site would not exist. He allowed me—and many others—to play in his sandbox, and for that I am eternally grateful. Best of luck in all of your future pursuits, Dave, and thanks for everything you've done for so many people in the baseball community.

Alex Skillin grew up in New England and now lives in Brooklyn. He has written for SB Nation, Beyond the Box Score, The Classical, SoxProspects.com and Fire Brand of the American League, among other places. A lifelong Red Sox fan, he is just counting down the days until Pedro's Hall of Fame induction speech.

I remember opening up the first Hardball Times Annual I ever read nearly 10 years ago and remarking at all the words spilled on baseball analysis in the middle of winter. It provided the perfect escape from those cold New England nights back to summer and the warm familiarity of blue skies and green grass. To be able to put some of my own words beside those of other talented writers in this year's Annual, to be able to write about, discuss and scrutinize baseball long after summer's gone and the season ends is as good as it gets.

Dave Studenmund would like to dedicate his contribution to the memory of his nephew, Scott Studenmund, who was killed in service of his country in Afghanistan this past June.

Jeff Sullivan has a job title with FanGraphs, although he doesn't know what it is. He likes the Mariners and lives in Portland, Ore., or as the locals refer to it, Portland.

They say it's always about the people, right? I've been blogging baseball for more than a decade. Several years back, I started to interact with Matthew Carruth, who wrote for THT and I believe routinely handled the Dartboard. Carruth was also a fan of the Mariners, and when PITCHf/x was getting launched, Carruth was invited to the first-ever PITCHf/x summit in San Francisco, and he asked if I'd be interested in coming along. I'd never met him in person before, but we had an incredible weekend and, out of that, we developed what I consider to be my best and closest friendship.

I know this seems like a peripheral anecdote, and I guess it is a peripheral anecdote, but the significance is this: were it not for THT, I wouldn't know my current best friend. And were it not for all the resulting sparks of inspiration, from bouncing ideas back and forth, I really don't know if I'd still be writing about baseball. THT, then, has meant a lot more than just your average Web site.

Matt Swartz writes for The Hardball Times, FanGraphs and MLB Trade Rumors. He has three degrees from the University of Pennsylvania, B.A.s in mathematics and economics and a Ph.D. in economics. Matt does the arbitration salary projection model for MLB Trade Rumors, and co-created the SIERA pitching statistic available at FanGraphs. He regularly consults for a major league team, in addition to working in his day job as an economist in the insurance industry. Matt is a native Philadelphian, and lives there now with his wife Laura and daughter Maya.

Studes has always been a source of creative ideas, constructive criticism and excellent advice. A couple years ago, Studes identified a topic that he thought I could write about, allowed me to bounce ideas off him, and helped me pick the strongest ones. After publishing them, he advocated for me to present at the SABR Analytics Conference, and subsequently published about my presentation himself to further expose the work he had already supported so much. This was not the first time that Studes advocated on my behalf, nor was it the last. In a field like sabermetrics where so much benefit could go to the selfish, Studes has been a tireless advocate and advisor to others, and our collective knowledge is far better for it.

Paul Swydan spends most of his time with his children, Xander and Jasmine.

A wise man once said, if you admire someone, you should go ahead and tell them. Admiration only begins to describe my feelings for Studes, who has trusted me with his baby, The Hardball Times, far beyond a level that I deserve. I'll try not to screw things up too badly. Thanks for everything, Studes. Please don't be a stranger.

Based out of Minneapolis, **David G. Temple** is the managing editor of Tech-Graphs and a contributor to FanGraphs. He has previously written for NotGraphs and *The Classical Magazine*. Dayn Perry once called him a Bible Made of Lasers.

The Hardball Times was always a must-read for me during my formative years of baseball fandom. So when I was approached to contribute, I was beyond excited. I was also very nervous and worried, but that has more to do with my general disposition than anything else.

I have both written and contributed podcasts for The Hardball Times. Through every step of the way, everyone I've dealt with has been kind, understanding, and very support-ive. The THT staff is a special one, that shows both on paper and electronic pages, as well as behind the scenes. Being a part of such a group has been an honor.

Kevin Tenenbaum is a senior mathematical sciences major and economics minor at Middlebury College. He has presented research at the SABR Analytics Confer-ence, been published in the *2014 Hardball Times Baseball Annual*, and interned for the Baltimore Orioles for the past two summers. He will join the Orioles' baseball opera-tions department in a full-time position upon his graduation in May.

Dave Studenmund was one of the first people that I met in the baseball analytics community. I had just arrived at the 2013 SABR Analytics Conference without knowing one person. I was one of the first people there in the morning for the Diamond Dollars Case Competition, for which Studes was a judge. Even though he was preparing to judge the competition and reuniting with old friends he had not seen in a while, he took the time to speak with a random college kid he had never heard of. I cannot speak enough about how much his effort meant to me, as I felt that I had made my first friend in baseball.

However, his kindness did not stop there. After the competition, when everyone had dispersed for lunch, I had no one to eat with. With nothing to lose, I asked Studes if it would be okay for me to go to lunch with him and the other two judges. While it would have been so easy for him to say no and move on with his day, he was very welcoming and allowed me to join them at lunch and included me in the conversation throughout the meal.

I cannot be more grateful than I am for everything that Studes has done for me over the last few years. I think it is safe to say that I would not be where I am today without his effort to make me feel welcome in a new community. For that I cannot thank him enough for all he has done.

Shane Tourtellotte is a refugee from the Northeast living in Asheville, N.C. He's published a few hundred thousand words of science fiction, but this didn't strike people as bizarre enough, so he has branched out into baseball. His tally of major-league stadiums visited currently stands at 14. Eleven of them are still standing.

I didn't mean to be a baseball writer. Thanks to Dave, it just happened that way.

Back in early 2012, I was someone with a good layman's grasp of sabermetrics, or maybe better, who got a little research itch. In my spare time, I wrote up an analysis of Jackie Robinson's steals of home, with an eye in advance to finding it a home somewhere online. I looked over some leading analytics sites, decided The Hardball Times was the best fit, and sent a query asking if they'd take guest pieces.

I was used to the timetable of print publication, where a response in one month is pretty good time. Dave wrote back in about two hours, redefining my concept of "pretty good time." When I did submit the piece about a month later (and I'd thought I was being so clever with my timing), Dave's acceptance came back in two days, and the piece was up on the site a week later.

With that introduction to the THT clan, the rest was almost pre-ordained. I did another spec article, and another, and by the opening weeks of the 2012 season I was officially on staff. Dave actually needed to make the invitation twice before I would accept. I needed to convince myself that I could produce regularly. He was not as skeptical of me.

Those early months of my initiation into The Hardball Times displayed a trait crucial to an editor, which is effectively what Dave was. Not just open to new writers at THT, Dave was zealous in bringing them in. Good as it is to have an experienced and dependable stable, it's the new blood, especially in a rising field such as baseball analytics, that keeps things vital.

Thanks to Dave Studenmund's work, The Hardball Times has been vital baseball reading for a good long while. I am humbled to be part of it, and fortunate that Dave opened the door so wide for me.

Steve Treder contributed a weekly column to The Hardball Times online from its founding in 2004 through 2011, and has been a co-author of many *Hardball Times Annual* and *Hardball Times Season Preview* books. His work has also been featured in *Nine*, *The National Pastime*, and other publications. He has frequently been a presenter at baseball forums such as the SABR National Convention, the Nine Spring Training Conference, and the Cooperstown Symposium.

In his day job, Steve is senior vice president at Western Management Group, a compensation consulting firm headquartered in Los Gatos, Calif. When Steve grows up, he hopes to play center field for the San Francisco Giants.

In my life, I have been involved in precious few projects as ambitious and as consistently successful as The Hardball Times. Organizing and managing a writing endeavor on the scale of THT is the furthest thing from easy: it's highly complicated, requiring the close coordination of the efforts of a diverse and widely scattered motley crew of (sometimes) tricky personalities, under the chronic pressure of pitiless deadlines and tempermental technology platforms.

Our man Studes is that very rare specimen who can take on such a challenge and make it at least appear to be easy. His patient-but-firm manner, his willingness to candidly deliver strong feedback, and his insightful vision are the essence of powerful leadership. All of us who have found such stimulation and enjoyment in reading THT over these many years, both online and in print, owe Studes endless gratitude.

Neil Weinberg is the site educator at FanGraphs, a contributor to The Hardball Times, the associate managing editor at Beyond The Box Score, and also writes enthusiastically about the Detroit Tigers at New English D. He has played nine fewer positions than Don Kelly at the major league level.

I don't have the fortune to know Studes personally, but The Hardball Times was one of the first Web sites that introduced me to sabermetrics and a group of people who cared about and thought about baseball in the way that I did. I wish I had a personal story to share about him, but either way, you can see his influence in every corner of the sabermetric world. I one day hope to shake his hand and call him "Mr. xFIP."

David Wiers is a writer at RotoGraphs and TechGraphs. He was once called "The nerdiest person at FanGraphs" by Dave Cameron, which given the hotly contested title, is clearly a compliment.

Since first coming across THT years ago, I was captivated by the knowledge and insight provided. After immediately purchasing as many Annuals and Season Previews as possible, it was like a Rosetta Stone or "eureka!" moment for me. I quickly realized things that used to be a mystery were now quantifiable. In a poor attempt to ape THT, I started writing in my spare time—I never dared dream I'd be contributing to these pages—and eventually found my own path. I'd like to thank THT in general and Dave Studenmund in particular for giving this nerd a clearer direction on where to focus my spreadsheet abilities.

In his day job, **Jesse Wolfersberger** is the director of consumer insights for GroupM Next, the innovation unit of media giant GroupM. In his ever dwindling free time, he writes for FanGraphs and The Hardball Times. He has a master's degree in economics from the University of Missouri, and lives in St. Louis with his wife, daughter and dog.

All any baseball analyst hopes is to advance sabermetrics on some level, to kick the ball a little farther down the road so that the next guy can kick it even farther. Dave Studenmund has kicked it farther than most, and it has been an honor and a pleasure working with him.

Bradley Woodrum's writing credits include FanGraphs, ESPN, NotGraphs and DRaysBay. He currently writes for The Hardball Times, Banknotes Industries and Cubs Stats. In his free time, he goes for long runs and thinks about the enormity of the universe. And if you think about it, trees are kind of like this tiny little fungus growing on the Earth.

In the world of writing, you need good editors to succeed. You need leaders who have a vision for a united product and the courage to let writers go crazy from time to time. The Annual wouldn't be what it is without Studes, and for that, all of baseball owes him. Thanks, man!

Miles Wray has reviewed books on sports for McSweeney's Internet Tendency, *Ploughshares Literary Journal* and The Allrounder. During the 2014 season, he reviewed every episode of MTV2's baseball-meets-pop-culture show "Off the Bat" for *The Classical*. He lives in Seattle, but is not a Mariners fan, which has no doubt done wonders for his mental health.

Dear Studes: Thanks so much for creating a platform for writers and readers young and old to think about this game we love in so many imaginative, creative ways. You've influenced all of us with your spirit of inquisition. Happy trails!

Craig Wright worked 21 years in major league baseball in player evaluation and pioneering the use of scientific methodology in the decisions of baseball operations. In retirement he researches and writes "Pages from Baseball's Past," a popular subscription story series on the history of the game.

I've never met Dave in person and I would feel strange saying that I know him. But the simple truth is that there was something that came through in his correspondence that made me instinctively like him. I get requests pretty much every year to write something for this or that publication, and for various reasons—usually time constraints—I turn them down. No one was more successful in getting me to contribute, and to repeatedly contribute, to their publication than Dave was with The Hardball Times. I'm still a bit mystified as to how he managed it!

Matthew Yaspan is a junior at Tufts University, where he dual majors in computer science and economics. Growing up in New York, he's loved baseball and the New York Mets from an early age and dabbled in pitching into college, where he now plays club ball. His dream is to be a LOOGY for the Long Island Ducks, provided that Dontrelle Willis be the only other option out of the bullpen. When not doing work for FanGraphs and the Hardball Times, Matthew is also a director of baseball analysis at Tufts, a group dedicated to research and discussion of the game.

Like many strapping youths of the early aughts, I got into sabermetrics after reading Moneyball. *I was enamored with this idea that baseball wasn't already a known quantity and that there was more to discover about the game. I didn't know what to do with the whole notion that there is a new way of looking at baseball until I stumbled upon The Hardball Times. I was immediately hooked. I have read THT pretty religiously since then, and am constantly amazed by the consistently rising quality. Baseball analysis makes up a much larger portion of my time than I am willing to admit, and without THT I'd likely go through some sort of withdrawal.*

I had the pleasure of meeting Dave Studenmund at the SABR Analytics Conference in Phoenix. His kind and curious demeanor re-affirmed to me what I like most about the sabermetric community. Sabermetrics lie on a junction between hardcore analytics, keen intuition, and most importantly, love for a game and camaraderie among fans. Studenmund really captured all of those aspects in my brief encounter with him, and I truly appreciate it.

Jeff Zimmerman is pretty sure the only people to check this bio will be two kids, Ruby and Cole, to see if their names made it in again.

I found The Hardball Times, especially the Annual, *must-read material when I first started researching. Dave made sure it was always high-quality material. My first two correspondences with Dave were him politely turning down my submitted crap. Eventually, he seemed to tolerate my work and it has been a pleasure working with him. Dave, thanks for keeping the high standards with everything you do.*

Made in the USA
Charleston, SC
01 March 2015